Lecture Notes in Computer Science   8772

Commenced Publication in 1973
Founding and Former Series Editors:
Gerhard Goos, Juris Hartmanis, and Jan van Leeuwen

Michele Mosca (Ed.)

Post-Quantum Cryptography

6th International Workshop, PQCrypto 2014
Waterloo, ON, Canada, October 1-3, 2014
Proceedings

 Springer

Volume Editor

Michele Mosca
University of Waterloo
Institute for Quantum Computing
200 University Avenue West
Waterloo, ON N2L 3G1, Canada
E-mail: mmosca@uwaterloo.ca

ISSN 0302-9743   e-ISSN 1611-3349
ISBN 978-3-319-11658-7   e-ISBN 978-3-319-11659-4
DOI 10.1007/978-3-319-11659-4
Springer Cham Heidelberg New York Dordrecht London

Library of Congress Control Number: 2014948669

LNCS Sublibrary: SL 4 – Security and Cryptology

Typesetting: Camera-ready by author, data conversion by Scientific Publishing Services, Chennai, India

Printed on acid-free paper

Springer is part of Springer Science+Business Media (www.springer.com)

Preface

PQCrypto 2014, the 6th International Workshop on Post-Quantum Cryptography was held in Waterloo, Ontario, Canada, during 1–3 October 2014.

On the 20th anniversary of Shor's algorithms for breaking factoring and discrete log based cryptosystems, there is a new landscape of quantum tools and intensifying efforts worldwide to build large-scale quantum computers. The aim of PQCrypto is to serve as a forum for researchers to present results and exchange ideas on the topic of cryptography in an era with large-scale quantum computers. The workshop was preceded by a summer school from 29–30 September 2014.

The workshop attracted 37 submissions, of which the Program Committee selected 16 for publication in the workshop proceedings. The accepted papers dealt with the topics of code-based cryptography, lattice-based cryptography, multivariate-cryptography, isogeny-based cryptography, security proof frameworks, cryptanalysis, and implementations. The Program Committee included 26 subject-matter experts from 10 countries.

The workshop included four invited talks by Lily Chen (NIST), Nicolas Gisin (Université de Genève), Matteo Mariantoni (University of Waterloo), and Vinod Vaikuntanathan (MIT), tours of the experimental facilities at the Institute for Quantum Computing, and a recent results session.

I am very grateful to all the Program Committee members for generously contributing their time, knowledge and expertise. Many thanks also to the external reviewers who assisted in the process.

I wish to thank the generous sponsors and partners of PQCrypto 2014 who made it possible to host this event and support the invited speakers and other participants.

Profound thanks are also due to Alfred Menezes for his organizational effort and general guidance as the general chair and to Kim Simmermaker and the Institute for Quantum Computing staff for their logistical support.

July 2014   Michele Mosca

Organization

General Chair

Alfred Menezes   University of Waterloo, Canada

Program Chair

Michele Mosca   University of Waterloo, Canada

Steering Committee

Daniel J. Bernstein   University of Illinois at Chicago, USA and
                                    Technische Universiteit Eindhoven,
                                    The Netherlands
Johannes Buchmann   Technische Universität Darmstadt, Germany
Claude Crépeau   McGill University, Canada
Jintai Ding   University of Cincinnati, USA
Philippe Gaborit   University of Limoges, France
Tanja Lange   Technische Universiteit Eindhoven,
                                    The Netherlands
Daniele Micciancio   University of California at San Diego, USA
Michele Mosca   University of Waterloo, Canada
Nicolas Sendrier   Inria, France
Shigeo Tsujii   Chuo University, Japan
Bo-Yin Yang   Academia Sinica, Taiwan

Program Committee

Paulo Barreto   University of São Paulo, Brazil
Daniel J. Bernstein   University of Illinois at Chicago, USA and TU
                                    Eindhoven, The Netherlands
Johannes Buchmann   TU Darmstadt, Germany
Claude Crépeau   McGill University, Canada
Jintai Ding   University of Cincinnati, USA
Philippe Gaborit   University of Limoges, France
Tim Güneysu   Ruhr University of Bochum, Germany
Sean Hallgren   Pennsylvania State University, USA
Nadia Heninger   University of Pennsylvania, USA
David Jao   University of Waterloo, Canada
Tanja Lange   TU Eindhoven, The Netherlands

Yi-Kai Liu	NIST, USA
Vadim Lyubashevsky	ENS Paris, France
Michele Mosca	University of Waterloo and Perimeter Institute, Canada
Bart Preneel	KU Leuven, Belgium
Martin Rötteler	Microsoft Research, USA
Nicolas Sendrier	Inria, France
Daniel Smith-Tone	University of Louisville and NIST, USA
Douglas Stebila	QUT, Australia
Damien Stehlé	ENS Lyon, France
Rainer Steinwandt	Florida Atlantic University, USA
Douglas Stinson	University of Waterloo, Canada
Tsuyoshi Takagi	Kyushu University, Japan
Enrico Thomae	operational services GmbH & Co. KG, Germany
Jean-Pierre Tillich	Inria, France
Bo-Yin Yang	Academia Sinica, Taiwan

External Reviewers

Martin Albrecht	Ruud Pellikaan
André Chailloux	Christiane Peters
Julia Chaulet	Albrecht Petzoldt
Jérémie Detrey	Thomas Pöppelmann
Gus Gutoski	Olivier Ruatta
Andreas Hülsing	Peter Schwabe
Stephen Jordan	Fang Song
Zhenhua Liu	Alan Szepieniec
Rafael Misoczki	Frederik Vercauteren
Dustin Moody	Ingo von Maurich
Svetla Nikova	Takanori Yasuda

Partners and Sponsors

CryptoWorks21
Institute for Quantum Computing, University of Waterloo
Microsoft Research
National Science Foundation
Perimeter Institute for Theoretical Physics
The Fields Institute for Research in Mathematical Sciences
Tutte Institute for Mathematics and Computing

Table of Contents

Sealing the Leak on Classical NTRU Signatures

Carlos Aguilar Melchor[1], Xavier Boyen[2], Jean-Christophe Deneuville[1], and Philippe Gaborit[1]

[1] XLIM-DMI, Université de Limoges, France
[2] QUT, Brisbane, Australia

Abstract. Initial attempts to obtain lattice based signatures were closely related to reducing a vector modulo the fundamental parallelepiped of a secret basis (like GGH [9], or NTRUSign [12]). This approach leaked some information on the secret, namely the shape of the parallelepiped, which has been exploited on practical attacks [24]. NTRUSign was an extremely efficient scheme, and thus there has been a noticeable interest on developing countermeasures to the attacks, but with little success [6].

In [8] Gentry, Peikert and Vaikuntanathan proposed a randomized version of Babai's nearest plane algorithm such that the distribution of a reduced vector modulo a secret parallelepiped only depended on the size of the base used. Using this algorithm and generating large, close to uniform, public keys they managed to get provably secure GGH-like lattice-based signatures. Recently, Stehlé and Steinfeld obtained a provably secure scheme very close to NTRUSign [26] (from a theoretical point of view).

In this paper we present an alternative approach to seal the leak of NTRUSign. Instead of modifying the lattices and algorithms used, we do a classic leaky NTRUSign signature and hide it with gaussian noise using techniques present in Lyubashevsky's signatures. Our main contributions are thus a set of strong NTRUSign parameters, obtained by taking into account latest known attacks against the scheme, a statistical way to hide the leaky NTRU signature so that this particular instantiation of CVP-based signature scheme becomes zero-knowledge and secure against forgeries, based on the worst-case hardness of the $\tilde{\mathcal{O}}(N^{1.5})$-Shortest Independent Vector Problem over NTRU lattices. Finally, we give a set of concrete parameters to gauge the efficiency of the obtained signature scheme.

Keywords: Lattice-based Cryptography, Digital Signatures, NTRUSign, Provable Security, SIS.

1 Introduction

Lattice based cryptography has met growing interest since the seminal work of Ajtai [1] which introduced the so called worst-case to average-case reductions. Based upon this work, a long list of cryptographic primitives such as One Way Functions, Collision-Resistant Hash Functions, Digital Signatures, or Identification schemes have been revisited to provide more confidence about security.

M. Mosca (Ed.): PQCrypto 2014, LNCS 8772, pp. 1–21, 2014.

The most efficient known digital signature scheme provably secure is BLISS [5][1] which leads to signatures of about 5kb[2] for a security level of 128 bits.

Digital signatures have shown great promise since 1997, when was introduced GGH [9]. The most famous particular instantiation of GGH is NTRUSign, which uses convolution modular lattices. The particularity of those schemes is their lack of strong worst-case to average-case security reductions, but they offer amazing performances regarding classical schemes based on number theory or discrete logarithm. For instance, for a 128 bit security level, a NTRUSign signature would be only 1784 bits long (see [11]).

NTRUSign, first known as NSS [13], was first introduced at EUROCRYPT'01 by Hoffstein, Pipher and Silverman. It was amazingly fast and benefited from small keys due to the cyclic structure of the underlying convolution modular lattices that were used. The authors were aware that their scheme was vulnerable to transcript attacks *i.e.* wasn't zero-knowledge, but unfortunately they overestimated its length, and Nguyen and Regev succeeded in breaking the scheme in 2006 [24] by a nice gradient descent over the even moment polynomials. Initially, their attack required about 100.000 NTRU signatures to recover the hidden parallelepiped that reveals the secret basis, but still due to the cyclic structure of convolution modular lattices, they were able to shrink this threshold to about only 400 signatures for a claimed security level of 80 bits. In order to tackle this issue, several heuristical countermeasures were proposed such as the use of perturbations [12] and the deformation of the fundamental parallelepiped [15], but none of them were capable to resist to the improved attack by Ducas and Nguyen [6].

1.1   Our Contribution

We revisit NTRUSign in order to provide it with a zero-knowledge proof. Our technique is inspired from Lyubashevsky's scheme [19], where the secret key $\mathbf{S}$ consists of a matrix in $\{-d, \ldots, d\}^{m \times k}$, the message is hashed to a vector $\mathbf{c} \leftarrow \{-1, 0, 1\}^{k}$ such that $\|\mathbf{c}\|_1 \leq \kappa$, and the signature consists of $\mathbf{Sc}$ shifted by a mask $\mathbf{y} \xleftarrow{\$} D_{\sigma}^m$ where D_{σ}^m represents the discrete gaussian distribution in dimension m with standard deviation σ.

Instead of hiding $\mathbf{Sc}$, we get a leaky signature from NTRUSign, and then use this signature as the secret and hide it with a well chosen $\mathbf{y}$. The critical technicality resides in the choice of the dimension N and the standard deviation σ : if it was chosen too small, the secret isn't properly hidden, and our modification doesn't seal any leak, if σ is too big, so will be our signatures and our scheme loses in efficiency and practicality.

We note that unlike other provably secure signature schemes such as GPV [8] or [25], we do not modify the initial NTRU signature scheme, except by choosing public parameters more conservatively, and thus keep its inherent size and computational efficiency. Of course masking the signature in a second step comes at

---

[1] Which improves [19] with a better rejection sampling.

[2] For the space-optimized version, see Table 3 of [5] for more details.

a price, but we manage to get signature of size $\approx 10kb$ together with public and secret keys respectively around 7000 and 1500 kb.

We choose to hide NTRU signatures with a noise based on the assumption that the leak in the signatures is exploitable but that there are no structural attacks against the public NTRU key (and thus we suppose that sealing the leak is enough to secure the scheme). This is based on the observation that the research community has published no noticeable structural attacks on NTRU lattices in the last decade and that problems such as SIS do not seem to be easier than in random lattices (if we take into account the gap induced by the small secret key).

1.2 Organization of the Paper

In section 2, we present the basic elements and notations used in NTRUSign and Lyubashevsky's signature scheme, then describe these schemes respectively in sections 3 and 4. Finally, we present the scheme we propose in section 5 along with its security proofs and sets of parameters.

2 Background and Problems

In this section, we introduce basics of lattice-based cryptography. Nevertheless, due to space restriction, some of them will be omitted and we refer the reader to [23] for further details and proofs.

2.1 Notation

Sets. Throughout this paper, $\mathbb{Z}$ will denote the set of integer numbers, and for $q \in \mathbb{Z}$, $\mathbb{Z}_q$ will denote the set of integers taken modulo q, in the set $\left[-\frac{q}{2}; \frac{q}{2}\right)$. We will make heavy use of the notation $\mathcal{R}_q$ to represent $\mathbb{Z}_q[X]/(X^N - 1)$, the ring of polynomials of degree less than N, modulo q and $X^N - 1$. Vectors and/or polynomials will be represented with bold-face letters, for any $\mathbf{x} \in \mathcal{R}_q$, we will use either its polynomial notation $\mathbf{x} = \sum_{i=0}^{N-1} x_i \cdot X^i$ or its vector representation $\mathbf{x} = (x_0, x_1, \ldots, x_{N-1})^t$. Matrices such as the public key will be represented with bold-face capital letters $\mathbf{A} \in \mathbb{Z}_q^{N \times 2N}$.

In section 3, the NTRUSign secret polynomials $\mathbf{f}, \mathbf{g}$ will be sampled from a particular subset $\mathcal{T}(d)$ of $\mathcal{R}_q$, which consists of polynomials $\mathbf{f}$ of degree strictly less that N, with exactly $d + 1$ coefficients equal to 1, d equal to -1 and the $N - 2d - 1$ others equal to 0. All logarithms will be based 2 unless explicitly mentioned.

Norms. For any $\mathbf{s}, \mathbf{t} \in \mathcal{R}_q$, we will make use of several norms :

- The centered norm : $\|\mathbf{s}\|_c^2 = \sum_{i=0}^{N-1} s_i^2 - \frac{1}{N} \left(\sum_{i=0}^{N-1} s_i\right)^2 = N \cdot \mathrm{Variance}(s_i)$
- The balanced norm : $\|(\mathbf{s}, \mathbf{t})\|_\nu^2 = \|\mathbf{s}\|_c^2 + \nu^2 \cdot \|\mathbf{t}\|_c^2$

- The euclidian norm : $\|\mathbf{s}\|_2^2 = \sum_{i=0}^{N-1} s_i^2$, or just $\|\mathbf{s}\|^2$ for simplicity as this norm is the most standard in lattice-based cryptography

The first and second norms are somehow typical to NTRU, and don't give many intuition on the actual length of a vector, in the common (euclidian) sense. Therefore, we describe a method to *experimentally* translate a balanced norm into a euclidian one with arbitrary desired probability. As $\|\mathbf{s}\|_c = \sigma_{\mathbf{s}}\sqrt{N}$ where $\sigma_{\mathbf{s}}$ is the standard deviation of the s_is, each s_i is approximately $\sigma_{\mathbf{s}}$, and by lemma 2.3.2 we have

$$\|\mathbf{s}\|_2 \leq \alpha \cdot \sigma_{\mathbf{s}}\sqrt{N} \text{ with probability } 1 - 2^{-k}$$

where k is the security parameter and the corresponding α can be read in table 1. Even if the s_is are not sampled according to a gaussian, it is possible to upper bound $\|\mathbf{s}\|_2$ during the NTRU signing process. This allows us to set two versions of parameters in our scheme, a speed-optimized one and a size-optimized one.

2.2 Digital Signatures

For completeness, we recall the definition of a Digital Signature scheme.

Definition 2.2.1 (Signature Scheme). *A signature scheme is composed of 3 polynomial-time algorithms* (K, S, V) :

1. *KeyGen K : which given a security parameter 1^k as input returns a couple of keys* (pk, sk)
2. *Sign S : which given the secret key sk and a message μ returns a signature s of this message*
3. *Verify V : which given the public key pk, the signature s and the message μ, ensures that this signature was indeed generated using sk*

such that for any $(pk, sk) \leftarrow K(1^k)$, $Pr[V(pk, \mu, S(sk, \mu)) = 1] = 1$.

There are two ways to attack a signature scheme, either try to create a signature from other couples (μ, s) and the public key pk, or recover the secret key sk directly from pk and eventually some signed messages. The former idea leads to the following definition :

Definition 2.2.2 (Forgery). *A signature scheme* (K, S, V) *is said to be secure against forgeries, if for any polynomial-time adversary $\mathcal{A}$ who has access to pk and couples* $(\mu_1, s_1), \ldots, (\mu_n, s_n)$ *of its choosing, $\mathcal{A}$ only has a negligible probability (depending on the security parameter k) to create a couple* $(\mu \neq \mu_i, s')$ *such that $V(pk, \mu, s') = 1$, that is to say a valid signature.*

2.3 Discrete Normal Distribution

In this section, we define the Discrete Normal Distribution and describe some of its desirable properties, that fit particularly well with lattices.

Definition 2.3.1 (Continuous Normal Distribution). *The Continuous Normal Distribution over* $\mathbb{R}^{2N}$ *centered at* $\mathbf{v}$ *with standard deviation* σ *is defined by*

$$\rho_{\mathbf{v},\sigma}^{2N}(\mathbf{x}) = (\frac{1}{\sigma\sqrt{2\pi}})^{2N} \cdot \exp(-\frac{\|\mathbf{x} - \mathbf{v}\|_2^2}{2\sigma^2}).$$

In order to make this distribution fitting with lattices and obtain a probability function, we need to scale this distribution by the lattice quantity $\rho_{\mathbf{0},\sigma}^{2N}(\mathbb{Z}^{2N}) = \sum_{\mathbf{x}\in\mathbb{Z}^{2N}} \rho_{\mathbf{0},\sigma}^{2N}(\mathbf{x})$. This quantity does not depend on the choice of the vector.

Definition 2.3.2 (Discrete Normal Distribution). *The Discrete Normal Distribution over* $\mathbb{Z}^{2N}$ *centered at* $\mathbf{v}$ *with standard deviation* σ *is defined by* $D_{\mathbf{v},\sigma}^{2N}(\mathbf{x}) = \rho_{\mathbf{v},\sigma}^{2N}(\mathbf{x})/\rho_{\mathbf{v},\sigma}^{2N}(\mathbb{Z}^{2N})$.

The next lemma gives us an idea of how big the standard deviation must be to ensure that the inner product of two vectors doesn't overflow a certain amount. This lemma is crucial to determine our signature size in table 3 with overwhelming probability.

Lemma 2.3.1 ([19]).

$$\forall \mathbf{v} \in \mathbb{R}^{2N}, \forall \sigma, r > 0, \text{we have } Pr\left[|\langle \mathbf{x}, \mathbf{v}\rangle| > r; \mathbf{x} \xleftarrow{\$} D_\sigma^{2N}\right] \le 2e^{-\frac{r^2}{2\|\mathbf{v}\|^2\sigma^2}}.$$

Optimally, we will set $r = \alpha \cdot \|\mathbf{v}\|\sigma$. Table 1 shows how big α should be to ensure k bits of security. We also need a few more material to prove that our NTRU signature will be correctly hidden by our mask. This material is given by the following lemma.

Lemma 2.3.2 ([19]).

1. $\forall \alpha > 0, Pr\left[|x| > \alpha\sigma; x \xleftarrow{\$} D_\sigma^1\right] \le 2e^{-\frac{\alpha^2}{2}}$
2. $\forall \eta \ge 1, Pr\left[\|\mathbf{x}\| > \eta\sigma\sqrt{2N}; \mathbf{x} \xleftarrow{\$} D_\sigma^{2N}\right] < \eta^{2N}e^{N(1-\eta^2))}$
3. $\forall \mathbf{x} \in \mathbb{Z}^{2N}$ *and* $\sigma \ge \frac{3}{\sqrt{2\pi}}$, *we have* $D_\sigma^{2N}(\mathbf{x}) \le 2^{-2N}$

Table 1. $\alpha = \lceil\sqrt{2(k+1)\ln(2)}\rceil$ as a function of the security level k

Security parameter k	80	100	112	128	160
Gap factor α	11	12	13	14	15

For our purposes, as the mask $\mathbf{y}$ is sampled from a Discrete Normal Distribution, we might have to re-sample several times before obtaining a valid signature, but still, we want our signature procedure to terminate, in a reasonable (polynomial) time. This is ensured by the next lemma, whose proof is essentially detailed in [19] for a security level of $k = 100$ bits. We extend the proof of this lemma (in appendix A.1) to make it fitting better with different security levels.

Lemma 2.3.3 ([19] extended). *For any* $\mathbf{v} \in \mathbb{Z}^{2N}$ *and* $\sigma = \omega(\|\mathbf{v}\|_2 \sqrt{\log_2(2N)})$, *we have*

$$Pr\left[D_\sigma^{2N}(\mathbf{x})/D_{\mathbf{v},\sigma}^{2N}(\mathbf{x}) = \mathcal{O}(1); \mathbf{x} \xleftarrow{\$} D_\sigma^{2N}\right] = 1 - 2^{-\omega(\log_2(2N))}$$

and more concretely, $\forall \mathbf{v} \in \mathbb{Z}^{2N}$, *if* $\sigma = \alpha\|\mathbf{v}\|$ *for some positive* α, *then*

$$Pr\left[D_\sigma^{2N}(\mathbf{x})/D_{\mathbf{v},\sigma}^{2N}(\mathbf{x}) < e^{1+1/(2\alpha^2)}; \mathbf{x} \xleftarrow{\$} D_\sigma^{2N}\right] > 1 - 2^{-k}$$

This lemma ensures us that Lyubashevsky's layer of the signing procedure will be called at most $M = e^{1+1/(2\alpha^2)}$ times with probability at least $1-2^{-k}$. Keeping this repetition rate down is of major importance especially as this layer involves a NTRUSign procedure which is itself also a loop. In table 3, we provide two versions of parameters for each security level. In the first one, the NTRUSign part is generated in only one round with overwhelming probability, before applying the rejection step with $M \approx 2.8$, leading to a speed-optimized version. In the second one, we allow the generation of the NTRU signature to take at most 5 rounds whilst reducing its norm. This implies more rejection steps ($M \approx 7.5$) but allows us to shrink the signature sizes by approximately 15%.

To prove the security of our scheme, we also need the following rejection sampling lemma, which will be used in the proof of theorem 2.3.5 that will help us getting our security reduction to SIS.

Lemma 2.3.4 ([19]). *For any set* V, *and probability distributions* $h : V \to \mathbb{R}$ *and* $f : \mathbb{Z}^{2N} \to \mathbb{R}$, *if* $g_v : \mathbb{Z}^{2N} \to \mathbb{R}$ *is a family of probability distributions indexed by* $v \in V$ *such that* $\exists M \in \mathbb{R} \ / \ \forall v \in V, Pr[Mg_v(\mathbf{z}) \geq f(\mathbf{z}); \mathbf{z} \xleftarrow{\$} f] \geq 1 - \epsilon$ *then the outputs of algorithms* $\mathcal{A}$ *and* $\mathcal{F}$

Algorithm $\mathcal{A}$	Algorithm $\mathcal{F}$
1: $v \xleftarrow{\$} h$	*1:* $v \xleftarrow{\$} h$
2: $\mathbf{z} \xleftarrow{\$} g_v$	*2:* $\mathbf{z} \xleftarrow{\$} f$
3: output $(\mathbf{z}, v)$ *with probability* $\min\left(\frac{f(\mathbf{z})}{Mg_v(\mathbf{z})}, 1\right)$	*3: output* $(\mathbf{z}, v)$ *with probability* $1/M$

are within statistical distance ϵ/M.

The next theorem is a direct consequence of lemmas 2.3.3 and 2.3.4 by replacing V by the subset of $\mathbb{Z}^{2N}$ of vector $\mathbf{v}$ of length at most T, f by D_σ^{2N} and g_v by $D_{\mathbf{v},\sigma}^{2N}$.

Theorem 2.3.5 ([19]) *Let* $V = \{\mathbf{v} \in \mathbb{Z}^{2N}; \|\mathbf{v}\| \leq T\}$, $\sigma = \omega(T\sqrt{\log 2N}) \in \mathbb{R}$ *and* $h : V \to \mathbb{R}$ *a probability distribution. Then* $\exists M = \mathcal{O}(1)$ *such that distributions of algorithms* $\mathcal{A}$ *and* $\mathcal{F}$ *below are within statistical distance* $\frac{2^{-\omega(\log 2N)}}{M}$. *Moreover,* $\mathcal{A}$ *outputs something with probability at least* $\frac{1-2^{-\omega(\log 2N)}}{M}$

Algorithm $\mathcal{A}$	Algorithm $\mathcal{F}$
1: $\mathbf{v} \xleftarrow{\$} h$	*1:* $\mathbf{v} \xleftarrow{\$} h$
2: $\mathbf{z} \xleftarrow{\$} g_\mathbf{v}$	*2:* $\mathbf{z} \xleftarrow{\$} f$
3: output $(\mathbf{z}, \mathbf{v})$ *with probability* $\min\left(\frac{f(\mathbf{z})}{Mg_\mathbf{v}(\mathbf{z})}, 1\right)$	*3: output* $(\mathbf{z}, \mathbf{v})$ *with probability* $1/M$

2.4   Average-Case SIS Problems

Problems. The last part of this background section describes the main average-case lattice problem we will base our signature scheme upon, namely the Short Integer Solution (SIS) Problem, which is a least as hard as the worst-case of Shortest Independent Vector Problem (SIVP) [1] up to a polynomial approximation factor.

Definition 2.4.1 (ℓ_2-SIS$_{q,N,2N,\beta}$ problem). *For any* $\mathbf{A} \in \mathbb{Z}_q^{N \times 2N}$, *the* ℓ_2-$SIS_{q,N,2N,\beta}$ *problem consists in finding a vector* $\mathbf{v} \in \mathbb{Z}_q^{2N} \setminus \{0\}$ *such that* $\mathbf{Av} = \mathbf{0}$ *and* $\|\mathbf{v}\|_2 \leq \beta$.

Relations between parameters q, N and β will be discussed later in this section as they condition the length of the shortest expected vector, but we can already mention that for a ℓ_2-SIS$_{q,N,2N,\beta}$ solution to exist, we need to set $\beta \geq \sqrt{2Nq}$.

Definition 2.4.2 (SIS$_{q,N,2N,d}$ distribution). *Given a matrix* $\mathbf{A} \in \mathbb{Z}_q^{N \times 2N}$, *and a random* $\mathbf{v} \in \mathbb{Z}_q^{2N}$, *output* $(\mathbf{A}, \mathbf{Av} \mod q)$.

Definition 2.4.3 (Search SIS$_{q,N,2N,d}$). *Given* $(\mathbf{A}, \mathbf{t}) \in \mathbb{Z}_q^{N \times 2N} \times \mathbb{Z}_q^N$, *find* $\mathbf{v} \in \{-d, \ldots, 0, \ldots, d\}^{2N}$ *such that* $\mathbf{Av} = \mathbf{t}$.

Definition 2.4.4 (Decisional SIS$_{q,N,2N,d}$). *Given* $(\mathbf{A}, \mathbf{t}) \in \mathbb{Z}_q^{N \times 2N} \times \mathbb{Z}_q^N$, *decide whether it comes from the* $SIS_{q,N,2N,d}$ *distribution or the uniform distribution over* $\mathbb{Z}_q^{N \times 2N} \times \mathbb{Z}_q^N$ *with non-negligible advantage.*

Relations between These Problems. We now recall existing relations between the problems described above, together with relationships between their parameters which somehow strengthen or weaken these problems. First, it is rather intuitive that the smaller d, the harder the problem, but this remark doesn't take the modulus q into account. We can see the matrix multiplication by $\mathbf{A} \in \mathbb{Z}_q^{N \times 2N}$ as a linear map whose domain is $\mathbb{Z}_q^{2N}$ (of size q^{2N}) and range is $\mathbb{Z}_q^N$ (of size q^N). So by constraining the domain to $\mathbb{Z}_d^{2N}$, we need d to be of order $\sqrt{q}$ for domain and range to be in one-to-one correspondence (even if it is not a sufficient condition). As a consequence, when $d \ll \sqrt{q}$ there will be only one $\mathbf{v} \in \{-d, \ldots, 0, \ldots, d\}^{2N}$ satisfying $\mathbf{Av} = \mathbf{t}$ with high probability, which makes it easier to distinguish between the SIS$_{q,N,2N,d}$ distribution and the uniform one. On the other hand, increasing d far beyond $\sqrt{q}$ leaves room for multiple solutions to the Search SIS$_{q,N,2N,d}$ Problem with high probability. Therefore, we can reasonably expect the hardest SIS$_{q,N,2N,d}$ instances to rely where $d \approx \sqrt{q}$.

Besides relationships between those parameters, there are reductions from some of these problems to others. For instance, as it is often the case between search and decisional problems, one can build a distinguisher from an oracle solving Decisional SIS$_{q,N,2N,d}$ to solve the search version, and that is what the following theorem states :

Theorem 2.4.6 ([16, 21]) *For any* $d \in \mathcal{O}(N)$, *there is a polynomial-time reduction from solving Search* $SIS_{q,N,2N,d}$ *to solving Decisional* $SIS_{q,N,2N,d}$.

Actually, the best (known) way to solve the search version of SIS appears to be solving the decisional version. However, the next lemma gives us confidence about the hardness of the decisional SIS problem when the solution is allowed to be larger and larger, which translates the fact that the SIS distribution comes closer and closer to the uniform distribution.

Lemma 2.4.7 ([19]). *For any $\alpha \geq 0$ such that $\gcd(2\alpha + 1, q) = 1$, there is a polynomial-time reduction from solving Decisional $SIS_{q,N,2N,d}$ to solving Decisional $SIS_{q,N,2N,(2\alpha+1)d+\alpha}$.*

As mentioned in [23], when the dimension equals twice the rank ($m = 2N$), and above all if β is small enough, the actual best known way to solve Decisional $SIS_{q,N,2N,d}$ is to solve the ℓ_2-$SIS_{q,N,2N,\beta}$ problem.

Lemma 2.4.8 ([23]). *If $4d\beta \leq q$, there is a polynomial-time reduction from solving Decisional $SIS_{q,N,2N,d}$ to solving ℓ_2-$SIS_{q,N,2N,\beta}$.*

As a consequence, it has been shown in [22, 19] that for ℓ_2-$SIS_{q,N,2N,\beta}$ to be hard, one has to ensure that the following inequality is satisfied for any desired security level k :

$$2\beta\sqrt{N \cdot \frac{d(d+1)}{3}} > \frac{q}{\pi}\sqrt{k \cdot \ln(2)} \tag{1}$$

This lemma already gives us a first restriction for setting the parameters. Indeed, by rewriting the above inequality, we have $4 \cdot \left(\frac{d\beta}{q}\right)^2 \cdot \frac{N(d+1)\pi^2}{3\ln(2)} > k$, and as $\frac{4\pi^2}{3\ln(2)} \approx 4^2$ and $\frac{4d\beta}{q} \leq 1$, this condition means that $N \cdot (d+1)$ is greater than k by some multiplicative gap. We now discuss about another kind of restriction due to the expected length of "the" shortest vector in a given convolution modular lattice (*i.e* Gaussian Heuristic) relatively to lattice basis reduction techniques.

Since its introduction in 1982 by Lenstra, Lenstra and Lovász [17] with the LLL algorithm, lattice reduction has known great applications and generalizations. Among all those techniques lives a perpetual trade-off between the running time of the reduction algorithm and the quality of the (eventual) output, which is gauged by the Hermit Factor δ. This factor plays a crucial role in the hardness of the ℓ_2-$SIS_{q,N,2N,\beta}$ problem in the sense that lattice reduction algorithms can find vectors $\mathbf{v} \in \mathbb{Z}_q^{2N}$ such that $\mathbf{Av} = \mathbf{0}$ and $\|\mathbf{v}\|_2 \leq \delta^{2N}\sqrt{q}$ [7]. Even if $\delta \approx 1.007$ seems to be a lower bound for reasonable future [4], deepest explorations on this factor have been made in [18], and more precise approximations have been extrapolated for different security levels. Parameter δ in table 4 has been set sticking to these extrapolations.

Further analysis led Micciancio and Regev [23] to the conclusion that the SIS problem *does not* become that harder by increasing the number of columns. Actually, they show that one can find a lattice vector $\mathbf{v}$ such that

$$\|\mathbf{v}\| \approx \min\left(q, 2^{2\sqrt{N \log q \log \delta}}\right) \tag{2}$$

and $\mathbf{Av} = \mathbf{0}$ using only $\sqrt{N \log q / \log \delta}$ of the $2N$ columns of the matrix $\mathbf{A}$. This bound will gives us another restriction when setting our parameters in section 5.

3   General Overview of NTRUSign

In this section, we briefly describe the NTRUSign scheme. For a complete description of the scheme, we refer the reader to [10, 11]. The basic set for NTRUSign is $\mathcal{R}_q = \mathbb{Z}_q/(X^N - 1)$ with addition and polynomial multiplication modulo $X^N - 1$, also known as convolution product and denoted by $*$:

$$(\mathbf{f} * \mathbf{g})(X) = \sum_{k=0}^{N-1} \left(\sum_{i+j \equiv k \mod N} f_i g_i \right) X^k \tag{3}$$

The public and private keys will be matrices $\mathbf{P}$, and $\mathbf{S}$ defined by :

$$\mathbf{P} = \begin{pmatrix} 1\,0\dots0 & h_0 & h_{N-1}\dots h_1 \\ 0\,1\dots0 & h_1 & h_0 \quad\dots h_2 \\ \vdots\,\vdots\ddots\vdots & \vdots & \vdots \quad\ddots\ \vdots \\ 0\,0\dots1 & h_{N-1}\,h_{N-2}\dots h_0 \\ \hline 0\,0\,0\,0 & q & 0\quad\dots\ 0 \\ 0\,0\,0\,0 & 0 & q\quad\dots\ 0 \\ \vdots\,\vdots\ddots\vdots & \vdots & \vdots\quad\ddots\ \vdots \\ 0\,0\dots0 & 0 & 0\quad\dots\ q \end{pmatrix} \qquad \mathbf{S} = \begin{pmatrix} f_0 & f_{N-1}\dots f_1 & F_0 & F_{N-1}\dots F_1 \\ f_1 & f_0\ \ \dots f_2 & F_0 & F_{N-1}\dots F_1 \\ \vdots & \vdots\quad\ddots\ \vdots & \vdots & \vdots\quad\ddots\ \vdots \\ f_{N-1} & f_{N-2}\dots f_0 & F_{N-1}\,F_{N-2}\dots F_0 \\ \hline g_0 & g_{N-1}\dots g_1 & G_0 & G_{N-1}\dots G_1 \\ g_1 & g_0\ \dots g_2 & G_0 & G_{N-1}\dots G_1 \\ \vdots & \vdots\quad\ddots\ \vdots & \vdots & \vdots\quad\ddots\ \vdots \\ g_{N-1}\,g_{N-2}\dots g_0 & G_{N-1}\,G_{N-2}\dots G_0 \end{pmatrix} \tag{4}$$

where $\mathbf{h} = \mathbf{f}^{-1} * \mathbf{g} \mod q$ for $\mathbf{f}, \mathbf{g} \in \mathcal{R}_q$, $\mathbf{F}, \mathbf{G} \in \mathcal{R}_q$ are given by the *keyGen* algorithm 1, and verify $\mathbf{f} * \mathbf{G} - \mathbf{g} * \mathbf{F} = q$. As operations are performed modulo q and as $(\mathbf{F}, \mathbf{G})$ can be obtained efficiently from $(\mathbf{f}, \mathbf{g})$ using [12], we will denote $\mathbf{P} = (\mathbf{1}\ \mathbf{h})$ and $\mathbf{S} = (\mathbf{f}\ \mathbf{g})$ for short. The NTRU lattice is :

$$\Lambda_q(\mathbf{A}) = \{(\mathbf{y_1}, \mathbf{y_2})/\mathbf{y_2} = \mathbf{y_1} * \mathbf{h} \mod q\} \tag{5}$$

Algorithms. We now recall the algorithms used in NTRUSign. More sophisticated versions of this signature scheme have been elaborated, such as the one with perturbations [12] or the deformation of the fundamental parallelepiped [15] to counter the attack of [24], but all these upgrades have been broken with the later improved attack of [6]. Therefore, we will further use the basic instantiation of NTRUSign for our scheme, which offers greater performances together with smaller keys. We will discuss the security of our scheme in section 5.

Key generation and signing procedures are described respectively in algorithms 1 and 2. The NTRU signature $\mathbf{s} \in \mathcal{R}_q$ is a simple Babaï's round-off [2] of the target $(\mathbf{0}, \mathbf{m})$ using the secret key sk, where $\mathbf{m} = H(\mu)$ is the hash of the message μ to be signed by $H : \{0,1\}^* \to \mathcal{R}_q$. In order to process this round-off, for any $x \in \mathbb{R}$ we will denote by $\lfloor x \rceil$ the nearest integer to x so that $\{x\} = x - \lfloor x \rceil \in (-\frac{1}{2}, \frac{1}{2}]$. By extension, for any $\mathbf{x} \in \mathcal{R}_q$, $\{\mathbf{x}\}$ will denote the previous operation applied to every x_i. Due to the particular structure of the NTRU lattice and to the fact that the NTRU signature is a lattice vector, giving $\mathbf{s}$ as the signature suffices to reconstruct the right part using the public key. This trick permits to save half of the space needed to represent the NTRU signature.

Algorithm 1: KeyGen(N, q, d, $\mathcal{N}$, ν)

Input: N, q, d, $\mathcal{N}$, and ν
Output: $pk = \mathbf{h} = \mathbf{f}^{-1} * \mathbf{g} \mod q$
  and $sk = \mathbf{f}, \mathbf{g}$
begin
　repeat
　　$\mathbf{f} \xleftarrow{\$} \mathcal{T}(d)$, $\mathbf{g} \xleftarrow{\$} \mathcal{T}(d)$;
　until $\mathbf{f}$ *is invertible in* $\mathcal{R}_q$;
　$\mathbf{h} = \mathbf{g} * \mathbf{f}^{-1}$;
　return $pk = \begin{pmatrix} 1 & \mathbf{h} \\ 0 & \mathbf{q} \end{pmatrix}$,
　$sk = \begin{pmatrix} \mathbf{f} & \mathbf{F} \\ \mathbf{g} & \mathbf{G} \end{pmatrix}$;

Algorithm 2: NTRUSign(pk, sk, μ)

Input: Public and private keys, and
  $\mu \in \{0,1\}^*$ the message to
  sign
Output: $\mathbf{s}$ the NTRU signature
begin
　$cpt \leftarrow 0$;
　repeat
　　$cpt \leftarrow cpt + 1$;
　　$\mathbf{m} \leftarrow H(\mu, cpt) \in \mathcal{R}_q$;
　　$(\mathbf{x}, \mathbf{y}) = (0, \mathbf{m}) \cdot \begin{pmatrix} \mathbf{G} & -\mathbf{F} \\ -\mathbf{g} & \mathbf{f} \end{pmatrix} / q$;
　　$\mathbf{s} = -\{\mathbf{x}\} * \mathbf{f} - \{\mathbf{y}\} * \mathbf{g}$;
　until $\|(\mathbf{s}, \mathbf{s} * \mathbf{h} - \mathbf{m})\|_\nu \leq \mathcal{N}$;
　return $(\mathbf{s}, cpt)$;

Algorithm 3: Verify($pk = \mathbf{h}, \mathbf{s}, cpt, \mu$)

Input: Public key pk, the signature $\mathbf{s}$, and the message $\mu \in \{0,1\}^*$
Output: *true* if and only if $\mathbf{s}$ is a valid signature of μ
begin
　$\mathbf{m} = H(\mu, cpt)$;
　if $\|(\mathbf{s}, \mathbf{s} * \mathbf{h} - \mathbf{m})\|_\nu \leq \mathcal{N}$ **then**
　　return *true*;
　else
　　return *false*;

Polynomials $\mathbf{F}$ and $\mathbf{G}$ in algorithm 1 can be obtained efficiently using the technique described in [12], but as we are using the transpose NTRU lattice, those polynomials are not even used for signing nor verifying the signature. So in the case of a constrained environment, one can just skip this computation. Nevertheless, $\mathbf{F}$ and $\mathbf{G}$ play a role in the size of the error when rounding-off the target. The technique of [12] permits to find those polynomials in such a way that $\|\mathbf{F}\| \approx \|\mathbf{G}\| \approx \sqrt{\frac{N}{12}}\|\mathbf{f}\|$ so that the error when signing using sk is of size approximately $(\sqrt{\frac{N}{6}} + \nu\frac{N}{6\sqrt{2}})\|\mathbf{f}\|$. As a comparison, an invalid signer trying to sign using pk instead of sk would generate an error of magnitude $\nu\sqrt{\frac{N}{12}}q$.

Table 2. New NTRUSign parameters, $\rho = 1$, no perturbation

k	N	d	q	ν	$\mathcal{N}$	ω_{cmb}	c	ω_{lk}	ω_{frg}	γ	ω_{lf}	R	L
100	431	34	2^{10}	0.16686	141	167	3.714	187	172	0.0516	415	131	180
112	479	42	2^{10}	0.15828	165	200	4.232	209	137	0.0558	470	157	200
128	541	61	2^{11}	0.14894	211	269	3.711	239	329	0.0460	541	207	226
160	617	57	2^{11}	0.13946	217	269	3.709	272	360	0.0431	627	210	258

Parameters. Setting concrete NTRUSign parameters for a given security level seems to be an unclear task to perform. Nevertheless, the authors of [10] provide a generic algorithm to generate such parameters, given the security parameter k, the signing tolerance ρ^3, and an upper bound N_{max} on the degree of the polynomials $\mathbf{f}$ and $\mathbf{g}$. Even if this algorithm doesn't take into account best known attacks, it can provide one with a hint of how the parameters should look like, relatively to one another. Therefore we will use it to get N, q, d, $\mathcal{N}$, and ν, and then check that best known attacks are out of range. We will not care about the transcript length as the fix we propose hides the leaky part of the signature, and an adversary would not learn anything more from issued signatures.

4   General Overview of Lyubashevsky's Scheme

In this section, we recall briefly the signature scheme presented by Lyubashevsky at EuroCrypt'12, and refer the reader to the original paper [19] for more details. The most efficient instantiations of this scheme rely on the average-case hardness of two problems : the $\mathrm{SIS}_{q,n,m,d}$ decisional problem and the $\ell_2\text{-}\mathrm{SIS}_{q,n,m,\beta}$ problem, which are at least as hard as the worst-case of the $\mathcal{O}(n^{1.5})$-SIVP [1].

---

[3] If $\mathcal{E}$ is the expected size of a signature, the verifying process should fail for every signature whose size is greater than $\rho\mathcal{E}$. Notice that the author also use one in [19], namely η. We will be tempted to set $\rho = \eta$ in next sections.

Algorithm 4: KeyGen(n, m, k, q)

Input: n, m, k, q
Output: $pk = (\mathbf{A}, \mathbf{T}) \in \mathbb{Z}_q^{n \times m} \times \mathbb{Z}_q^{n \times k}$ and $sk = \mathbf{S} \in \mathbb{Z}_q^{m \times k}$

begin

$\quad \mathbf{S} \xleftarrow{\$} \{-d, \ldots, 0, \ldots, d\}^{m \times k};$

$\quad \mathbf{A} \xleftarrow{\$} \mathbb{Z}_q^{n \times m};$

$\quad \mathbf{T} \leftarrow \mathbf{AS};$

$\quad$ **return** $pk = (\mathbf{A}, \mathbf{T}), sk = \mathbf{S};$

Algorithm 5: Sign(pk, sk, μ)

Input: Public and private keys, and $\mu \in \{0, 1\}^*$ the message to sign
Output: $(\mathbf{z}, \mathbf{c})$ the signature

begin

$\quad \mathbf{y} \xleftarrow{\$} D_\sigma^m;$

$\quad \mathbf{c} \leftarrow H(\mathbf{Ay}, \mu);$

$\quad \mathbf{z} \leftarrow \mathbf{Sc} + \mathbf{y};$

$\quad$ **return** $(\mathbf{z}, \mathbf{c})$ *with probability*

$\quad \min \left(\frac{D_\sigma^m(\mathbf{z})}{M \cdot D_{\mathbf{Sc}, \sigma}^m(\mathbf{z})}, 1 \right);$

Algorithm 6: Verify$(pk, (\mathbf{z}, \mathbf{c}), \mu)$

Input: Public key, message μ, and the signature $(\mathbf{z}, \mathbf{c})$ to check
Output: *true* if and only if $(\mathbf{z}, \mathbf{c})$ is a valid signature of μ

begin

$\quad$ **if** $H(\mathbf{Az} - \mathbf{Tc}, \mu) = \mathbf{c}$ *and* $\|\mathbf{z}\| \leq \eta\sigma\sqrt{m}$ **then**

$\quad\quad$ **return** *true*;

$\quad$ **else**

$\quad\quad$ **return** *false*;

As mentioned by the author, key sizes can be shrunk by a factor k using more structured matrices and relying on the ring version of the SIS problem, but we will skip this detail in this section for simplicity. Public and private keys are respectively uniformly random matrices $\mathbf{A} \in \mathbb{Z}_q^{n \times m}$ and $\mathbf{S} \in \{-d, \ldots, 0, \ldots, d\}^{m \times k}$ and the signature process invokes a random oracle $H : \{0, 1\}^* \rightarrow \left\{ \mathbf{v} : \mathbf{v} \in \{0, 1\}^k, \|\mathbf{v}\|_1 \leq \kappa \right\}$. A signature $(\mathbf{z}, \mathbf{c})$ of a message μ corresponds to a combination of the secret key and the hash of this message, shifted by a commitment value also used in the random oracle.

5   Description of Our Scheme

5.1   Putting the Pieces Together

Before exposing our scheme, we want to recall an important property over the NTRU lattice that we will make use of. We denote :

$$\Lambda_q^\perp(\mathbf{P}) = \left\{ (\mathbf{y_1}, \mathbf{y_2}) / (\mathbf{1} \quad \mathbf{h}) \cdot (\mathbf{y_1} \quad \mathbf{y_2})^t = \mathbf{0} \mod q \right\} = \left\{ (-\mathbf{h} * \mathbf{x} \mod q, \mathbf{x}), \mathbf{x} \in \mathbb{Z}_q^N \right\} \tag{6}$$

Then one can see $\Lambda_q^\perp(\mathbf{P}) = q \cdot \Lambda_q(\mathbf{P})^*$, and $\Lambda_q(\mathbf{P}) = q \cdot \Lambda_q^\perp(\mathbf{P})^*$. If we borrow the notation from code-based cryptography, if $\Lambda_q(\mathbf{P})$ is generate by $\mathbf{P} = (\mathbf{1}, \mathbf{h})$ then $\Lambda_q^\perp(\mathbf{P})$ is generated by $(\mathbf{h}, -\mathbf{1})$.

As the key generation part of our scheme is exclusively constituted by the NTRUSign key generation process, we use the algorithm described in [10] to get N, q, d, $\mathcal{N}$, and ν, then invoke algorithm 1 for our keyGen procedure, to get the public and private matrices $\mathbf{P}$ and $\mathbf{S}$ as depicted in algorithm 7.

To sign a message $\mu \in \{0,1\}^*$, we will need a regular random oracle $H : \{0,1\}^* \rightarrow \mathcal{R}_q$. To add some randomness to our signature, the oracle's input will be an element of $\mathcal{R}_q$ represented under a bit string concatenated with our message μ. We then NTRUSign the oracle's output to get our leaky sample, which we shift by a mask $(\mathbf{y_1}, \mathbf{y_2})$ large enough to statistically hide this leak. Finally, we apply a rejection sampling step to ensure that the overall signature follows the expected distribution.

Algorithm 7: KeyGen(N, q, d, $\mathcal{N}$, and ν)

Input: N, q, d, $\mathcal{N}$, and ν
Output: $pk = \mathbf{h} = \mathbf{g} * \mathbf{f}^{-1} \mod q$
  and $sk = \mathbf{f}, \mathbf{g}$
begin
> **repeat**
>> $\mathbf{f} \xleftarrow{\$} \mathcal{T}(d)$, $\mathbf{g} \xleftarrow{\$} \mathcal{T}(d)$;
>
> **until** $\mathbf{f}$ *is invertible in* $\mathcal{R}_q$;
> $\mathbf{h} = \mathbf{g} * \mathbf{f}^{-1}$;
> **return** $\mathbf{P} = (-\mathbf{h}, 1)$, $\mathbf{S} = (\mathbf{f}, \mathbf{g})$;

Algorithm 8: Sign($\mathbf{P}, \mathbf{S}, \mu$)

Input: Public and private keys, and
  $\mu \in \{0,1\}^*$ the message to
  sign
Output: $(\mathbf{x_1}, \mathbf{x_2})$, $\mathbf{e}$ the signature
begin
> $\mathbf{y_1} \xleftarrow{\$} D_\sigma^N$, $\mathbf{y_2} \xleftarrow{\$} D_\sigma^N$;
> $\mathbf{e} = H(\mathbf{P}(\mathbf{y_1}, \mathbf{y_2}), \mu) = $
> $H(\mathbf{y_2} - \mathbf{h} * \mathbf{y_1}, \mu)$;
> $(\mathbf{s}, \mathbf{t}) = \text{NTRUSign}_\mathbf{S}(\mathbf{0}, \mathbf{e})$;
> $(\mathbf{x_1}, \mathbf{x_2}) = $
> $(\mathbf{0}, \mathbf{e}) - (\mathbf{s}, \mathbf{t}) + (\mathbf{y_1}, \mathbf{y_2})$;

return $(\mathbf{x_1}, \mathbf{x_2})$, $\mathbf{e}$ *with probability*
$$\min\left(\frac{D_\sigma^{2N}(\mathbf{x})}{M \cdot D_{(-\mathbf{s}, \mathbf{e}-\mathbf{t}), \sigma}^{2N}(\mathbf{x})}, 1 \right);$$

Algorithm 9: Verify($\mathbf{P}, (\mathbf{x_1}, \mathbf{x_2}), \mathbf{e}, \mu$)

Input: Public key $\mathbf{P}$, a signature $(\mathbf{x_1}, \mathbf{x_2})$, $\mathbf{e}$, and a message μ
Output: *true* if and only if $(\mathbf{x_1}, \mathbf{x_2})$, $\mathbf{e}$ is a valid signature of μ
begin
> **if** $\|(\mathbf{x_1}, \mathbf{x_2})\|_2 \leq \eta\sigma\sqrt{2N}$ *and* $H(\mathbf{P} \cdot (\mathbf{x_1}, \mathbf{x_2}) - \mathbf{e}, \mu) = \mathbf{e}$ **then**
>> **return** *true*;
>
> **else**
>> **return** *false;*

We insist on the fact that in the original scheme *with perturbations*, the aim was to sign the message μ enough times so that the transcript an adversary could collect with couples of messages and signatures is short enough to make all secret key recovery techniques fail. The main difference in our scheme consists in hiding the leaky part with something larger so that it becomes indistinguishable, whether than sign it again and again. In other words, the leaky part of NTRUSign plays the role of the secret key in [19].

5.2   Sets of Parameters

Hereafter is a set of parameters for our signature scheme, given different security levels. One interesting aspect of those sets is that we had to raise q and N for our NTRUSign part to be secure, but due to the small norm of our NTRU signature, this q is not raised as much as in [19]. This results in the nice property of lowering key and signature sizes.

Table 3. Parameters, signature and key sizes for our scheme, given the security level k

Security parameter (bits) k	100	100	112	112	128	128	160	160
Optimized for	Size	Speed	Size	Speed	Size	Speed	Size	Speed
N	431	431	479	479	541	541	617	617
d	34	34	42	42	61	61	57	57
$\log_2(q)$	16	16	16	16	16	16	16	16
η (lemma 2.3.2)	1.296	1.296	1.297	1.297	1.299	1.299	1.314	1.314
ν	0.16686	0.16686	0.15828	0.15828	0.14894	0.14894	0.13946	0.13946
$\mathcal{N}$	109	139	128	165	160	213	165	218
α (lemma 2.3.1)	6	12	6.5	13	7	14	7.5	15
$\sigma = \eta\alpha\mathcal{N}$	848	2162	1080	2783	1455	3874	1627	4297
$M = e^{1+1/(2\alpha^2)}$ (lemma 2.3.3)	7.492	2.728	7.477	2.726	7.465	2.725	7.455	2.724
signature size (bits) $\approx 2N\log_2(\alpha\sigma)$	10700	12700	12300	14600	14500	17100	16800	19800
pk size (bits) $\approx N\log_2(q)$	6900	6900	7700	7700	8700	8700	9900	9900
sk size (bits) $\approx 2N\log_2(3)$	1400	1400	1550	1550	1750	1750	2000	2000

5.3   Security of Our Scheme

In this section, k will represent the security parameter, typically $k = 80$ for a "toy" security, $k = 100$ or 112 for a current security, and $k = 128$ to 160 for a "strong" security. Due to space restrictions, we will only mention the different known kinds of attack the reader can find in the literature. For further details, we refer to [11, 20, 6, 14] for the NTRUSign part, and to [19, 18, 23] for Lyuba-shevsky's scheme. Due to the hybridness of our scheme, potential attacks could be of three types, that we exposed in what follows, before tackling them.

The first one consists in attacking the NTRU lattice by trying to find back the private key $(\mathbf{f}, \mathbf{g})$ only from the public key $\mathbf{h} = \mathbf{g} * \mathbf{f}^{-1}$ (and eventually some signatures after Lyubashevsky's layer). Even if there is no theoretical proof on the intractability of this attack, there hasn't been (to the best of our knowledge) any efficient way to do so neither. Parameters given in table 3 have been chosen so that someone succeeding in doing so would achieve a lattice reduction with better Hermit factors than those described in 4 respectively to the security parameter k. Such a good algorithm could obviously be used to solve worst-case of lattice problems on general convolution modular lattices. A second way to break our signature scheme, still by finding out the secret key, could be trying to isolate the NTRU signature inside our signature to find enough leaky parts to then proceed to a [6]-like attack. This issue is addressed by Theorem 2.3.5. Finally, we show that if an adversary succeed in creating a forgery in polynomial-time, then we can use this forgery to solve the SIS problem, which is the main theorem (5.3.1) of this section.

Regarding attacks against the NTRUSign, all parameters have been heighten so they ensure way more than k bits of security. We are aware that some attacks might lower the security level [20, 7, 14, 6], but also due to our lack of knowledge on how to benefit from the singular structure of NTRU lattices, we take a conservative gap between claimed and effective security. Nevertheless, all parameters given in table 2 were set in such a way that lattice reduction techniques are meant to fail, either by finding a short vector too long, either by a computational complexity blow up. Also due to recent attacks such as [14, 7, 6], the NTRUSign parameters presented in [11] don't reach the claimed security. Therefore, we ran the Baseline Parameter Generation Algorithm of [10], and integrated the most recent known attacks. As one can notice, we intentionally took a "huge" degree N, and a big q for two reasons. It first gives more confidence about the security of the underlying NTRU lattice, and it was also necessary for proofs to work after applying Lyubashevsky's layer to our scheme.

As far as we know, lattice-reduction over $\Lambda_q^\perp(\mathbf{A})$ is the most efficient technique to solve random instances of knapsack problems. Experiments in [7] led to the ability of finding a vector $\mathbf{v} \in \Lambda_q^\perp(\mathbf{A})$ whose norm is at most $\|\mathbf{v}\|_2 \leq \delta^{2N} \cdot \sqrt{q}$, for δ depending on the lattice-reduction algorithm which is used (see below). Experiments from Micciancio and Regev [23] conducted to a minimum of $\delta^m \cdot q^{n/m} \approx \min(q, 2^{2\sqrt{N \log_2(q) \log_2(\delta)}})$ for $m \approx \sqrt{N \log_2(q)/\log_2(\delta)}$.

In 2011, Lindner and Peikert [18] achieved to give an approximation of the best δ reachable for a given security level k, using a conservative approximation on BKZ's running time :

$$t_{BKZ}(\delta) = \log_2(T_{BKZ}(\delta)) = 1.8/\log_2(\delta) - 110 \tag{7}$$

where $T_{BKZ}(\delta)$ is the running time of BKZ in second, on their machine. So assuming one can achieve 2^{30} operations per second on a "standard" computer, to determine δ given the security parameter k, we have :

$$\log_2(\delta) := \frac{1.8}{\log_2(\frac{T_{BKZ}(\delta)}{2^{30}}) + 110} = \frac{1.8}{k - 30 + 110} = \frac{1.8}{k + 80} \tag{8}$$

This equation gives us a way to get δ as a function of the security parameter k, see table 4. Similarly to [19], in order to hide properly our leaky part $(\mathbf{0}, \mathbf{e}) - (\mathbf{s}, \mathbf{t})$, we will use Lemmas 2.3.1 and 2.3.2 to get a proper α.

Table 4. δ and α as a function of the security level k

k	100	112	128	160
δ	1.00696	1.00652	1.00602	1.00521
α	12	13	14	15

Against Forgeries. In this section, we give a short overview of the material that will be needed to base our signature scheme upon the SIS problem over random NTRU lattices. This leads to a signature scheme based on the worst-case hardness of the $\tilde{\mathcal{O}}(N^{1.5})$-SIVP problem over general convolutional modular lattices.

Hybrid 1

Sign$(\mathbf{P}, \mathbf{S}, \mu)$

1. $\mathbf{y_1} \xleftarrow{\$} D_\sigma^N$, $\mathbf{y_2} \xleftarrow{\$} D_\sigma^N$
2. $\mathbf{e} \xleftarrow{\$} \mathcal{R}_q$
3. $(\mathbf{s}, \mathbf{t}) = \text{NTRUSign}_\mathbf{S}(0, \mathbf{e})$
4. $(\mathbf{x_1}, \mathbf{x_2}) = (0, \mathbf{e}) - (\mathbf{s}, \mathbf{t}) + (\mathbf{y_1}, \mathbf{y_2})$
5. with probability $\min\left(\frac{D_\sigma^{2N}(\mathbf{x})}{M \cdot D_{(-\mathbf{s}, \mathbf{e}-\mathbf{t}), \sigma}^{2N}(\mathbf{x})}, 1\right)$:

   – Output $(\mathbf{x_1}, \mathbf{x_2}), \mathbf{e}$
   – Program $H(\mathbf{P} \cdot (\mathbf{x_1}, \mathbf{x_2}) - \mathbf{e}, \mu) = \mathbf{e}$

Hybrid 2

Sign$(\mathbf{P}, \mathbf{S}, \mu)$

1. $\mathbf{e} \xleftarrow{\$} \mathcal{R}_q$
2. $(\mathbf{x_1}, \mathbf{x_2}) \xleftarrow{\$} D_\sigma^{2N}$
3. with probability $1/M$:
   – Output $(\mathbf{x_1}, \mathbf{x_2}), \mathbf{e}$
   – Program $H(\mathbf{P} \cdot (\mathbf{x_1}, \mathbf{x_2}) - \mathbf{e}, \mu) = \mathbf{e}$

Fig. 1. Signing Hybrids

We now expose the core of the reduction, which allows us to base the security of our signature scheme upon the ℓ_2-SIS$_{q,N,2N,\beta}$ Problem of general NTRU lattices. Our main theorem will be proved by two lemmas, mostly proved in [19], but revisited in appendix A in some of the details in order to fit best with our sets of parameters.

Theorem 5.3.1 ([19] revisited) *Assume there is polynomial-time forger $\mathcal{F}$, which makes at most s (resp. h) queries to the signing (resp. random) oracle, who breaks our signature scheme (with parameters such those in Table 3), then there is a polynomial-time algorithm to solve the ℓ_2-SIS$_{q,N,2N,\beta}$ Problem for $\beta = 2\eta\sigma\sqrt{2N}$ with probability $\approx \frac{\delta^2}{h+s}$. Moreover, the signing algorithm 8 produces a signature with probability $\approx \frac{1}{M}$ and the verifying algorithm 9 accepts the signature produced by an honest signer with probability at least $1 - 2^{-2N}$.*

Proof. We begin the proof by showing that our signature algorithm 8 is statistically close (within distance $\epsilon = s(h + s) \cdot 2^{-N+1} + s \cdot \frac{2^{-\omega(\log_2 2N)}}{M}$ by Lemma 5.3.2) to the one in Hybrid 2 in Figure 1. Given that Hybrid 2 outputs something with probability $1/M$, our signing algorithm will output something too with probability $(1 - \epsilon)/M$. Then by Lemma 5.3.3, we show that if a forger $\mathcal{F}$ succeeds in forging with probability δ when the signing algorithm is replaced by the one in Hybrid 2, then we can use $\mathcal{F}$ to come up with a non-zero lattice vector $\mathbf{v}$ such that $\|\mathbf{v}\| \leq 2\eta\sigma\sqrt{2N}$ and $\mathbf{Pv} = 0$ with probability at least $\left(\delta - 2^{-k}\right)\left(\frac{\delta - 2^{-k}}{h+s} - 2^{-k}\right)$. $\square$

Lemma 5.3.2 ([19] revisited). *Let $\mathcal{D}$ be a distinguisher who can query the random oracle H and either the actual signing algorithm 8 or Hybrid 2 in Figure 1. If he makes h queries to H and s queries to the signing algorithm that he has access to, then for all but a $e^{-\Omega(N)}$ fraction of all possible matrices $\mathbf{P}$, his advantage of distinguishing the actual signing algorithm from the one in Hybrid 2 is at most $s(h+s) \cdot 2^{-N+1} + s \cdot \frac{2^{-\omega(\log_2 2N)}}{M}$.*

Lemma 5.3.3 ([19] revisited). *Suppose there exists a polynomial-time forger $\mathcal{F}$ who makes at most h queries to the signer in Hybrid 2, s queries to the random oracle H, and succeeds in forging with probability δ. Then there exists an algorithm of the same time-complexity as $\mathcal{F}$ that for a given $\mathbf{P} \xleftarrow{\$} \mathbb{Z}_q^{N \times 2N}$ finds a non-zero $\mathbf{v}$ such that $\|\mathbf{v}\|_2 \leq 2\eta\sigma\sqrt{2N}$ and $\mathbf{Pv} = \mathbf{0}$ with probability at least*

$$\left(\delta - 2^{-k}\right) \left(\frac{\delta - 2^{-k}}{h+s} - 2^{-k}\right).$$

6 Conclusion

In this work, we described a method for sealing NTRUSign signatures' leak, based on the worst-case hardness of standard problems over ideal lattices. This method differs from existing heuristic countermeasures such the use of perturbations [12] or the deformation of the parallelepiped [15] - both broken [6] - but also from provably secure modifications of NTRUSign like [26] which uses gaussian sampling techniques in order to not disclose the secret basis [8]. Moreover, this technique seems to be sufficiently generic to be applied on GGH signatures. Details on this will be provided in a longer version of this paper.

We show that it is actually possible to use the rejection sampling technique from [19] instead of gaussian sampling to achieve zero-knowledgeness, while keeping most of NTRUSign's efficiency. Moreover, parameter refinements allowed us to lower the rejection rate, leading to performance improvements regarding [19], together with smaller signature and secret key sizes.

It might be possible to improve the rejection sampling procedure even more using techniques such those in [5], but it seems necessary to break the public key's particular shape to do so. Therefore, it is still an open question whether the resulting benefit in the signature size would worth the key sizes growth.

Acknowledgment. The authors thank Léo Ducas for helpful discussions on rejection sampling, and the anonymous PQCrypto reviewers for their valuable comments.

References

[1] Ajtai, M.: Generating hard instances of lattice problems (extended abstract). In: Proceedings of the Twenty-Eighth Annual ACM Symposium on the Theory of Computing, pp. 99–108. ACM (1996)

[2] Babai, L.: On lovász' lattice reduction and the nearest lattice point problem (shortened version). In: Mehlhorn, K. (ed.) STACS 1985. LNCS, vol. 182, pp. 13–20. Springer, Heidelberg (1985)

[3] Bellare, M., Neven, G.: Multi-signatures in the plain public-key model and a general forking lemma. In: Proceedings of the 13th ACM Conference on Computer and Communications Security, CCS 2006, pp. 390–399. ACM, New York (2006)

[4] Chen, Y., Nguyen, P.Q.: Bkz 2.0: Better lattice security estimates. In: Lee, D.H., Wang, X. (eds.) ASIACRYPT 2011. LNCS, vol. 7073, pp. 1–20. Springer, Heidelberg (2011)

[5] Ducas, L., Durmus, A., Lepoint, T., Lyubashevsky, V.: Lattice signatures and bimodal gaussians. In: Canetti, R., Garay, J.A. (eds.) CRYPTO 2013, Part I. LNCS, vol. 8042, pp. 40–56. Springer, Heidelberg (2013)

[6] Ducas, L., Nguyen, P.Q.: Learning a zonotope and more: Cryptanalysis of NTRUSign countermeasures. In: Wang, X., Sako, K. (eds.) ASIACRYPT 2012. LNCS, vol. 7658, pp. 433–450. Springer, Heidelberg (2012)

[7] Gama, N., Nguyen, P.Q.: Predicting Lattice Reduction. In: Smart, N.P. (ed.) EUROCRYPT 2008. LNCS, vol. 4965, pp. 31–51. Springer, Heidelberg (2008)

[8] Gentry, C., Peikert, C., Vaikuntanathan, V.: Trapdoors for hard lattices and new cryptographic constructions. In: STOC, pp. 197–206 (2008)

[9] Goldreich, O., Goldwasser, S., Halevi, S.: Public-key cryptosystems from lattice reduction problems. In: Kaliski Jr., B.S. (ed.) CRYPTO 1997. LNCS, vol. 1294, pp. 112–131. Springer, Heidelberg (1997)

[10] Hoffstein, J., Howgrave-graham, N., Pipher, J., Silverman, J.H., Whyte, W.: Performance Improvements and a Baseline Parameter Generation Algorithm for NTRUSign. In: Proc. of Workshop on Mathematical Problems and Techniques in Cryptology, pp. 99–126 (2005)

[11] Hoffstein, J., Howgrave-Graham, N., Pipher, J., Whyte, W.: Practical lattice-based cryptography: NTRUEncrypt and NTRUSign. In: Nguyen, P.Q., et al. (eds.) The LLL algorithm. Survey and Applications. Information Security and Cryptography, pp. 349–390. Springer, Dordrecht (2010)

[12] Hoffstein, J., Howgrave-Graham, N., Pipher, J., Silverman, J.H., Whyte, W.: NTRUSIGN: Digital signatures using the NTRU lattice. In: Joye, M. (ed.) CT-RSA 2003. LNCS, vol. 2612, pp. 122–140. Springer, Heidelberg (2003)

[13] Hoffstein, J., Pipher, J., Silverman, J.H.: NSS: An NTRU lattice-based signature scheme. In: Pfitzmann, B. (ed.) EUROCRYPT 2001. LNCS, vol. 2045, pp. 211–228. Springer, Heidelberg (2001)

[14] Howgrave-Graham, N.: A hybrid lattice-reduction and meet-in-the-middle attack against NTRU. In: Menezes, A. (ed.) CRYPTO 2007. LNCS, vol. 4622, pp. 150–169. Springer, Heidelberg (2007)

[15] Hu, Y., Wang, B., He, W.: NTRUsign with a new perturbation. IEEE Trans. Inf. Theor. 54(7), 3216–3221 (2008)

[16] Impagliazzo, R., Naor, M.: Efficient cryptographic schemes provably as secure as subset sum. Journal of Cryptology 9, 236–241 (1996)

[17] Lenstra, H.J., Lenstra, A., Lovász, L.: Factoring polynomials with rational coefficients. Mathematische Annalen 261, 515–534 (1982)

[18] Lindner, R., Peikert, C.: Better key sizes (and attacks) for LWE-based encryption. In: Kiayias, A. (ed.) CT-RSA 2011. LNCS, vol. 6558, pp. 319–339. Springer, Heidelberg (2011)

[19] Lyubashevsky, V.: Lattice signatures without trapdoors. In: Pointcheval, D., Johansson, T. (eds.) EUROCRYPT 2012. LNCS, vol. 7237, pp. 738–755. Springer, Heidelberg (2012)

[20] May, A., Silverman, J.H.: Dimension reduction methods for convolution modular lattices. In: Silverman, J.H. (ed.) CaLC 2001. LNCS, vol. 2146, pp. 110–125. Springer, Heidelberg (2001)

[21] Micciancio, D., Mol, P.: Pseudorandom knapsacks and the sample complexity of LWE search-to-decision reductions. In: Rogaway, P. (ed.) CRYPTO 2011. LNCS, vol. 6841, pp. 465–484. Springer, Heidelberg (2011)

[22] Micciancio, D., Regev, O.: Worst-case to Average-case reductions based on Gaussian measure. SIAM Journal on Computing 37(1), 267–302 (2007); Preliminary version in FOCS 2004

[23] Micciancio, D., Regev, O.: Lattice-based Cryptography. In: Bernstein, D., Buchmann, J., Dahmen, E. (eds.) Post-Quantum Cryptography, pp. 147–191. Springer, Heidelberg (2009)

[24] Nguyên, P.Q., Regev, O.: Learning a parallelepiped: Cryptanalysis of GGH and NTRU signatures. In: Vaudenay, S. (ed.) EUROCRYPT 2006. LNCS, vol. 4004, pp. 271–288. Springer, Heidelberg (2006)

[25] Stehlé, D., Steinfeld, R.: Making NTRU as secure as worst-case problems over ideal lattices. In: Paterson, K.G. (ed.) EUROCRYPT 2011. LNCS, vol. 6632, pp. 27–47. Springer, Heidelberg (2011)

[26] Stehlé, D., Steinfeld, R.: Making NTRUencrypt and NTRUsign as secure as standard worst-case problems over ideal lattices. Cryptology ePrint Archive, Report 2013/004 (2013) http://eprint.iacr.org/

A   Proofs

A.1   Section 2

Most of the lemmas of Section 2 are proved in [19]. We therefore refer the reader to the original paper for these proofs. Nevertheless, we adapted lemma 2.3.3 to make bounds tighter with respect to different security levels. We prove the correctness of our modification :

Proof.

$$D_\sigma^{2N}(\mathbf{x})/D_{\mathbf{v},\sigma}^{2N}(\mathbf{x}) = \rho_\sigma^{2N}(\mathbf{x})/\rho_{\mathbf{v},\sigma}^{2N}(\mathbf{x}) = \exp\left(\frac{\|\mathbf{x}-\mathbf{v}\|^2 - \|\mathbf{x}\|^2}{2\sigma^2}\right) = \exp\left(\frac{\|\mathbf{v}\|^2 - 2\langle\mathbf{x},\mathbf{v}\rangle}{2\sigma^2}\right)$$

By lemma 2.3.1 and using the fact that $\sigma = \omega(\|\mathbf{v}\|\sqrt{\log(2N)})$, with probability $1 - 2^{-\omega(\log(2N))}$ we have

$$\exp\left(\frac{\|\mathbf{v}\|^2 - 2\langle\mathbf{x},\mathbf{v}\rangle}{2\sigma^2}\right) < \exp\left(\frac{\|\mathbf{v}\|^2 + \omega(\sigma\|\mathbf{v}\|\sqrt{\log(2N)})}{2\sigma^2}\right) = \mathcal{O}(1).$$

And more precisely, by setting $r = \alpha\|\mathbf{v}\|\sigma$ in lemma 2.3.1 with α determined by the security parameter k in table 1, we obtain with probability $1 - 2^{-k}$ that

$$\exp\left(\frac{\|\mathbf{v}\|^2 - 2\langle\mathbf{x},\mathbf{v}\rangle}{2\sigma^2}\right) < \exp\left(\frac{\|\mathbf{v}\|^2 + 2\alpha\|\mathbf{v}\|\sigma}{2\sigma^2}\right) = \exp\left(\frac{\|\mathbf{v}\|^2}{2\sigma^2} + \frac{\alpha\|\mathbf{v}\|}{\sigma}\right) \overset{\sigma=\alpha\|\mathbf{v}\|}{=} e^{1+1/(2\alpha^2)}.$$

$\square$

A.2   Proofs of Section 5

We begin with the proof of lemma 5.3.2, which states that our actual signing algorithm 8 is indistinguishable from Hybrid 2 depicted in Figure 1, using Hybrid 1 as an intermediate step.

Proof. First, let us prove that $\mathcal{D}$ has an advantage of at most $s(h+s) \cdot 2^{-N+1}$ of distinguishing between the actual signature scheme 8 and Hybrid 1. The only difference between those algorithms is the output of the random oracle H. It is chosen uniformly at random from $\mathcal{R}_q$ in Hybrid 1, rather than according to $H(\mathbf{Py}, \mu)$ for $y \xleftarrow{\$} D_q^{2N}$ in the real signing algorithm. Random oracle in Hybrid 1 is then programmed to answer $H(\mathbf{Px} - \mathbf{e}, \mu) = H(\mathbf{Py}, \mu)$ without checking whether $(\mathbf{Py}, \mu)$ was already queried or not. Since $\mathcal{D}$ calls H (resp. algorithm 8) h (resp s) times, at most $s + h$ values of $(\mathbf{Py}, \mu)$ will be set. We now bound the probability of generating such an already set value. Using lemma 2.3.2, we can see that for any
$$\mathbf{t} \in \mathbb{Z}_q^N,$$

$$Pr[\mathbf{Py} = \mathbf{t}; y \xleftarrow{\$} D_q^{2N}] = Pr[\mathbf{y_1} = (\mathbf{t} - \mathbf{h} * \mathbf{y_0}); y \xleftarrow{\$} D_q^{2N}] \leq \max_{\mathbf{t'} \in \mathbb{Z}_q^N} Pr[\mathbf{y_1} = \mathbf{t'}; \mathbf{y_1} \xleftarrow{\$} D_q^N] \leq 2^{-N}.$$

Therefore, if Hybrid 1 is called s times with the probability of getting a collision begging less than $(s + h) \cdot 2^{-N+1}$ for each call, then the probability of coming up with a collision after s calls is at most $s(s + h) \cdot 2^{-N+1}$.

We pursue by showing that the outputs of Hybrids 1 and 2 are statistically within distance $\frac{2^{-\omega(\log_2 2N)}}{M}$. As noticed in [19], this is an almost straightforward consequence of theorem 2.3.5 : assuming both Hybrids output $(\mathbf{x}, (-\mathbf{s}, \mathbf{e} - \mathbf{t}))$ with respective probabilities $\min\left(\frac{D_\sigma^{2N}(\mathbf{x})}{M \cdot D_{(-\mathbf{s}, \mathbf{e} - \mathbf{t}), \sigma}^{2N}(\mathbf{x})}, 1\right)$ for Hybrid 1 and $1/M$ for Hybrid 2, they respectively play the role of $\mathcal{A}$ and $\mathcal{F}$ (with $T = \eta \alpha \mathcal{N}$). Even if both Hybrids only output $\mathbf{e}$, this does not increase the statistical distance because given $\mathbf{e}$, one can generate $(-\mathbf{s}, \mathbf{e} - \mathbf{t})$ such that $\mathbf{P}(-\mathbf{s}, \mathbf{e} - \mathbf{t}) = \mathbf{e}$ simply by NTRUSigning $(\mathbf{0}, \mathbf{e})$, and this will have the exact same distribution as the $\mathbf{e}$ in both Hybrids. Finally, as the signing oracle is called s times, the statistical distance between the two Hybrids is at most $s \cdot \frac{2^{-\omega(\log_2 2N)}}{M}$, or more concretely $s \cdot \frac{2^{-k}}{M}$. The claim in the lemma is obtained by summing both distances.   □

We now prove lemma 5.3.3, which provides us with a ℓ_2-SIS$_{q,N,2N,\beta}$ solver using a polynomial-time successful forger.

Proof. Let $t = h + s$ be the number of calls to the random oracle H during $\mathcal{F}$'s attack. H can be either queried by the forger or programmed by the signing algorithm when $\mathcal{F}$ asks for some message to be signed. We pick random coins ϕ (resp. ψ) for the forger (resp. the signer), along with $\mathbf{r_1}, \ldots, \mathbf{r_t} \leftarrow \mathcal{R}_q$, which will correspond to the H's responses. We now consider a subroutine $\mathcal{A}$, which on input $(\mathbf{P}, \phi, \psi, \mathbf{r_1}, \ldots, \mathbf{r_t})$ initializes $\mathcal{F}$ by giving it $\mathbf{P}$ and ϕ and run it. Each time $\mathcal{F}$ asks for a signature, $\mathcal{A}$ runs Hybrid 2 using the signer's coins ψ to get a signature, and H is programmed to answer with the first unused $\mathbf{r}_i \in (\mathbf{r}_1, \ldots, \mathbf{r}_t)$. $\mathcal{A}$ keeps track of the answered $\mathbf{r}_i$ in case $\mathcal{F}$ queries the same message to be signed again. Similarly, if $\mathcal{F}$ queries directly the random oracle, H will answer with the first unused $\mathbf{r}_i \in (\mathbf{r}_1, \ldots, \mathbf{r}_t)$, unless the query was already made. When $\mathcal{F}$ ends and eventually come up with an output (with probability δ), $\mathcal{A}$ simply forwards $\mathcal{F}$'s output.

With probability δ, $\mathcal{F}$ succeeds in forging, coming up with $(\mathbf{x}, \mathbf{e})$ satisfying $\|\mathbf{x}\| \leq \eta\sigma\sqrt{2N}$ and $H(\mathbf{Px} - \mathbf{e}, \mu) = \mathbf{e}$ for some message μ. If H was not queried nor programmed on some input $\mathbf{w} = \mathbf{Px} - \mathbf{e}$, then $\mathcal{F}$ has only a $1/|\mathcal{R}_q| = q^{-N}$ (*i.e. negligible*) chance of generating a $\mathbf{e}$ such that $\mathbf{e} = H(\mathbf{w}, \mu)$. Therefore, $\mathcal{F}$ has at least a $\delta - q^{-N}$ chance of succeeding in a forgery with $\mathbf{e}$ being one of the $\mathbf{r}_i$'s. Assume $\mathbf{e} = \mathbf{r}_j$, we are left with two cases : $\mathbf{r}_j$ is a response to a random oracle query made by $\mathcal{F}$, or it was program during the signing procedure invoked by $\mathcal{A}$.

Let first assume that the random oracle was programmed to answer $H(\mathbf{Px}' - \mathbf{e}, \mu') = \mathbf{e}$ on input μ'. If $\mathcal{F}$ succeeds in forging $(\mathbf{x}, \mathbf{e})$ for some (possibly different) message μ, then $H(\mathbf{Px}' - \mathbf{e}, \mu') = H(\mathbf{Px} - \mathbf{e}, \mu)$. If $\mu \neq \mu'$ or $\mathbf{Px}' - \mathbf{e} \neq \mathbf{Px} - \mathbf{e}$, then $\mathcal{F}$ found a pre-image of $\mathbf{r}_j$. Therefore, $\mu = \mu'$ and $\mathbf{Px}' - \mathbf{e} = \mathbf{Px} - \mathbf{e}$, so that $\mathbf{P}(\mathbf{x} - \mathbf{x}') = \mathbf{0}$. We know that $\mathbf{x} - \mathbf{x}' \neq \mathbf{0}$ (because otherwise $(\mathbf{x}, \mathbf{e})$ and $(\mathbf{x}', \mathbf{e})$ sign the same message μ), and since $\|\mathbf{x}\|_2, \|\mathbf{x}'\|_2 \leq \eta\sigma\sqrt{2N}$, we have that $\|\mathbf{x} - \mathbf{x}'\| \leq 2\eta\sigma\sqrt{2N}$.

Let now assume that $\mathbf{r}_j$ was a response of the random oracle invoked by $\mathcal{F}$. We start by recording $\mathcal{F}$'s output $(\mathbf{x}, \mathbf{r}_j)$ for the message μ, then generate fresh random elements $\mathbf{r}'_j, \ldots, \mathbf{r}'_t \leftarrow \mathcal{R}_q$. We then run $\mathcal{A}$ again with input $(\mathbf{P}, \phi, \psi, \mathbf{r}_1, \ldots, \mathbf{r}_{j-1}, \mathbf{r}'_j, \ldots, \mathbf{r}'_t)$, and by the General Forking Lemma [3], we obtain that the probability that $\mathbf{r}'_j \neq \mathbf{r}_j$ and the forger uses the random oracle response $\mathbf{r}'_j$ (and the query associated to it) in its forgery is at least

$$\left(\delta - \frac{1}{|\mathcal{R}_q|}\right)\left(\frac{\delta - 1/|\mathcal{R}_q|}{t} - \frac{1}{|\mathcal{R}_q|}\right),$$

and thus with the above probability, $\mathcal{F}$ outputs a signature $(\mathbf{x}', \mathbf{r}'_j)$ of the message μ and $\mathbf{Px} - \mathbf{e} = \mathbf{Px}' - \mathbf{e}'$ where we let $\mathbf{e} = \mathbf{r}_j$ and $\mathbf{e}' = \mathbf{r}'_j$. By rearranging terms in the above equality we obtain

$$\mathbf{P}(\mathbf{x} - \mathbf{x}') - \overbrace{(\mathbf{e} - \mathbf{e}')}^{\mathbf{P}\left((0,\mathbf{e}) - (0,\mathbf{e}') - \left((\mathbf{s},\mathbf{t}) - (\mathbf{s}',\mathbf{t}')\right)\right)} = \mathbf{0}$$
$$\mathbf{P}(\mathbf{y} - \mathbf{y}') = \mathbf{0} \qquad (9)$$

But since $H(\mathbf{Py}, \mu) = \mathbf{e} = \mathbf{r}_j \neq \mathbf{r}'_j = \mathbf{e}' = H(\mathbf{Py}', \mu)$, necessarily $\mathbf{y} \neq \mathbf{y}'$, and as $\|\mathbf{y}\|_2, \|\mathbf{y}'\|_2 \leq \eta\sigma\sqrt{2N}$, we finally have that $\|\mathbf{y} - \mathbf{y}'\|_2 \leq 2\eta\sigma\sqrt{2N}$ with probability

$$\left(\delta - 2^{-k}\right)\left(\frac{\delta - 2^{-k}}{h + s} - 2^{-k}\right).$$

$\square$

On the Efficiency of Provably Secure NTRU

Daniel Cabarcas[1], Patrick Weiden[2], and Johannes Buchmann[2]

[1] Universidad Nacional de Colombia sede Medellín, Medellín, Colombia
dcabarc@unal.edu.co
[2] Technische Universität Darmstadt, Darmstadt, Germany
{pweiden,buchmann}@cdc.informatik.tu-darmstadt.de

Abstract. It is still a challenge to find a lattice-based public-key encryption scheme that combines efficiency (as e.g. NTRUEncrypt) with a very strong security guarantee (as e.g. the ring-LWE based scheme of Lyubashevsky, Peikert, and Regev LPR-LWE). Stehlé and Steinfeld (EUROCRYPT 11) presented a provably secure variant of NTRUEncrypt (pNE), perhaps the first step towards addressing the challenge. In this paper we thoroughly assess the efficiency of pNE, and investigate whether it can meet those presumed extremes. We show how to select parameters that provide a given security level and we explain how to instantiate pNE. As we compare our instantiation of pNE to NTRUEncrypt and LPR-LWE, we find that pNE is still inferior to both due to the very wide Gaussian distribution used in its key generation.

Keywords: Public-Key Encryption, Efficiency, NTRUEncrypt, Lattice, Learning With Errors, and Discrete Gaussian Distribution.

1 Introduction

Public-key encryption (PKE) based on lattice problems has attracted a lot of attention in the last decade. This is in part due to the need for alternatives to traditional PKE. Most PKE schemes in use today rely on the hardness of either factoring or computing discrete logarithms. However, the trustworthiness of these assumptions has been eroding by improvements in factoring algorithms and by polynomial time quantum algorithms that solve both problems.

The success of lattice-based PKE has also its own virtues. Among lattice-based encryption schemes one can find NTRUEncrypt, which is competitive in terms of practical efficiency with well established PKEs like RSA [17]. Although the most efficient attacks against NTRUEncrypt use lattice algorithms, there exists no formal proof relating the security of the scheme to a lattice problem.

There are also lattice-based PKE schemes such as Regev's [32], that allow for a worst- to average-case reduction from well established lattice problems. Regev proposed a scheme that is secure as long as the learning with errors problem (LWE) is hard on average, and he shows that the LWE problem is as hard as solving a well established lattice problem in its worst case. His original reduction was a quantum reduction, yet more recently it was shown that a classical reduction is also possible [5]. These worst- to average-case reductions

M. Mosca (Ed.): PQCrypto 2014, LNCS 8772, pp. 22–39, 2014.

have also been used to prove other related problems hard, such as the ring-LWE problem [25] and small parameter variants [26], and subsequently, other provably secure PKE schemes have been proposed [36,13,25,23,8]. In any case, the worst-to average-case reduction is considered a very strong security guarantee because it proves that breaking a randomly chosen instance of the scheme is as hard as solving the hardest instance of a well established lattice problem.

The construction of a lattice-based PKE scheme that has both properties —strong security and practical efficiency— is still an interesting challenge. At Eurocrypt 2011, Stehlé and Steinfeld made a first step towards solving this challenge by presenting a provably secure NTRU-variant [35], which we refer to as pNE. The pNE scheme permits a worst- to average-case reduction. Its similarity to NTRUEncrypt raises the questions of how efficient pNE is and of how far the scheme closes the efficiency gap between NTRUEncrypt and a provably secure scheme. Although the authors of pNE state that an instantiation of pNE is likely to be less efficient than NTRUEncrypt, it is still important to determine how much it closes this gap. Moreover, a recent homomorphic implementation of pNE [4] seem to suggest that pNE can be rather efficient.

The pNE and NTRUEncrypt schemes are structurally very similar. Operations take place in the quotient ring $R_q = \mathbb{Z}_q[x]/\Phi(x)$, where q is a moderately large integer and $\Phi(x)$ is a degree n polynomial. The secret key $\mathbf{f}$ is sampled from R_q and the public key $\mathbf{h}$ is computed as $\mathbf{h} = p\mathbf{g}/\mathbf{f} \in R_q$, where p is a small integer and $\mathbf{g}$ is also sampled from R_q. Then a message $\mathbf{m} \in R_p$ is encrypted by sampling small elements $\mathbf{e}, \mathbf{e}'$ in R_q, and computing the ciphertext $\mathbf{c} := \mathbf{h}\mathbf{e} + p\mathbf{e}' + \mathbf{m} \in R_q$. The main difference between pNE and NTRUEncrypt is the distribution used to sample $\mathbf{f}$ and $\mathbf{g}$. Stehlé and Steinfeld show that if $\mathbf{f}$ and $\mathbf{g}$ are sampled from a discrete Gaussian distribution with a large parameter σ, instead of being sampled uniformly at random from a set of small norm polynomials, the public key $\mathbf{h}$ is statistically close to uniform [35]. They then show that the ciphertext is indistinguishable from random assuming the hardness of the LWE problem on average. Finally, they rely on Regev's [32] worst- to average-case reduction from well established lattice problems to conclude that pNE is secure as long as some lattice problems are hard in the worst case.

Our Contribution. In this paper we answer the question of how efficient pNE is and of how far the scheme closes the efficiency gap between NTRUEncrypt and a provably secure scheme. We do so by presenting a thorough assessment of the efficiency of pNE. In order to achieve this, we address five important problems that are of interest in their own right.

1. We show how to select parameters that provide an expected security level. We do not rely on the worst-case hardness in this context because it is unknown how tight the worst- to average-case reduction is. We rather analyze a well-known attack against the average-case problem underlying pNE and deduce the corresponding security level. For example, a lattice dimension of 2048 is required for a bit security level of 144. Although the security level is

not grounded on the worst- to average-case reduction, we make sure it holds for the chosen parameters.

2. Next, we explain how to implement pNE. In particular, we discuss how to adapt best known discrete Gaussian samplers to fit the needs of pNE and we compare their efficiency.

3. We present experimental data on the performance of pNE. It shows that our pNE implementation is over 100 times slower and requires 24 times larger keys than an implementation of NTRUEncrypt by Security Innovation Inc. We consider this gap too large to be overcome through optimization alone.

4. We then move on to compare pNE with the ring-LWE based scheme of Lyubashevsky, Peikert, and Regev [25] (LPR-LWE). We chose LPR-LWE because it appears to be one of the most efficient provably secure lattice-based PKE schemes, based on the parameter selection by Lindner and Peikert [23] and its implementation by Göttert et al. [15]. In order to allow for a fair comparison, we use an analogous method to derive the LPR-LWE parameters and we implement it using the same procedures as in the pNE implementation. This is possible because pNE and LPR-LWE are structurally similar and rely on the same security assumption. It turns out that LPR-LWE is still superior over pNE. LPR-LWE is more than 5 times faster than pNE and pNE uses keys more than 12 times larger than LPR-LWE.

5. Finally, through a careful analysis, we conclude that the main reason pNE is still less efficient than the other schemes is the very wide Gaussian distribution used in key generation, and the unexpected influence this has on the practical security of the scheme.

Related Work. In a related work, Bos et al. [4] analyze the efficiency of a leveled homomorphic encryption scheme based on pNE. We discuss their results in more detail at the end of Section 4. In this paper we do not analyze the performance of NTRUEncrypt since several works highlight its efficiency, see for example [17,29,20]. There has been less scrutiny over LPR-LWE. Although Göttert et al. [15] tested it in software and hardware, the parameters they consider do not support a worst- to average-case reduction (see [23]). In this paper we analyze LPR-LWE's efficiency for a parameter set that does support such a reduction. Finally, we compare the efficiency of four Gaussian samplers over the integers to use the best for our implementation of pNE. The samplers we consider were proposed by Gentry et al. [14], Peikert [30], Knuth and Yao [22] (adapted in [12]), and Buchmann et al. [7]. The samplers of Ducas et al. [11] and (a discrete variant) of Karney [21] we did not consider in this paper due to their less practical efficiency as stated by the authors.

Organization. This paper is organized as follows. Section 2 introduces notation and background material. Section 3 explains how to select parameters that provide an expected security level. Section 4 briefly describes our implementation of pNE, presents experimental data on its performance, and compares it with both NTRUEncrypt and LPR-LWE. Finally, Section 5 analyzes the efficiency of pNE and draws a conclusion about its main source of inefficiency.

2   Preliminaries

In this section we recall some of the background necessary to support the remainder of the paper. We first describe the assumed hard problem that the pNE scheme relies on, namely the ring-LWE problem. Next, we describe Gaussian sampling techniques, an important building block for implementing pNE. Finally, we describe the pNE scheme itself.

2.1   The Ring-LWE Problem

The security of pNE relies on the assumption that the learning with errors problem over rings (ring-LWE) is hard. The ring-LWE problem was introduced by Lyubashevsky, Peikert and Regev [25] as an adaptation of the LWE problem [32] to ideal lattices.

The *decisional ring-LWE problem* is parametrized by a positive integer q, a polynomial $\Phi(x) \in \mathbb{Z}[x]$, and a noise distribution χ on $R_q = \mathbb{Z}_q[x]/(\Phi(x))$. For $\mathbf{s} \in R_q$, define $A_{\mathbf{s}}$ to be the distribution of pairs $(\mathbf{a}, \mathbf{b})$, where $\mathbf{a}$ is uniformly chosen in R_q and $\mathbf{b} = \mathbf{as} + \mathbf{e}$, with $\mathbf{e}$ sampled from χ. The decisional ring-LWE problem is defined as follows: For a uniformly random $\mathbf{s} \in R_q$ (which is kept secret) and given arbitrarily many samples $(\mathbf{a}, \mathbf{b})$, determine whether the samples come from $A_{\mathbf{s}}$, or whether they are uniformly distributed in $R_q \times R_q$. The search variant is to determine $\mathbf{s}$ given arbitrarily many samples from $A_{\mathbf{s}}$. For certain parameters, there is a quantum reduction from worst-case classical lattice problems over ideal lattices to the average-case ring-LWE problem [25].

Several algorithms have been proposed to solve the LWE and ring-LWE problems, see for example [27,23,2,1,24]. Some of these algorithms rely on lattice-basis reductions by algorithms such as BKZ [33] or BKZ 2.0 [9]. Another approach is based on the BKW algorithm [3], a method for solving the learning parity with noise problem. Pruned-enumeration has also been proved to be a viable option [24]. Some algorithms take advantage of the ring structure (e.g. [31]), others are oblivious to it.

In this paper we base all practical security estimates on the well established distinguishing attack [27] using BKZ. Although other attacks might be more effective, it is outside the scope of this paper to compare the effectiveness of the different attacks. Lindner and Peikert [23] heuristically estimate that the running time of the distinguishing attack using BKZ is

$$\log(t_\epsilon) = 1.8/\log(\delta_\epsilon) - 110 \,, \tag{1}$$

where δ_ϵ is the so called *Hermite factor* (see Appendix A for more details.) The expression $\log(\delta_\epsilon)$ is polynomial in n, thus $\log(t_\epsilon)$ is also polynomial in n, and therefore t_ϵ is exponential in n. It is also worth noticing that $\log(t_\epsilon)$ is of the order of $1/\log(q)$, a fact that will play an important role in Section 5, where we analyze pNE's efficiency.

2.2 Sampling Discrete Gaussians

For a vector $\mathbf{v} \in \mathbb{R}^n$, a positive real σ, and a lattice $\mathcal{L} \subset \mathbb{R}^n$, let $D_{\mathcal{L},\mathbf{v},\sigma}$ denote the n-dimensional discrete Gaussian distribution over $\mathcal{L}$, centered at $\mathbf{v}$, with parameter σ. For $x \in \mathcal{L}$, $D_{\mathcal{L},\mathbf{v},\sigma}$ assigns probability

$$D_{\mathcal{L},\mathbf{v},\sigma}(\mathbf{x}) := \frac{\rho_{\mathbf{v},\sigma}(\mathbf{x})}{\sum\limits_{\mathbf{z} \in \mathcal{L}} \rho_{\mathbf{v},\sigma}(\mathbf{z})}$$

with $\rho_{\mathbf{v},\sigma}(\mathbf{x}) = \exp\left(-\frac{1}{2} \|\mathbf{x} - \mathbf{v}\|^2 / \sigma^2\right)$. For brevity we write $D_{\mathcal{L},\sigma}$ for $D_{\mathcal{L},\mathbf{0},\sigma}$ and ρ_σ for $\rho_{\mathbf{0},\sigma}$.[1] For practical reasons, we will use a spheric Gaussian distribution, where each coordinate is sampled independently according to the discrete Gaussian distribution $D_{\mathbb{Z},\sigma}$ over the integers, and we rely on the fact that $\sum_{z \in \mathbb{Z}} \rho_\sigma(z)$ is constant and hence $D_{\mathbb{Z},\sigma}$ is proportional to ρ_σ.

Several methods have been proposed to sample values from $D_{\mathbb{Z},\sigma}$. We consider the following sampling algorithms: rejection sampling [14], inverting the cumulative distribution function (CDF) [30], the Knuth-Yao algorithm [22,12], and the Ziggurat algorithm [7]. Besides those, there have been developed two other methods quite recently [11,21], which we omit here since the authors state that their methods are slower in practice than existing ones.

We briefly recall the different methods listed above. Let k be some positive real number.[2] In the rejection sampling method, one samples points (x, y) inside the rectangle $B := [-k\sigma, k\sigma] \cap \mathbb{Z} \times [0, 1)$ uniformly at random and outputs x whenever (x, y) is below the graph of ρ_σ.[3] The Ziggurat algorithm is a more advanced rejection sampling algorithm in B. In a precomputation step, one divides the graph of ρ_σ into a partition of horizontal rectangles. Then, one first chooses one of the rectangles and samples a point (x, y) with integer x-coordinate inside this rectangle next (both uniformly at random). Depending on the location inside the rectangle, either x is directly output, rejection sampling is needed or the process is restarted. In the inverse CDF method one precomputes the CDF values $p_z = \Pr[D_{\mathbb{Z},\sigma} \leq z]$ for all integers $z \in [-k\sigma, k\sigma)$. Then, one samples y uniformly at random in $[0, 1)$ and outputs $x \in [-k\sigma, k\sigma) \cap \mathbb{Z}$ such that $y \in [p_{x-1}, p_x)$. In the Knuth-Yao algorithm one constructs in advance a tree using the binary expansion of the probabilities $\rho_\sigma(z)$ for $z \in [-k\sigma, k\sigma) \cap \mathbb{Z}$ up to some predefined precision. During the sampling process, one walks down the binary tree, using

---

[1] Some authors use a slightly different definition $\rho_{\mathbf{v},s}(\mathbf{x}) = \exp\left(-\pi \|\mathbf{x} - \mathbf{v}\|^2 / s^2\right)$. The two definitions are equivalent with $s = \sqrt{2\pi} \cdot \sigma$.

[2] The parameter k affects the distribution and the running time: A larger k yields a better fit to $D_{\mathbb{Z},\sigma}$, but increases both storage and rejection rate (and thus running time). Gentry et al. proved that the rejection rate (see description of rejection sampling) is proportional to k and independent of σ [14]. Moreover, they showed that for $k = \omega(\sqrt{\log(n)})$ the output distribution is statistically close to $D_{\mathbb{Z},\sigma}$.

[3] An equivalent view is that one first samples an integer x uniformly at random in the interval $[-k\sigma, k\sigma)$. Then, with probability $\rho_\sigma(x)$ one outputs x, otherwise one restarts.

one uniformly chosen bit at each step to decide which child to move to, and finally outputs the integer of the reached leaf.

2.3 Stehlé and Steinfeld's pNE Scheme

We briefly recall Stehlé and Steinfeld's provably secure encryption scheme pNE [35], which is specified by the following public parameters:

- dimension $n > 8$, a power of 2, which determines the cyclotomic polynomial $\Phi(x) = x^n + 1$ and the quotient ring $R = \mathbb{Z}[x]/\Phi(x)$,
- a prime $q > 5$ such that $q \equiv 1 \bmod 2n$, which determines the ciphertext space $R_q = \mathbb{Z}_q[x]/\Phi(x)$,
- a polynomial $p \in R$ such that p is invertible in R_q and has small coefficients (typically $p = 2$, $p = 3$ or $p = x + 2$), which determines the message space $\mathcal{P} = R/pR$,
- a ring-LWE noise distribution χ,
- and a positive real σ that determines the (n-dimensional sperical) discrete Gaussian distribution $D_{\mathbb{Z}^n, \sigma}$ used in key generation.

The scheme pNE = (KeyGen, Encrypt, Decrypt) is defined as follows.

KeyGen: Sample $\mathbf{f}' \leftarrow D_{\mathbb{Z}^n, \sigma}$, let $\mathbf{f} = p\mathbf{f}' + 1 \bmod q$; if $\mathbf{f} \notin R_q^\times$ resample. Sample $\mathbf{g} \leftarrow D_{\mathbb{Z}^n, \sigma}$; if $\mathbf{g} \notin R_q^\times$ resample. The secret key is $\mathbf{f}$ and the public key is $\mathbf{h} := p\mathbf{g}/\mathbf{f} \in R_q$.

Encrypt(h, m): Sample $\mathbf{e}, \mathbf{e}' \leftarrow \chi$, and return the ciphertext $\mathbf{c} := \mathbf{h}\mathbf{e} + p\mathbf{e}' + \mathbf{m} \in R_q$.

Decrypt(f, c): Compute $\mathbf{c}' := \mathbf{f} \cdot \mathbf{c} \in R_q$ and return $\mathbf{c}' \bmod p$.

Stehlé and Steinfeld show that pNE is secure as long as some classical lattice problems are hard to solve on quantum computers [35]. First they show that for certain parameter choices, the public key $\mathbf{h}$ is statistically close to uniform. Then, they show that $\mathbf{h}\mathbf{e} + p\mathbf{e}'$ is basically a sample from a ring-LWE distribution, and hence an IND-CPA attack on pNE can be used to solve ring-LWE. Then, by the worst- to average-case quantum reduction [25], the hardness result follows.[4]

Stehlé and Steinfeld also show that there exist parameter choices for which decryption correctly recovers the plaintext [35]. Let $\mathbf{c}'' = p(\mathbf{g}\mathbf{e} + \mathbf{e}'\mathbf{f}) + \mathbf{f}\mathbf{m} \in R$. If $\|\mathbf{c}''\|_\infty < q/2$, no wrapping around q occurs, and thus $\mathbf{c}' = \mathbf{c}'' \bmod q = \mathbf{c}''$ and decryption recovers the message $\mathbf{m}$ always.

For pNE to be both secure and correct, the parameters need to be chosen carefully. On the one hand, for the public key $\mathbf{h}$ to be statistically close to uniform, a large parameter σ is required. On the other hand, a large σ increases the size of $\mathbf{c}''$ and hence forces a larger modulus q for decryption to work. Balancing this conflicting forces is an important achievement of the authors of pNE. This balancing act is also decisive for pNE's efficiency as we will show in the following sections.

---

[4] Here we rely on the original security proof by Stehlé and Steinfeld [35]. However, Brakerski et al. [5] quite recently established a classical worst- to average-case reduction that might apply in this case.

3   Parameter Selection for pNE

We propose concrete parameters for pNE so that it is both correct and secure. For correctness, we name a range of values for the modulus q that guarantee a negligible error rate. Next, we show how to select parameters that provide an expected security level.

- Fix n to be a power of two.
- Fix $p = 2$. This choice provides a useful message space and causes the least possible expansion on the noise.
- Set χ to be the discrete Gaussian distribution $D_{\mathbb{Z}^n, r}$ for some real r (see below). Elements can be efficiently drawn from this distribution and moreover, with n a power of two and $\Phi(x) = x^n + 1$, the ring-LWE noise distribution can be spherical, and the worst-case reduction still holds [25].
- Set $r = \sqrt{2n/\pi}$, so that ring-LWE is as hard as lattice problems in the worst-case (see [25] for details).
- Set $\sigma = 2n\sqrt{\ln(8nq)}q$. With this, the public key is statistically close to uniform, thus an IND-CPA attack implies solving an instance of ring-LWE [35].
- Choose a prime $q \in [dn^6 \ln(n), 2dn^6 \ln(n)]$, such that $q \equiv 1 \bmod 2n$. We show in Lemma 3 below that $d = 25830$ guarantees correctness of the scheme. Experimentally, we obtain a lower value $d = 2^9$.

Table 1 shows some sets of parameter values computed as described above.

Table 1. Parameter values for pNE, security and error rate estimates. For given values of n, columns two through four show values for parameters q, σ and r that specify an instance of pNE. For a given set of parameters, column seven shows the estimated running time of a distinguishing attack, and columns five and six show the advantage and corresponding Hermite factor, respectively, under which such running time is achieved. Column eight shows the equivalent bit security and column nine the error rate.

Parameters			Advantage	Hermite	Attack time	Equiv. bit	Error
n	$\log q$	$\log \sigma$	r	$\log(1/\epsilon)$	factor δ_ϵ	$\log(T)$ [s]	security	rate
1024	71,90	49,89	25,53	2,72	1,0102	16	38	$O(2^{-n})$
2048	77,28	53,63	36,11	4,63	1,0055	122	144	$O(2^{-n})$
4096	83,30	57,70	51,06	7,85	1,0030	315	338	$O(2^{-n})$

The following two results will be used to prove the correctness of pNE for the proposed parameters.

Lemma 1 ([35], Lemma 11). *Let $n \geq 8$ be a power of two such that $\Phi(x) = x^n + 1$ splits into n linear factors modulo a prime $q \geq 8n$. Let $\sigma \geq \sqrt{2n \ln(6n)/\pi} \cdot q^{1/n}$ and let $p = 2$. The polynomials $\mathbf{f}$ and $\mathbf{g}$, generated by the KeyGen algorithm, satisfy, with probability $\geq 1 - 2^{-n+3}$,*

$$\|\mathbf{f}\| \leq 8\sqrt{n} \cdot \sigma \quad and \quad \|\mathbf{g}\| \leq \sqrt{n} \cdot \sigma .$$

Lemma 2 ([28], Lemma 3.1). *Let $n \in \mathbb{N}$. For any real $r = \omega(\sqrt{\log(n)})$, the probability that a polynomial $\mathbf{e}$ chosen according to $D_{\mathbb{Z}^n, r}$ has norm $\|\mathbf{e}\| > r\sqrt{n}$ is $\leq 2^{-n+1}$.*

The following lemma establishes the correctness of pNE for the proposed parameters.

Lemma 3. *Let $p = 2$, n a power of two s.t. $log(n) \geq 3$, $r = \sqrt{2n/\pi}$, $\chi = D_{\mathbb{Z}^n, r}$, $\sigma = 2n\sqrt{\ln(8nq)q}$, and $d \geq 25830$. If q is a prime in $[dn^6 \ln(n), 2dn^6 \ln(n)]$, then pNE correctly recovers plaintexts with probability greater or equal to $1 - 2^{-n+6}$.*

Proof. Let $\mathbf{c}'' = p(\mathbf{ge} + \mathbf{e}'\mathbf{f}) + \mathbf{fm} \in R$. Decryption recovers $\mathbf{m}$ if $\|\mathbf{c}''\|_\infty < q/2$. From Lemma 1, we have that $\|\mathbf{g}\|_2 \leq \sqrt{n} \cdot \sigma$ and $\|\mathbf{f}\|_2 \leq 8\sqrt{n} \cdot \sigma$ with probability $\geq 1 - 2^{-n+3}$. Furthermore, it is $\|p\mathbf{g}\|_2 \leq \sqrt{2n} \cdot \sigma$ and $\|p\mathbf{f}\|_2 \leq 8\sqrt{2n} \cdot \sigma$, both with probability $\geq 1 - 2^{-n+3}$. We also have that

$$\|p\mathbf{ge}\|_\infty \leq \|p\mathbf{ge}\|_2 \leq \sqrt{n}\|p\mathbf{g}\|_2\|\mathbf{e}\|_2 .$$

Since $\mathbf{e}$ is drawn from $D_{\mathbb{Z}^n, r}$, it follows from Lemma 2 that $\|\mathbf{e}\|_2 \leq \sqrt{n} \cdot r$ with probability $\geq 1 - 2^{-n+1}$. It follows that $\|p\mathbf{ge}\|_\infty \leq \sqrt{2n} \cdot n\sigma r$ with probability $\geq 1 - 2^{-n+4}$. Similarly, $\|p\mathbf{e}'\mathbf{f}\|_\infty \leq 8\sqrt{2n} \cdot n\sigma r$ with probability $\geq 1 - 2^{-n+4}$. Also, $\|\mathbf{fm}\|_\infty \leq \|\mathbf{fm}\|_2 \leq \sqrt{n}\|\mathbf{f}\|_2\|\mathbf{m}\|_2 = \sqrt{n}\|2\mathbf{f}' + 1\|_2\|\mathbf{m}\|_2$. Since $\mathbf{f}' \leftarrow D_{\mathbb{Z}^n, \sigma}$, $\|2\mathbf{f}' + 1\|_2 \leq \sqrt{2n} \cdot \sigma$ with probability $\geq 1 - 2^{-n+1}$. Since $\mathbf{m} \in R_2$, $\|\mathbf{m}\|_2 \leq \sqrt{n}$. Thus $\|\mathbf{fm}\|_\infty \leq \sqrt{2n} \cdot n\sigma$ with probability $\geq 1 - 2^{-n+1}$. Then

$$\|\mathbf{c}''\|_\infty \leq \sqrt{2n} \cdot n\sigma(9r + 1),$$
$$\text{with probability} \geq 1 - 2^{-n+6} . \tag{2}$$

Assuming $\log(n) \geq 3$ and with $r = \sqrt{2n/\pi}$, we have that

$$(9r + 1)^2 \leq \alpha n \text{ with } \alpha = \left(9\sqrt{2/\pi} + 1/\sqrt{2^3}\right)^2 . \tag{3}$$

Now, suppose $dn^6 \ln(n) \leq q \leq 2dn^6 \ln(n)$ for some $d \geq 1$. Then

$$\ln(8nq) \leq \ln(16n^8 d) \leq \beta(d) \ln(n),$$
$$\text{with } \beta(d) = 8 + \frac{\ln(16) + \ln(d)}{\ln(2^3)} . \tag{4}$$

Then, from (2), (3) and (4), it follows that

$$\|2\mathbf{c}''\|_\infty^2 \leq \left(2\sqrt{2n} \cdot n\sigma(9r + 1)\right)^2$$
$$\leq 8n^3\sigma^2\alpha n$$
$$\leq 32\alpha\beta(d)n^6 \ln(n)q .$$

Since $\beta(d) = \mathcal{O}(\ln(d))$, there exists $D \geq 0$ such that for $d \geq D$, $32\alpha\beta(d) \leq d$, and thus $\|2\mathbf{c}''\|_\infty^2 \leq dn^6 \ln(n)q \leq q^2$, and the result follows. We compute the smallest such D by numerical means to be approximately 25830, and it follows that for any $d \geq 25830$ the bound holds.   □

Next, for each set of parameters, we calculate a bit security level, based on the distinguishing attack against LWE described in Appendix A. Notice that we do not rely on the worst-case hardness to determine the bit security level of the scheme. This is because it is unknown how tight the worst- to average-case reduction is. We rather analyze the efficiency of the distinguishing attack against the average-case problem underlying pNE. We acknowledge that this approach does not imply that those worst-case lattice problems are hard. However, it provides a plausible estimate for the practical hardness of the average-case problem.

The running time t_ϵ of the distinguishing attack in (1) depends on the desired advantage ϵ. Since an adversary can choose ϵ within a reasonable range, we define the total time of an attack as

$$T = \min\{t_\epsilon/\epsilon \mid \epsilon \in (2^{-80}, 1)\},$$

which we approximate numerically.

From the total time of an attack, we then compute a bit security level b, following the methodology of Howgrave-Graham [19]. Note that the attack time described in Appendix A was estimated by Lindner and Peikert on a 2.3 GHz PC [23]. Assuming that a single block-cipher encryption takes 500 clock cycles, it would take $2^b \cdot \frac{500}{2.3 \times 10^9}$ seconds to attack a b-bit block-cipher using brute-force. From this, we obtain that the bit security of a cryptosystem, that can be attacked in no less than T seconds, is given by

$$b = \log(T) + \log\left(2.3 \times 10^9\right) - \log(500).$$

Table 1 shows the bit security level for each set of parameters, as well as the distinguishing advantage and corresponding Hermite factor that minimizes the total attack time.

4   Instantiation and Performance of pNE

In this section we first briefly describe our implementation of pNE, then we present experimental data on its performance, and finally we compare pNE with both NTRUEncrypt and LPR-LWE.

We implemented pNE in C++ using the Number Theory Library (NTL, [34]) for arithmetic in R_q together with the GNU Multiple Precision Arithmetic Library (GMP, [16]) for large integer arithmetic. NTL uses the fast Fourier transform (FFT) for multiplication in the ring R_q. All experiments were performed on a Sun XFire 4440 server with 16 Quad-Core AMD Opteron(tm) Processor 8356 CPUs running at 2.3GHz, having 64GB of memory and running 64bit Debian 7.1. For our experiments we only used one of the 16 cores. We compiled our implementations using GCC v4.7.2-5, NTL v5.5.2-2, and GMP v2:5.0.5+dfsg-2.

In key generation of pNE we must check that $\mathbf{f}$ and $\mathbf{g}$ are invertible in R_q. This is done by choosing $\mathbf{f}, \mathbf{g}$ uniformly at random from R_q and using the native GCD implementation of NTL to test their invertibility. Lemma 10 in [35] proves that the "resample rate" is less or equal to n/q. Our experiments confirm that the resample rate is very small ($< 1/1000$) for our choice of parameters.

Besides R_q arithmetic, the main challenge for implementing pNE is instantiating the Gaussian sampler used in key generation and encryption. We implemented the methods listed in Section 2.2 or adapted provided source code, where available, and tested the implementations in terms of memory size and speed. We also considered two variants of rejection sampling, namely computing ρ_σ on demand and precomputing all possible values of ρ_σ. First, we tested the methods for the rather small value $r = \sqrt{2n/\pi}$ of the Gaussian parameter used in the ring-LWE noise distribution $\chi = D_{\mathbb{Z}^n, r}$ in pNE's Encrypt function. From Table 2, which shows timings and storage requirements for this setting, the Knuth-Yao algorithm appears to be the most efficient algorithm regarding speed. Second, for the much larger value $\sigma \approx 2^8 n^4 \ln^2(n)$ in pNE's KeyGen algorithm, the only method suitable is rejection sampling with ρ_σ computed on demand due to its minimalist storage requirement.

Table 2. Experimental comparison of discrete Gaussian sampling techniques for parameter $\sigma = \sqrt{2n/\pi}$. For each dimension n and each method, the table shows running time in milliseconds and storage in kilobytes. For all n, we used the same Ziggurat with 8192 rectangles in regard to experiments in [7], and for Knuth-Yao we used a precision of 128 bits.

Parameters		Rej. on-demand		Rej precomp.		Inv. CDF		Knuth-Yao		Ziggurat	
n	σ	time	storage	time	storage	time	storage	time	storage	time	storage
1024	25.53	149	0	2.60	4.09	1.07	4.09	0.56	16.47	1.92	262.21
2048	36.11	437	0	6.86	6.36	1.98	6.36	1.03	50.97	2.42	262.21
4096	51.06	1200	0	19.66	9.80	4.04	9.80	2.04	78.69	7.03	262.21

In the remainder of this section we present experimental data on the performance of pNE and compare it to NTRUEncrypt and LPR-LWE's. Table 3 shows timings and sizes for our implementation of pNE.

Table 3. Experimental performance of pNE. For a given set of parameters, column seven shows public key, secret key and ciphertext size in kilobytes, and column eight shows the ciphertext to plaintext ratio. Columns nine to eleven show the running times for KeyGen, Encrypt, and Decrypt in milliseconds, respectively.

Parameters						Sizes [kB]		Running times [ms]		
n	$\log q$	$\log \sigma$	r	bit sec	err rate	pk = sk = ct	ct/pt	KeyGen	Encrypt	Decrypt
1024	71.90	49.89	25.53	38	$O(2^{-n})$	9.22	72	763	5.60	4.12
2048	77.28	53.63	36.11	144	$O(2^{-n})$	19.97	78	1731	12.09	9.51
4096	83.30	57.70	51.06	338	$O(2^{-n})$	43.01	84	3820	26.70	21.37

For comparison, we collected recent figures about NTRUEncrypt in the literature, and we present them in Table 4 (see also Figure 1 for a comparison with pNE and LPR-LWE).

Table 4. Security and performance of NTRUEncrypt with $q = 2048$ and $p = 3$ on a 2GHz CPU. Security estimates were taken from [18] and efficiency measures were provided in private communication by William Whyte of Security Innovation Inc.

n	bit sec	Sizes [kB]			ct/pt	Running times [ms]	
		pk	sk	pt		Encrypt	Decrypt
401	112	0.55	0.20	0.10	11	0.09	0.19
439	128	0.60	0.22	0.11	11	0.10	0.20
743	256	1.02	0.37	0.19	11	0.20	0.40

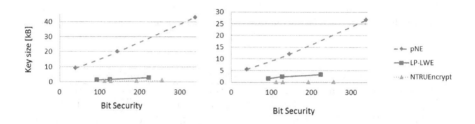

Fig. 1. Encryption running time and public key size against bit security for pNE, NTRUEncrypt and LPR-LWE (parameters as in Tables 3, 4 and 6)

Our pNE implementation is more than 100 times slower and requires 24 times larger keys than an implementation of NTRUEncrypt by Security Innovation Inc. We consider this gap too large to be overcome through optimization of pNE's implementation.

We then move on to compare pNE to the ring-LWE based scheme of Lyubashevsky, Peikert, and Regev [25] (LPR-LWE), which appears to be the most efficient provably secure lattice-based PKE scheme [15]. In order to obtain comparable data, we adapted the implementation by Göttert et al. [15] so as to make it as close as possible to our implementation of pNE. In particular, we use the same Gaussian sampler and the same library for polynomial arithmetic. Table 5 summarizes the results.

Comparing our implementations of pNE with that of LPR-LWE, we conclude that LPR-LWE is significantly more efficient. Take for example pNE with $n = 2048$ which offers 144 bit security and LPR-LWE with $n = 256$ which offers 151 bit security. The public key of pNE is 26 times larger and the secret key 52 times larger. Moreover, key generation of pNE is over 1000 times slower than

Table 5. Experimental performance of LPR-LWE with parameters as proposed by Lindner and Peikert [23]

Parameters					Sizes [kB]			Running times [ms]		
n	q	s	bit sec	error rate	pk = ct	sk	ct/pt	KeyGen	Encrypt	Decrypt
192	4093	8.87	100	1%	0.58	0.29	12	0.79	1.25	0.49
256	4093	8.35	151	1%	0.77	0.38	12	0.98	1.52	0.59
320	4093	8.00	199	1%	0.96	0.48	12	1.40	2.25	0.92

that of LPR-LWE, encryption is over 7 times slower and decryption over 15 times slower.

There are two caveats to this apparently disproportionate difference between pNE and LPR-LWE. First, the error rate of LPR-LWE is very high, at around 1%, while the error rate of pNE is negligible. A 1% error rate could be problematic in a realistic deployment. Second, the Gaussian parameter s in LPR-LWE is small.[5] The worst- to average-case reduction requires $s \geq 2\sqrt{n}$. Moreover, values of s below $\sqrt{n}$ lead to subexponential attacks [2] (see also [10] for other attacks for bounded distribution).[6]

In order to provide a more fair comparison between pNE and LPR-LWE, we computed parameters that guarantee negligible error rate and the worst-to average-case reduction to hold. We follow a methodology adapted from [23] to setup the parameters. We fix n, set $s = 2\sqrt{n}$ and $\delta = 2^{-n}$. Then we find $c > 1$ such that $c \cdot \exp\left((1 - c^2)/2\right) = 1/2$. We then choose the smallest prime q greater than $4cs^2\sqrt{n \ln(2/\delta)}/(\sqrt{2} \cdot \pi)$. These choices guarantee negligible error rate. Finally, we calculate security based on the distinguishing attack as we did for the pNE scheme.

Table 6. Experimental performance of LPR-LWE with conservative parameters that guarantee negligible error rate and the worst- to average-case reduction to hold

Parameters					Sizes [kB]			Running times [ms]		
n	q	s	bit sec	error rate	pk = ct	sk	ct/pt	KeyGen	Encrypt	Decrypt
256	378353	32.00	92	$O(2^{-n})$	1.22	0.61	19	1.02	1.56	0.59
320	590921	35.77	126	$O(2^{-n})$	1.60	0.80	20	1.46	2.36	0.92
512	1511821	45.25	223	$O(2^{-n})$	2.69	1.34	21	2.09	3.29	1.16

Table 6 summarizes the results. It shows parameters that provide low, medium, and high levels of security, as well as experimental data on storage requirements and running times. Although these results show a narrower gap between pNE

---

[5] In order to be consistent with the notation in [23], here s is the Gaussian parameter for $\rho_s(\mathbf{x}) = \exp\left(-\pi \|\mathbf{x}\|^2 / s^2\right)$ (see Section 2.2).

[6] This is true despite recent results showing the LWE problem hard for small parameters [26], because LPR-LWE does not meet the requirements of the new results [8].

and LPR-LWE, a significant difference in favor of LPR-LWE persists. This difference can also be seen in Figure 1, which depicts encryption running time and public key size against bit security for pNE, LPR-LWE and NTRUEncrypt.

On a recent paper, Bos et al. [4] analyze the efficiency of a leveled homomorphic encryption scheme based on pNE, call it H-pNE. It is difficult to derive a conclusion about pNE's efficiency from the single measurement of their related scheme. However, their results seem to indicate that H-pNE's efficiency is competitive to that of other provably secure ring-LWE homomorphic encryption schemes. We claim that this does not contradict our findings. They report that their H-pNE implementation is about ten times faster than an implementation of a scheme by Brakerski and Vaikuntanathan [6], which is closely related to LPR-LWE. They justify the performance increase partially on better hardware and an optimized implementation. But there are two more factors they do not mention. First, in order to allow homomorphic operations, one must choose a large modulus q to allow additional noise growth. This is true for a homomorphic version of pNE as well as for a homomorphic version of other schemes. Thus, they are comparing schemes with equally high modulus q, while in our analysis we compare to an instance of LPR-LWE with a much smaller q. This means that, while a homomorphic variant of pNE might be comparatively efficient, pNE is less efficient as a stand-alone encryption scheme. The second factor is that the parameter choices they highlight allow for a single multiplicative level of H-pNE, against four levels for the scheme by Brakerski and Vaikuntanathan. This asymmetry is not discussed in the paper by Bos et al.

5   Efficiency Analysis of pNE

We have seen in Section 4 that pNE is less efficient than LPR-LWE or NTRUEncrypt. In this section we analyze why this is the case.

The size of pNE's public key, secret key and ciphertext is given by $n \lceil \log q \rceil$ bits, which is the space required to store one element of R_q. The ciphertext to plaintext ratio is given by $\lceil \log q \rceil$ because a plaintext is encoded into an element of $R_p = R_2$ which stores up to n bits and it is encrypted into an element of R_q of size $n \lceil \log q \rceil$.

In order to better understand the running time of pNE we run experiments for $\log(n) = 4, \ldots, 16$. The results presented in Figure 2 seem to indicate that the running time of the KeyGen, Encrypt and Decrypt algorithms is proportional to $n \log(n) \log(q)$. Actually, we found a strong correlation between their running time and $n \log(n) \log(q)$ in our experiments (Pearson product moment correlation coefficient $r > 0.999$). This confirms that polynomial multiplication and division can be performed in $O(n \log n)$ scalar operations using FFT.

Table 7 shows a breakdown of the running time of key generation, encryption and decryption into their most time-consuming subroutines. The table shows that close to 90% of key generation is spent sampling $\mathbf{f}$ and $\mathbf{g}$ according to a discrete Gaussian distribution, while computing $\mathbf{h}$ takes around 10% of the time.

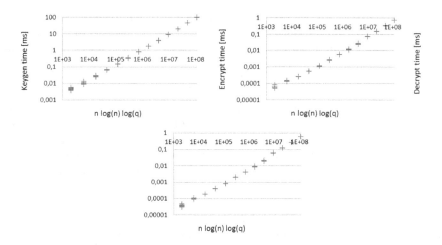

Fig. 2. Running time in milliseconds of pNE's KeyGen, Encrypt and Decrypt versus $n \log(n) \log(q)$, for $\log(n) = 4, \ldots, 16$, respectively

For encryption the tendency is reversed, with little under 20% of the total time spent on sampling Gaussian elements, while computing the ciphertext **c** takes a little bit over 80% of the time. This is in part thanks to the efficiency of the Knuth-Yao sampler, which is not possible to be used in key generation. In the case of decryption, the operations in R_q take more than 90% of the time, while the reduction mod p only takes around 5%.

Table 7. Running time breakdown of pNE

n	Key Generation		Encryption		Decryption	
	sampling	arithmetic	sampling	arithmetic	arithmetic	mod p reduction
1024	90.10%	9.90%	18.71%	81.29%	93.83%	6.17%
2048	89.71%	10.29%	16.16%	83.84%	93.65%	6.35%
4096	89.30%	10.70%	14.63%	85.37%	95.39%	4.61%

Although efficiency improvements are certainly possible, the gap between pNE and the other two schemes is too large to be surmounted by optimization alone. In order to understand why this gap is so large we take a closer look at the schemes. The only differences between pNE and NTRUEncrypt are:

i) Operations are performed modulo $x^n + 1$ instead of $x^n - 1$.
ii) The integer modulus q is chosen to be a prime instead of a power of 2.
iii) The secret key polynomials **f** and **g** are sampled from a discrete Gaussian distribution with parameter $\sigma = 2n\sqrt{\ln(8nq)q}$ instead of being sampled uniformly at random from a set of small norm polynomials.

iv) The ciphertext is $\mathbf{c} = \mathbf{h}\mathbf{e} + p\mathbf{e}' + \mathbf{m}$ with $\mathbf{e}, \mathbf{e}'$ sampled from a discrete Gaussian distribution with parameter $r = \sqrt{2n/\pi}$, instead of $\mathbf{c} = \mathbf{h}\phi + \mathbf{m}$ with ϕ sampled uniformly at random from a set of small norm polynomials.

Differences i), ii), and iv) cannot be decisive because they are features of LPR-LWE as well, and the latter is much more efficient than pNE. We argue that the main source of inefficiency lays on difference iii). More precisely, efficiency of pNE is hampered in several ways by the large value of σ required to make the public key statistically close to uniform. As shown in the proof of Lemma 3, a large σ induces a large modulus q to allow correct decryption. A large q directly impacts the running times of KeyGen, Encrypt and Decrypt, as they are all proportional to $n \log(n) \log(q)$, as well as it impacts the key sizes, which are proportional to $n \log(q)$.

But large q has an even more decisive negative effect on practical security. From the equations in Appendix A, one can conclude that the running time t of the distinguishing attack depends on q as $\log(t) = \mathcal{O}(1/\log(q))$. Thus, a large q makes the scheme less secure, forcing a large dimension n to obtain a given security level. A large n has an even more dramatic effect on the efficiency of the cryptosystem. Table 8 illustrates the effect of the parameter σ on the efficiency of pNE.

Table 8. Efficiency and security measures of pNE for different values of the parameter σ. Bit security is calculated based on the distinguishing attack and does not take into consideration attacks that may exploit the departure from the security proof.

Parameters				Sizes [kB]		Running times [ms]		
n	$\log(\sigma)$	$\log(q)$	bit sec	pk = sk = ct	ct/pt	KeyGen	Encrypt	Decrypt
512	49	69.22	-22	4.48	70	336	2.58	2.00
512	29	49.71	10	3.20	50	320	2.20	1.59
512	9	29.37	103	1.92	30	305	1.79	1.21
1024	49	71.90	38	9.22	72	759	5.63	4.13
1024	29	51.99	98	6.66	52	737	4.88	3.43
1024	9	31.24	265	4.10	32	689	3.73	2.42

The negative effect that a "wide" Gaussian has on the security of pNE seems counterintuitive as one would expect that a larger key space improves security. Yet, it is the main force dragging pNE's efficiency. It is unclear to us at the moment whether this can be improved while preserving pNE's strong security guarantee —its worst- to average-case reduction.

Acknowledgements. This work was partially supported by CASED (www.cased.de). We would like to thank Rachid Elbansarkhani, Andreas Hülsing, Michael Schneider, Damien Stehlé, William Whyte and zgr Dagdelen for useful discussions.

References

1. Albrecht, M.R., Cid, C., Faugère, J.C., Fitzpatrick, R., Perret, L.: On the complexity of the BKW algorithm on LWE. Cryptology ePrint Archive, Report 2012/636 (2012), http://eprint.iacr.org/2012/636/
2. Arora, S., Ge, R.: New algorithms for learning in presence of errors. In: Aceto, L., Henzinger, M., Sgall, J. (eds.) ICALP 2011, Part I. LNCS, vol. 6755, pp. 403–415. Springer, Heidelberg (2011)
3. Blum, A., Kalai, A., Wasserman, H.: Noise-tolerant learning, the parity problem, and the statistical query model. J. ACM 50(4), 506–519 (2003)
4. Bos, J., Lauter, K., Loftus, J., Naehrig, M.: Improved security for a ring-based fully homomorphic encryption scheme. In: Stam, M. (ed.) IMACC 2013. LNCS, vol. 8308, pp. 45–64. Springer, Heidelberg (2013)
5. Brakerski, Z., Langlois, A., Peikert, C., Regev, O., Stehlé, D.: Classical hardness of learning with errors. In: Proceedings of the 45th Annual ACM Symposium on Theory of Computing, STOC 2013, pp. 575–584. ACM, New York (2013)
6. Brakerski, Z., Vaikuntanathan, V.: Fully homomorphic encryption from ring-LWE and security for key dependent messages. In: Rogaway, P. (ed.) CRYPTO 2011. LNCS, vol. 6841, pp. 505–524. Springer, Heidelberg (2011)
7. Buchmann, J., Cabarcas, D., Göpfert, F., Hülsing, A., Weiden, P.: Discrete ziggurat: A time-memory trade-off for sampling from a gaussian distribution over the integers. In: Lange, T., Lauter, K., Lisoněk, P. (eds.) SAC 2013. LNCS, vol. 8282, pp. 402–417. Springer, Heidelberg (2014)
8. Cabarcas, D., Göpfert, F., Weiden, P.: Provably secure LWE-encryption with uniform secret. Cryptology ePrint Archive, Report 2013/164 (2013), http://eprint.iacr.org/2013/164
9. Chen, Y., Nguyen, P.Q.: BKZ 2.0: Better lattice security estimates. In: Lee, D.H., Wang, X. (eds.) ASIACRYPT 2011. LNCS, vol. 7073, pp. 1–20. Springer, Heidelberg (2011)
10. Ding, J.: Solving LWE problem with bounded errors in polynomial time. Cryptology ePrint Archive, Report 2010/558 (2010), http://eprint.iacr.org/2010/558/
11. Ducas, L., Durmus, A., Lepoint, T., Lyubashevsky, V.: Lattice signatures and bimodal gaussians. In: Canetti, R., Garay, J.A. (eds.) CRYPTO 2013, Part I. LNCS, vol. 8042, pp. 40–56. Springer, Heidelberg (2013), http://dx.doi.org/10.1007/978-3-642-40041-4_3
12. Galbraith, S.D., Dwarakanath, N.C.: Efficient sampling from discrete Gaussians for lattice-based cryptography on a constrained device (2012), preprint available at http://www.math.auckland.ac.nz/~sgal018/gen-gaussians.pdf
13. Gentry, C., Halevi, S., Vaikuntanathan, V.: A simple BGN-type cryptosystem from LWE. In: Gilbert, H. (ed.) EUROCRYPT 2010. LNCS, vol. 6110, pp. 506–522. Springer, Heidelberg (2010), http://dx.doi.org/10.1007/978-3-642-13190-5_26
14. Gentry, C., Peikert, C., Vaikuntanathan, V.: Trapdoors for hard lattices and new cryptographic constructions. In: Ladner, R.E., Dwork, C. (eds.) 40th Annual ACM Symposium on Theory of Computing, pp. 197–206. ACM Press (May 2006)
15. Göttert, N., Feller, T., Schneider, M., Buchmann, J., Huss, S.A.: On the design of hardware building blocks for modern lattice-based encryption schemes. In: Prouff, E., Schaumont, P. (eds.) CHES 2012. LNCS, vol. 7428, pp. 512–529. Springer, Heidelberg (2012)

16. Granlund, T.: The GNU multiple precision arithmetic library, http://gmplib.org/
17. Hoffstein, J., Pipher, J., Silverman, J.H.: NTRU: A ring-based public key cryptosystem. In: Buhler, J.P. (ed.) ANTS 1998. LNCS, vol. 1423, pp. 267–288. Springer, Heidelberg (1998)
18. Hoffstein, J., Pipher, J., Whyte, W.: A note on hybrid resistant parameter selection for NTRUEncrypt (2010) (unpublished)
19. Howgrave-Graham, N.: A hybrid lattice-reduction and meet-in-the-middle attack against NTRU. In: Menezes, A. (ed.) CRYPTO 2007. LNCS, vol. 4622, pp. 150–169. Springer, Heidelberg (2007)
20. Kaps, J.P.: Cryptography for Ultra-Low Power Devices. Ph.D. thesis, Worcester Polytechnic Institute (2006)
21. Karney, C.F.F.: Sampling exactly from the normal distribution. Tech. rep., SRI International (March 2013), http://arxiv.org/abs/1303.6257
22. Knuth, D.E., Yao, A.C.: The complexity of non uniform random number generation. In: Algorithms and Complexity: New Directions and Recent Results, pp. 357–428 (1976)
23. Lindner, R., Peikert, C.: Better key sizes (and attacks) for LWE-based encryption. In: Kiayias, A. (ed.) CT-RSA 2011. LNCS, vol. 6558, pp. 319–339. Springer, Heidelberg (2011)
24. Liu, M., Nguyen, P.Q.: Solving BDD by enumeration: An update. In: Dawson, E. (ed.) CT-RSA 2013. LNCS, vol. 7779, pp. 293–309. Springer, Heidelberg (2013)
25. Lyubashevsky, V., Peikert, C., Regev, O.: On ideal lattices and learning with errors over rings. In: Gilbert, H. (ed.) EUROCRYPT 2010. LNCS, vol. 6110, pp. 1–23. Springer, Heidelberg (2010)
26. Micciancio, D., Peikert, C.: Hardness of SIS and LWE with small parameters. In: Canetti, R., Garay, J.A. (eds.) CRYPTO 2013, Part I. LNCS, vol. 8042, pp. 21–39. Springer, Heidelberg (2013), http://dx.doi.org/10.1007/978-3-642-40041-4_2
27. Micciancio, D., Regev, O.: Lattice-based cryptography. In: Bernstein, D.J., Buchmann, J.A., Dahmen, E. (eds.) Post-Quantum Cryptography, pp. 147–191. Springer (2008)
28. Naehrig, M., Lauter, K., Vaikuntanathan, V.: Can homomorphic encryption be practical? In: Proceedings of the 3rd ACM Cloud Computing Security Workshop, CCSW 2011, pp. 113–124. ACM, New York (2011)
29. O'Rourke, C., Sunar, B.: Achieving NTRU with Montgomery multiplication. IEEE Transactions on Computers 52(4), 440–448 (2003)
30. Peikert, C.: An efficient and parallel Gaussian sampler for lattices. In: Rabin, T. (ed.) CRYPTO 2010. LNCS, vol. 6223, pp. 80–97. Springer, Heidelberg (2010)
31. Plantard, T., Susilo, W., Zhang, Z.: Lattice reduction for modular knapsack. In: Knudsen, L.R., Wu, H. (eds.) SAC 2012. LNCS, vol. 7707, pp. 275–286. Springer, Heidelberg (2013), http://dx.doi.org/10.1007/978-3-642-35999-6_18
32. Regev, O.: On lattices, learning with errors, random linear codes, and cryptography. In: Gabow, H.N., Fagin, R. (eds.) 37th Annual ACM Symposium on Theory of Computing, pp. 84–93. ACM Press (May 2005)
33. Schnorr, C.P., Euchner, M.: Lattice basis reduction: Improved practical algorithms and solving subset sum problems. Mathematical Programming 66, 181–199 (1994)
34. Shoup, V.: Number theory library (NTL) for C++, http://www.shoup.net/ntl/
35. Stehlé, D., Steinfeld, R.: Making NTRU as secure as worst-case problems over ideal lattices. In: Paterson, K.G. (ed.) EUROCRYPT 2011. LNCS, vol. 6632, pp. 27–47. Springer, Heidelberg (2011)

36. Stehlé, D., Steinfeld, R., Tanaka, K., Xagawa, K.: Efficient public key encryption based on ideal lattices. In: Matsui, M. (ed.) ASIACRYPT 2009. LNCS, vol. 5912, pp. 617–635. Springer, Heidelberg (2009), http://dx.doi.org/10.1007/978-3-642-10366-7_36

A   Distinguishing Attack

For the sake of simplicity we will consider the distinguishing attack only against LWE, and not against ring-LWE. In LWE, the samples are constructed as (A, b) with $b = A^\top s + e$, where $A \leftarrow \mathbb{Z}_q^{n \times m}$ and $s \leftarrow \mathbb{Z}_q^n$ are chosen uniformly at random. The ring-LWE problem can be seen as a variant of LWE in which the matrix A has a special structure, where the structure depends on the first part of the ring-LWE samples $\mathbf{a}$ and the underlying ring R_q. We assume that the distinguishing attack does not take advantage of this special structure.

The bottleneck of the distinguishing attack is the computation of a short vector in the lattice

$$\Lambda_q^\perp(A) := \{y \in \mathbb{Z}^m \mid Ay \equiv 0 \bmod q\}.$$

If the distribution χ is a discrete Gaussian, then the advantage of the distinguishing attack is close to $\epsilon = \exp(-2(\pi c r/q)^2)$, where c is the length of the shortest vector the adversary is able to find, and r is the parameter of the discrete Gaussian distribution [23]. The shortest vectors are of length $\delta^m q^{n/m}$, where δ is the so called *Hermite factor*. This length is minimized for $m = \sqrt{n \log(q)/\log(\delta)}$; thus, the shortest vectors we can expect to produce are of length $2^{2\sqrt{n \log(q) \log(\delta)}}$.

The running time of state-of-the-art lattice reduction algorithms (e.g. BKZ) is determined by the Hermite factor δ. In order to obtain an advantage greater or equal to ϵ we need to be able to compute vectors of length less or equal to

$$c_\epsilon = \frac{q}{\pi r} \sqrt{\frac{\ln(1/\epsilon)}{2}} \,,$$

for which we require a Hermite factor not greater than

$$\delta_\epsilon = 2^{\frac{\log^2(c_\epsilon)}{4n \log q}} \,.$$

Lindner and Peikert [23] heuristically estimate that the running time of the distinguishing attack using BKZ is

$$\log(t_\epsilon) = 1.8/\log(\delta_\epsilon) - 110 \,.$$

A Polynomial-Time Algorithm for Solving a Class of Underdetermined Multivariate Quadratic Equations over Fields of Odd Characteristics

Chen-Mou Cheng[1], Yasufumi Hashimoto[2], Hiroyuki Miura[1], and Tsuyoshi Takagi[1]

[1] Kyushu University, Fukuoka-shi, 819-0395, Japan
{ccheng,takagi}@imi.kyushu-u.ac.jp
ma212042@math.kyushu-u.ac.jp
[2] University of the Ryukyus, Okinawa-ken, 903-0213, Japan
hashimoto@math.u-ryukyu.ac.jp,

Abstract. Following up a series of works by Kipnis-Patarin-Goubin, Courtois-Goubin-Meier-Tacier, and Thomae-Wolf, in PQCrypto 2013 Miura, Hashimoto, and Takagi proposed an efficient algorithm for solving a class of underdetermined multivariate quadratic equations. Their algorithm does not use any generic Gröbner-basis solving techniques and asymptotically requires the least degree of underdeterminedness among all similar algorithms in the current literature. Building on top of their work, in this paper we focus on solving polynomially underdetermined multivariate quadratic equations over fields of odd characteristics. We show that we can further improve the applicable range of the Miura-Hashimoto-Takagi algorithm essentially for free. Furthermore, we show how to allow a certain degree of trade-off between applicable range and running time. Last but not least, we show that the running time of the improved algorithm is actually polynomial in number of equations and variables. To the best of our knowledge, this is the first result showing that this class of polynomially underdetermined multivariate quadratic equations over fields of odd characteristics can be solved in polynomial time.

Keywords: multivariate cryptography, quadratic equation solving over finite fields, underdetermined system solving.

M. Mosca (Ed.): PQCrypto 2014, LNCS 8772, pp. 40–58, 2014.

1   Introduction

Let q be a power of a prime number and $\mathbb{F}_q$ the finite field of q elements. For natural numbers n, m, let $f_1, \ldots, f_m$ be a set of quadratic polynomials over $\mathbb{F}_q$:

$$
\begin{cases}
f_1(x_1, \ldots, x_n) = \displaystyle\sum_{1 \leq i \leq j \leq n} a_{1,i,j} x_i x_j + \sum_{1 \leq i \leq n} b_{1,i} x_i + c_1, \\[2mm]
f_2(x_1, \ldots, x_n) = \displaystyle\sum_{1 \leq i \leq j \leq n} a_{2,i,j} x_i x_j + \sum_{1 \leq i \leq n} b_{2,i} x_i + c_2, \\[2mm]
\quad\vdots \\[1mm]
f_m(x_1, \ldots, x_n) = \displaystyle\sum_{1 \leq i \leq j \leq n} a_{m,i,j} x_i x_j + \sum_{1 \leq i \leq n} b_{m,i} x_i + c_m,
\end{cases}
$$

where $a_{i,j,k}$, $b_{i,j}$, and c_i are in $\mathbb{F}_q$. The "MQ problem" of solving m multivariate quadratic equations in n variables over $\mathbb{F}_q$ is the problem of finding a set of $\mathbb{F}_q$ roots $(\tilde{x}_1, \ldots, \tilde{x}_n) \in \mathbb{F}_q^n$ such that $f_1(\tilde{x}_1, \ldots, \tilde{x}_n) = \cdots = f_m(\tilde{x}_1, \ldots, \tilde{x}_n) = 0$.

It is well-known that if $m \approx n$, then such a problem is NP-complete for random polynomial equations over a finite field [10]. This result has many applications, e.g., it is a basis for the security of Multivariate Public Key Cryptography (MPKC). Starting from the seminal work by Matsumoto and Imai [13], MPKC has attracted a lot of attention in the cryptologic research community. There has been success in constructing encryption schemes such as HFE [16]; signature schemes such as UOV [11], TTS [22], and Rainbow [6]; as well as identification schemes such as the Sakumoto-Shirai-Hiwatari scheme [17]. Moreover, to this date we do not know the existence of any quantum algorithms that can solve the MQ problem for the case of $m \approx n$ in polynomial time, which makes MPKC a candidate for post-quantum cryptography.

Certainly, polynomials used in MPKC must have trapdoors to allow, e.g., efficient decryption by a private-key holder and hence cannot be random. In fact, we have seen several (and will most likely continue to see more) successful attacks that exploit structural weaknesses in these trapdoors, such as the Patarin attack on the original Matsumoto-Imai scheme [15], as well as rank attacks [12] and the derivatives. The history of MPKC has been marked by sequences of attempts and failures, through which we develop more confidence on those schemes that have survived.

In contrast to structural attacks, algorithms that attempt to directly solve the MQ problem present a generic attack to MPKC. For example, there have been successes on HFE [9] and QUAD [21] using Gröbner-basis solvers [7,8,4]. Determining the complexity of such algorithms is important because it can determine the security of "well-designed" MPKC schemes. Here by well-designedness we mean that solving the MQ problem can be reduced to breaking such a scheme from a theoretical point of view. Or, alternatively, we believe that such a scheme can withstand all structural attacks from a practical point of view. In either case, direct solvers are arguably the only feasible attack against such a well-designed MPKC scheme. Furthermore, such direct solvers are also an important subroutine in cryptanalysis of MPKC, and better understanding of their complexity often leads to insight into, e.g., security of schemes with certain special structures [5].

As a result, there have been several studies on the complexity of solving the MQ problem. Such complexity certainly depends on the relation between m and n. A simple case is that if the system is heavily overdetermined, e.g., $m \geq n(n+1)/2$ over $\mathbb{F}_2$, then we can simply linearize and solve it in polynomial time. On the other end of the spectrum, if the system is heavily underdetermined, e.g., $n \geq m(m+1)$ over $\mathbb{F}_2$, then we also have efficient polynomial-time solvers such as Kipnis-Patarin-Goubin [11], Courtois-Goubin-Meier-Tacier [3], and Miura-Hashimoto-Takagi [14]. *Although it is unlikely that we can use any of these algorithms to break a realistic MPKC scheme, they are certainly interesting and can help us better understand the nature of solving the MQ problem.* The interested reader is referred to Figure 4 on page 15 of Thomae's PhD dissertation [19] for a nice graph showing the complexities of solving 11 equations with various numbers of variables over $\mathbb{F}_{2^k}$ for large enough k using the F5 algorithm [8]. We can clearly see a pattern of rise and fall of complexities as we move from underdetermined to overdetermined systems.

The situation is, however, quite different when it comes to fields of odd characteristics. For example, the Courtois-Goubin-Meier-Tacier algorithm can have polynomial time complexity, in which case we require that there are exponentially many variables than there are equations [3]. Alternatively, if we require a polynomial relation between the number of variables and that of equations, then the best running time is still exponential by using Kipnis-Patarin-Goubin [11], Thomae-Wolf [20], or Miura-Hashimoto-Takagi [14]. To help see the big picture, we summarize several recent results in the current literature in Table 1.

Table 1. Comparison of the applicable ranges and time complexities of several recent results over fields of odd characteristics

Algorithm	Applicable range	Complexity
Kipnis-Patarin-Goubin [11]	$n \geq m(m+1)$	Exponential
Courtois-Goubin-Meier [3]	$n \geq 2^{m/7}m(m+1)$	Polynomial
Courtois-Goubin-Meier [3]	$n \geq 2^{m/7}(m+1)$	Exponential
Thomae-Wolf [20]	$n > m$	Exponential
Miura-Hashimoto-Takagi [14]	$n \geq m(m+3)/2$	Exponential
This work	$n \geq m(m+1)/2$	Polynomial

Clearly, there is a significant gap between the cases over fields of even vs. odd characteristics. *In this paper, we attempt to close this gap by focusing on solving polynomially underdetermined MQ problem over fields of odd characteristics.* Currently, the best result is obtained by the Miura-Hashimoto-Takagi algorithm, as asymptotically it requires the least degree of underdeterminedness while avoiding the use of expensive, generic Gröbner-basis solver. As we shall discuss in more detail in Section 2, the algorithm can essentially be viewed as a way of obtaining a generalization of row echelon form for MQ problem. Our main contributions include that we can further improve the applicable range of the algorithm to $n \geq m(m + 1)/2$ essentially *for free*. Furthermore, we show how to allow a certain degree of *trade-off* between applicable range and running time. Last but not least, the running time of the improved algorithm is actually *polynomial* in number of equations and variables if we are allowed to use a *linear* amount of extra memory. *To the best of our knowledge, this is the first result showing that this class of polynomially underdetermined MQ problem over fields of odd characteristics can be solved in polynomial time.*

2 The Miura-Hashimoto-Takagi Algorithm Revisited

In this section, we give an overview of the state-of-the-art Miura-Hashimoto-Takagi algorithm for the sake of completeness. We begin by recalling that a nondegenerate system of m *linear* equations in m variables over a field is in row echelon form if it has the following form:

$$
\begin{cases}
f_1(x_1, \ldots, x_m) = x_1 + \sum_{2 \leq i \leq m} b_{1,i} x_i, \\
\quad \vdots \\
f_{m-2}(x_1, \ldots, x_m) = x_{m-2} + b_{m-2,m-1} x_{m-1} + b_{m-2,m} x_m, \\
f_{m-1}(x_1, \ldots, x_m) = x_{m-1} + b_{m-1,m} x_m, \\
f_m(x_1, \ldots, x_m) = x_m.
\end{cases}
$$

Such a form allows efficient solution by recursively solving the last equation and back-substituting. The Miura-Hashimoto-Takagi algorithm can essentially be viewed as a way of obtaining a generalization of row echelon form for *quadratic* equations. Recall that in the algorithm, the top-left $m \times m$ submatrices of the quadratic coefficients have the following forms at the end of Step m [14]:

$$
\begin{pmatrix} 0 \\ & 0 \\ & & 0 \\ & & & \ddots \\ & & & & 0 \\ & & & & & * \end{pmatrix},
\begin{pmatrix} 0 \\ & 0 \\ & & \ddots \\ & & & 0 \\ & & & & * \\ & & & & & * \end{pmatrix},
\begin{pmatrix} 0 \\ & \ddots \\ & & 0 \\ & & & * \\ & & & & * \\ & & & & & * \end{pmatrix}, \ldots,
\begin{pmatrix} * \\ & \\ & * \\ & \\ \end{pmatrix}.
$$

$$\tag{1}$$

At this point, the entire system may look like:

$$
\begin{cases}
f_1(x_1,\ldots,x_n) = x_m^2 + \sum_{1\leq i\leq m} x_i L_{1,i}(x_{m+1},\ldots,x_n) + Q_{1,2}(x_{m+1},\ldots,x_n), \\[2mm]
f_2(x_1,\ldots,x_n) = x_{m-1}^2 + Q_{2,1}(x_m) \\
\qquad\qquad\quad + \sum_{1\leq i\leq m} x_i L_{2,i}(x_{m+1},\ldots,x_n) + Q_{2,2}(x_{m+1},\ldots,x_n), \\[2mm]
f_3(x_1,\ldots,x_n) = x_{m-2}^2 + Q_{3,1}(x_{m-1},x_m) \\
\qquad\qquad\quad + \sum_{1\leq i\leq m} x_i L_{3,i}(x_{m+1},\ldots,x_n) + Q_{3,2}(x_{m+1},\ldots,x_n), \\[2mm]
\qquad\qquad \vdots \\[2mm]
f_m(x_1,\ldots,x_n) = x_1^2 + Q_{m,1}(x_2,\ldots,x_m) \\
\qquad\qquad\quad + \sum_{1\leq i\leq m} x_i L_{m,i}(x_{m+1},\ldots,x_n) + Q_{m,2}(x_{m+1},\ldots,x_n),
\end{cases}
\tag{2}
$$

where $L_{i,j}$ and $Q_{i,j}$ are some linear and quadratic polynomials, respectively. *Note that some equations may have x_i instead of x_i^2 as the leading term, which happens roughly with probability $1/q$ [14].*

Next in Step $m+1$, $\{L_{i,j} : \forall 1 \leq i \leq m, 1 \leq j < i\}$ are further eliminated by appropriate choice of $x_{m+1},\ldots,x_n$, resulting in

$$
\begin{cases}
x_m^2 - \lambda_1 = 0, \\
x_{m-1}^2 + \tilde{Q}_2(x_m) - \lambda_2 = 0, \\
x_{m-2}^2 + \tilde{Q}_3(x_{m-1},x_m) - \lambda_3 = 0, \\
\qquad\qquad \vdots \\
x_1^2 + \tilde{Q}_m(x_2,\ldots,x_m) - \lambda_m = 0,
\end{cases}
\tag{3}
$$

which is then recursively solved in Step $m+2$ by solving from the top and back-substituting.

In the case of linear equations, one can simply perform Gaussian elimination to obtain a matrix in row echelon form. This does not work for quadratic equations because there are more coefficients than can be eliminated by straightforward Gaussian elimination. Instead, in Steps 1 through m of the Miura-Hashimoto-Takagi algorithm, one performs a series of change-of-variable transformations on the system to be solved. This is equivalent to performing a series of elementary row/column operations simultaneously on the matrices of quadratic coefficients and bringing them to the forms as shown in Equation (1), which is possible as long as the system is sufficiently underdetermined [14].

A Toy Example. Here we give a toy example to help understand how the Miura-Hashimoto-Takagi algorithm works. Let us consider the following system over $\mathbb{F}_7$:

$$
\begin{cases}
f_1(x_1,\ldots,x_6) = 3x_1^2 + 6x_1x_3 + x_1x_4 + 3x_1x_5 + 5x_1x_6 + 4x_2^2 + 4x_2x_3 \\
\qquad\qquad\quad + 6x_2x_4 + 2x_2x_5 + 3x_2x_6 + 4x_3^2 + x_3x_4 + 6x_3x_6 \\
\qquad\qquad\quad + 6x_4^2 + 4x_4x_5 + 3x_4x_6 + 6x_5^2 + 4x_5x_6 + 2x_6^2 = 0, \\
f_2(x_1,\ldots,x_6) = 2x_1^2 + 3x_1x_2 + 3x_1x_3 + x_1x_4 + 6x_1x_5 + 2x_1x_6 + x_2^2 \\
\qquad\qquad\quad + 4x_2x_3 + 5x_2x_4 + x_2x_5 + 2x_3^2 + 2x_3x_4 + 6x_3x_5 \\
\qquad\qquad\quad + x_4^2 + 4x_4x_5 + 2x_4x_6 + 2x_5^2 + 5x_5x_6 + 6x_6^2 = 0.
\end{cases}
$$

The quadratic coefficients of f_1 and f_2 can be expressed by matrices F_1 and F_2, respectively:

$$
F_1 = \begin{pmatrix}
3 & 0 & 6 & 1 & 3 & 5 \\
0 & 4 & 4 & 6 & 2 & 3 \\
0 & 0 & 4 & 1 & 0 & 6 \\
0 & 0 & 0 & 6 & 4 & 3 \\
0 & 0 & 0 & 0 & 6 & 4 \\
0 & 0 & 0 & 0 & 0 & 2
\end{pmatrix}, F_2 = \begin{pmatrix}
2 & 3 & 3 & 1 & 6 & 2 \\
0 & 1 & 4 & 5 & 1 & 0 \\
0 & 0 & 2 & 2 & 6 & 0 \\
0 & 0 & 0 & 1 & 4 & 2 \\
0 & 0 & 0 & 0 & 2 & 5 \\
0 & 0 & 0 & 0 & 0 & 6
\end{pmatrix}.
$$

We can then proceed as follows.

Step 1.

$$
F_1 \mapsto F_1 - 5F_2 = \begin{pmatrix}
0 & 6 & 5 & 3 & 1 & 2 \\
0 & 6 & 5 & 2 & 4 & 3 \\
0 & 0 & 1 & 5 & 5 & 6 \\
0 & 0 & 0 & 1 & 5 & 0 \\
0 & 0 & 0 & 0 & 3 & 0 \\
0 & 0 & 0 & 0 & 0 & 0
\end{pmatrix}.
$$

Step 2. Consider the following change-of-variable transformation:

$$
T_2 = \begin{pmatrix}
1 & a_{1,2} & 0 & 0 & 0 & 0 \\
0 & 1 & 0 & 0 & 0 & 0 \\
0 & a_{3,2} & 1 & 0 & 0 & 0 \\
0 & a_{4,2} & 0 & 1 & 0 & 0 \\
0 & a_{5,2} & 0 & 0 & 1 & 0 \\
0 & a_{6,2} & 0 & 0 & 0 & 1
\end{pmatrix}.
$$

With T_2 applied to both f_1 and f_2, we require that

$$
\begin{cases}
5a_{3,2} + 3a_{4,2} + a_{5,2} + 2a_{6,2} + 6 = 0, \\
4a_{1,2} + 3a_{3,2} + a_{4,2} + 6a_{5,2} + 2a_{6,2} + 3 = 0.
\end{cases}
$$

There are many solutions, among which we can take, e.g., $(a_{1,2}, a_{3,2}, a_{4,2}, a_{5,2}, a_{6,2}) = (4, 3, 0, 0, 0)$. In this case, T_2 transforms F_1 and F_2 as follows:

$$F_1 \mapsto \begin{pmatrix} 0 & 0 & 5 & 3 & 1 & 2 \\ 0 & 2 & 0 & 1 & 2 & 1 \\ 0 & 3 & 1 & 5 & 5 & 6 \\ 0 & 0 & 0 & 1 & 5 & 0 \\ 0 & 0 & 0 & 0 & 3 & 0 \\ 0 & 0 & 0 & 0 & 0 & 0 \end{pmatrix}, F_2 \mapsto \begin{pmatrix} 2 & 6 & 3 & 1 & 6 & 2 \\ 1 & 6 & 1 & 1 & 1 & 1 \\ 0 & 6 & 2 & 2 & 6 & 0 \\ 0 & 0 & 0 & 1 & 4 & 2 \\ 0 & 0 & 0 & 0 & 2 & 5 \\ 0 & 0 & 0 & 0 & 0 & 6 \end{pmatrix},$$

and f_1 and f_2 become:

$$\begin{cases} 2x_2^2 + x_1(5x_3 + 3x_4 + x_5 + 2x_6) + x_2(3x_3 + x_4 + 2x_5 + x_6) + x_3^2 \\ \quad + 5x_3x_4 + 5x_3x_5 + 6x_3x_6 + x_4^2 + 5x_4x_5 + 3x_5^2 = 0, \\ 2x_1^2 + 6x_2^2 + x_1(3x_3 + x_4 + 6x_5 + 2x_6) + x_2(x_4 + x_5 + x_6) + 2x_3^2 \\ \quad + 2x_3x_4 + 6x_3x_5 + x_4^2 + 4x_4x_5 + 2x_4x_6 + 2x_5^2 + 5x_5x_6 + 6x_6^2 = 0. \end{cases}$$

Step 3. Now we need to solve:

$$\begin{cases} 5x_3 + 3x_4 + x_5 + 2x_6 = 0, \\ 3x_3 + x_4 + 2x_5 + x_6 = 0, \\ 3x_3 + x_4 + 6x_5 + 2x_6 = 0. \end{cases}$$

Again there are many solutions, among which we can take, e.g., $(x_3, x_4, x_5, x_6) = (1, 3, 3, 2)$ and arrive at:

$$\begin{cases} 2x_2^2 + 5 = 0, \\ 2x_1^2 + (6x_2^2 + x_2) + 1 = 0. \end{cases}$$

Step 4. From the first equation we see that $x_2^2 = 1$, solving which gives $x_2 = 1$ or 6. If we pick $x_2 = 6$ and substitute it into the second equation, then we get $x_1^2 = 4$, again solving which gives $x_1 = 2$ or 5. This can immediately give a solution $(x_1, x_2, x_3, x_4, x_5, x_6) = (2, 6, 1, 3, 3, 2)$, from which we can obtain a solution $(x_1, x_2, x_3, x_4, x_5, x_6) = (5, 6, 5, 3, 3, 2)$ to the original system by reversing T_2.

3   A First Improvement and Complexity Analysis

In this section, we first present an efficient time-memory trade-off for the Miura-Hashimoto-Takagi algorithm over fields of odd characteristics. We then prove that the proposed improvement has polynomial running time in number of equations and variables while using only linear amount of extra memory.

3.1 Root Finding on a Search Tree

Over fields of odd characteristics, the Miura-Hashimoto-Takagi algorithm was claimed to have an exponential time complexity $O(2^m n^w m (\log q)^2)$, where $2 \leq w \leq 3$ is the exponent of Gaussian elimination's time complexity, because the success probability of solving a system like Equation (3) is $2^{-m}(1 - q^{-m})$ [14]. We note that this explanation is indeed true if we use a naïve root finding algorithm in solving Equation 3. That is, whenever a resulted univariate equation in the process of solving Equation (3) has one or more roots in $\mathbb{F}_q$, we simply pick a random one, substitute it into all subsequent equations, and continue solving. Take the toy example in Section 2 as an example. There the equation $x_2^2 = 1$ has two roots in $\mathbb{F}_7$, namely, 1 and 6. Had we taken $x_2 = 1$ instead, we would not have been able to solve the system because this root would have led to $x_1^2 = 3$, which does not have any roots in $\mathbb{F}_7$. Since such a decision in solving x_i can change whether we can solve x_j for $j > i$, the success probability of solving the entire system of m equations drops exponentially in m, assuming such influence is essentially random.

Alternatively, we can *conceptually* collect all those $\mathbb{F}_q$ roots that we iteratively obtain and arrange them in a search tree, as shown in Figure 1.

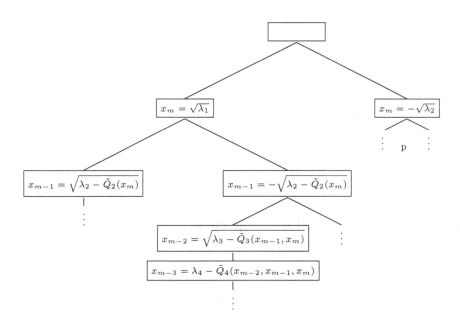

Fig. 1. Part of an example search tree formed by the $\mathbb{F}_q$ roots found in iteratively solving Equation (3)

We note that in this particular example, the fourth equation is degenerate, having x_{m-3} *instead of* x_{m-3}^2. In such a tree, we immediately see that the solution obtained at a child node depends on those at all its ancestors. With this in mind, we can then perform a *depth-first search* on this tree, as shown in Algorithm 1. If the tree has depth greater than m, then there exists a path from the root node to a leaf node of length at least m, meaning that we have found a solution for *all* $x_1, \ldots, x_m$. We declare a failure only when the tree does not have depth greater than m, which we will find out only after visiting all nodes in the tree.

Algorithm 1. Depth-first search on the tree formed by the $\mathbb{F}_q$ roots found in iteratively solving Equation (3)

```
 1: procedure DFS({f₁(xₖ), f₂(xₖ₋₁, xₖ), ..., fₖ(x₁, ..., xₖ)})
 2:     if k = 0 then
 3:         return SUCCESS
 4:     else
 5:         solve f₁(xₖ)
 6:         if f₁ has no 𝔽_q roots at all then
 7:             return FAILURE
 8:         else if f₁ has one 𝔽_q root x̃ then
 9:             substitute xₖ = x̃ into f₂, ..., fₖ
10:             return DFS({f₂, ..., fₖ})
11:         else                                    ▷ f₁ has two 𝔽_q roots x̃₁ and x̃₂
12:             substitute xₖ = x̃₁ into f₂, ..., fₖ and get g₂, ..., gₖ
13:             if DFS({g₂, ..., gₖ})=SUCCESS then
14:                 return SUCCESS
15:             else
16:                 substitute xₖ = x̃₂ into f₂, ..., fₖ
17:                 return DFS({f₂, ..., fₖ})
18:             end if
19:         end if
20:     end if
21: end procedure
```

3.2 Proof of Polynomial Running Time

How likely will we succeed in finding a solution for all $x_1, \ldots, x_m$? As we will show below, this success probability actually drops like $O(1/m)$ as m increases.

Lemma 1. *Assume that* $\lambda_1, \lambda_2, \ldots$, *and* $\tilde{Q}_2, \tilde{Q}_3, \ldots$ *in the search tree shown in Figure 1 are random. Let* $f(n)$ *denote the probability that the depth of this tree is greater than* n. *Then* $1/f \in O(n)$.

Proof. First, we will recursively analyze $p(n) = 1 - f(n)$, the probability that the height of the tree is smaller or equal to n, as follows. At the root node, there is a $1/q$ probability that the quadratic coefficient vanishes, and the Miura-Hashimoto-Takagi algorithm will make sure that the linear coefficient is nonzero. Hence, we will always be able to find a root and continue downward, in which case the probability of having a tree of height n is the same as that of $n-1$. In the other cases, there is a $1/2$ probability that the resulting univariate quadratic equation does not have any roots in $\mathbb{F}_q$, as well as $1/2$ probability that it has two roots in $\mathbb{F}_q$. In the latter case, in order to have a tree no taller than n, we will need to have *two* subtrees no taller than $n-1$. Therefore, p must satisfy a (nonlinear) recurrence relation

$$p(n+1) = \frac{q-1}{2q} + \frac{1}{q}p(n) + \frac{q-1}{2q}p^2(n).$$

Substituting $p(n) = 1 - f(n)$, we get the following recurrence relation for f:

$$f(n+1) = f(n) - \frac{q-1}{2q}f^2(n), \text{ with } f(1) = 1 - p(1) = \frac{q+1}{2q}. \tag{4}$$

Now we will show that $1/f \in O(n)$ by showing that $\lim_{n\to\infty} nf(n)$ exists and is a nonzero constant. Let $g(n) = \frac{q-1}{2q}nf(n)$. Then g satisfies

$$g(n+1) = \frac{n+1}{n}g(n)\left(1 - \frac{1}{n}g(n)\right), \text{ with } 0 < g(1) = \frac{q^2-1}{4q^2} < \frac{1}{2}. \tag{5}$$

We will show that $g(n)$ is appropriately bounded and monotonically increasing, and hence $\lim_{n\to\infty} g(n) = c$ for some nonzero constant c.

First, the boundedness of $g(n)$ can be shown by induction. We claim that for all natural numbers n,

$$0 < g(n) < \frac{n}{n+1}. \tag{6}$$

This is clearly true for $n = 1$ because $0 < g(1) < 1/2$. Now we assume that $0 < g(n) < n/(n+1)$. The right-hand side of Equation (5) is a quadratic formula $h(x) = \frac{n+1}{n}x(1 - x/n)$. For $0 \le x \le n/(n+1)$, the minimum of $h(x)$ is 0, which is achieved if and only if $x = 0$. Similarly, the maximum is

$$\frac{n+1}{n}\frac{n}{n+1}\left(1 - \frac{1}{n}\frac{n}{n+1}\right) = \frac{n}{n+1} < \frac{n+1}{n+2},$$

which is achieved if and only if $x = n/(n+1)$. Therefore, $0 < g(n+1) < (n+1)/(n+2)$, and we can conclude that $0 < g(n) < n/(n+1)$ for all natural numbers n.

Secondly, we can show that $g(n)$ is monotonically increasing by combining Equations (5) and (6):

$$\frac{g(n+1)}{g(n)} = \frac{n+1}{n}\left(1 - \frac{1}{n}g(n)\right) > \frac{n+1}{n}\left(1 - \frac{1}{n}\frac{n}{n+1}\right) = 1.$$

Therefore, we can further refine the bounds:

$$\frac{q^2-1}{4q^2} = g(1) \le g(n) < \frac{n}{n+1} < 1 \text{ for all natural numbers } n.$$

It follows that $g(n)$ must converge to some nonzero constant as n goes to infinity.
□

Next, we will also need to compute $\nu(n)$, the average number of nodes that we need to visit per solving attempt, in order to determine the overall time complexity. From the proof, we see that ν must satisfy the following recurrence relations:

$$\nu(n+1) = \frac{q-1}{2q} + \frac{1}{q}\left(\nu(n)+1\right) + \frac{q-1}{2q}\left(2\nu(n)+1\right) = 1 + \nu(n).$$

Since $\nu(1) = 1$, this means that $\nu(n) = n$. Putting it together, we conclude that the overall time complexity of the improved Miura-Hashimoto-Takagi algorithm is *polynomial*, as will be summarized in Theorem 1 in the next section.

Finally, the space complexity of depth-first search is linear in the longest path length searched, which will never exceed $m+1$ in our case. Therefore, the amount of extra memory used by Algorithm 1 is at most linear in m compared with that used the naïve root finding algorithm in the Miura-Hashimoto-Takagi algorithm, making our first improvement an efficient form of time-memory trade-off.

4   Two More Extensions in Applicable Range

In this section, we discuss how far we can push the applicable range of the Miura-Hashimoto-Takagi algorithm. That is, how underdetermined is sufficient over fields of odd characteristics? It has been shown that there are two determining factors [14]:

1. In Step $1 \leq t \leq m$, we need to eliminate $B_1(t) = \sum_{i=1}^{m} \min(i, t-1)$ coefficients using change-of-variable transformations by the other $n-1$ variables; Obviously the most stringent requirement here is $B_1(m) \leq n-1$, which in turn requires that $n \geq m(m+1)/2$.
2. In Step $m+1$, we need to make $L_{t,i} = 0$ for all $t \leq i \leq m$ in f_t. This means that in total, we need to make $B_2 = \sum_{t=1}^{m}(m-t+1)$ linear polynomials in $n-m$ variables vanish simultaneously. That is, we require that $n \geq m(m+3)/2$.

Together, we have the requirement that $n \geq m(m+3)/2$.

Our first insight is that we can actually have a slightly more relaxed requirement for n. Observe that, compared with solving Equation (2), it should be equally easy to solve the following system of quadratic equations *in a field of odd characteristics*:

$$\begin{cases} x_m^2 + L_{1,m}x_m + \lambda_1 = 0, \\ x_{m-1}^2 + L_{2,m-1}x_{m-1} + \lambda_2 + \tilde{Q}_2(x_m) = 0, \\ x_{m-2}^2 + L_{3,m-2}x_{m-2} + \lambda_3 + \tilde{Q}_3(x_{m-1}, x_m) = 0, \\ \qquad\qquad\qquad\vdots \\ x_1^2 + L_{m,1}x_1 + \lambda_m + \tilde{Q}_m(x_2, \ldots, x_m) = 0. \end{cases} \tag{7}$$

This means that instead of $\sum_{t=1}^{m}(m-t+1)$, we just need to cancel $\sum_{t=1}^{m}(m-t)$ linear polynomials. Therefore, the requirement on B_2 can be relaxed to $B_2 = \sum_{i=1}^{m}m(m-t) \leq n-m$, or equivalently, $n \geq m(m+1)/2$, matching that from B_1.

Furthermore, we observe that we can further relax this requirement to $n \geq m(m+1)/2 - b(b-1)/2$ at a cost superpolynomial in b. This can be achieved by making the following two modifications. First, in Step $1 \leq t \leq m$, we eliminate $B_1(t) = \sum_{i=1}^{m}\min(i, t-1, m-b)$ coefficients using change-of-variable transformations by the other $n-1$ variables. As a result, the top-left $m \times m$ submatrices of the quadratic coefficients will have the following forms at the end of Step m:

$$\underbrace{\begin{pmatrix} 0 & & & \\ & \ddots & & \\ & & 0 & \\ & & & * \\ & & * & \end{pmatrix}, \ldots, \begin{pmatrix} 0 & & & \\ & \ddots & & \\ & & 0 & \\ & & & * \\ & & * & \end{pmatrix}}_{b}, \underbrace{\begin{pmatrix} 0 & & & \\ & \ddots & & \\ & & * & \\ & & & \\ & * & & \end{pmatrix}, \ldots, \begin{pmatrix} * & & & \\ & & & \\ & & * & \\ & & & \end{pmatrix}}_{m-b}.$$

Again the limiting factor will be $B_1(m)$ if b is relatively small compared with m, in which case we have $B_1(m) = m(m+1)/2 - b(b+1) \leq n-1$. Secondly, in Step $m+1$, we make $L_{t,i} = 0$ for all $\max(t,b) < i \leq m$ in f_t. This means that in total, we need to make $B_2 = \sum_{t=1}^{m}(m - \max(t,b)) = m(m-1)/2 - b(b-1)/2$ linear polynomials in $n-m$ variables vanish simultaneously. Combining both requirements, we have $n \geq m(m+1)/2 - b(b-1)/2$, and we will need to solve the following system of quadratic equations:

$$\begin{cases} \tilde{Q}_1(x_{m-b+1}, \ldots, x_m) = 0, \\ \qquad\qquad \vdots \\ \tilde{Q}_b(x_{m-b+1}, \ldots, x_m) = 0, \\ x_{m-b}^2 + L_{b+1,m-b}x_{m-b} + \lambda_{b+1} + \tilde{Q}_{b+1}(x_{m-b+1}, \ldots, x_m) = 0, \\ \qquad\qquad \vdots \\ x_1^2 + L_{m,1}x_1 + \lambda_m + \tilde{Q}_m(x_2, \ldots, x_m) = 0. \end{cases}$$

We can use, for example, a Gröbner-basis solver to solve the first b generic-looking quadratic equations in b variables [23,1], but unfortunately the solving time is at least exponential in b.

Combining with the result of polynomial running time, we see that the extended Miura-Hashimoto-Takagi algorithm can actually provide better asymptotic performance than Thomae-Wolf. The latter also uses a Gröbner-basis solver to solve a system of $b' = m - \lfloor n/m \rfloor$ quadratic equations in as many variables [20]. We see that in the range where $n \approx m^2/2$, $b' \approx m/2$, and solving such a large system can be much more expensive than solving a system of b generic-looking quadratic equations in as many variables with $b \ll m$. Furthermore, it remains so even when we take $b \approx m/2$, in which case $n \gtrsim 3/8m^2$, whereas the Thomae-Wolf algorithm will need to solve systems of $b' \approx 5/8m$ equations in as many variables.

Finally, we are ready to state the main result of this paper in the following theorem.

Theorem 1. *For solving m multivariate quadratic equations in n variables over a finite field $\mathbb{F}_q$ of odd characteristics, the extended Miura-Hashimoto-Takagi algorithm has a time complexity $O(g(b)m^3 n^w (\log q)^2)$, where m, n, b are natural numbers with $n \geq m(m+1)/2 - b(b-1)/2$, $g(\cdot)$ accounts for the time complexity of a Gröbner-basis solver, and $2 \leq w \leq 3$ is the exponent of Gaussian elimination's time complexity.*

5   Preliminary Experimental Results and Concluding Remarks

We implemented both the original and the extended Miura-Hashimoto-Takagi algorithm over fields of odd characteristics in Magma [2] and Sage [18], respectively. We first summarize the experimental result of our Magma implementation of the original algorithm in Table 2. Here the experiments were carried out on an Intel Celeron processor running at 1.80 GHz with 4 GB of RAM using Magma V2.17-9 running on Microsoft Windows 8 (64-bit). The average was taken over 100,000 runs. We can see that in Table 2, the success probabilities indeed drop rather quickly even for n slightly larger than $m(m + 3)/2$.

Table 2. Running time and success probabilities of the original Miura-Hashimoto-Takagi algorithm over $\mathbb{F}_7$

m	n	Avg. time	Suc. prob.	$O(2^{-m})$	$O(1/m)$
4	16	3.25 ms	25.37%	6.25%	25.00%
11	84	183.56 ms	3.68%	4.88×10^{-4}	9.09%
28	434	32.23 sec	0.01%	3.73×10^{-9}	3.57%

In Table 3, we report the success probabilities of the extended Miura-Hashimoto-Takagi algorithm implemented in Sage for the cases of solving x equations in $x(x + 3)/2$ variables over $\mathbb{F}_7$, where $x = 1, \ldots, 10$. The second column in the table shows the probabilities predicted by Equation (4), whereas each of the entries in the third column represents the statistics obtained from solving 1,000 randomly generated systems. From this preliminary experimental result, it seems that Equation (4) does a fairly good job in predicting the success probability, which is strong evidence for our claim of polynomial running time for the extended Miura-Hashimoto-Takagi algorithm.

To conclude, the extended Miura-Hashimoto-Takagi algorithm closes a gap between solving a class of underdetermined MQ problem over fields of even

Table 3. Success probabilities of Step $m + 2$ in the extended Miura-Hashimoto-Takagi algorithm when solving x equations in $x(x + 3)/2$ variables over $\mathbb{F}_7$

x	$f(x)$	Exp.	Diff.
1	0.571	0.562	-2%
2	0.431	0.404	-6%
3	0.352	0.318	-10%
4	0.299	0.284	-5%
5	0.260	0.252	-3%
6	0.231	0.215	-7%
7	0.208	0.215	3%
8	0.190	0.156	-18%
9	0.174	0.168	-4%
10	0.161	0.141	-13%

vs. odd characteristics. Now as long as $n \geq m(m + 1)/2$, we have polynomial-time solvers for both the even and odd cases. This boundary, symmetric with the case of overdetermined MQ problem, seems *tight*. We suspect that any further breakthrough in time complexity beyond the extended Miura-Hashimoto-Takagi algorithm may require an entirely different approach.

Acknowledgments. This work was supported in part by Japan Society for the Promotion of Science via Grant-in-Aid for JSPS Fellows, no. 25-P13346 and Grant-in-Aid for Young Scientists (B), no. 26800020, as well as Strategic Information and Communications R&D Promotion Programme (SCOPE), no. 0159-0172.

References

1. Ars, G., Faugère, J.-C., Imai, H., Kawazoe, M., Sugita, M.: Comparison Between XL and Gröbner Basis Algorithms. In: Lee, P.J. (ed.) ASIACRYPT 2004. LNCS, vol. 3329, pp. 338–353. Springer, Heidelberg (2004)
2. Bosma, W., Cannon, J., Playoust, C.: The Magma algebra system. I. The user language. J. Symbolic Comput. 24(3-4), 235–265 (1997), http://dx.doi.org/10.1006/jsco.1996.0125, computational algebra and number theory, London (1993)
3. Courtois, N., Goubin, L., Meier, W., Tacier, J.-D.: Solving Underdefined Systems of Multivariate Quadratic Equations. In: Naccache, D., Paillier, P. (eds.) PKC 2002. LNCS, vol. 2274, pp. 211–227. Springer, Heidelberg (2002)
4. Courtois, N., Klimov, A.B., Patarin, J., Shamir, A.: Efficient Algorithms for Solving Overdefined Systems of Multivariate Polynomial Equations. In: Preneel, B. (ed.) EUROCRYPT 2000. LNCS, vol. 1807, pp. 392–407. Springer, Heidelberg (2000)
5. Ding, J., Hodges, T.J.: Inverting HFE Systems Is Quasi-Polynomial for All Fields. In: Rogaway, P. (ed.) CRYPTO 2011. LNCS, vol. 6841, pp. 724–742. Springer, Heidelberg (2011)
6. Ding, J., Schmidt, D.: Rainbow, a New Multivariable Polynomial Signature Scheme. In: Ioannidis, J., Keromytis, A.D., Yung, M. (eds.) ACNS 2005. LNCS, vol. 3531, pp. 164–175. Springer, Heidelberg (2005)

7. Faugère, J.C.: A new efficient algorithm for computing Gröbner bases (F4). Journal of Pure and Applied Algebra 139(13), 61–88 (1999), http://www.sciencedirect.com/science/article/pii/S0022404999000055
8. Faugère, J.C.: A new efficient algorithm for computing Gröbner bases without reduction to zero (F5). In: Proceedings of the 2002 International Symposium on Symbolic and Algebraic Computation, ISSAC 2002, pp. 75–83. ACM, New York (2002), http://doi.acm.org/10.1145/780506.780516
9. Faugère, J.-C., Joux, A.: Algebraic Cryptanalysis of Hidden Field Equation (HFE) Cryptosystems Using Gröbner Bases. In: Boneh, D. (ed.) CRYPTO 2003. LNCS, vol. 2729, pp. 44–60. Springer, Heidelberg (2003)
10. Garey, M.R., Johnson, D.S.: Computers and Intractability: A Guide to the Theory of NP-Completeness. W. H. Freeman (1979)
11. Kipnis, A., Patarin, J., Goubin, L.: Unbalanced Oil and Vinegar Signature Schemes. In: Stern, J. (ed.) EUROCRYPT 1999. LNCS, vol. 1592, pp. 206–222. Springer, Heidelberg (1999)
12. Kipnis, A., Shamir, A.: Cryptanalysis of the Oil & Vinegar Signature Scheme. In: Krawczyk, H. (ed.) CRYPTO 1998. LNCS, vol. 1462, pp. 257–266. Springer, Heidelberg (1998)
13. Matsumoto, T., Imai, H.: Public Quadratic Polynomial-Tuples for Efficient Signature-Verification and Message-Encryption. In: Günther, C.G. (ed.) EUROCRYPT 1988. LNCS, vol. 330, pp. 419–453. Springer, Heidelberg (1988)
14. Miura, H., Hashimoto, Y., Takagi, T.: Extended Algorithm for Solving Underdefined Multivariate Quadratic Equations. In: Gaborit, P. (ed.) PQCrypto 2013. LNCS, vol. 7932, pp. 118–135. Springer, Heidelberg (2013)
15. Patarin, J.: Cryptanalysis of the Matsumoto and Imai Public Key Scheme of Eurocrypt '88. In: Coppersmith, D. (ed.) CRYPTO 1995. LNCS, vol. 963, pp. 248–261. Springer, Heidelberg (1995)
16. Patarin, J.: Hidden Fields Equations (HFE) and Isomorphisms of Polynomials (IP): Two New Families of Asymmetric Algorithms. In: Maurer, U.M. (ed.) EUROCRYPT 1996. LNCS, vol. 1070, pp. 33–48. Springer, Heidelberg (1996)
17. Sakumoto, K., Shirai, T., Hiwatari, H.: Public-Key Identification Schemes Based on Multivariate Quadratic Polynomials. In: Rogaway, P. (ed.) CRYPTO 2011. LNCS, vol. 6841, pp. 706–723. Springer, Heidelberg (2011)
18. Stein, W., et al.: Sage Mathematics Software (Version 6.0). The Sage Development Team (2013), http://www.sagemath.org
19. Thomae, E.: About the security of multivariate quadratic public key schemes. Ph.D. thesis, Ruhr Universität Bochum (June 2013)
20. Thomae, E., Wolf, C.: Solving Underdetermined Systems of Multivariate Quadratic Equations Revisited. In: Fischlin, M., Buchmann, J., Manulis, M. (eds.) PKC 2012. LNCS, vol. 7293, pp. 156–171. Springer, Heidelberg (2012)
21. Yang, B.-Y., Chen, O.C.-H., Bernstein, D.J., Chen, J.-M.: Analysis of QUAD. In: Biryukov, A. (ed.) FSE 2007. LNCS, vol. 4593, pp. 290–308. Springer, Heidelberg (2007)
22. Yang, B.-Y., Chen, J.-M.: Building Secure Tame-like Multivariate Public-Key Cryptosystems: The New TTS. In: Boyd, C., González Nieto, J.M. (eds.) ACISP 2005. LNCS, vol. 3574, pp. 518–531. Springer, Heidelberg (2005)
23. Yang, B.-Y., Chen, J.-M., Courtois, N.T.: On Asymptotic Security Estimates in XL and Gröbner Bases-Related Algebraic Cryptanalysis. In: López, J., Qing, S., Okamoto, E. (eds.) ICICS 2004. LNCS, vol. 3269, pp. 401–413. Springer, Heidelberg (2004)

A   An Example Implementation in Magma

A.1   The Implementation

Step 1–m

```
Trans_step:=function(k,n,m,F);
T:=AssociativeArray(); Step:=1;
while Step le m do;
  if Step ge 2 then;
    CoeA:=AssociativeArray(); countA:=0;
    Coeb:=AssociativeArray(); countb:=0;
    for l:=1 to Step-1 do;
      for j:=1 to m-l+1 do;
        for i:=1 to n do;
          if i ne Step then; countA:=countA+1;
            CoeA[countA]:=F[j][l,i]+F[j][i,l];
          else; countb:=countb+1;
            Coeb[countb]:=F[j][l,Step]+F[j][Step,l];
          end if;
        end for;
      end for;
    end for;
    A:=Matrix(k,countb,n-1,[CoeA[i]:i in [1..countA]]);
    b:=Matrix(k,1,countb,[(-1)*Coeb[i]:i in [1..countb]]);
    x:=Solution(Transpose(A),b);
    T[Step]:=ScalarMatrix(k,n,1);
    for i:=1 to Step-1 do;
      T[Step][i,Step]:=x[1,i];
    end for;
    for i:=Step+1 to n do;
      T[Step][i,Step]:=x[1,i-1];
    end for;
    "T[",Step,"]="; T[Step];
    for i:=1 to m do;
      F[i]:=Transpose(T[Step])*F[i]*T[Step];
    end for;
  end if;
  if Step lt m then; c:=AssociativeArray();
    for i:=1 to m-Step do;
      c[i]:=F[i][Step,Step]/F[m-Step+1][Step,Step];
      F[i]:=F[i]-c[i]*F[m-Step+1];
    end for;
  end if;
  Step:=Step+1;
end while;
for i:=1 to m do; "F[",i,"]="; F[i]; end for;
```

```
return F,T;
end function;
```

Step $m + 1$

```
Linear_step:=function(k,n,m,F);
Lin:=AssociativeArray();
count:=0;
for i:=1 to m do;
  for j:=1 to m-i+1 do;
    for l:=m+1 to n do;
      count:=count+1;
      Lin[count]:=F[i][j,l]+F[i][l,j];
    end for;
  end for;
end for;
NumOfLin:=IntegerRing()!(count/(n-m));
LE:=Matrix(k,NumOfLin,n-m,[Lin[i]:i in [1..count]]);
L:=Kernel(Transpose(LE));
x:=BasisElement(L,1);
x:=Matrix(n-m,1,x);
"a Solution of Linear Equations is"; Transpose(x);
return F,x;
end function;
```

Step $m + 2$

```
Root_step:=function(k,n,m,F,G,T,x);
P<[y]>:=PolynomialRing(k,m);
vec:=AssociativeArray();
for i:=1 to n do;
  if i le m then; vec[i]:=y[i];
  else; vec[i]:=x[i-m,1]; end if;
end for;
Y:=Matrix(P,n,1,[vec[i]:i in[1..n]]);
for i:=1 to m do; G[i]:=ChangeRing(G[i],P); end for;
count:=0; i:=1;
while i le m do;
  H:=Transpose(Y)*G[i]*Y;
  a:=(G[i][m-i+1,m-i+1]*y[m-i+1]^2-H[1,1])/G[i][m-i+1,m-i+1];
  if IsSquare(a) eq false then;
    if i ne 1 then;
      if count eq 0 then;
        i:=i-1; Y[m-i+1,1]:=(-1)*Y[m-i+1,1];
        "Y[",m-i+1,"]=",Y[m-i+1,1]; count:=1;
      else; "error"; break;
```

```
        end if;
      else; "error"; break;
      end if;
    else;
      Y[m-i+1,1]:=Sqrt(a);
      "Y[",m-i+1,"]=",Y[m-i+1,1];
      count:=0;
    end if;
    i:=i+1;
  end while;
  "Y=",Transpose(Y);
  T[1]:=&*[T[i]:i in[2..m]]; T[1]:=ChangeRing(T[1],P);
  X:=T[1]*Y; "X=",Transpose(X);
  // Verification
  for i:=1 to m do;
    F[i]:=ChangeRing(F[i],P); F[i]:=Transpose(X)*F[i]*X;
  end for;
  Check:=Matrix(P,1,m,[F[i][1,1]: i in[1..m]]);
  if IsZero(Check) eq true then;
  return "OK."; else return "Failed."; end if;
  end function;
```

A.2   Example Calculation
System Parameters

```
k:=GF(7); n:=6; m:=2; F:=AssociativeArray();
F[1]:=Matrix(k,[[3,0,6,1,3,5],[0,4,4,6,2,3],[0,0,4,1,0,6],
[0,0,0,6,4,3],[0,0,0,0,6,4],[0,0,0,0,0,2]]);
F[2]:=Matrix(k,[[2,3,3,1,6,2],[0,1,4,5,1,0],[0,0,2,2,6,0],
[0,0,0,1,4,2],[0,0,0,0,2,5],[0,0,0,0,0,6]]);
```

Example Output

```
> G,T:=Trans_step(k,n,m,F);
T[ 2 ]=              F[ 1 ]=              F[ 2 ]=
[1 4 0 0 0 0]        [0 0 5 3 1 2]        [2 6 3 1 6 2]
[0 1 0 0 0 0]        [0 2 0 1 2 1]        [1 6 1 1 1 1]
[0 3 1 0 0 0]        [0 3 1 5 5 6]        [0 6 2 2 6 0]
[0 0 0 1 0 0]        [0 0 0 1 5 0]        [0 0 0 1 4 2]
[0 0 0 0 1 0]        [0 0 0 0 3 0]        [0 0 0 0 2 5]
[0 0 0 0 0 1]        [0 0 0 0 0 0]        [0 0 0 0 0 6]
> G,y:=Linear_step(k,n,m,G);
a Solution of Linear Equations is
[1 3 3 2]
> Root_step(k,n,m,F,G,T,y);
```

```
Y[ 2 ]= 1          Y=[2 6 1 3 3 2]
Y[ 2 ]= 6          X=[5 6 5 3 3 2]
Y[ 1 ]= 2          OK.
```

Differential Properties of the *HFE* Cryptosystem

Taylor Daniels[1] and Daniel Smith-Tone[1,2]

[1] Department of Mathematics, University of Louisville,
Louisville, Kentucky, USA
[2] National Institute of Standards and Technology,
Gaithersburg, Maryland, USA
tsdani02@louisville.edu, daniel.smith@nist.gov

Abstract. Multivariate Public Key Cryptography (MPKC) has been put forth as a possible post-quantum family of cryptographic schemes. These schemes lack provable security in the reduction theoretic sense, and so their security against yet undiscovered attacks remains uncertain. The effectiveness of differential attacks on various field-based systems has prompted the investigation of differential properties of multivariate schemes to determine the extent to which they are secure from differential adversaries. Due to its role as a basis for both encryption and signature schemes we contribute to this investigation focusing on the *HFE* cryptosystem. We derive the differential symmetric and invariant structure of the *HFE* central map and that of *HFE*⁻ and provide a collection of parameter sets which make these *HFE* systems provably secure against a differential symmetric or differential invariant attack.

1 Introduction and Outline

Along with the discovery of polytime quantum algorithms for factoring and computing discrete logarithms, see [1], came a rising interest in "quantum-resistant" cryptographic protocols. For the last two decades this interest has blossomed into a large international effort to develop post-quantum cryptography, a term which elicits visions of a post-apocalyptic world where quantum computing machines reign supreme. While progress in quantum computing indicates that such devices are not precluded by the laws of physics, it is not at all clear when we may see large-scale quantum computing devices becoming a cryptographic threat. Nevertheless, the potential and the uncertainty of the situation clearly establish the need for secure post-quantum options.

One of a few reasonable candidates for security in a quantum computing world is multivariate cryptography. We already rely heavily on the difficulty of inverting nonlinear systems of equations in symmetric cryptography, and we quite reasonably suspect that that security will remain in the quantum paradigm. Multivariate Public Key Cryptography (MPKC) has the added challenge of resisting quantum attack in the asymmetric setting.

M. Mosca (Ed.): PQCrypto 2014, LNCS 8772, pp. 59–75, 2014.

While it is difficult to be assured of a cryptosystems's post-quantum security in light of the continual evolution of the relatively young field of quantum algorithms, it is reasonable to start by developing schemes which resist classical attack and for which there is no known significant weakness in the quantum realm. Furthermore, the establishment of security metrics provide insight which educate us about the possibilities for attacks and the correct strategies for the development of cryptosystems.

In this vein, some classification metrics are introduced in [2,3] which can be utilized to rule out certain classes of attacks. While not reduction theoretic attacks, reducing the task of breaking the scheme to a known (or often suspected) hard problem, these metrics can be used to prove that certain classes of attacks fail or to illustrate specific computational challenges which an adversary must face to effect an attack.

Many attacks on multivariate public key cryptosystems can be viewed as differential attacks, in that they utilize some symmetric relation or some invariant property of the public polynomials. These attacks have proved effective in application to several cryptosystems. For instance, the attack on SFLASH, see [4], is an attack utilizing differential symmetry, the attack of Kipnis and Shamir [5] on the oil-and-vinegar scheme is actually an attack exploiting a differential invariant, even Patarin's initial attack on C^* [6] can be viewed as an exploitation of a trivial differential symmetry, see [3]. These attacks are evidence that the work in [2,3] is worthy of continuation and further development.

This task leads us to an investigation of the HFE family of schemes, see [7], and a characterization of the differential properties of some variants. Results similar to those of [2,3] will allow us to make conclusions about the differential security of HFE-derived schemes, and, in particular, provide some insight into the properties of some of its important variants such as HFE^- and $HFEv^-$, see [8] and [9].

To this end, we derive the differential symmetry and differential invariant structure of the central map of HFE. Specifically, we are able to bound the probability that an HFE or HFE^- primitive has a nontrivial differential structure and to provide parameter sets for which these schemes are provably secure against a restricted differential adversary. This result on the HFE and HFE^- primitives, in conjunction with degree of regularity results such as [10,11] provide a strong argument for the security of the HFE^- and $HFEv^-$ signature schemes, though more work is required to verify that the differential structure is not weakened by the vinegar modifier for practical parameters.

We note explicitly that the provided proof of security against a differential adversary for HFE is not an endorsement of HFE, a scheme thoroughly broken in [12,13]. The proof indicates that HFE cannot be broken by "differential means." The attack of [12] is a decidedly "rank" attack, referring to the fact that it relies heavily and necessarily on rank analysis. Furthermore, since rank methods have remained ineffective in breaking the general HFE^- and $HFEv^-$ schemes, the proofs provided for parameter sets of HFE^- schemes have greater significance.

The paper is organized as follows. First, we describe the notion of a differential adversary and discuss differential security. We then recall the HFE scheme from [7] and some of its history. In the following section, we examine linear differential symmetric relations for both the HFE and HFE^- schemes, deriving parameters to ensure the non-existence of such relations. We next review the notion of a differential invariant and a method of classifying differential invariants. We continue, analyzing the differential invariant structure of the HFE and HFE^- systems and providing parameters precluding the existence of a nontrivial differential invariant in the general case. Finally, we conclude, noting parameters which provide provable differential security.

2   The Differential Adversary

The discrete differential of a field map $f : \mathbb{F}_q^n \to \mathbb{F}_q^m$ is given by:

$$Df(y, x) = f(x + y) - f(x) - f(y) + f(0).$$

It is simply a normalized difference equation with variable interval. Several prominent cryptanalyses in the history of MPKC have utilized a symmetric relation of the discrete differential of the core map or subspaces which are left invariant under some action of the differential of the core map. Simple examples include the linearization equations attack of [7], which can be viewed as exploiting the relation $Df(f(x), f(x)) = 0$; the attack on balanced Oil-Vinegar, see [14,5]; and the SFLASH attack of [4]. Along with rank attacks, differential attacks have made the greatest impact on MPKC among structural key recovery attacks.

For the purpose of progress in security analysis in MPKC, we propose a model for a differential adversary. This model strives to capture the behaviors employed in all differential attacks and will hopefully be improved with time.

We will say that a *restricted differential adversary* $\mathcal{A}$ is a probabilistic Turing machine with access to a public key P which computes either

1. an affine map L such that $DP(Ly, x) + DP(y, Lx) = \Lambda_L DP(y, x)$, or
2. a pair of subspaces V and W with $dim(V) + dim(W) \geq n$ the number of variables, such that $DP(y, x) = 0$ for all $x \in V$ and $y \in W$,

and uses the solution to derive an equivalent private key.

An *unrestricted differential adversary* $\mathcal{A}$ is a probabilistic Turing machine with access to a public key P which computes either

1. a subspace $Z \subseteq \mathbb{F}_q^m$ of dimension at least two where m is the number of public equations and an affine map L such that $A(Ly, x) + A(y, Lx) = \Lambda_L A(y, x)$ for all $A = \sum_{i=0}^{m-1} z_i DP_i$ where $(z_0, z_1, \ldots, z_{m-1}) \in Z$, i.e. $A \in Span_Z(DP_i)$, or
2. a subspace $Z \subseteq \mathbb{F}_q^m$ of dimension at least two and a pair of subspaces V and W with $dim(V) + dim(W) \geq n$ the number of variables, such that $A(y, x) = 0$ for all $x \in V$, $y \in W$, and $A \in Span_Z(DP_i)$,

and uses the solution to derive an equivalent private key.

We note here a few things. Item number two in the definition of the unrestricted differential adversary has no meaning if the subspace Z is one dimensional. The significance of the subspace Z is that it allows the unrestricted differential adversary to target subspaces of the span of the public polynomials which were constructed in different ways, having different differential properties, see [15] for a particular example of such an attack. A proof of security against an unrestricted differential adversary is very challenging, however there is little interest in the distinction between an unrestricted differential adversary and a restricted differential adversary if the private polynomials of a scheme were not constructed with different methods, since trivial structure for proper subspaces Z is a generic property.

In the case of the restricted differential adversary it specifically suffices to prove that a core map f has no such L and no such (V, W) to guarantee that the restricted differential adversary's advantage for the cryptosystem with primitive f is zero. Item 1 of the restricted differential adversary above is discussed in more detail in Section 5 and item 2 in Section 6.

3   Useful Background Algebraic Results

For completeness, we present a collection of useful propositions and definitions which make the later proofs more streamlined.

Proposition 1. *If A, B are two $m \times n$ matrices, then $rank(A) = rank(B)$ if and only if there exist nonsingular matrices C, D, such that $A = CBD$.*

Proof. Let A be an $m \times n$ matrix of rank r. With row operations $(P, m \times m)$ we can get A into row echelon form, PA. Then we can use column operations $(Q, n \times n)$ to "zero-out" the remaining nonleading elements and permute the leading 1's to the first r columns. Thus PAQ is the $m \times n$ matrix with the $r \times r$ identity matrix in the upper-left region, and zeros everywhere else. Denote this matrix as I'. Thus $PAQ = I'$. We can also do this with B, so that $P'BQ' = I' = PAQ$. Thus $A = (P^{-1}P')B(Q'Q^{-1})$, with $P^{-1}P'$ and $Q'Q^{-1}$ nonsingular.

From this point forward we fix a finite field $\mathbb{F}_q$ and a finite extension $\mathbb{K}$ of degree n.

Definition 1. *We define the* minimal polynomial *of a subspace $V \subseteq \mathbb{K}$ as*

$$\mathcal{M}_V(x) = \prod_{v \in V} (x - v)$$

The term "minimal polynomial" is used since this is the polynomial of minimal degree of which every element of V is a root. We note that the equation $\mathcal{M}_V(x) = 0$ is an $\mathbb{F}_q$-linear equation.

Suppose that V has $\mathbb{F}_q$-dimension d, so that $|V| = q^d$. Then $\mathcal{M}_V(x)$ has degree q^d and must have the form

$$x^{q^d} + b_{d-1}x^{q^{d-1}} + \cdots + b_2 x^{q^2} + b_1 x^q + b_0 x \quad b_i \in \mathbb{K} \tag{1}$$

Proposition 2. *Let $T : \mathbb{K} \to \mathbb{K}$ be an $\mathbb{F}_q$-linear map. Let $\pi : \mathbb{K} \to \mathbb{K}$ be defined by $\pi x = \mathcal{M}_{ker(T)}(x)$. There exists a nonsingular $\mathbb{F}_q$-linear map $\tilde{T} : \mathbb{K} \to \mathbb{K}$ such that $Tx = \tilde{T}\pi x$.*

Proof. Clearly, π is an $\mathbb{F}_q$-linear map. Also clear is the fact that $ker(\pi) = ker(T)$. Since π and T are additive homomorphisms, each is constant on cosets of the kernel. Therefore we may define $\tilde{T}x = T\pi^{-1}(x)$ where $\pi^{-1}(x)$ is the preimage of x (a coset of the common kernel) under π. Evidently, $\tilde{T}$ is well-defined. Finally, $\tilde{T}\pi(x) = T\pi^{-1}(\pi x) = T(x + ker(T)) = Tx$.

In addition, we can characterize all functions from V to $\mathbb{K}$ (analogous to the coordinate ring $\overline{\mathbb{K}}[x]/\langle \mathcal{M}_V(x)\rangle$):

Proposition 3. *Let $\mathcal{F}_V$ be the ring of all functions from the $\mathbb{F}_q$-subspace V of $\mathbb{K}$ to $\mathbb{K}$. Then $\mathcal{F}_V$ is isomorphic to $\mathbb{K}[x]/\langle \mathcal{M}_V(x)\rangle$.*

Proof. The ring of all functions from $\mathbb{K}$ to itself is $\mathbb{K}[x]/\langle x^{q^n} - x\rangle$. Suppose that $f, g \in \mathbb{K}[x]/\langle x^{q^n} - x\rangle$ are identical on V. Then for all $v \in V$, v is a root of $(f - g)(x)$. Thus $(x - v)$ is a linear factor of $(f - g)(x)$ for all $v \in V$. Thus $\mathcal{M}_V(x)|(f - g)(x)$. Consequently, $\langle \mathcal{M}_V(x)\rangle$ is the ideal of functions which send V to zero. Thus $\mathbb{K}[x]/\langle x^{q^n} - x, \mathcal{M}_V(x)\rangle$ is the ring of nontrivial functions from V to $\mathbb{K}$. Since $\mathcal{M}_V(x)$ splits in $\mathbb{K}$, $\mathcal{M}_V(x)|x^{q^n} - x$. To see that all functions from V to $\mathbb{K}$ are polynomials note that there are $(q^n)^{q^d}$ functions from V (of $\mathbb{F}_q$-dimension d) to $\mathbb{K}$, and $|\mathbb{K}[x]/\langle \mathcal{M}_V(x)\rangle| = (q^n)^{q^d}$.

4   HFE

The Hidden Field Equations (HFE) scheme was first presented by Patarin in [7] as a method of avoiding his linearization equations attack on the C^* scheme of Matsumoto and Imai, see [6] and [16]. The basic idea of the system is to use the butterfly construction to hide an easily invertible polynomial over an extension field.

More specifically, let $\mathbb{F}_q$ be a finite field and let $\mathbb{K}$ be a degree n extension of $\mathbb{F}_q$. Given an easily invertible "quadratic" map $f : \mathbb{K} \to \mathbb{K}$, quadratic in the sense that f is a sum of products of pairs of $\mathbb{F}_q$-linear functions of x, one constructs a system of quadratic formulae over $\mathbb{F}_q$ by composing two $\mathbb{F}_q$-affine transformations $T, U : \mathbb{K} \to \mathbb{K}$ thusly, $P = T \circ f \circ U$, and then expressing the composition over the base field, $\mathbb{F}_q$. Explicitly any such "core" map f has the form:

$$f(x) = \sum_{\substack{i \leq j \\ q^i + q^j < D}} \alpha_{i,j} x^{q^i + q^j} + \sum_{\substack{i \\ q^i < D}} \beta_i x^{q^i} + \gamma,$$

with the degree bound D established to allow for easy inversion.

To encrypt given the public key $P(x)$, one simply evaluates every public polynomial at the plaintext vector $x \in \mathbb{F}_q^n \approx \mathbb{K}$. Decryption is accomplished by inverting each of the three private components individually. The most interesting inversion is that of f, which is inverted via a polynomial system solver such as the Berlekamp algorithm.

In [7], Patarin presented a couple of HFE challenges to be used as benchmarks for progress in cryptanalyzing HFE and HFE^-. HFE challenge 1 was broken in 2003, see [17], via an algebraic attack which allows the direct inversion of the system of equations. This attack was specialized in the sense that it took advantage of the choices of the coefficients of f as well as the characteristic of $\mathbb{F}_q$.

In 2011, HFE was broken for all characteristics altogether in [12], in a vast improvement of the Kipnis-Shamir attack of [18]. The attack breaks the original HFE for all practical parameters as well as several variants, including projected HFE and Multi-HFE, by what amounts to a sophisticated rank analysis of the central map via the public polynomials. Notably, the attack can *not* break HFE^- or $HFEv^-$.

5   Linear Differential Symmetry

5.1   Symmetry for HFE

In [4], the SFLASH signature scheme was broken by exploiting a symmetric relation of the differential of the public key. This relation was inherited from the core map of the scheme. Specifically, a linear differential symmetry is an equation in which linear maps are applied to the differential in such a way that the equation is linear in the unknown coefficients of the linear maps. We can always express the symmetry in the following form:

$$Df(My, x) + Df(y, Mx) = \Lambda_M Df(y, x), \tag{2}$$

where M and Λ_M are linear maps. To evaluate the potential for a differential symmetric attack on HFE, we consider conditions for the existence of a linear differential symmetry on the core map f of an HFE scheme.

Consider the differential of the core map:

$$Df(y, x) = \sum_{\substack{i \leq j \\ q^i + q^j < D}} \alpha_{i,j}(y^{q^i} x^{q^j} + y^{q^j} x^{q^i}). \tag{3}$$

Df is a $\mathbb{K}$-bilinear form. We choose a convenient representation for $\mathbb{K}$:

$$x \mapsto \begin{bmatrix} x \\ x^q \\ \vdots \\ x^{q^{n-1}} \end{bmatrix}.$$

Under this representation we can express Df as the $n \times n$ symmetric matrix with (i, j)th and (j, i)th entries $\alpha_{i,j}$ for $i \neq j$ and (i, i)th entry $2\alpha_{i,i}$ (which may be zero depending on the characteristic of $\mathbb{K}$).

Since any linear map $M : \mathbb{K} \to \mathbb{K}$ can be written $Mx = \sum_{i=0}^{n-1} m_i x^{q^i}$, under our representation M can be expressed:

$$M = \begin{bmatrix} m_0 & m_1 & \cdots & m_{n-1} \\ m_{n-1}^q & m_0^q & \cdots & m_{n-2}^q \\ \vdots & \vdots & \ddots & \vdots \\ m_1^{q^{n-1}} & m_2^{q^{n-1}} & \cdots & m_0^{q^{n-1}} \end{bmatrix}.$$

In this representation, we have the formula

$$Df(My, x) + Df(y, Mx) = y(M^T Df + DfM)x. \tag{4}$$

Consider the action of Λ_M on Df. $\Lambda_M Df(y, x) = \sum_{k=0}^{n-1} \lambda_k Df(y, x)^{q^k}$. Notice specifically that in our representation the matrix for Df^{q^k} is the same as the matrix representing Df shifted to the right and down k units with all entries raised to the q^kth power. This shift is due to the fact that

$$Df(y, x)^{q^k} = \sum_{\substack{i \leq j \\ q^i + q^j < D}} \alpha_{i,j}^{q^k} (y^{q^{i+k}} x^{q^{j+k}} + y^{q^{j+k}} x^{q^{i+k}}).$$

Specifically, the (i, j)th entry of Df^{q^k} is $\alpha_{i-k,j-k}^{q^k}$ if $i \neq j$, and (i, i)th entry $(2\alpha_{i-k,i-k})^{q^k} = 2\alpha_{i-k,i-k}^{q^k}$ (0 in characteristic two).

Thus the possibility of a differential symmetry can be deduced simply by setting the matrix $M^T Df + DfM$ equal to the matrix $\Lambda_M Df$. With certain constraints it is easy to deduce whether there exists a solution.

Theorem 1. *Let $f(x)$ be an HFE polynomial (in particular f is not a monomial function). Suppose that f has the following properties:*

1. no power of q is repeated among the exponents of f, and
2. the difference of the powers of q in each exponent is unique.

Then f has no nontrivial differential symmetry.

Proof. First consider computing DfM. From the condition on the monomials of f, Df has at most a single nonzero entry in any row or column. Therefore each row of DfM is a multiple of a row in M. In particular, if $\alpha_{i,j} x^{q^i + q^j}$ is a monomial of f, then the ith row of DfM is

$$\left[\alpha_{i,j} m_{-j}^{q^j} \ \alpha_{i,j} m_{1-j}^{q^j} \ \cdots \ \alpha_{i,j} m_{-1-j}^{q^j} \right],$$

and the jth row is

$$\left[\alpha_{i,j} m_{-i}^{q^i} \ \alpha_{i,j} m_{1-i}^{q^i} \ \cdots \ \alpha_{i,j} m_{-1-i}^{q^i} \right].$$

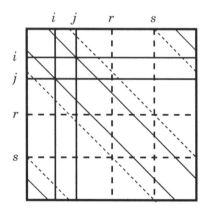

Fig. 1. Graphical representation of the equation $M^T Df + DfM = \Lambda_M Df$ for the HFE polynomial $f(x) = \alpha_{i,j} x^{q^i + q^j} + \alpha_{r,s} x^{q^r + q^s}$. Horizontal and vertical lines represent nonzero entries in $M^T Df + DfM$ while diagonal lines represent nonzero entries in $\Lambda_M Df$. Solid lines correspond to the (i,j) monomial while dotted lines correspond to the (r,s) monomial.

Consider the ith row of $M^T Df + DfM$. For all k not occurring as a power of q in f, the (i,k)th entry is $\alpha_{i,j} m_{k-j}^{q^j}$. Consider the (i,j)th entry of $M^T Df + DfM$. This quantity is the sum of the (i,j)th entry of DfM and the (j,i)th entry, specifically $\alpha_{i,j}(m_0^{q^i} + m_0^{q^j})$. Let $\alpha_{r,s} x^{q^r + q^s}$ be another monomial of f. Then the (i,r)th entry of $M^T Df + DfM$ is $\alpha_{i,j} m_{r-j}^{q^j} + \alpha_{r,s} m_{i-s}^{q^s}$, and the (i,s)th entry is $\alpha_{i,j} m_{s-j}^{q^j} + \alpha_{r,s} m_{i-r}^{q^r}$.

In $\Lambda_M Df$, for all $\alpha_{i,j} x^{q^i + q^j}$ a monomial in f, the $(i+k, j+k)$th entry is equal to the $(j+k, i+k)$th entry and takes the value $\alpha_{i,j}^{q^k} \lambda_k$ while all other entries are zero.

Therefore consider the elements in the ith row of the equation $M^T Df + DfM = \Lambda_M Df$. For every monomial $\alpha_{r,s} x^{q^r + q^s}$ in f, we have that the $s - r + i$th element and the $r - s + i$th element of row i in $\Lambda_M Df$ are nonzero. All other entries of that row are zero. Therefore, for all k not occurring as a power of q in f or as a difference of the powers of q in an exponent of a monomial in f plus i, $m_{k-j} = 0$. Given the condition that the differences of powers of q in the exponents are unique, and the equations $m_{k-t} = 0$ for all other t occurring as powers of q, we obtain $m_i = 0$ for all $i \neq 0$. Therefore M is a multiplication map. But as proven in Theorem 2 in [19], if $m_0 \notin \mathbb{F}_q$ this implies that the polynomial is a C^* monomial, a contradiction. Thus M is simply multiplying by a scalar which induces a symmetry for every map $g : \mathbb{K} \to \mathbb{K}$. Thus f has no nontrivial differential symmetry.

5.2   Symmetry for HFE^-

We can extend the result of the previous section to reveal the differential symmetric structure of HFE^-. The specific difference in the proof is merely placing the operator π, a projection on to a subspace, in (4).

$$\pi \left[M^T Df + DfM \right] = \Lambda_M \left[Df \right]. \tag{5}$$

We handle the general case of a codimension r projection explicitly.

Theorem 2. *Let $\mathbb{K}$ be a prime extension of $\mathbb{F}_q$ and let $\pi : \mathbb{K} \to \mathbb{K}$ be a codimension r projection. Let $f : \mathbb{K} \to \mathbb{K}$ be a nontrivial HFE polynomial with degree bound $D < q^{n/2}$, let P_f be the multiset of powers of q occurring in the exponents of f, and let S_f be the multiset of differences of the powers of q in the exponent of each monomial summand of f. Suppose that f has the following properties:*

1. P_f is a set,
2. S_f is a set, and
3. for all $i \in P_f$ the Lee distance between $(i + S_f) \setminus P_f$ and P_f is at least $r + 1$.

Then if $D(\pi \circ f)(My, x) + D(\pi \circ f)(y, Mx) = \Lambda_M Df(y, x)$, then $Mx = m_0 x$ for some $m_0 \in \mathbb{F}_q$. Thus $\pi \circ f$ has no nontrivial differential symmetry.

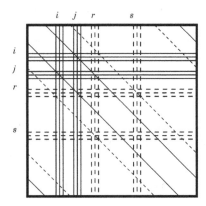

Fig. 2. Graphical representation of the equation $\pi \left[M^T Df + DfM \right] = \Lambda_M Df$ for the HFE polynomial $f(x) = \alpha_{i,j} x^{q^i + q^j} + \alpha_{r,s} x^{q^r + q^s}$, where $\pi x = ax + bx^q + x^{q^2}$. Horizontal and vertical lines represent nonzero entries in $\pi \left[M^T Df + DfM \right]$ while diagonal lines represent nonzero entries in $\Lambda_M Df$. Solid lines correspond to the (i, j) monomial while dotted lines correspond to the (r, s) monomial.

Proof. Due to the effect of T and by Proposition 2, we may without loss of generality assume that $\pi x = \sum_{b=0}^{r} a_b x^{q^b}$ with $a_r = 1$. Therefore, the matrix form of $\pi \left[M^T Df + DfM \right]$ is easily derived from the matrix form of $M^T Df + DfM$.

The action of raising to the power of q results in each element of the matrix raised to the power of q and transposed one row down and one column to the right.

Let $\alpha_{i,j} x^{q^i + q^j}$ be a monomial summand of f. We observe that the (i, k)th entry of $\pi \left[M^T Df + Df M \right]$ for $k \notin P_f \cup (1 + P_f) \cup \cdots \cup (r + P_f) \cup (i + S_f)$ is $m_{k-j}^{q^j}$ while the corresponding entry of $\Lambda_M Df$ is zero. Therefore $m_k = 0$ for all $k \in (-j + P_f) \cup (1 - j + P_f) \cup \cdots \cup (r - j + P_f) \cup (i - j + S_f)$. The remaining entries of $\pi \left[M^T Df + Df M \right]$ produce the relations $2m_{i-j} = 0$, $m_{i-j+1}^{q^j} + m_{i-j-1}^{q^{j+1}} = 0$, and so on corresponding to the (i, k)th entry for $k \in P_f \cup (1 + P_f) \cup \cdots \cup (r + P_f) \cup (i + S_f)$. From these we derive that $m_k = 0$ for all $k \notin (i - j + [S_f \cup \{0\}])$.

By symmetry, we have that $m_k = 0$ for all $k \notin (r - s + [S_f \cup \{0\}])$ for all monomial summands $\alpha_{r,s} x^{q^r + q^s}$. We search for an element $g \in \mathbb{Z}_n$ where n is prime by hypothesis such that g is in every such set. Since for every $a \in S_f$ we have that $-a \in S_f$, a necessary condition is that S_f is closed under addition by g. Since every nonzero g is a generator of $\mathbb{Z}_n$, we must have that $g = 0$, since otherwise we contradict the fact that $D < q^{n/2}$. Thus $Mx = m_0 x$, and we may apply Theorem 2 from [19] in the case $m_0 \notin \mathbb{F}_q$ to conclude that $\pi \circ f$ is a quadratic monomial map. Since f is a nontrivial HFE polynomial, we have that $m_0 \in \mathbb{F}_q$.

We note that the conditions of the above theorem are very easy to check, though for very small D they may be difficult to satisfy and there may be some issues regarding a lack of entropy in the private key space. With proper selection of the extension, however, it is unlikely that this adjustment will lead to a successful attack based on the morphism of polynomials problem, in a similar vein to [20].

6   Differential Invariants

The discrete differential Df is a symmetric, bilinear *function* on $\mathbb{F}_q^n$ (using the vector space representation of $\mathbb{K}$), but each coordinate of Df is a symmetric, bilinear *form* on $\mathbb{K}$. Because of this, we may express each coordinate of Df, $[Df(y, x)]_i$ as

$$[Df(y, x)]_i = y^T Df_i x.$$

Maintaining our definitions of $\mathbb{K}$ and f, we define a "first order differential invariant" of f.

Definition 1. *Let $f : \mathbb{K} \to \mathbb{K}$ be a function. A* differential invariant *of f is a subspace $V \subseteq \mathbb{K}$ with the property that there is a subspace $W \subseteq \mathbb{K}$ such that $dim(W) \leq dim(V)$ and $\forall A \in Span_{\mathbb{F}_q}(Df_i)$, $AV \subseteq W$.*

Informally speaking, a function has a differential invariant if the image of a subspace under all differential coordinate forms lies in a fixed subspace of dimension no larger. This definition captures the notion of *simultaneous invariants*, subspaces which are simultaneously invariant subspaces of Df_i for all i, and detects when large subspaces are acted upon linearly.

If we assume the existence of a first order differential invariant V, we can define a corresponding subspace $V^\perp$ as the set of all elements $x \in \mathbb{K}$ such that the dot product $\langle x, Av \rangle = 0 \ \forall v \in V, \forall A \in Span(Df_i)$. This is not quite the usual definition of an orthogonal complement. $V^\perp$ is not the set of everything orthogonal to V, but rather everything orthogonal to AV, which may or may not be in V.

With our definitions of V and $V^\perp$, we can establish the following useful result. Assume there is a first order differential invariant $V \subseteq \mathbb{K}$, and pick a linear projection $M : \mathbb{K} \to V$ and another linear projection $M^\perp : \mathbb{K} \to V^\perp$. Examining one of the differential coordinate-forms,

$$[Df(M^\perp y, Mx)]_i = (M^\perp y)^T (Df_i(Mx)) \qquad (6)$$

Since $M^\perp y$ is in $V^\perp$, and $Df_i Mx \in AV$, we must then have that

$$[Df(M^\perp y, Mx)]_i = (M^\perp a)^T (Df_i(Mx)) = 0 \qquad (7)$$

The "i" in Df_i did not matter, meaning that for all i (from 1 to n), i.e. for all coordinates of Df, the above equation is true. We can then simply say that:

$$\forall y, x \in \mathbb{K}, Df(M^\perp y, Mx) = 0 \quad \text{or equivalently,} \quad Df(M^\perp \mathbb{K}, M\mathbb{K}) = 0 \qquad (8)$$

This fact will restrict what M and $M^\perp$ can be. We can make our investigation of $M, M^\perp$ easier by employing Proposition 1. Our idea is to express $M^\perp = SMT$, where S may be singular, but T is nonsingular (or vice versa if $rank(M) < rank(M^\perp)$).

Without loss of generality, due to the symmetry of Df, we may assume that $rank(M^\perp) \leq rank(M)$. If the ranks are equal, then we may apply Proposition 1 and write $M^\perp = SMT$, with S and T nonsingular. If $rank(M^\perp) < rank(M)$, compose M with a singular matrix X so that $rank(XM) = rank(M^\perp)$, and *then* apply the result so that $M^\perp = S(XM)T$. Then we can express $M^\perp = S'MT$, where S' is singular. The matrix T is included to ensure that the kernels of $M, M^\perp$ are properly aligned. Restating our differential result (8) in this manner, we have that if $M^\perp = SMT$, and $M : \mathbb{K} \to V$, then

$$\forall x, y \in \mathbb{K}, Df(SMTy, MTx) = 0 \qquad (9)$$

7 Differential Invariant Structure

7.1 HFE

If f has non-trivial invariant V we know that $\forall A \in Span(Df_i)$, $dim(AV) \leq dim(V)$. Since the dot-product is non-degenerate on $\mathbb{K}$, and remembering that $V^\perp$ is defined slightly differently, we can say $dim(V^\perp) + dim(AV) = n$. This fact implies that $dim(V^\perp) + dim(V) \geq n$, so either $dim(V^\perp) \geq n/2$ or $dim(V) \geq n/2$, possibly both.

If $dim(V) \geq n/2$, we maintain $MT : \mathbb{K} \to V$ and characterize $S : V \to V^{\perp}$. If we deduce S maps V to $\{0\}$, that is, $V^{\perp} = \{0\}$, this would mean $dim(AV) = n$ and consequently $AV = \mathbb{K}$. If $V \neq \mathbb{K}$, we contradict $dim(AV) \leq dim(V)$, and if $V = \mathbb{K}$, we contradict the non-triviality of V.

If $dim(V^{\perp}) \geq n/2$, we take $M'T' : \mathbb{K} \to V^{\perp}$ instead and characterize $S' : V^{\perp} \to V$. If S' is the zero map on $V^{\perp}$, i.e. $S'V^{\perp} = V = \{0\}$, then we contradict the non-triviality of V.

Without loss of generality we assume $dim(V) \geq n/2$ because the following analysis and results can be achieved just as easily if we have $dim(V^{\perp}) \geq n/2$.

For notational convenience, we now fix $MTx = \hat{x}$, $MTy = \hat{y}$, $MT\mathbb{K} = V$, and $d = dim(V)$. Starting with the core map

$$f(x) = \sum_{\substack{i \leq j \\ q^i + q^j < D}} \alpha_{i,j} x^{q^i + q^j} + \sum_{\substack{i \\ q^i < D}} \beta_i x^{q^i} + \gamma,$$

we compute:

$$Df(S\hat{y}, \hat{x}) = \sum_{\substack{i \leq j \\ q^i + q^j < D}} \alpha_{i,j} \left[(S\hat{y})^{q^i} \hat{x}^{q^j} + (S\hat{y})^{q^j} \hat{x}^{q^i} \right]. \tag{10}$$

For practical parameters, D is far smaller than $|V|$, see for example [7], and so for $Df(S\hat{y}, \hat{x}) = 0$, every coefficient of $\hat{x}^{q^j}$ must be in $\langle \mathcal{M}_V(\hat{y}) \rangle$. Expanding (10) we obtain:

$$\begin{aligned} Df(S\hat{y}, \hat{x}) &= \sum_{\substack{i \leq j \\ q^i + q^j < D}} \alpha_{i,j} \left[(S\hat{y})^{q^i} \hat{x}^{q^j} + (S\hat{y})^{q^j} \hat{x}^{q^i} \right] \\ &= \sum_{\substack{i,j \\ q^i + q^j < D}} \left[(\alpha_{i,j} + \alpha_{j,i}) (S\hat{y})^{q^i} \right] \hat{x}^{q^j}, \end{aligned} \tag{11}$$

where we specifically note in the last expression that if $i \neq j$ exactly one of $\alpha_{i,j}$ and $\alpha_{j,i}$ may be nonzero. Thus for each j such that $q^j < D$ we have the following polynomial:

$$\sum_{i : q^i + q^j < D} (\alpha_{i,j} + \alpha_{j,i})(S\hat{y})^{q^i}. \tag{12}$$

The membership of the jth polynomial of the form (12) in $\langle \mathcal{M}_V(\hat{y}) \rangle$ provides the relation

$$\sum_{i : q^i + q^j < D} (\alpha_{i,j} + \alpha_{j,i})(S\hat{y})^{q^i} = 0. \tag{13}$$

Relation (13) has $\ell = \lfloor log_q(D) \rfloor$ degrees of freedom on S as a linear action on V. Therefore, there are $d - \ell$ $\mathbb{F}_q$-linearly independent relations on S from a single monomial of (11). For a practically chosen D, two linearly independent relations of this form on S force S to be the zero map on V. Consequently, we have that $V^{\perp} = \{0\}$, a contradiction. Specifically, the probability that two such given relations are independent is approximately $1 - q^{-n\ell}$; thus with very high probability f has no differential invariant structure.

In particular, we provide a specific strategy for provably eliminating differential invariants.

Theorem 3. *Let f be an HFE polynomial with degree bound $D < q^{n/2}$. If there is a power of q which is unique, f has no non-trivial invariant structure.*

Proof. Assume by way of contradiction that f has a non-trivial differential invariant. Let j be the unique power of q occurring in an exponent in f. By the above discussion it suffices to analyze membership of the jth polynomial of the form (12) in $\langle \mathcal{M}_V(\hat{y}) \rangle$. Given the condition on j, this polynomial has the form $(\alpha_{rj} + \alpha_{jr})(S\hat{y})^{q^r}$. If this polynomial is in $\langle \mathcal{M}_V(\hat{y}) \rangle$, then so is $S\hat{y}$, since $\mathcal{M}_V(\hat{y})$ has no repeated factors, and we have $SV = \{0\}$, a contradiction.

7.2 HFE^-

Deriving the differential invariant structure for HFE^- follows a nearly identical line of reasoning. The clear distinction is that since the definition of the differential invariant depends on the span of the differentials of the public polynomials, there is greater freedom to have an invariant when there are fewer public polynomials. For specificity, we analyze the case in which a single public equation is removed, though importantly, a very similar though notationally messy analysis is easy to derive in the general case.

Once again, considering the effects of T and Proposition 2, it suffices to analyze $\pi \circ f$ where $\pi x = x + x^q$. Notice that we have:

$$
\begin{aligned}
\pi \circ f(x) = \sum_{\substack{i \leq j \\ q^i + q^j < D}} \alpha_{i,j} x^{q^i + q^j} + \sum_{\substack{i \\ q^i < D}} \beta_i x^{q^i} + \gamma \\
+ \sum_{\substack{i \leq j \\ q^i + q^j < D}} \alpha_{i,j}^q x^{q^{i+1} + q^{j+1}} + \sum_{\substack{i \\ q^i < D}} \beta_i^q x^{q^{i+1}} + \gamma^q,
\end{aligned}
\tag{14}
$$

and therefore,

$$
\begin{aligned}
D(\pi \circ f)(S\hat{y}, \hat{x}) = \sum_{\substack{i \leq j \\ q^i + q^j < D}} \alpha_{i,j} \left[(S\hat{y})^{q^i} \hat{x}^{q^j} + (S\hat{y})^{q^j} \hat{x}^{q^i} \right] \\
+ \sum_{\substack{i \leq j \\ q^i + q^j < D}} \alpha_{i,j}^q \left[(S\hat{y})^{q^{i+1}} \hat{x}^{q^{j+1}} + (S\hat{y})^{q^{j+1}} \hat{x}^{q^{i+1}} \right].
\end{aligned}
\tag{15}
$$

Again, we may collect terms with respect to the powers of $\hat{x}$, and obtain polynomials in $S\hat{y}$.

$$
D(\pi \circ f)(S\hat{y}, \hat{x}) = \sum_j p_j(S\hat{y}) \hat{x}^{q^j}.
\tag{16}
$$

Setting this quantity equal to zero, we see that a differential invariant is only possible when $p_j(S\hat{y}) \in \langle \mathcal{M}_V(\hat{y}) \rangle$ for all j. Here we note that an equation of the form (16) occurs for any projection π, though the structure of the polynomials p_j depend on the corank of π and the structure of f.

Despite the added difficulty of the minus modifier, we can prove the nonexistence of nontrivial differential invariants for HFE^- under conditions very similar to those provided in the previous subsection.

Theorem 4. *Let f be an HFE polynomial with degree bound $D < q^{n/2}$. Let π be the codimension r projection $\pi x = \sum_{b=0}^{r} a_b x^{q^b}$ where $a_r = 1$. If there is a power k of q which is unique and $k-1, k-2, \ldots, k-r$ does not occur as a power of q in any quadratic monomial summand, $\pi \circ f$ has no non-trivial invariant structure.*

Proof. By the above condition, there is a power k such that the "coefficient" of $\hat{x}^{q^k}$ in (16) is p_k. Moreover, the condition on k that $k-1, k-2, \ldots, k-r$ do not occur implies that p_k is derived from a single summand in (15). Applying the argument from Theorem 3, we have that $SV = \{0\}$, and therefore there is no nontrivial differential invariant of $\pi \circ f$.

As an immediate corollary, we can derive a very easy condition for the nonexistence of nontrivial differential invariants for practical HFE^- schemes.

Corollary 1. *Let f be an HFE polynomial with degree bound $D < q^{n/2}$. If $r < n/2$ public equations are removed and the smallest power of q in any quadratic monomial summand of f occurs only once, the public key has no non-trivial differential invariant structure.*

Proof. Apply Theorem 4 with k the specified smallest power of q.

It is easy to see that the result if also valid if we replace the word "smallest" by "largest." Informally, the important condition is that $log_q(D) + r < n$.

8   IP, Degree of Regularity, Other Factors

The restrictions suggested in Theorems 1, 2, 3, and 4 reduce the entropy of the private key space, which might raise concerns about vulnerability to attacks based on a "guess-then-IP" strategy, to direct inversion via Gröbner bases. As it turns out, for even modest parameters these issues are not realized. Moreover, the theorems are not "tight," meaning that they are merely simple ways of eliminating differential symmetric and invariant weakness. Given a private HFE polynomial, one can check directly for conditions which guarantee the nonexistence of a differential symmetry or invariant.

Consider, for example, using the parameter set for HFE Challenge 2; specifically, we have $q = 16, n = 36, r = 4$, and $D = 4352 = 16^2 + 16^3$. Thus $\mathbb{K} = \mathbb{F}_{16^{36}}$, and our HFE map must have the form :

$$f(x) = \sum_{i \leq j \leq 3, i \neq 3} \alpha_{i,j} x^{q^i + q^j} + \sum_{i \leq 3} \beta_i x^{q^i} + \gamma$$

We may choose $\alpha_{1,2}$ and $\alpha_{0,3}$ to be the only non-zero α, therefore we obtain the distinct powers of q $P_f = \{0, 1, 2, 3\}$ and differences $S_f = \{-3, -1, 1, 3\}$. By Corollary 1, f has no nontrivial differential invariant structure. One may also consider the system of equations arising from setting $\pi x = x^{q^4} + ax^{q^3} + bx^{q^2} + cx^q + dx$ in (5). Using similar analysis as in Theorem 2, we derive that the only possible solution is when $Mx = m_0 x$ for $m_0 \in \mathbb{F}_q$; therefore, f has no nontrivial differential symmetric structure and thus this instantiation of HFE^- is secure against a restricted differential adversary. The private key space is reduced from containing q^{13n} HFE polynomials to only containing q^{7n} such maps, though $q^n(q^n - 1)$ of these may be seen to be equivalent keys (counting equivalence classes of keys intersected with polynomials of this form), via the additive and big sustainers of [21]. Therefore, there are roughly q^{5n} nonequivalent polynomials with only $\alpha_{1,2}$ and $\alpha_{0,3}$ nonzero among the α.

For weak parameters, in particular when the $\alpha_{i,j}$ are chosen from the base field, an attack based on the IP problem is presented in [20]. The symmetries used in that method, however, are not present when both $\alpha_{1,2}$ and $\alpha_{0,3}$ are chosen randomly from $\mathbb{K}$. While we may consider the coefficient of $\alpha_{1,2}$ to be "absorbed" by the affine map T, the effect of the remaining coefficient breaks the symmetry. Without the commutativity of the Frobenius map with the HFE polynomial, the parameters supplied are out of range for an IP-based attack.

Another concern is that the rank of the scheme may be so low as to make the scheme susceptible to attack via Gröbner basis methods. However, using the theorem from [22], we compute the degree of regularity of the adjusted scheme to be:

$$\frac{(16 - 1)4}{2} + 2 = 32,$$

based on the fact that the rank of the central map is only four. Using the formula from [23], we obtain an estimated complexity of

$$\binom{36 + 32}{32}^{\omega}$$

where $\omega = 2.3766$. Thus, we estimate the complexity of directly inverting this concrete example to be $O(2^{153})$. Note, the attack of [12] is not feasible here since this is an HFE^- scheme, see section 8.1 in [12].

9   Conclusion

For eighteen years, HFE has been studied, influencing cryptanalysis, symbolic computation, and the development of new cryptographic schemes. Though the original HFE scheme is broken for all practical parameters, as a platform for the development of various signature schemes, HFE has excelled, utilizing several modifiers to spawn new systems, some of which are leading candidates for secure post-quantum signatures.

Our analysis contributes to the HFE legacy, elucidating the differential structure inherent to the core map. The results indicate that given practical parameters, many HFE-derived systems lack non-trivial differential invariant structure. Further, we have established that with a simple choice of parameters we can *provably* eliminate non-trivial differential symmetric and invariant structure while maintaining security against attacks exploiting a diminished private key space. In particular, there is a parameter space for which HFE^- is provably secure against a restricted differential adversary.

References

1. Shor, P.W.: Polynomial-time algorithms for prime factorization and discrete logarithms on a quantum computer. SIAM J. Sci. Stat. Comp. 26, 1484 (1997)
2. Smith-Tone, D.: On the differential security of multivariate public key cryptosystems. In: Yang, B.-Y. (ed.) PQCrypto 2011. LNCS, vol. 7071, pp. 130–142. Springer, Heidelberg (2011)
3. Perlner, R.A., Smith-Tone, D.: A classification of differential invariants for multivariate post-quantum cryptosystems. In: [24], pp. 165–173
4. Dubois, V., Fouque, P.-A., Shamir, A., Stern, J.: Practical cryptanalysis of SFLASH. In: Menezes, A. (ed.) CRYPTO 2007. LNCS, vol. 4622, pp. 1–12. Springer, Heidelberg (2007)
5. Kipnis, A., Shamir, A.: Cryptanalysis of the oil & vinegar signature scheme. In: Krawczyk, H. (ed.) CRYPTO 1998. LNCS, vol. 1462, pp. 257–266. Springer, Heidelberg (1998)
6. Patarin, J.: Cryptoanalysis of the Matsumoto and Imai Public Key Scheme of Eurocrypt'88. In: Coppersmith, D. (ed.) CRYPTO 1995. LNCS, vol. 963, pp. 248–261. Springer, Heidelberg (1995)
7. Patarin, J.: Hidden fields equations (HFE) and isomorphisms of polynomials (IP): Two new families of asymmetric algorithms. In: Maurer, U.M. (ed.) EUROCRYPT 1996. LNCS, vol. 1070, pp. 33–48. Springer, Heidelberg (1996)
8. Patarin, J., Goubin, L., Courtois, N.T.: C $^*_{-+}$ and HM: Variations around two schemes of T.Matsumoto and H.Imai. In: Ohta, K., Pei, D. (eds.) ASIACRYPT 1998. LNCS, vol. 1514, pp. 35–50. Springer, Heidelberg (1998)
9. Patarin, J., Courtois, N., Goubin, L.: Quartz, 128-bit long digital signatures. In: Naccache, D. (ed.) CT-RSA 2001. LNCS, vol. 2020, pp. 282–297. Springer, Heidelberg (2001)
10. Ding, J., Kleinjung, T.: Degree of regularity for hfe-. IACR Cryptology ePrint Archive 2011, 570 (2011)
11. Ding, J., Yang, B.Y.: Degree of regularity for hfev and hfev-. In: [24] pp. 52–66
12. Bettale, L., Faugère, J.C., Perret, L.: Cryptanalysis of hfe, multi-hfe and variants for odd and even characteristic. Des. Codes Cryptography 69(1), 1–52 (2013)
13. Granboulan, L., Joux, A., Stern, J.: Inverting hfe is quasipolynomial. In: Dwork, C. (ed.) CRYPTO 2006. LNCS, vol. 4117, pp. 345–356. Springer, Heidelberg (2006)
14. Patarin, J.: The oil and vinegar algorithm for signatures. Presented at the Dagsthul Workshop on Cryptography (1997)

15. Moody, D., Perlner, R.A., Smith-Tone, D.: An asymptotically optimal structural attack on the abc multivariate encryption scheme. In: Mosca, M. (ed.) PQCrypto 2014. LNCS, vol. 8772, Springer, Heidelberg (2014)
16. Matsumoto, T., Imai, H.: Public Quadratic Polynominal-Tuples for Efficient Signature-Verification and Message-Encryption. In: Günther, C.G. (ed.) EUROCRYPT 1988. LNCS, vol. 330, pp. 419–453. Springer, Heidelberg (1988)
17. Faugère, J.-C., Joux, A.: Algebraic cryptanalysis of hidden field equation (HFE) cryptosystems using gröbner bases. In: Boneh, D. (ed.) CRYPTO 2003. LNCS, vol. 2729, pp. 44–60. Springer, Heidelberg (2003)
18. Kipnis, A., Shamir, A.: Cryptanalysis of the HFE public key cryptosystem by relinearization. In: Wiener, M. (ed.) CRYPTO 1999. LNCS, vol. 1666, pp. 19–30. Springer, Heidelberg (1999)
19. Smith-Tone, D.: Properties of the discrete differential with cryptographic applications. In: Sendrier, N. (ed.) PQCrypto 2010. LNCS, vol. 6061, pp. 1–12. Springer, Heidelberg (2010)
20. Bouillaguet, C., Fouque, P.A., Joux, A., Treger, J.: A family of weak keys in hfe and the corresponding practical key-recovery. J. Mathematical Cryptology 5, 247–275 (2012)
21. Wolf, C., Preneel, B.: Equivalent keys in multivariate quadratic public key systems. J. Mathematical Cryptology 4, 375–415 (2011)
22. Ding, J., Hodges, T.J.: Inverting hfe systems is quasi-polynomial for all fields. In: Rogaway, P. (ed.) CRYPTO 2011. LNCS, vol. 6841, pp. 724–742. Springer, Heidelberg (2011)
23. Bardet, M., Faugere, J.C., Salvy, B.: On the complexity of gröbner basis computation of semi-regular overdetermined algebraic equations. In: Proceedings of the International Conference on Polynomial System Solving (2004)
24. Gaborit, P. (ed.): PQCrypto 2013. LNCS, vol. 7932. Springer, Heidelberg (2013)

The Cubic Simple Matrix Encryption Scheme

Jintai Ding[1], Albrecht Petzoldt[2], and Lih-chung Wang[3]

[1] University of Cincinnati, Ohio, USA and Academia Sinica, Taiwan
[2] TU Darmstadt, Germany
[3] National Dong Hwa University, Taiwan
{jintai.ding,lihchungwang}@gmail.com,
apetzoldt@cdc.informatik.tu-darmstadt.de

Abstract. In this paper, we propose an improved version of the Simple Matrix encryption scheme of PQCrypto2013. The main goal of our construction is to build a system with even stronger security claims. By using square matrices with random quadratic polynomials, we can claim that breaking the system using algebraic attacks is at least as hard as solving a set of random quadratic equations. Furthermore, due to the use of random polynomials in the matrix A, Rank attacks against our scheme are not feasible.

Keywords: Multivariate Cryptography, Simple Matrix Encryption Scheme, Provable Security.

1   Introduction

Cryptographic techniques are an essential tool to guarantee the security of communication in modern society. Today, the security of nearly all of the cryptographic schemes used in practice is based on number theoretic problems such as factoring large integers and solving discrete logarithms. The best known schemes in this area are RSA [20], DSA and ECC. However, schemes like these will become insecure as soon as large enough quantum computers arrive. The reason for this is Shor's algorithm [21], which solves number theoretic problems such as integer factorization and discrete logarithms in polynomial time on a quantum computer. Therefore, one needs alternatives to those classical public key schemes which are based on mathematical problems not affected by quantum computer attacks.

Besides lattice, code and hash based cryptosystems, multivariate cryptography is one of the main candidates for this [1]. Multivariate schemes are very fast and require only modest computational resources, which makes them attractive for the use on low cost devices like smart cards and RFID chips [2,4]. However, while there exist many practical multivariate signature schemes [9,13,18], the number of efficient and secure multivariate encryption schemes is somewhat limited.

M. Mosca (Ed.): PQCrypto 2014, LNCS 8772, pp. 76–87, 2014.

At PQCrypto 2013, Tao et al. proposed a new MPKC for encryption called Simple Matrix (or ABC) encryption scheme, which resists all known attacks against multivariate schemes. However, decryption errors occur with non negligible probability.

In this paper, we propose an improved version of the ABC scheme. The main goal of our approach is to increase the security of the scheme even further. We achieve this by using square matrices with random quadratic polynomials, by which we obtain a cubic map as the public key. We claim that an algebraic attack on our scheme is at least as hard as solving a random quadratic system of the same size. Furthermore, due to the use of random polynomials in the matrix A, the matrices associated to the central map are of high rank, which prevents the use of Rank attacks against our scheme.

The rest of this paper is organized as follows. In Section 2 we describe the basic ABC encryption scheme as proposed in [22]. Section 3 introduces our cubic version of the ABC scheme. In Section 4 we discuss the security of our scheme, whereas Section 5 proposes concrete parameter sets for the cubic ABC encryption scheme. In Section 6 we describe shortly a technique to decrease the probability of decryption failures. Finally, Section 7 concludes the paper.

2 The Basic ABC Encryption Scheme

In this section we introduce the ABC encryption scheme as proposed by Tao et al. in [22]. Before we come to the description of the scheme itself, we start with a short overview of the main concepts of multivariate cryptography.

2.1 Multivariate Cryptography

The basic objects of multivariate cryptography are systems of multivariate quadratic polynomials (see equation (1)).

$$p^{(1)}(x_1,\ldots,x_n) = \sum_{i=1}^{n}\sum_{j=i}^{n} p_{ij}^{(1)} \cdot x_i x_j + \sum_{i=1}^{n} p_i^{(1)} \cdot x_i + p_0^{(1)}$$

$$p^{(2)}(x_1,\ldots,x_n) = \sum_{i=1}^{n}\sum_{j=i}^{n} p_{ij}^{(2)} \cdot x_i x_j + \sum_{i=1}^{n} p_i^{(2)} \cdot x_i + p_0^{(2)}$$

$$\vdots$$

$$p^{(m)}(x_1,\ldots,x_n) = \sum_{i=1}^{n}\sum_{j=i}^{n} p_{ij}^{(m)} \cdot x_i x_j + \sum_{i=1}^{n} p_i^{(m)} \cdot x_i + p_0^{(m)}. \tag{1}$$

The security of multivariate schemes is based on the

Problem MQ: Given m multivariate quadratic polynomials $p^{(1)}(\mathbf{x}), \ldots, p^{(m)}(\mathbf{x})$ as shown in equation (1), find a vector $\bar{\mathbf{x}} = (\bar{x}_1, \ldots, \bar{x}_n)$ such that $p^{(1)}(\bar{\mathbf{x}}) = \ldots = p^{(m)}(\bar{\mathbf{x}}) = 0$.

The MQ problem (for $m \approx n$) is proven to be NP-hard even for quadratic polynomials over the field GF(2) [12].

To build a public key cryptosystem based on the MQ problem, one starts with an easily invertible quadratic map $\mathcal{F} : \mathbb{F}^n \to \mathbb{F}^m$ (central map). To hide the structure of $\mathcal{F}$ in the public key, one composes it with two invertible affine (or linear) maps $\mathcal{L}_1 : \mathbb{F}^n \to \mathbb{F}^n$ and $\mathcal{L}_2 : \mathbb{F}^m \to \mathbb{F}^m$.

The *public key* is therefore given by $\bar{\mathcal{F}} = \mathcal{L}_2 \circ \mathcal{F} \circ \mathcal{L}_1$.

The *private key* consists of $\mathcal{L}_1$, $\mathcal{F}$ and $\mathcal{L}_2$ and therefore allows to invert the public key.

In this paper we concentrate on multivariate encryption schemes. The standard encryption/decryption process works as shown in Figure 1.

Encryption

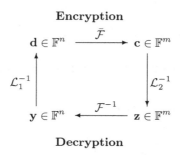

Decryption

Fig. 1. General workflow of multivariate encryption schemes

Encryption: To encrypt a message $\mathbf{d} \in \mathbb{F}^n$, one simply computes $\mathbf{c} = \bar{\mathcal{F}}(\mathbf{d})$. The ciphertext of the message $\mathbf{d}$ is $\mathbf{c} \in \mathbb{F}^m$.

Decryption: To decrypt the ciphertext $\mathbf{c} \in \mathbb{F}^m$, one computes recursively $\mathbf{z} = \mathcal{L}_2^{-1}(\mathbf{c})$, $\mathbf{y} = \mathcal{F}^{-1}(\mathbf{z})$ and $\mathbf{d} = \mathcal{L}_1^{-1}(\mathbf{y})$. $\mathbf{d} \in \mathbb{F}^n$ is the plaintext corresponding to the ciphertext $\mathbf{c}$.

Since, for multivariate encryption schemes, we have $m \geq n$, the preimage of the vector $\mathbf{z}$ under the central map $\mathcal{F}$ and therefore the decrypted plaintext is unique.

An overview of existing multivariate schemes can be found in [8].

2.2   The ABC Encryption Scheme of [22]

The original Simple Matrix encryption scheme as proposed by Tao et al. can be described as follows.

Key Generation: Let $\mathbb{F}$ be a finite field with q elements. For a parameter $s \in \mathbb{N}$ we set $n = s^2$ and $m = 2 \cdot n$ and define three matrices A, B and C of the form

$$
A = \begin{pmatrix} x_1 & \cdots & x_s \\ \vdots & & \vdots \\ x_{(s-1)\cdot s+1} & \cdots & x_n \end{pmatrix}, \; B = \begin{pmatrix} b_1 & \cdots & b_s \\ \vdots & & \vdots \\ b_{(s-1)\cdot s+1} & \cdots & b_n \end{pmatrix}, \; C = \begin{pmatrix} c_1 & \cdots & c_s \\ \vdots & & \vdots \\ c_{(s-1)\cdot s+1} & \cdots & c_n \end{pmatrix}.
$$

Here, $x_1, \ldots, x_n$ are the linear monomials of the multivariate polynomial ring $\mathbb{F}[x_1, \ldots, x_n]$, whereas $b_1, \ldots, b_n$ and $c_1, \ldots, c_n$ are randomly chosen linear combinations of $x_1, \ldots, x_n$.

One computes $E_1 = A \cdot B$ and $E_2 = A \cdot C$. The central map $\mathcal{F}$ of the scheme consists of the m components of E_1 and E_2.

The *public key* of the scheme is the composed map $\bar{\mathcal{F}} = \mathcal{L}_2 \circ \mathcal{F} \circ \mathcal{L}_1 : \mathbb{F}^n \to \mathbb{F}^m$ with two randomly chosen invertible linear maps $\mathcal{L}_2 : \mathbb{F}^m \to \mathbb{F}^m$ and $\mathcal{L}_1 : \mathbb{F}^n \to \mathbb{F}^n$, the *private key* consists of the matrices B and C and the linear maps $\mathcal{L}_1$ and $\mathcal{L}_2$.

Encryption: To encrypt a message $\mathbf{d} \in \mathbb{F}^n$, one simply computes $\mathbf{c} = \bar{\mathcal{F}}(\mathbf{d}) \in \mathbb{F}^m$.

Decryption: To decrypt a ciphertext $\mathbf{c} \in \mathbb{F}^m$, one has to perform the following three steps.

1. Compute $\mathbf{z} = \mathcal{L}_2^{-1}(\mathbf{c})$. The elements of the vector $\mathbf{z} \in \mathbb{F}^m$ are written into matrices $\bar{E}_1$ and $\bar{E}_2$ as follows.

$$
\bar{E}_1 = \begin{pmatrix} z_1 & \cdots & z_s \\ \vdots & & \vdots \\ z_{(s-1)\cdot s+1} & \cdots & z_n \end{pmatrix}, \; \bar{E}_2 = \begin{pmatrix} z_{n+1} & \cdots & z_{n+s} \\ \vdots & & \vdots \\ z_{n+(s-1)\cdot s+1} & \cdots & z_m \end{pmatrix}.
$$

2. In the second step one has to find a vector $\mathbf{y} = (y_1, \ldots, y_n)$ such that $\mathcal{F}(\mathbf{y}) = \mathbf{z}$. To do this, one has to distinguish four cases.
   - If $\bar{E}_1$ is invertible, one considers the equation $B \cdot \bar{E}_1^{-1} \cdot \bar{E}_2 - C = 0$. Therefore one gets n linear equations in the n variables $y_1, \ldots, y_n$.
   - If $\bar{E}_1$ is not invertible, but $\bar{E}_2$ is invertible, one considers the equation $C \cdot \bar{E}_2^{-1} \cdot \bar{E}_1 - B = 0$. One gets n linear equations in the n variables.
   - If none of $\bar{E}_1$ and $\bar{E}_2$ is invertible, but $\bar{A} = A(\mathbf{y})$ is invertible, one considers the relations $\bar{A}^{-1} \cdot \bar{E}_1 - B = 0$ and $\bar{A}^{-1} \cdot \bar{E}_2 - C = 0$. One interprets the elements of $\bar{A}^{-1}$ as new variables $w_1, \ldots, w_n$ and therefore gets m linear equations in the m variables $w_1, \ldots, w_n, y_1, \ldots, y_n$.
   - If none of $\bar{E}_1$, $\bar{E}_2$ and $\bar{A}$ is invertible, there occurs a decryption failure.
3. Finally, one computes the plaintext by $\mathbf{d} = \mathcal{L}_1^{-1}(y_1, \ldots, y_n)$.

The probability of a decryption failure occurring in the second step is about $\frac{1}{q}$.

It might happen that the linear systems in the second step of the decryption process have multiple solutions $\mathbf{y}^{(1)}, \ldots, \mathbf{y}^{(\ell)}$. In this case one has to perform the third step for each of these solutions to get a set of possible plaintexts $\mathbf{d}^{(1)}, \ldots, \mathbf{d}^{(\ell)}$. By encrypting these plaintexts one can test which of them corresponds to the given ciphertext $\mathbf{c}$.

3   The New Cubic Encryption Scheme

The new cubic Simple Matrix encryption scheme can be described as follows.

Key Generation: Let $\mathbb{F}$ be a finite field with q elements. For a parameter $s \in \mathbb{N}$ we set $n = s^2$ and $m = 2 \cdot n$ and define three matrices A, B and C of the form

$$
A = \begin{pmatrix} p_1 & \cdots & p_s \\ \vdots & \vdots & \vdots \\ p_{(s-1)\cdot s+1} & \cdots & p_n \end{pmatrix}, \ B = \begin{pmatrix} b_1 & \cdots & b_s \\ \vdots & \vdots & \vdots \\ b_{(s-1)\cdot s+1} & \cdots & b_n \end{pmatrix}, \ C = \begin{pmatrix} c_1 & \cdots & c_s \\ \vdots & \vdots & \vdots \\ c_{(s-1)\cdot s+1} & \cdots & c_n \end{pmatrix}.
$$

Here, $p_1, \ldots, p_n$ are random quadratic polynomials, whereas $b_1, \ldots, b_s$ and $c_1, \ldots, c_n$ are randomly chosen linear combinations of $x_1, \ldots, x_n$.

One computes $E_1 = A \cdot B$ and $E_2 = A \cdot C$. The central map $\mathcal{F}$ of the scheme consists of the m components of E_1 and E_2.

The *public key* of the scheme is the composed map $\bar{\mathcal{F}} = \mathcal{L}_2 \circ \mathcal{F} \circ \mathcal{L}_1 : \mathbb{F}^n \to \mathbb{F}^m$ with two randomly chosen invertible linear maps $\mathcal{L}_2 : \mathbb{F}^m \to \mathbb{F}^m$ and $\mathcal{L}_1 : \mathbb{F}^n \to \mathbb{F}^n$, the *private key* consists of the matrices B and C and the linear maps $\mathcal{L}_1$ and $\mathcal{L}_2$.

Encryption: To encrypt a message $\mathbf{d} \in \mathbb{F}^n$, one simply computes $\mathbf{c} = \bar{\mathcal{F}}(\mathbf{d}) \in \mathbb{F}^m$.

Decryption: To decrypt a ciphertext $\mathbf{c} \in \mathbb{F}^m$, one has to perform the following three steps.

1. Compute $\mathbf{z} = \mathcal{L}_2^{-1}(\mathbf{c})$. The elements of the vector $\mathbf{z} \in \mathbb{F}^m$ are written into matrices $\bar{E}_1$ and $\bar{E}_2$ as follows.

$$
\bar{E}_1 = \begin{pmatrix} z_1 & \cdots & z_s \\ \vdots & & \vdots \\ z_{(s-1)\cdot s+1} & \cdots & z_n \end{pmatrix}, \ \bar{E}_2 = \begin{pmatrix} z_{n+1} & \cdots & z_{n+s} \\ \vdots & & \vdots \\ z_{n+(s-1)\cdot s+1} & \cdots & z_m \end{pmatrix}.
$$

2. In the second step one has to find a vector $\mathbf{y} = (y_1, \ldots, y_n)$ such that $\mathcal{F}(\mathbf{y}) = \mathbf{z}$. To do this, one has to distinguish four cases:

   - If $\bar{E}_1$ is invertible, one considers the equation $B \cdot \bar{E}_1^{-1} \cdot \bar{E}_2 - C = 0$. Therefore one gets n linear equations in the n variables $y_1, \ldots, y_n$.
   - If $\bar{E}_1$ is not invertible, but $\bar{E}_2$ is invertible, one considers the equation $C \cdot \bar{E}_2^{-1} \cdot \bar{E}_1 - B = 0$. One gets n linear equations in the n variables.
   - If none of $\bar{E}_1$ and $\bar{E}_2$ is invertible, but $\bar{A} = A(\mathbf{y})$ is invertible, one considers the relations $\bar{A}^{-1} \cdot \bar{E}_1 - B = 0$ and $\bar{A}^{-1} \cdot \bar{E}_2 - C = 0$. One interprets the elements of $\bar{A}^{-1}$ as new variables $w_1, \ldots, w_n$ and therefore gets m linear equations in the m variables $w_1, \ldots, w_n, y_1, \ldots, y_n$.
   - If none of $\bar{E}_1$, $\bar{E}_2$ and $\bar{A}$ is invertible, there occurs a decryption failure.

3. Finally, one computes the plaintext by $\mathbf{d} = \mathcal{L}_1^{-1}(y_1, \ldots, y_n)$.

The probability of a decryption failure occurring in the second step is about $\frac{1}{q}$.

It might happen that the linear systems in the second step have multiple solutions $\mathbf{y}^{(1)}, \ldots, \mathbf{y}^{(\ell)}$. In this case one has to perform the third step of the decryption process for each of these solutions to get a set of possible plaintexts $\mathbf{d}^{(1)}, \ldots, \mathbf{d}^{(\ell)}$. By encrypting these plaintexts one can test which of them corresponds to the given ciphertext $\mathbf{c}$.

4   Security Analysis

4.1   Rank Attacks

Rank attacks are one of the major threats against multivariate encryption schemes. There are two different versions of this attack. The first one is called the MinRank attack or LowRank attack as proposed by Goubin et al. in [11]. The other one is called the HighRank Attack [5].

The goal of the MinRank attack is to find a linear combination of the components of the public key of minimal rank r. In the context of e.g. HFE such a polynomial of low rank corresponds to a central polynomial. By finding those linear combinations of low rank an attacker can recover the linear map $\mathcal{L}_2$ and therefore the secret key of the scheme.

In the High Rank Attack, the attacker tries to find linear combinations corresponding to variables which appear in the central polynomials the smallest number of times. In a scheme like Rainbow these are the oil variables of the last layer. By repeating this attack for the other layers, the attacker can recover the linear map $\mathcal{L}_1$ and therefore the secret key of the scheme.

However, in the case of the cubic Simple Matrix encryption scheme, the elements of the matrix A are randomly chosen multivariate quadratic polynomials. Therefore, their rank is close to n and all variables appear in each of the central polynomials approximately the same number of times. This shows that rank attacks can not be used to attack the cubic Simple Matrix encryption scheme.

4.2 Algebraic Attacks

In a direct attack (message recovery attack) the attacker tries to solve the public system $\mathcal{F}(\mathbf{d}) = \mathbf{c}$ for the plaintext $\mathbf{d}$. To achieve this, the attacker can use either a Gröbner Basis method such as F_4[10] or a system solving algorithm like XL or one of its variants like mutant XL [6,7,17,16].

When attacking our scheme, the attacker is faced with a system of $m = 2n$ multivariate cubic polynomials in n variables. As described in the section above, this system was obtained by multiplying a matrix A containing randomly chosen multivariate quadratic polynomials with matrices B and C containing linear ones (when neglecting the linear transformations $\mathcal{L}_1$ and $\mathcal{L}_2$). We make the following claim:

Claim: Solving the cubic public system of our scheme is asymptotically at least as hard as solving a multivariate quadratic system with randomly chosen coefficients.

To justify this claim, let us assume that an attacker wants to solve the equation $E_2(\mathbf{x}) = \mathbf{y}$, where $E_2 = A \cdot C$ and $\mathbf{y}$ is some matrix in $\mathbb{F}^{s \times s}$. Let us further assume that an oracle $\mathcal{O}$ gives the attacker the values of the elements of C (without revealing the inner structure of this matrix), i.e. the oracle gives him a matrix $\bar{C} \in \mathbb{F}^{s \times s}$ with $\bar{C} = C(\mathbf{x})$. So the attacker obtains a system of linear combinations in the elements of the matrix A. By solving this system by Gaussian elimination, the attacker finally gets a system $A(\mathbf{x}) = \mathbf{y} \cdot \bar{C}^{-1}$. But to get the values of $(x_1, \ldots, x_n)$, the attacker still has to solve a system of multivariate quadratic equations with randomly chosen coefficients.

A much more interesting heuristic argument goes as follows.

Let us denote the polynomial entries of the matrix A by $A_{ij}(\mathbf{x})$ and similarly the polynomial entries of E_1 and E_2 by $E_{1,ij}(\mathbf{x})$ and $E_{2,ij}(\mathbf{x})$. And we denote the entries of B and C by $B_{ij}(\mathbf{x})$ and $C_{ij}(\mathbf{x})$ respectively. Clearly we have that

$$E_{1,ij}(\mathbf{x}) = \sum_{l=1}^{s} A_{il}(\mathbf{x}) \cdot B_{lj}(\mathbf{x}),$$

$$E_{2,ij}(\mathbf{x}) = \sum_{l=1}^{s} A_{il}(\mathbf{x}) \cdot C_{lj}(\mathbf{x}).$$

In the case of quadratic systems, it is a common assumption that the complexity of solving the system is actually determined by the structure of the ideal generated by the homogeneous part of highest degree, namely the degree 2 part of the polynomials.

In our case this means that the complexity of solving the system

$$A_{ij}(\mathbf{x}) = D_{ij},$$

is actually determined by the structure of the ideal generated by the homogeneous polynomials $\bar{A}_{ij}(\mathbf{x})$, which are the quadratic part of $A_{ij}(\mathbf{x})$. We call this ideal I_A.

Now let us look at the system $E_{1,ij}(\mathbf{x}) = D_{1,ij}$, and $E_{2,ij}(\mathbf{x}) = D_{2,ij}$. In this case the complexity should be dominated by the structure of the homogeneous part of degree 3, which is given by

$$\bar{E}_{1,ij}(\mathbf{x}) = \sum_{l=1}^{s} \bar{A}_{il}(\mathbf{x}) \cdot \bar{B}_{lj}(\mathbf{x}) \text{ and}$$

$$\bar{E}_{2,ij}(\mathbf{x}) = \sum_{l=1}^{s} \bar{A}_{il}(\mathbf{x}) \cdot \bar{C}_{lj}(\mathbf{x}),$$

where $\bar{B}_{ij}$ and $\bar{C}_{ij}$ are the homogeneous linear parts of B_{ij} and C_{ij} respectively. We call this ideal I_E. If we now look that the generators of this ideal, we immediately reach the conclusion that

$$I_E \subset I_A.$$

Furthermore, the generators of I_E are nothing but elements in the space spanned by the elements generated in the first step of the XL algorithm if applied to I_A, since $\bar{B}_{ij}(\mathbf{x})$ and $\bar{C}_{ij}(\mathbf{x})$ are nothing but linear functions. From this perspective, we therefore speculate that in general or precisely asymptotically (when s is too small it might be different), the complexity of solving the public systems of the cubic Simple Matrix encryption scheme should be harder or at least as hard as solving a quadratic system with randomly chosen coefficients of size $n \times n$.

This heuristic analysis is very speculative, however it is very exciting in the sense that it actually hints that maybe we can derive a certain form of provable security for our new system, which is something we have never seen before.

Additionally to these theoretical considerations, we carried out a number of experiments with MAGMA, which contains an efficient implementation of Faugeres F_4 algorithm [10]. For this, we created, for different parameter sets, the public system of both the cubic Simple Matrix encryption scheme and the original ABC scheme of [22] and solved these systems using the MAGMA command **Variety**. We repeated each of these experiments ten times.

Table 1. Direct attack against the cubic Simple Matrix encryption scheme

		GF(2^8)				GF(2^{16})			
	(s, m, n)	$(2, 4, 8)$	$(3, 9, 18)$	$(4, 16, 32)$	$(5, 25, 50)$	$(2, 4, 8)$	$(3, 9, 18)$	$(4, 16, 32)$	$(5, 25, 50)$
our scheme	d_{reg}	5	6	7	-	5	6	7	-
	time(s)	0.8	15.4	-	-	1.2	23.7	-	-
	memory(MB)	5.2	18.3	ooM [1]	-	8.4	27.1	ooM [1]	-
ABC	d_{reg}	-	4	5	6	-	4	5	6
scheme	time(s)	-	0.02	3.5	17,588	-	0.1	5.7	23,264
of [22]	memory(MB)	-	3.4	8.1	1,112	-	7.4	23.1	3,214

[1] out of memory

As we see from the table, for the same value of s the degree of regularity is at least higher by two than that of the original Simple Matrix encryption scheme. Therefore, to obtain the same security level, we can decrease the value of s by 2 (compared to [22]).

Here we would like to point out that, due to the fact that we can only perform experiments for very small s, we can not really say anything precise about our speculations.

5 Parameter Proposals

Based on our security analysis presented in the previous section, we propose the following parameters for our cubic version of the Simple Matrix encryption scheme. For the fields GF(2^8) and GF(2^{16}), to be on the conservative side, we suggest

- $s = 7$ for a security level of 80 bit and
- $s = 8$ for a security level of 100 bit

These parameter proposals are obtained by the following analysis:

As Table 1 shows, the degree of regularity of solving the public system increases linearly with s. We can therefore assume that for $s = 7$ the degree of regularity is greater or equal to 10, while for $s = 8$ it is given by 11. We can therefore (for $s = 7$) estimate the number of homogeneous monomials of highest degree in the solving step of F_4 by

$$T = \binom{n + d_{\mathrm{reg}}}{d_{\mathrm{reg}}} \geq 2^{35.8}.$$

The number of non-zero monomials in every polynomial is given by

$$\tau = \binom{n + 3}{3} \geq 2^{14.4}.$$

Therefore we can estimate the complexity of a direct attack against the cubic Simple Matrix Encryption scheme by

$$\text{Complexity}_{\text{direct attack}}(s = 7) \geq 3 \cdot \tau \cdot T^2 \geq 2^{88}. \tag{2}$$

For $s = 8$ we get $T \geq 2^{42.2}$, $\tau \geq 2^{15.5}$ and therefore

$$\text{Complexity}_{\text{direct attack}}(s = 8) \geq 3 \cdot \tau \cdot T^2 \geq 2^{102}. \tag{3}$$

Table 2 shows for our 4 parameter sets key sizes of the cubic Simple Matrix encryption scheme as well as the probability of a failure occurring during the decryption process.

Table 2. Parameters and key sizes of the cubic Simple Matrix encryption scheme

security level (bit)	parameters $(\mathbb{F}, s, n, m)$	input size (bit)	output size (bit)	public key size (kB)	private key size(kB)	probability of decryption failure
80	$(GF(2^8),7,49,98)$	392	784	2,115	72.7	2^{-8}
	$(GF(2^{16},7,49,98)$	784	1,568	4,230	145.4	2^{-16}
100	$(GF(2^8),8,64,128)$	512	1,024	5,988	154	2^{-8}
	$(GF(2^{16},8,64,128)$	1,024	2,048	11,976	308	2^{-16}

Here, we would like to further speculate actually that even for the case of $s = 5$ and $s = 6$, the scheme might provide a good security level for practical applications. But this needs much better support evidence, which we still do not have.

6 Decreasing the Probability of Decryption Failures

As Table 2 shows, the probability of failures occuring during the decryption process of our scheme is non negligible. To decrease this probability, we can use the technique presented in [23]. The basic idea of this is to use non square matrices for A, B and C. In particular, A is chosen to be an $r \times s$ $(r < s)$ matrix containing random quadratic polynomials, while the matrices B and C (containing linear combinations of $x_1, \ldots, x_n$) are of size $s \times u$. Decryption remains possible, as long as the rank of the matrix A is at least r. The probability of this is given by

$$\Pr(\text{Rank}(A) \geq r) = 1 - \left(1 - \frac{1}{q^s}\right) \cdot \left(1 - \frac{1}{q^{s-1}}\right) \cdot \ldots \cdot \left(1 - \frac{1}{q^{s-r+1}}\right) \approx \frac{1}{q^{s-r+1}}.$$

By choosing the parameters r and s of the scheme in an appropriate way, it is possible to decrease the probability of decryption failures arbitrarily.

In [23] it was shown that by this strategy the security of the scheme against known attacks is not weakened. However, as it comes to provable security, we do not exactly know what happens. In this field, there has still much work to be done.

However, there are other ways to reduce the probability of decryption failures. For example, we can simply encrypt the message twice. In the second run, we encode the message with a public invertible affine transformation over the ring $\mathbb{Z}_{256}$ (integers mod 256) and then encrypt the encoded message with our scheme. Since an affine transformation over the ring $\mathbb{Z}_{256}$ is algebraically complicated with respect to the Galois field GF(256), we can not join these two encryptions as a larger low-degree algebraic system. If necessary, one can even encrypt the message several times. We will demonstrate the ways to reduce decryption failures in our further work.

7   Conclusion and Future Work

In this paper we proposed a cubic version of the Simple Matrix encryption scheme of PQCrypto 2013 [22]. By using a matrix A whose elements are randomly chosen multivariate quadratic polynomials, we increase the security of the original Simple Matrix scheme even further. Our construction completely eliminates the possibility of Rank attacks against our scheme. Furthermore, we speculate that breaking our scheme using direct attacks is as least as hard as solving a quadratic system with randomly chosen coefficients. Future work includes decreasing the probability of decryption failures and a formal proof of our security claim.

Acknowledgements. The first author was partially supported by the CAS/SAFEA International Partnership Program for Creative Research Teams.

References

1. Bernstein, D.J., Buchmann, J., Dahmen, E. (eds.): Post Quantum Cryptography. Springer (2009)
2. Bogdanov, A., Eisenbarth, T., Rupp, A., Wolf, C.: Time-area optimized public-key engines: MQ-cryptosystems as replacement for elliptic curves? In: Oswald, E., Rohatgi, P. (eds.) CHES 2008. LNCS, vol. 5154, pp. 45–61. Springer, Heidelberg (2008)
3. Bardet, M., Faugere, J.-C., Salvy, B.: On the complexity of Gröbner basis computation of semi-regular overdetermined algebraic equations. In: ICPSS, pp. 71–75 (2004)
4. Chen, A.I.T., Chen, M.-S., Chen, T.-R., Cheng, C.-M., Ding, J., Kuo, E.L.-H., Lee, F.Y.-S., Yang, B.-Y.: SSE implementation of multivariate pkcs on modern x86 cpus. In: Clavier, C., Gaj, K. (eds.) CHES 2009. LNCS, vol. 5747, pp. 33–48. Springer, Heidelberg (2009)
5. Coppersmith, D., Stern, J., Vaudenay, S.: Attacks on the Birational Permutation Signature Schemes. In: Stinson, D.R. (ed.) CRYPTO 1993. LNCS, vol. 773, pp. 435–443. Springer, Heidelberg (1994)

6. Courtois, N.T., Klimov, A., Patarin, J., Shamir, A.: Efficient algorithms for solving overdefined systems of multivariate polynomial equations. In: Preneel, B. (ed.) EUROCRYPT 2000. LNCS, vol. 1807, pp. 392–407. Springer, Heidelberg (2000)
7. Ding, J., Buchmann, J., Mohamed, M.S.E., Mohamed, W.S.A.E., Weinmann, R.-P.: Mutant XL. Talk at the First International Conference on Symbolic Computation and Cryptography (SCC 2008), Beijing (2008)
8. Ding, J., Gower, J.E., Schmidt, D.S.: Multivariate Public Key Cryptosystems. Springer (2006)
9. Ding, J., Schmidt, D.: Rainbow, a new multivariable polynomial signature scheme. In: Ioannidis, J., Keromytis, A.D., Yung, M. (eds.) ACNS 2005. LNCS, vol. 3531, pp. 164–175. Springer, Heidelberg (2005)
10. Faugere, J.C.: A new efficient algorithm for computing Gröbner bases (F4). Journal of Pure and Applied Algebra 139, 61–88 (1999)
11. Goubin, L., Courtois, N.: Cryptanalysis of the TTM Cryptosystem. In: Okamoto, T. (ed.) ASIACRYPT 2000. LNCS, vol. 1976, pp. 44–57. Springer, Heidelberg (2000)
12. Garey, M.R., Johnson, D.S.: Computers and Intractability: A Guide to the Theory of NP-Completeness. W.H. Freeman and Company (1979)
13. Kipnis, A., Patarin, J., Goubin, L.: Unbalanced Oil and Vinegar Signature Schemes. In: Stern, J. (ed.) EUROCRYPT 1999. LNCS, vol. 1592, pp. 206–222. Springer, Heidelberg (1999)
14. Kipnis, A., Shamir, A.: Cryptanalysis of the HFE Public Key Cryptosystem by Relinearization. In: Wiener, M. (ed.) CRYPTO 1999. LNCS, vol. 1666, pp. 19–30. Springer, Heidelberg (1999)
15. Matsumoto, T., Imai, H.: Public quadratic polynomial-tuples for efficient signature-verification and message-encryption. In: Günther, C.G. (ed.) EUROCRYPT 1988. LNCS, vol. 330, pp. 419–453. Springer, Heidelberg (1988)
16. Mohamed, M.S.E., Cabarcas, D., Ding, J., Buchmann, J., Bulygin, S.: MXL$_3$: An efficient algorithm for computing Gröbner bases of zero-dimensional ideals. In: Lee, D., Hong, S. (eds.) ICISC 2009. LNCS, vol. 5984, pp. 87–100. Springer, Heidelberg (2010)
17. Mohamed, M.S.E., Mohamed, W.S.A.E., Ding, J., Buchmann, J.: MXL2: Solving polynomial equations over GF(2) using an improved mutant strategy. In: Buchmann, J., Ding, J. (eds.) PQCrypto 2008. LNCS, vol. 5299, pp. 203–215. Springer, Heidelberg (2008)
18. Patarin, J., Courtois, N., Goubin, L.: QUARTZ, 128-Bit Long Digital Signatures. In: Naccache, D. (ed.) CT-RSA 2001. LNCS, vol. 2020, pp. 282–297. Springer, Heidelberg (2001)
19. Patarin, J.: Cryptanalysis of the Matsumoto and Imai Public Key Scheme of Eurocrypt '88. In: Coppersmith, D. (ed.) CRYPTO 1995. LNCS, vol. 963, pp. 248–261. Springer, Heidelberg (1995)
20. Rivest, R.L., Shamir, A., Adleman, L.: A Method for Obtaining Digital Signatures and Public-Key Cryptosystems. Commun. ACM 21(2), 120–126 (1978)
21. Shor, P.: Polynomial-Time Algorithms for Prime Factorization and Discrete Logarithms on a Quantum Computer. SIAM J. Comput. 26(5), 1484–1509
22. Tao, C., Diene, A., Tang, S., Ding, J.: Simple Matrix Scheme for Encryption. In: Gaborit, P. (ed.) PQCrypto 2013. LNCS, vol. 7932, pp. 231–242. Springer, Heidelberg (2013)
23. Tao, C., Petzoldt, A., Ding, J.: SimpleMatrix - An MPKC for Encryption (to appear)

RankSign: An Efficient Signature Algorithm Based on the Rank Metric

Philippe Gaborit[1], Olivier Ruatta[1], Julien Schrek[1], and Gilles Zémor[2]

[1] Université de Limoges, XLIM-DMI,
123, Av. Albert Thomas
87060 Limoges Cedex, France
{gaborit,schrek,ruatta}@unilim.fr
[2] Université de Bordeaux,
Institut de Mathématiques, UMR 5251
zemor@math.u-bordeaux.fr

Abstract. In this paper we propose a new approach to code-based signatures that makes use in particular of rank metric codes. When the classical approach consists in finding the unique preimage of a syndrome through a decoding algorithm, we propose to introduce the notion of mixed decoding of erasures and errors for building signature schemes. In that case the difficult problem becomes, as is the case in lattice-based cryptography, finding a preimage of weight above the Gilbert-Varshamov bound (case where many solutions occur) rather than finding a unique preimage of weight below the Gilbert-Varshamov bound. The paper describes RankSign: a new signature algorithm for the rank metric based on a new mixed algorithm for decoding erasures and errors for the recently introduced Low Rank Parity Check (LRPC) codes. We explain how it is possible (depending on choices of parameters) to obtain a full decoding algorithm which is able to find a preimage of reasonable rank weight for any random syndrome with a very strong probability. We study the semantic security of our signature algorithm and show how it is possible to reduce the unforgeability to direct attacks on the public matrix, so that no information leaks through signatures. Finally, we give several examples of parameters for our scheme, some of which with public key of size $11,520$ bits and signature of size 1728 bits. Moreover the scheme can be very fast for small base fields.

Keywords: post-quantum cryptography, signature algorithm, code-based cryptography, rank metric.

1 Introduction

In recent years there has been a burst of activity regarding post-quantum cryptography, the attractiveness of which has become even more obvious since the recent attacks on the discrete logarithm problem in small characteristic [4]: it shows that the emergence of new attacks on classical cryptographic systems is always a possibility and that it is important to seriously consider alternatives to existing cryptosystems.

M. Mosca (Ed.): PQCrypto 2014, LNCS 8772, pp. 88–107, 2014.

Among potential candidates for alternative cryptography, lattice-based and code-based cryptography are strong candidates; in this paper we consider the signature problem for code-based cryptography and especially rank metric based cryptography. The problem of finding an efficient signature algorithm has been a major challenge for code-based cryptography since its introduction in 1978 by McEliece. Signing with error-correcting codes can be achieved in different ways: the CFS algorithm [7] considers extreme parameters of Goppa codes to obtain a class of codes in which a non-negligeable part of random syndromes are invertible. This scheme has a very small signature size, however it is rather slow and the public key is very large. Another possibility is to use the Fiat-Shamir heuristic to turn a zero-knowledge authentication scheme (like the Stern authentication scheme [32]) into a signature scheme. This approach leads to very small public keys of a few hundred bits and is rather fast, but the signature size in itself is large (about 100,000b), so that overall no wholly satisfying scheme is known.

Classical code-based cryptography relies on the Hamming distance but it is also possible to use another metric: the rank metric. This metric introduced in 1985 by Gabidulin [12] is very different from the Hamming distance. The rank metric has received in recent years a very strong attention from the coding community because of its relevance to network coding. Moreover, this metric can also be used for cryptography. Indeed it is possible to construct rank-analogues of Reed-Solomon codes: the Gabidulin codes. Gabidulin codes inspired early cryptosystems, like the GPT cryposystem ([13]), but they turned out to be inherently vulnerable because of the very strong structure of the underlying codes. More recently, by considering an approach similar to NTRU [21](and also MDPC codes [27]) constructing a very efficient cryptosystem based on weakly structured rank codes was shown to be possible [14]. However, in terms of signatures based on the rank metric, only systems that use Fiat-Shamir are presently known [15]. Overall the main appeal of rank-metric based cryptography is that the complexity of the best known attack grows very fast with the size of parameters: contrary to (Hamming) code-based and to lattice-based cryptography, it is possible to obtain *a general instance of the rank decoding problem* with size only a few thousands bits for a (say) 2^{80} security, when such sizes of parameters can be obtained only with additional structure (quasi-cyclic for instance) for code-based or lattice based cryptography.

An interesting point in code-based cryptography is that in general the security of the protocols relies on finding small weight vectors *below* the Gilbert-Varshamov bound (the typical minimum weight of a random code). This is noticeably different from lattice based cryptography for which it is very common for the security of a signature algorithm [20,26] to rely on the capacity to approximate a random vector far beyond its closest lattice vector element (the Gap-CVP problem).

Traditionally, this approach was not developed for code-based cryptography since no decoding algorithm is known that decodes beyond the Gilbert-Varshamov bound: since this problem implies many solutions for decoding, it is somewhat marginal for the coding community for which the goal is almost always to find the most probable codeword or a short list of most likely codewords.

Our Contribution

The main contribution of this paper is the introduction of a new way of considering code-based signatures, by introducing the idea that it is possible to invert a random syndrome not below the Gilbert-Varshamov bound, but above it. The approach is similar in spirit to what is done in lattice-based cryptography. We describe a new algorithm for LRPC codes, a recently introduced class of rank codes, the new algorithm permits in practice decoding both errors and (generalized) rank erasures. This new algorithm enables us to approximate a syndrome beyond the Gilbert-Varshamov bound. The algorithm is a unique decoder (not a list decoder) but can give different solutions depending on the choice of the erasure. We explain precisely in which conditions one can obtain successful decoding for any given syndrome and give the related probabilistic analysis. Based on this error/erasure algorithm we propose a new signature scheme RankSign. We give conditions for which no information leakage is possible from real signatures obtained through our scheme. This point is very important since information leaking from real signatures was the weakness through which the NTRUSign scheme came to be attacked [22,8,30]. Finally, we give examples of parameters: they are rather versatile, and their size depends on a bound on the amount of potentially leaked information. In some cases one obtains public keys of size 11,000 bits with signatures of length 1728 bits, moreover the scheme is rather fast.

The paper is organized as follows: Section 2 recalls basic facts on the rank metric, Section 3 introduces LRPC codes and describes a new mixed algorithm for decoding (generalized) erasures and errors, and studies its behaviour, Section 4 shows how to use them for cryptography, and lastly, Section 5 and 6 consider security and parameters for these schemes.

2   Background on Rank Metric Codes and Cryptography

2.1   Definitions and Notation

Notation: Let q be a power of a prime p, m an integer and let V_n be a n dimensional vector space over the finite field $GF(q^m)$. Let $\beta = (\beta_1, \ldots, \beta_m)$ be a basis of $GF(q^m)$ over $GF(q)$. Let $\mathcal{F}_i$ be the map from $GF(q^m)$ to $GF(q)$ where $\mathcal{F}_i(x)$ is the i-th coordinate of x in the basis β.

To any $v = (v_1, \ldots, v_n)$ in V_n we associate the matrix $\overline{v} \in \mathcal{M}_{m,n}(F_q)$ in which $\overline{v}_{i,j} = \mathcal{F}_i(v_j)$. The rank weight of a vector v can be defined as the rank of the associated matrix $\overline{v}$. If we name this value rank(v) we can define a distance between two vectors x, y through the formula $d_r(x, y) = \text{rank}(x - y)$. *Isometry for rank metric:* in a context of rank metric codes, the notion of isometry is different from Hamming distance: when for Hamming distance isometries are permutation matrices, for rank metric the isometries are invertible $n \times n$ matrices on the base field $GF(q)$ (indeed these matrices, usually denoted by P, do not change the rank of a codeword). We refer to [24] for more details on codes for the rank distance.

A rank code C of length n and dimension k over $GF(q^m)$ is a subspace of dimension k of $GF(q^m)$ viewed as a (rank) metric space. The minimum rank distance of the code C is the minimum rank of non-zero vectors of the code. In the following, C is a rank metric code of length n and dimension k over $GF(q^m)$. The matrix G denotes a $k \times n$ generator matrix of C and H one of its parity check matrices.

Definition 1. *Let $x = (x_1, x_2, \cdots, x_n) \in GF(q^m)^n$ be a vector of rank r. We denote E the $GF(q)$-sub vector space of $GF(q^m)$ generated by $x_1, x_2, \cdots, x_n$. The vector space E is called the* **support** *of x.*

Remark 1. The notions of support of a code word for the Hamming distance and that introduced in definition 1 are different but they share a common principle: in both cases, suppose one is given a syndrome s and that there exists a low weight vector x such that $H.x^t = s$, then, if the support of x is known, it is possible to recover all the coordinate values of x by solving a linear system.

Definition 2. *Let e be an error vector of rank r and error support space E. We call* **generalized erasure of dimension** *t of the error e, a subspace T of dimension t of its error support E.*

The notion of erasure for Hamming distance corresponds to knowing a particular position of the error vector (hence some partial information on the support), in the rank distance case, the support of the error being a subspace E, the equivalent notion of erasure (also denoted generalized erasure) is therefore the knowledge of a subspace T of the error support E.

2.2 Bounds for Rank Metric Codes

The classical bounds for the Hamming metric have straightforward rank metric analogues, since two of them are of interest for the paper we recall them below.

Rank Gilbert-Varshamov Bound. [GVR] The number of elements $S(m, q, t)$ of a sphere of radius t in $GF(q^m)^n$, is equal to the number of $m \times n$ q-ary matrices of rank t. For $t = 0$ $S_0 = 1$, for $t \geq 1$ we have (see [24]):

$$S(n, m, q, t) = \prod_{j=0}^{t-1} \frac{(q^n - q^j)(q^m - q^j)}{q^t - q^j}$$

From this we deduce the volume of a ball $B(n, m, q, t)$ of radius t in $GF(q^m)$ to be:

$$B(n, m, q, t) = \sum_{i=0}^{t} S(n, m, q, i)$$

In the linear case the Rank Gilbert-Varshamov bound $GVR(n, k, m, q)$ for a $[n, k]$ linear code over $GF(q^m)$ is then defined as the smallest integer t such that $B(n, m, q, t) \geq q^{m(n-k)}$.

The Gilbert-Varshamov bound for a rank code C with dual matrix H, corresponds to the smallest rank weight r for which, for any syndrome s, there exists on the average a word x of rank weight r such that $H.x^t = s$. To give an idea of the behaviour of this bound, it can be shown that, asymptotically in the case $m = n$ ([24]): $\frac{GVR(n,k,m,q)}{n} \sim 1 - \sqrt{\frac{k}{n}}$.

Singleton Bound. The classical Singleton bound for a linear $[n, k]$ rank code of minimum rank r over $GF(q^m)$ works in the same way as for linear codes (by finding an information set) and reads $r \leq 1 + n - k$: in the case when $n > m$ this bound can be rewritten as $r \leq 1 + \lfloor \frac{(n-k)m}{n} \rfloor$ [24]. Codes achieving this bound are called Maximum Rank Distance codes (MRD).

2.3   Cryptography and Rank Codes

The main use of rank codes in the cryptographic context is through the rank analogue of the classical syndrome decoding problem.

Rank Syndrome Decoding Problem (RSD). Let H be a $(n-k) \times n$ matrix over $GF(q^m)$ with $k \leq n$, and let $s \in GF(q^m)^{n-k}$ and an integer r. The problem is: does there exist an element $x \in GF(q^m)^n$ such that $\text{rank}(x) \leq r$ and $Hx^t = s$.

Progress on computational complexity of this problem, which was stayed unknown for more than 20 years, was recently provided in [17] in which the authors give a randomized reduction to the Syndrome Decoding problem in Hamming distance: more precisely they prove that if there exists a polynomial algorithm which solves the RSD problem, then $NP = RP$, which is very unlikely. Their results also extend to the case of the approximation of the rank distance of a code by a constant.

Besides the theoretical hardness of the RSD problem, practical attacks on the problem have a complexity which increases very fast with the parameters.

There exist several types of generic attacks on the problem:

- **Combinatorial Attacks:** these attacks are usually the best ones for small values of q (typically $q = 2$) and when n and k are not too small (typically 30 and more), when q increases, the combinatorial aspect makes them less efficient. The first non-trivial attack on the problem was proposed by Chabaud and Stern [6] in 1996, then in 2002 Ourivski and Johannson [28] improved the previous attack and proposed a new attack, meanwhile these two attacks did not take into account the value of n in the exponent. Very recently the two previous attacks were generalized in [16] by Gaborit et al. in $(n - k)^3 m^3 q^{(r-1)\lfloor \frac{(k+1)m}{n} \rfloor})$ and take the value of n into account and were used to break some repaired versions of the GPT crypyosystem.

- **Algebraic Attacks and Levy-Perret Attack:** the particular nature of the rank metric makes it a natural field for algebraic attacks and solving by Groebner basis, since these attacks are largely independent of the value of q and in some cases may also be largely independent of m. There exist different types of algebraic equation settings: the first one by Levy and Perret [23] in 2006 considers a quadratic setting by taking as unknowns the support E of the error and the error coordinates regarding E, there is also the Kernel attack by [9] and the minor approach which consists in considering multivariate equations of degree $r + 1$ obtained from minors of matrices [10], and more recently the annulator setting by Gaborit et al. in [16] (which is valid on certain type of parameters but may not be independent on m). In our context for some of the parameters considered in the end of the paper, the Levy-Perret attack is the most efficient one to consider. The attack works as follows: suppose one starts from a $[n, k]$ rank codes over $GF(q^m)$ and we want to solve the RSD problem for an error e of rank weight r, the idea of the attack is to consider the support E of e as unknowns together with the error coordinates, it gives $nr + m(r - 1)$ unknowns and $m(2(n - k) - 1)$ equations from the syndrome equations. One obtains a quadratic system, on which one can use Groebner basis. All the complexities for Grobner basis attacks are estimated through the very nice program of L. Bettale [5]. In practice this attack becomes too costly whenever $r \geq 4$ for not too small n and k.

The Case of More Than One Solution: Approximating Beyond the GVR Bound

In code based cryptography there is usually only one solution to the syndrome problem (for instance for the McEliece scheme), now in this situation we are interested in the case when there are a large number of solutions. This case is reminiscent of lattice-based cryptography when one tries to approximate as much as possible a given syndrome by a word of weight as low as possible.

Even though the recent results of [17] show that the problem of approximation of the rank distance remains hard, there are cases for which the problem is easy, that we want to consider.

It is helpful to first consider the situation of a binary linear $[n, k]$ Hamming metric code. Given a random element of length $n - k$ of the syndrome space, we know that with high probability there exists a word that has this particular syndrome and whose weight is on the GV bound. This word is usually hard to find, however. Now what is the lowest minimum weight for which it is easy to find such a word ? A simple approach consists in taking $n - k$ random columns of the parity-check matrix (a potential support of the solution word) and inverting the associated matrix, multiplying by the syndrome gives us a solution of weight $(n - k)/2$ on average. In fact it is difficult to do better than this without a super-polynomial increase in complexity.

Now for the rank metric, one can apply the same approach: suppose one starts from a random $[n, k]$ code over $GF(q^m)$ and that one searches for a word of small rank weight r with a given syndrome. One fixes (as in the Hamming case) a potential support for the word - here a subspace of dimension r of $GF(q^m)$ - and one tries to find a solution. Let $x = (x_1, \cdots, x_n)$ be a solution vector, so that $H.x^t = s$. If we consider the syndrome equations induced in the small field $GF(q)$, there are $n.r$ unknowns and $m.(n - k)$ equations. Hence it is possible (with a good probability) to solve the system whenever $nr \geq m(n - k)$, therefore it is possible to find in probabilistic polynomial time a solution to a typical instance of the RSD problem whenever $r \geq \lceil \frac{m(n-k)}{n} \rceil$, which corresponds to the Singleton bound. This proves the following proposition:

Proposition 1. *There is a probabilistic polynomial time algorithm that solves random instances of the RSD problem in polynomial time when $r \geq \lceil \frac{m(n-k)}{n} \rceil$.*

For a rank weight r below this bound, the best known attacks are, as in the Hamming distance case, obtained by considering the cost of finding a word of rank r divided by the number of potential solutions: $\frac{B(n,k,m,q)}{q^{m(n-k)}}$. In practice the complexity we find is coherent with this.

3   Approximating a Random Syndrome Beyond the GVR Bound with LRPC Codes

3.1   Decoding Algorithm in Rank Metric

The rank metric has received a lot of attention in the context of network coding [31]. There exist very few algorithms, however, for decoding codes in the rank metric. The most well known $[n, k]$ codes which are decodable are the Gabidulin codes [12]. These codes can correct up to $\frac{n-k}{2}$ errors, and have been proposed for encryption: but since they cannot decode up to the GVR bound, they do not seem suitable for full decoding in the spirit of [7] for signature algorithms. Another more recent family of decodable codes are the LRPC codes [14], these codes are defined through a low rank matrix.

Definition 3. *A Low Rank Parity Check (LRPC) code of rank d, length n and dimension k over $GF(q^m)$ is a code defined by an $(n-k) \times n$ parity check matrix $H = (h_{ij})$, such that all its coordinates h_{ij} belong to the same $GF(q)$-subspace F of dimension d of $GF(q^m)$. We denote by $\{F_1, F_2, \cdots, F_d\}$ a basis of F.*

These codes can decode with a good probability up to $\frac{n-k}{d}$ errors, they can be used for encryption [14], but since they can decode only up to $\frac{n-k}{2}$ errors at best, they also seems unsuitable for signature algorithms.

3.2   Using LRPC Codes to Approximate a Random Syndrome Beyond the GVR Bound

High Level Overview. The traditional approach for decoding random syndromes, that is used by the CFS scheme for instance, consists in taking advantage of the decoding properties of a code (e.g. a Goppa code) and considering parameters for which the proportion of decodable vectors – the decodable density – is not too low. For the Hamming metric, this approach leads to very flat dual matrices, i.e, codes with high rate and very low Hamming distance. In the rank metric case, this approach leads to very small decodable densities and does not work in practice. However, it is possible to proceed otherwise. It turns out that the decoding algorithm of LRPC codes can be adapted so that it is possible to decode not only errors but also (generalized) erasures. This new decoding algorithm allows us to decode more rank errors since the support is then partially known. In that case since the size of the balls depends directly on the dimension of the support, it leads to a dramatic increase of the size of the decodable balls. Semantically, what happens is that the signer can fix an erasure space, which relaxes the condition for finding a preimage. This approach works because in the particular case of our algorithm, it is possible to consider the erasure space at no cost in terms of error correction: to put it differently, the situation for LRPC codes is different from traditional Hamming metric codes for which "an error equals two erasures".

In practice it is possible to find parameters (not flat at all) for which it is possible to decode a random syndrome with the constraint that its support contains a fixed random subspace. Fixing part of the rank-support of the error, (the generalized erasure) allows us more rank-errors. For suitable parameters, the approach works then as follows: for a given random syndrome-space element s, one chooses a random subspace T of fixed dimension t (a generalized erasure of Definition 2), and the algorithm returns a small rank-weight word, whose rank-support E contains T, and whose syndrome is the given element s. Of course, there is no unicity of the error e since different choices of T lead to different errors e, which implies that the rank of the returned error is above the GVR bound: it is however only just above the GVR bound for the right choice of parameters.

LRPC Decoding with Errors and Generalized Erasures

Setting: Let an $[n, k]$ LRPC code be defined by an $(n - k) \times n$ parity-check matrix H whose entries lie in a space $F \subset GF(q^m)$ of small dimension d. Let t and r' be two parameters such that

$$r' \leq \frac{n - k}{d}.$$

Set $r = t + r'$. Given an element of the syndrome space s, we will be looking for a rank r vector e of $GF(q^m)^n$ with syndrome s. We first look for an acceptable subspace E of dimension r of $GF(q^m)$ and then solve the linear system $H.e^t = s$ where $e \in E^n$. To this end we choose a random subspace T of dimension t of $GF(q^m)$ and impose the condition $T \subset E$.

The subspace T being fixed, we now describe the set of decodable elements of the syndrome space. We will then see how to decode them.

Definition 4. *Let F_1 and F_2 be two fixed linearly independent elements of the space F. We shall say that an element $s \in GF(q^m)^{n-k}$ of the syndrome space is T-decodable if there exists a rank r subspace E of $GF(q^m)$ satisfying the following conditions.*

(i) $\dim\langle FE\rangle = \dim F \dim E$,
(ii) $\dim(F_1^{-1}\langle FE\rangle \cap F_2^{-1}\langle FE\rangle) = \dim E$,
(iii) *the coordinates of* s *all belong to the space* $\langle FE\rangle$ *and together with the elements of the space* $\langle FT\rangle$ *they generate the whole of* $\langle FE\rangle$.

Decoding Algorithm. We now argue that if a syndrome s is T-decodable, we can effectively find e of rank r such that $H.e^t = s$. We first determine the required support space E. Since the decoder knows the subspaces F and T, he has access to the product space $\langle FT\rangle$. He can then construct the subspace S generated by $\langle FT\rangle$ and the coordinates of s. Condition (iii) of T-decodability ensures that the subspace S is equal to $\langle FE\rangle$ for some E, and since

$$F_1^{-1}\langle FE\rangle \cap F_2^{-1}\langle FE\rangle \supset E,$$

condition (ii) implies that E is uniquely determined and that the decoder recovers E by computing the intersection of subspaces $F_1^{-1}S \cap F_2^{-1}S$.

It remains to justify that once the subspace E is found, we can always find e of support E such that $H.e^t = s$. This will be the case if the mapping

$$E^n \to \langle FE\rangle^{n-k} \tag{1}$$
$$e \mapsto H.e^t$$

can be shown to be surjective. Extend $\{F_1, F_2\}$ to a basis $\{F_1, \cdots, F_d\}$ of F and let $\{E_1, \cdots, E_r\}$ be a basis of E. Notice that the system $H.e^t = s$ can be rewritten formally as a linear system in the small field $GF(q)$ where the coordinates of e and the elements of H are written in the basis $\{E_1, \cdots, E_r\}$ and $\{F_1, \cdots, F_d\}$ respectively, and where the syndrome coordinates are written in the product basis $\{E_1.F_1, \cdots, E_r.F_d\}$. We therefore have a linear system with $n.r$ unknowns and $(n-k).rd$ equations over $GF(q)$ that is defined by an $(n.r) \times (n-k)rd$ formal matrix H_f (say) whose coefficients depend only on H (see [14] for more details on how to obtain H_f from H).

We now see that the matrix H can be easily chosen so that the matrix H_f is of maximal rank $n.r$, which makes the mapping (1) surjective, *for any subspace* E of dimension d satisfying condition (i) of T-decodability.

Remark 2

1. For applications, we will consider only the case where $nr = (n-k)rd$, meaning that the mapping (1) is always one-to-one.
2. The system $H.e^t = s$ can be formally inverted through the matrix H_f and stored in a pre-processing phase, so that the decoding complexity is only the complexity of multiplication by the preprocessed square matrix H_f^{-1} of dimension $nr \times nr$, rather than the cubic cost of a matrix inersion for each decoding.
3. In principle, the decoder could derive the support E by computing

$$E = F_1^{-1}S \cap \cdots \cap F_d^{-1}S \tag{2}$$

rather than simply $E = F_1^{-1}S \cap F_2^{-1}S$, and the procedure would work in the same way in cases when (2) holds but not the simpler condition (ii). This potentially increases the set of decodable syndromes, but the gain is somewhat marginal and condition (ii) makes the forthcoming analysis simpler. For similar reasons, when conditions (i)–(iii) are not all satisfied, we do not attempt to decode even if there are cases when it stays feasible.

4. In term of computation, the elements of the extension field $GF(q^m)$ are represented as polynomials of degree $m - 1$ and all operations are done modulo a fixed irreducible polynomial. Since $GF(q^m)$ is a m-dimensional vectr space over $GF(q)$ it is possible to fix a $GF(q)$-basis $\beta = (\beta_1, \cdots, \beta_m)$ of $GF(q^m)$. A $GF(q)$-subspace of $GF(q^m)$ of dimension d consists in d vectors of length m over $GF(q)$, such a subspace can be seen as a $d \times m$ matrix over $GF(q)$.

Figure 1 summarizes the decoding algorithm. Note that the decoder can easily check conditions (i)–(iii), and that a decoding failure is declared when they are not satisfied.

Input: $T = \langle T_1, \cdots, T_t \rangle$ a subspace of $GF(q^m)$ of dimension t, H an $(n-k) \times n$ matrix with elements in a subspace $F = \langle F_1, \cdots, F_d \rangle$ of dimension d, and $s \in GF(q^m)^{n-k}$.
Output: a vector $e = (e_1, \ldots e_n)$ such that $s = H.e^t$, with $e_i \in E$, E a subspace of dimension $\dim E = r = t + \frac{n-k}{d}$ satisfying $T \subset E$.

1. **Syndrome computations**
   a) Compute a basis $B = \{F_1 T_1, \cdots, F_d T_t\}$ of the product space $\langle F.T \rangle$.
   b) Compute the subspace $S = \langle B \cup \{s_1, \cdots, s_{n-k}\} \rangle$.

2. **Recovering the support E of the error**
   Compute the support of the error $E = F_1^{-1}S \cap F_2^{-1}S$, and compute a basis $\{E_1, E_2, \cdots, E_r\}$ of E.

3. **Recovering the error vector $e = (e_1, \ldots, e_n)$**
   For $1 \leq i \leq n$, write $e_i = \sum_{i=1}^{n} e_{ij} E_j$, solve the system $H.e^t = s$, where the equations $H.e^t$ and the syndrome coordinates s_i are written as elements of the product space $P = \langle E.F \rangle$ in the basis $\{F_1 E_1, \cdots, F_1 E_r, \cdots, F_d E_1, \cdots, F_d E_r\}$. The system has nr unknowns (the e_{ij}) in $GF(q)$ and $(n - k).rd$ equations from the syndrome.

Fig. 1. Algorithm 1: a general errors/erasures decoding algorithm for LRPC codes

Complexity of the Decoding Algorithm of Fig. 1. Steps 1 and 2 of the decoding algorithm are simple linear algebra computations over $GF(q)$ (moreover the values of F_i^{-1} can be preprocessed since the F_i are fixed), whose cost is dominated by Step 3. The cost of Step 3 is the cost of solving a linear algebra system with $n.r$ unknowns in $GF(q)$, for a $n.r \times n.r$ matrix H_f obtained from the matrix H. The a priori cost is then $O((nr)^3)$ operations in $GF(q)$, but in fact, it is possible to use the same trick as in [14] and to write the matrix H_f of the system formally, so that the matrix H_f of the system to solve is always the same and hence the matrix H_f^{-1} can be preprocessed. Therefore the cost of the inversion is just the cost a matrix-vector product with the preprocessed matrix H_f^{-1} for a complexity of $O((nr)^2)$ operations in $GF(q)$, (see details of this approach in [14]).

3.3 Proportion of Decodable Syndromes for Unique Decoding of LRPC Codes

Signature algorithms based on codes all inject the message space in some way into the syndrome space and then decode them to form a signature. We should therefore estimate the proportion of decodable syndromes. The classical decoding approach tells us to look for a preimage by H that sits on the Gilbert-Varshamov bound: for typical random codes, a preimage typically exists and is (almost) unique. Computing such a preimage is a challenge, however. In our case, we are looking for a preimage above the Gilbert-Varshamov bound, for which many preimages exist, but for a fixed (erasure) subspace T, decoding becomes unique again. In the following, we count the number of T-decodable syndromes and show that for some adequate parameter choices, their proportion can be made to be close to 1. It will be convenient to use the following notation.

Definition 5. *For a subspace T of $GF(q^m)$ of dimension t, denote by $\mathcal{E}(T)$ the number of subspaces of dimension $r = r' + t$ that contain T.*

Lemma 1. *We have*

$$\mathcal{E}(T) = \prod_{i=0}^{r'-1} \left(\frac{q^{m-t-i} - 1}{q^{i+1} - 1} \right)$$

Proof. Consider the case where $r = t+1$, we need to construct distinct subspaces of dimension $t + 1$ containing T. This can be done by adjoining an element of $GF(q^m)$ modulo the subspace T, which gives $(q^m - q^t)/(q^{t+1} - q^t) = (q^{m-t} - 1)/(q - 1)$ possibilities. Now any subspace of dimension $t + 1$ contains $q^{t+1} - 1$ supspaces of dimension t containing T. A repetition of this approach $r' - 1$ times gives the formula. (see also [25] p.630). □

Theorem 1. *The number $\mathcal{T}(t, r, d, m)$ of T-decodable syndromes satisfies the upper bound:*
$$\mathcal{T}(t, r, d, m) \leq \mathcal{E}(T)q^{rd(n-k)}.$$

Furthermore, under the conditions $r(2d - 1) \leq m$ and

$$\dim\langle FT \rangle = \dim F \dim T, \tag{3}$$
$$\dim(F_1^{-1}F + F_2^{-1}F) = 2\dim F - 1 = 2d - 1, \tag{4}$$

we also have the lower bound:

$$\left(1 - \frac{1}{q-1}\right)^2 \mathcal{E}(T)q^{rd(n-k)} \leq \mathcal{T}(t, r, d, m).$$

Note that condition (4) depends only on the subspace F and can be ensured quite easily when designing the matrix H. Random spaces F with random elements F_1 and F_2 will typically have this property. Condition (3) depends on the choice of the subspace T: for a random subspace T condition (3) holds with probability very close to 1.

The proof of Theorem 1 will be given in the full version of this paper.

Remark 3

1. It can be shown with a finer analysis that the term $(1 - 1(q - 1))^2$ in the lower bound can be improved to a quantity close to $1 - 1(q - 1)$.
2. For large q, Theorem 1 shows that, for most choices of T, the density of T-decodable syndromes essentially equals

$$\frac{\mathcal{E}(T)q^{rd(n-k)}}{q^{m(n-k)}} \approx q^{(r-t)(m-r)+(n-k)(rd-m)}. \tag{5}$$

Remarkably, it is possible to choose sets of parameters (m, t, r, d), with $(n - k) = d(r - t)$, such that the exponent in (5) equals zero, which gives a density very close to 1.

Example of Parameters with Density Almost 1: For $q = 2^8, m = 18, n = 16, k = 8, t = 2, r' = 4$, the algorithm decodes up to $r = t + r' = 6$ for a fixed random partial support T of dimension 2. The GVR bound for a random $[16, 8]$ code with $m = 18$ is 5, the Singleton bound is 8, we see that the decoding radius 6 is therefore just above the GVR bound at 5 and smaller than the Singleton bound at 8. Moreover one can notice that if parameters (m, t, r, d) satisfy the two equations $(r - t)(m - r) + (n - k)(rd - m) = 0$ and $(n - k) = d(r - t)$ (the case for which the density is almost 1), then for any integer α greater than 1, the parameter set $(\alpha m, \alpha t, \alpha r, d)$ satisfies the same equations, and hence for a given d one obtains an infinite family of parameters with density almost 1.

Decoding in Practice. In practice it is simple to find sets of parameters for which the density of decodable syndromes is very close to 1, i.e. such that $(r - t)(m - r) + (n - k)(rd - m) = 0$.

4 *RankSign*, a Signature Scheme for Rank Metric Based on Augmented LRPC Codes

We saw in the previous section how to construct a matrix H of an LRPC code, with a unique support decoding, which opens the way for a signature algorithm. In practice the best decoding results are obtained for $d = 2$: the natural strategy is to define for the public key a matrix $H' = AHP$, where A is a random $(n - k) \times (n - k)$ invertible matrix in the extension field and P is an invertible $n \times n$ matrix in the small field. However, it is easily possible for a cryptanalyst to recover the words of small weight $d = 2$ in H' and it is therefore necessary to hide the matrix H in another way. In what follows we present a simple type of masking: *RankSign* which consists in adding a few random columns to H. Other more complex types of masking are also possible, which will be described in the full version of the paper.

Suppose one has a fixed support T of dimension t. We consider the public matrix $H' = A(R|H)P$ with R a random $(n-k) \times t'$ matrix in $GF(q^m)$. We will typically take $t' = t$ but one could envisage other values of t'. We denote by *augmented LRPC codes* such codes with parity-check matrices $H' = A(R|H)P$.

Starting from a partial support T that has been randomly chosen and is then fixed, the signature consists in decoding not a random s but the syndrome $s' = s - R.(e_1, \cdots, e_t)^t$ for e_i random independent elements of T.

The overall rank of the solution vector e is still $r = t + r'$. the masking gives us that the minimum rank-weight of the code generated by the rows of H' is $t + d$ rather than purely d: therefore recovering the hidden structure involves finding relatively large minimum weight vectors in a code. In practice we consider $d = 2$ and H is a $n/2 \times n$ matrix with all coordinates in a space F of dimension 2. Moreover for $\{F_1, F_2\}$ a basis of F, we choose the matrix H such that when H is written in the basis $\{F_1, F_2\}$, one obtains a $n \times n$ invertible matrix (of maximal rank) over $GF(q)$. It can be done easily. Figure 2 describes the scheme, where $||$ denotes concatenation.

---

1. **Secret key:** an augmented LRPC code over $GF(q^m)$ with parity-check matrix $(R|H)$ of size $(n-k) \times (n+t)$ which can decode r' errors and t generalized erasures: a randomly chosen $(n-k) \times (n-k)$ matrix A that is invertible in $GF(q^m)$ a randomly chosen $(n+t) \times (n+t)$ matrix P invertible in $GF(q)$.
2. **Public key:** the matrix $H' = A(R|H)P$, a small integer value l, a hash function *hash*.
3. **Signature of a message** M:
   a) *initialization*: seed $\leftarrow \{0, 1\}^l$, pick t random independent elements $(e_1, \cdots, e_t)$ of $GF(q^m)$
   b) *syndrome*: $s \leftarrow hash(M||seed) \in GF(q^m)^{n-k}$
   c) decode by the LRPC matrix H, the syndrome $s' = A^{-1}.s^T - R.(e_1, \cdots, e_t)^T$ with erasure space $T = \langle e_1, \cdots, e_t \rangle$ and r' errors by Algorithm 1.
   d) if the decoding algorithm works and returns a word $(e_{t+1}, \cdots, e_{n+t})$ of weight $r = t + r'$, signature=$((e_1, \cdots, e_{n+t}).(P^T)^{-1}, seed)$, else return to a).
4. **Verification:** Verify that $Rank(e) = r = t + r'$ and $H'.e^T = s = hash(M||seed)$.

Fig. 2. The *RankSign* signature algorithm

Parameters: *Public key size:* $(k+t)(n-k)mLog_2(q)$ *Signature size:* $(m+n+t)rLog_2(q)$.

Complexity of the Signature Algorithm

Signature Complexity: The main step of the signature algorithm consists in decoding the value s'. The cost of the signature can therefore be separated in two parts: the computation of s' and the cost of the decoding of s'. The cost of the computation of s' is dominated by the cost of the matrix-vector product $A^{-1}.s^T$:

$(n-k) \times (n+t)$ operations in $GF(q^m)$. The cost of the decoding algorithm described in Section 3.2 is $O((r.(n+t))^2)$ operations in $GF(q)$. Overall the cost of the computation of s' is dominant and the overall cost of the signature is $(n-k) \times (n+t)$ operations in $GF(q^m)$. Notice that the cost of multiplications in $GF(q^m)$ which can be computed trivially in $O(m^2)$ operations over $GF(q)$ can be optimized in $mLog_2(m)Log_2(Log_2(m))$ operations over $GF(q)$ ([18]).

Verification Complexity: The cost of the verification is the cost of a syndrome computation and the cost of checking the weight of the signature, hence $(n-k) \times (n+t)$ operations in $GF(q^m)$.

The length l of the seed can be taken as $\frac{80}{Log_2(q)}$ for instance.

5   Security Analysis of the Scheme

5.1   Security of Augmented LRPC Codes

In the previous section we defined augmented-LRPC with dual matrix $H' = A(R|H)P$, we now formulate the problem Ind-LRPC codes (Ind-LRPC) on the security of these codes:

Problem [Ind-LRPC]. *Given an augmented LRPC code, is it possible to distinguish it from a random code with the same parameters ?*

We now make the following assumption on the problem that we discuss in the following:

Assumption: *the Ind-LRPC problem is difficult to solve*

Discussion on the Assumption: The family of augmented LRPC codes is not of course a family of random codes, but they are weakly structured codes: the main point being that they have a parity-check matrix one part of which consists only in low rank coordinates the other part consisting in random entries. The attacker never has direct access to the LRPC matrix H, which is hidden by the augmented part.

The minimum weight of augmented LRPC codes is smaller than the GVR bound, hence natural attacks consist in trying to use their special structure to attack them. There exist general attacks for recovering the minimum weight of a code (see Section 2.3) but these attacks have a fast increasing complexity especially when the size of the base field $GF(q)$ increases. We first list obvious classical attack for recovering the structure of the augmented-LRPC codes and then describe specific attacks.

• *Previously Known Structural Attacks for Rank Codes.* The main structural attack for the rank metric is the Overbeck attack on the GPT cryptosystem [29], the attack consists in considering concatenated public matrices $G^q, G^{q^2}, ..., G^{q^{n-k-1}}$, in that case the particular structure of Gabidulin codes enables one to find a concatenated matrix with a rank default; this is due to the particular structure of the Gabidulin codes and the fact that for Gabidulin codes G^{q^i} is very close to $G^{q^{i+1}}$. In the case of LRPC codes, since the rows are taken randomly in a small space, this attack makes no sense, and cannot be generalized.

• *Dual Attack: Attack on the Dual Matrix H':* another approach consists in finding directly words of small weight induced by the structure of the code, from which one can hope to recover the global structure. For augmented LRPC codes, the rank of the minimum weight words is $d+t$: d for LRPC and t for the masking. This attack becomes very hard when t increases, even for low t. For instance for $t = 2$ and $d = 2$ it gives a minimum weight of 4, which for most parameters n and k is already out of reach of the best known attacks on the rank syndrome decoding (see Section 2).

• *Attack on the Isometry Matrix P:* remember that for rank metric codes, the isometry matrix *is not a permutation matrix* but an invertible matrix on the base field $GF(q)$. The attacker can then try to guess the action of P on H, since d is usually small negating this action may permit to attack directly a code of rank d. Since d is small it is enough to guess the resulting action of P on $n - k + 3$ columns by considering only the action of P coming from the first t columns of the matrix R - the only columns which may increase the rank-, it means guessing $(n - k + 3) \times t$ elements of $GF(q)$ (since coordinates of P are in $GF(q)$, hence a complexity of $q^{(n-k+3)t}$. In general this attack is not efficient, as soon as q is not small (for instance $q = 256$).

• *Attack on Recovering the Support:* an attacker may also try to recover directly an element of the support, for instance in the case of $d = 2$, for F the error support generate by $\{F_1, F_2\}$, up to a constant, one can rewrite F as generated by 1 and $F_2.F_1^{-1}$. Then the attacker can try to guess the particular element $F_2.F_1^{-1}$, recover F and solve a linear system in the coordinates of the elements of H. The complexity of this attack is hence $q^m.(nd)^3$, in the most favourable case when $d = 2$, this attack is exponential and becomes infeasible for q not too small.

• *Differential Support Attack:* it is also possible to search for attacks, directly based on the specific structure of the augmented LRPC codes. The general idea of the differential support attack is to consider the vector space V on the base field $GF(q)$ generated by the elements of a row of the augmented matrix H' and to find a couple (x, x') of elements of V such that $\frac{x'}{x} \in F$ the support of the LRPC code. The complexity of the attack is at least $q^{(n-k)(d-1)+t}$, the detail of the attack will be described in the full version of the paper. In practice this exponential attack is often the best attack to recover the structure of the code and distinguish the augmented LRPC code from a random code.

Conclusion on the Hardness of the Ind-LRPC Problem

We saw that there were many ways to attack the Ind-LRPC problem, in particular because of the rich structure of the rank metric, meanwhile the previous analysis of general known attacks shows that these attacks are all exponential with a strong dependency on the size of q. Moreover we also considered very specific attack (like the differential support attack) related to the particular structure of the augmented LRPC codes which deeply uses the structure of the code. This analysis seems to show that the Ind-LRPC problem is indeed difficult, with all known attacks being exponential. In practice it is easy to find parameters which resist to all these attacks.

5.2 Information Leakage

We considered in previous attacks the case where no additional information was known besides the public parameters. Often the most efficient attacks on signatures is to recover the hidden structure of the public key by using information leaking from real signatures. This for instance is what happened in the case of NTRUSign: the secret key is not directly attacked, but the information leaked from real signatures enables one to recover successfully the hidden structure. We show in the following that with our masking scheme no such phenomenon can occur, since we prove that, if an attacker can break the signature scheme for public augmented matrices with the help of information leaking from a number of (approximately) q real signatures, then he can also break the scheme just as efficiently *without* any authentic signatures.

Theorem 2 below states the unleakibility of signatures. It essentially states that valid signatures leak no information on the secret key. More precisely, under the random oracle model, there exists a polynomial time algorithm that takes as input the public matrix H' and, produces couples (m, σ), where m is a message and σ a valid signature for m when one's only access to the hashing oracle is through the simulator, and this with the same probability distribution as those output by the authentic signature algorithm. Therefore whatever forgery can be achieved from the knowledge of H' and a list of valid signed messages, can be simulated and reproduced with the public matrix H' as only input.

Theorem 2. *For any algorithm $\mathcal{A}$ that leads to a forged signature using $N \leq q/2$ authentic signatures, there is an algorithm $\mathcal{A}'$ with the same complexity that leads to a forgery using only the public key as input and without any authentic signatures.*

Proof. (main idea) the main idea of the proof is that it is possible to prove that it is possible to simulate couples (x', y') where x' is a hashed value of a message M and y' is the associated signature, so that an attacker cannot distinguish between real (message,signature) obtained from the signer and simulated couples. The proof relies on the fact that parameters of the signature are chosen such that any random syndrome value has a unique preimage with probability $1/q$. The full version of the proof will be given in the long version of the paper. □

5.3 Unforgeability

Corollary 1. *The RankSign signature scheme is secure in the ROM against existential forgery with adaptive chosen-message attack under the Ind-LRPC assumption.*

Proof. Our main Theorem 2 and its proof, show that with the sole knowledge of the public key it is possible to simulate new (message,signature) couples with the same success probability as when given valid (message,signature) couples whenever the number of such couples is less than $q/2$. Hence it means that given less than $q/2$ signatures (chosen or given), an attacker cannot do better than an attacker who knows only the public key (the matrix of a code). And in that case, under the Ind-LRPC indistinguishability assumption of augmented LRPC codes with random codes, it implies that forging a false signature in the ROM (ie: being able to approximate a random syndrome for the augmented LRPC class of codes) means being able to decode a random rank code. Parameters of the scheme are hence chosen with large q and suitable code parameters for which it is difficult to decode a random code and to distinguish augmented LRPC codes from random codes.   □

6   Practical Security, Parameters and Implementation

6.1   Parameters Setting

The parameters have to be chosen so that the LRPC code considered is decodable for errors and erasures as in Section 3.2, and such that the parameters correspond to a proportion of decodable syndromes which is almost 1, as explained in Section 3.3. Parameters (m, t, r, d, n, k) have hence to fulfill the conditions given by results of Section 3.2 and 3.3. Notice that as explained in Section 3.3, for a given set of parameters (m, t, r, d) which fulfills the conditions, the set $(\alpha m, \alpha t, \alpha r, d)$ for α an integer, will also fulfill the conditions. Moreover for a given set of parameters, it is possible to consider different fields $GF(q)$ without modifying the fact that the density of decodable syndromes is almost 1. Moreover the set of parameters have to be resistant to all known attacks described in Section 5.

6.2   Examples of Parameters

In the following we give in Table 1 some examples of parameters. The parameters are adjusted to resist all previously known attacks. The security reduction holds for up to $q/2$ signatures, hence if one considers $q = 2^{40}$ it means we are protected against leakage for up to 2^{40} obtained authentic signatures. such an amount of signatures is very difficult to obtain in real life, moreover if one multiplies by the amount of time necessary to obtain a signature (about 2^{30} for $q = 2^{40}$) we clearly see that obtaining such a number of authentic signatures is out of reach, and it justifies our security reduction.

    We also give parameters for q lower than 2^{40}: in that case the reduction is weaker in the sense that it does not exclude an information leakage attack for sufficiently many signatures. However, such an information leakage attack seems difficult to obtain anyway, and these parameters can be seen as challenges for our system.

    In the table the considered codes are $[n+t, k+t]$ codes which give a signature of rank r. The dual code H' is a $[n+t, n-k]$ code which contains words of rank $d+t$. In the table 'LP' stands for the logarithmic complexity of the algebraic Levy-Perret attack, for instance in the case $n = 16$, one gets a $[18, 8]$ code in which one searches for words of rank 4, it gives 270 quadratic equations for 126 unknowns, with a theoretical complexity of 2^{120} from [5] (remember that for a random quadratic system over $GF(2)$ with n unknowns and $2n$ equations the complexity is roughly 2^n operations inthe base field $GF(2)$. The complexity of a direct attack for searching low weight words of weight $d + t$ with combinatorial attacks (see section 2.3) is given in 'Dual'. At last 'DS' stands for the differential support attack of section 5.1 and 'DA' stands for the direct attack on the signature in which one searches directly for a forgery for a word of weight r in a $[n + t, k + t]$ code. In the table the number of augmented columns is usually t except for the last example for which one adds 2 columns rather than $t = 5$.

The analysis of the security complexities shows that the best attack (in bold in the table) depends on the given parameters: when q is large the algebraic attacks are better since they do not really depends on q, when d increases the decoding algorithm is less efficient and then one get closer from the Singleton bound and direct forgery for the signature becomes easier. For other parameters, usually the specific structural attack differential support attack DS is better.

Table 1. Examples of parameters for the RankSign signature scheme

n	n-k	m	q	d	t	r'	r	GVR	Sing	pk	sign	LP	Dual	DS	DA
16	8	18	2^{40}	2	2	4	6	5	8	57600	8640	**130**	1096	400	776
16	8	18	2^{8}	2	2	4	6	5	8	11520	1728	110	233	**80**	168
16	8	18	2^{16}	2	2	4	6	5	8	23040	3456	**120**	448	160	320
20	10	24	2^{8}	2	3	5	8	6	10	24960	3008	190	370	**104**	226
27	9	20	2^{6}	3	2	3	5	4	7	23328	1470	170	187	**120**	129
48	12	40	2^{4}	4	5	3	8	6	10	78720	2976	> 600	340	164	**114**
50	10	42	2^{4}	5	5	2	7	5	9	70560	2800	> 600	240	180	**104**

6.3   Implementation Results

We implemented our scheme on a Intel Core i5-4200U CPU 1.60GHz processor, in a non optimized way for two sets of parameters over $GF(2^8)$ of Table 1 for security 2^{80} and 2^{104}, in the C language (with the MPFQ library for finite fields computations), the results were as follows:

Table 2. Implementation time for two sets of parameters

n	n-k	m	q	d	signature time (ms)	verification time (ms)	security (bits)
16	8	18	2^{8}	2	2.75	4.4	80
20	10	24	2^{8}	2	6.13	12	104

The results obtained follow the complexity of Section 4 and compare very well to other signatures.

7 Conclusion

In this paper we introduced a new approach to devising signatures with coding theory and in particular in the rank metric, by proposing to decode both erasures and errors rather than simply errors. This approach enables one to return a small weight word beyond the Gilbert-Varshamov bound rather than below. We proposed a new efficient algorithm for decoding LRPC codes which makes this approach possible. We then proposed a signature scheme based on this algorithm and the full decoding of a random syndrome beyond the Gilbert-Varshamov bound. We also showed that it was possible to protect our system against leakage from authentic signatures. Overall we propose different types of parameters, some of which are rather small. The parameters we propose compares very well to other existing signature schemes on coding theory as the CFS scheme for instance.

References

1. Berger, T.P., Cayrel, P.-L., Gaborit, P., Otmani, A.: Reducing Key Length of the McEliece Cryptosystem. In: Preneel, B. (ed.) AFRICACRYPT 2009. LNCS, vol. 5580, pp. 77–97. Springer, Heidelberg (2009)
2. Berger, T., Loidreau, P.: Designing an Efficient and Secure Public-Key Cryptosystem Based on Reducible Rank Codes. In: Canteaut, A., Viswanathan, K. (eds.) INDOCRYPT 2004. LNCS, vol. 3348, pp. 218–229. Springer, Heidelberg (2004)
3. Bettale, L., Faugère, J.-C., Perret, L.: Hybrid approach for solving multivariate systems over finite fields. J. Mathematical Cryptology 3(3), 177–197 (2009)
4. Barbulescu, R., Gaudry, P., Joux, A., Thomé, E.: A quasi-polynomial algorithm for discrete logarithm in finite fields of small characteristic. eprint iacr 2013/400
5. http://www-polsys.lip6.fr/~bettale/hybrid
6. Chabaud, F., Stern, J.: The Cryptographic Security of the Syndrome Decoding Problem for Rank Distance Codes. In: Kim, K.-c., Matsumoto, T. (eds.) ASIACRYPT 1996. LNCS, vol. 1163, pp. 368–381. Springer, Heidelberg (1996)
7. Courtois, N.T., Finiasz, M., Sendrier, N.: How to achieve a mcEliece-based digital signature scheme. In: Boyd, C. (ed.) ASIACRYPT 2001. LNCS, vol. 2248, pp. 157–174. Springer, Heidelberg (2001)
8. Ducas, L., Nguyen, P.Q.: Learning a Zonotope and More: Cryptanalysis of NTRUSign Countermeasures. In: Wang, X., Sako, K. (eds.) ASIACRYPT 2012. LNCS, vol. 7658, pp. 433–450. Springer, Heidelberg (2012)
9. Faugère, J.-C., Levy-dit-Vehel, F., Perret, L.: Cryptanalysis of MinRank. In: Wagner, D. (ed.) CRYPTO 2008. LNCS, vol. 5157, pp. 280–296. Springer, Heidelberg (2008)
10. Faugère, J.-C., El Din, M.S., Spaenlehauer, P.-J.: Computing loci of rank defects of linear matrices using Grbner bases and applications to cryptology. In: ISSAC 2010, pp. 257–264 (2010)
11. Faugère, J.-C., Otmani, A., Perret, L., Tillich, J.-P.: Algebraic Cryptanalysis of McEliece Variants with Compact Keys. In: Gilbert, H. (ed.) EUROCRYPT 2010. LNCS, vol. 6110, pp. 279–298. Springer, Heidelberg (2010)
12. Gabidulin, E.M.: Theory of Codes with Maximum Rank Distance. Probl. Peredachi Inf. (21), 3–16 (1985)

13. Gabidulin, E.M., Paramonov, A.V., Tretjakov, O.V.: Ideals over a non-commutative ring and their application in cryptology. In: Davies, D.W. (ed.) EUROCRYPT 1991. LNCS, vol. 547, pp. 482–489. Springer, Heidelberg (1991)
14. Gaborit, P., Murat, G., Ruatta, O., Zmor, G.: Low Rank Parity Check Codes and their application in cryptography. Published in Workshop Codes and Cryptography (WCC 2013), Bergen (2013), http://www.selmer.uib.no/WCC2013/pdfs/Gaborit.pdf
15. Gaborit, P., Schrek, J., Zémor, G.: Full Cryptanalysis of the Chen Identification Protocol. In: Yang, B.-Y. (ed.) PQCrypto 2011. LNCS, vol. 7071, pp. 35–50. Springer, Heidelberg (2011)
16. Gaborit, P., Ruatta, O., Schrek, J.: On the complexity of the rank syndrome decoding problem, eprint, http://arxiv.org/abs/1301.1026
17. Gaborit, P., Zémor, G.: On the hardness of the syndrome decoding and minimum distance problems for rank metric (preprint, 2014), http://arxiv.org/abs/1404.3482
18. von zur Gathen, J., Gerhard, J.: Modern computer algebra. Cambridge University Press (2003)
19. Gentry, C., Peikert, C., Vaikuntanathan, V.: Trapdoors for hard lattices and new cryptographic constructions. In: STOC 2008, pp. 197–206 (2008)
20. Goldreich, O., Goldwasser, S., Halevi, S.: Public-Key Cryptosystems from Lattice Reduction Problems. In: Kaliski Jr., B.S. (ed.) CRYPTO 1997. LNCS, vol. 1294, pp. 112–131. Springer, Heidelberg (1997)
21. Hoffstein, J., Pipher, J., Silverman, J.H.: NTRU: A Ring-Based Public Key Cryptosystem. In: Buhler, J.P. (ed.) ANTS 1998. LNCS, vol. 1423, pp. 267–288. Springer, Heidelberg (1998)
22. Hoffstein, J., Howgrave-Graham, N., Pipher, J., Silverman, J.H., Whyte, W.: NTRUSIGN: Digital Signatures Using the NTRU Lattice. In: Joye, M. (ed.) CT-RSA 2003. LNCS, vol. 2612, pp. 122–140. Springer, Heidelberg (2003)
23. Levy-dit-Vehel, F., Perret, L.: Algebraic decoding of rank metric codes. In: Proceedings of YACC 2006 (2006)
24. Loidreau, P.: Properties of codes in rank metric, http://arxiv.org/abs/cs/0610057
25. MacWilliams, J., Sloane, N.J.A.: The theory of error correcting codes. North Holland, Ninth impression (1977)
26. Micciancio, D., Regev, O.: Lattice-based Cryptography. In: Bernstein, D.J., Buchmann, J. (eds.) Post-quantum Cryptography. Springer (2008)
27. Misoczki, R., Tillich, J.-P., Sendrier, N., Barreto, P.S.L.M.: MDPC-McEliece: New McEliece variants from moderate density parity-check codes. IACR Cryptology ePrint Archive, 2012:409 (2012)
28. Ourivski, A.V., Johansson, T.: New Technique for Decoding Codes in the Rank Metric and Its Cryptography Applications. Probl. Inf. Transm(38), 237–246 (2002)
29. Overbeck, R.: Structural attacks for public key cryptosystems based on Gabidulin codes. J. Cryptology 21(2), 280–301 (2008)
30. Nguyên, P.Q., Regev, O.: Learning a Parallelepiped: Cryptanalysis of GGH and NTRU Signatures. In: Vaudenay, S. (ed.) EUROCRYPT 2006. LNCS, vol. 4004, pp. 271–288. Springer, Heidelberg (2006)
31. Silva, D., Kschishang, Kötter, R.: Communication over Finite-Field Matrix Channels. IEEE Trans. Inf. Theory 56, 1296–1305 (2010)
32. Stern, J.: A new paradigm for public key identification. IEEE Transactions on Information Theory, IT 42(6), 2757–2768 (1996)

Cryptanalysis of the Multivariate Signature Scheme Proposed in PQCrypto 2013

Yasufumi Hashimoto

Department of Mathematical Sciences, University of the Ryukyus

Abstract. In PQCrypto 2013, Yasuda, Takagi and Sakurai proposed a new signature scheme as one of multivariate public key cryptosystems (MPKCs). This scheme (called YTS) is based on the fact that there are two isometry classes of non-degenerate quadratic forms on a vector space with a prescribed dimension. The advantage of YTS is its efficiency. In fact, its signature generation is eight or nine times faster than Rainbow of similar size. For the security, it is known that the direct attack, the IP attack and the min-rank attack are applicable on YTS, and the running times are exponential time for the first and the second attacks and subexponential time for the third attack. In the present paper, we give a new attack on YTS using an approach similar to the diagonalization of a matrix. Our attack works in polynomial time and it actually recovers equivalent secret keys of YTS having 140-bits security againt min-rank attack in several minutes.

Keywords: multivariate public key cryptosystems, signature scheme, quadratic forms, post-quantum cryptography.

1 Introduction

A Multivariate Public Key Cryptosystem (MPKC) is a cryptosystem whose public key is a set of multivariate quadratic polynomials over a finite field. It is known that the problem of solving systems of randomly chosen multivariate quadratic equations over a finite field is NP-hard [14]. Then MPKC is considered as one of candidates of public key cryptosystems which can resist against the quantum attacks. MPKC also has advantage for efficiency compared with RSA and ECC. In fact, Chen et al. [5] presented several MPKC implementations on modern x86 CPUs which are more efficint than RSA and ECC. Until now, various MPKCs have been proposed, e.g. MI [24], HFE [27], Sflash [1], UOV [20], Rainbow [7], TTS [29]. On the other hand, various attacks on MPKCs (e.g. the direct attacks [9,10,2], the rank attacks [6,11,16,18,21,29], the differential attacks [8,12,13] and the UOV attacks [20,22]) also have been proposed, and some MPKCs were shown to be insecure against (one of) these attacks [26,22,9,8].

Recently in PQCrypto 2013, Yasuda, Takagi and Sakurai [30] proposed a new signature scheme as one of MPKCs. This scheme (called YTS) is based on the fact that there are two isometry classes of non-degenerate quadratic forms on a vector space with a prescribed dimension [28]. There have been no MPKCs

M. Mosca (Ed.): PQCrypto 2014, LNCS 8772, pp. 108–125, 2014.

similar to YTS. The advantage of YTS is that its signature generation is fast. In fact, it is eight or nine times faster than Rainbow of similar size. For the security, it is known that the direct attack [9,10,2], the IP attack [27] and the min-rank attack [29] are applicable on YTS and the running times are exponential times for the first and the second attacks and subexponential time for the third attack [30]. Then (at the time of PQCrypto 2013), YTS was considered to be secure enough under suitable parameter selections.

The aim in the present paper is to study the structure of YTS in detail and propose a new attack on YTS. The coefficient matrices of the quadratic forms in the central map of YTS are described by extensions of sparse smaller matrices. Then, taking two linear sums of coefficient matrices of quadratic forms in the public key and multiplying the one and the inversion of the other, the attacker gets a matrix conjugate to a matrix extended from a smaller matrix. By using an approach similar to the diagonalization of this matrix, the attacker can recover partial information of the secret keys. After that, taking several elementary operations in linear algebra, the attacker can recover equivalent secret keys in polynomial time. Actually, we experimentally succeed to recover equivalent secret keys of YTS having 140-bits security against the min-rank attacks [30] in several minutes (see Section 5). This means that YTS is not secure at all and it must be repaired for practical use.

2   Notations

Throughout in this paper, we use the following notations.

q: a power of odd prime.
k: a finite field of order q.

For an integer $r \geq 1$,

$M_r(k)$: the set of $r \times r$ matrices of k-entries.

$SM_r(k)$: the set of $r \times r$ symmetric matrices of k-entries.

$I_r \in M_r(k)$: the identity matrix.

For a matrix A,

A^t: the transpose of A.

For $1 \leq i, j \leq r$,

$E_{ij} \in SM_r(k)$: the symmetric matrix whose $(i,j), (j,i)$ entries are 1 and other entries are 0, namely

$$E_{11} := \begin{pmatrix} 1 & \\ & \end{pmatrix}, \quad E_{12} := \begin{pmatrix} & 1 \\ 1 & \end{pmatrix}, \quad \ldots, \quad E_{rr} := \begin{pmatrix} & \\ & 1 \end{pmatrix}.$$

For $L_1 \in M_{r_1}(k), \ldots, L_u \in M_{r_u}(k)$,

$$L_1 \oplus \cdots \oplus L_u := \begin{pmatrix} L_1 & & \\ & \ddots & \\ & & L_u \end{pmatrix} \in M_{r_1 + \cdots + r_u}(k),$$

$$L_1^{\oplus u} := \underbrace{L_1 \oplus \cdots \oplus L_1}_{u} \in M_{r_1 u}(k).$$

For $A = \begin{pmatrix} a_{11} & \cdots & a_{1r_1} \\ \vdots & \ddots & \vdots \\ a_{r_1 1} & \cdots & a_{r_1 r_1} \end{pmatrix} \in M_{r_1}(k)$ and $B \in M_{r_2}(k)$,

$$A \otimes B := \begin{pmatrix} a_{11}B & \cdots & a_{1r_1}B \\ \vdots & \ddots & \vdots \\ a_{r_1 1}B & \cdots & a_{r_1 r_1}B \end{pmatrix} \in M_{r_1 r_2}(k).$$

For a monic polynomial $g(t) := c_0 + c_1 t + \cdots + c_{r-1} t^{r-1} + t^r$ of degree r,

$$C(g) := \begin{cases} (-c_0), & (r = 1), \\ \begin{pmatrix} 0 & \cdots & 0 & -c_0 \\ 1 & & 0 & -c_1 \\ & \ddots & & \vdots \\ 0 & & 1 & -c_{r-1} \end{pmatrix}, & (r \geq 2). \end{cases}$$

For $A = \begin{pmatrix} a_{11} & \cdots & a_{1r} \\ \vdots & \ddots & \vdots \\ a_{r1} & \cdots & a_{rr} \end{pmatrix} \in M_r(k)$ and $B = \begin{pmatrix} b_{11} & \cdots & b_{r1} \\ \vdots & \ddots & \vdots \\ b_{r1} & \cdots & b_{rr} \end{pmatrix} \in SM_r(k),$

$$\phi(A) := (a_{11}, a_{21}, \ldots, a_{r1}, a_{12}, \ldots, \ldots, a_{rr})^t \in k^{r^2},$$
$$\psi(B) := (b_{11}, b_{21}, \ldots, b_{r1}, b_{22}, \ldots, \ldots, b_{rr})^t \in k^{r(r+1)/2}.$$

3   The Signature Scheme YTS

In this section, we give a short survey of the signature scheme YTS [30].

3.1   Construction of the Scheme

In a multivariate public key cryptosystem (MPKC), the public key is a set of multivariate quadratic polynomials

$$f_1(x_1, \cdots, x_n) = \sum_{1 \leq i \leq j \leq n} a_{ij}^{(1)} x_i x_j + \sum_{1 \leq i \leq n} b_i^{(1)} x_i + c^{(1)},$$

$$\vdots$$

$$f_m(x_1, \cdots, x_n) = \sum_{1 \leq i \leq j \leq n} a_{ij}^{(m)} x_i x_j + \sum_{1 \leq i \leq n} b_i^{(m)} x_i + c^{(m)},$$

over a finite field. The quadratic polynomials for YTS [30] are constructed as follows.

```
─────────────── The signature scheme YTS ───────────────
```

Let $r \geq 1$ be an integer and denote $n := r^2$, $m := r(r+1)/2$. For $X \in M_r(k)$, put

$$U_1(X) := X^t I_r X (= X^t X), \qquad U_\delta(X) := X^t \begin{pmatrix} I_{r-1} & \\ & \delta \end{pmatrix} X,$$

where δ is an element in k such that $\delta \neq \alpha^2$ for any $\alpha \in k$.

Secret Keys: Two invertible affine transforms $S : k^n \to k^n$, $T : k^m \to k^m$ and an invertible matrix $B \in M_r(k)$. Note that, for $x \in k^n$ and $y \in k^m$, $S(x)$ and $T(y)$ are given by

$$S(x) = S_0 x + s, \qquad T(y) = T_0 y + t \tag{1}$$

where $S_0 \in M_n(k), T_0 \in M_m(k)$ are invertible matrices and $s \in k^n, t \in k^m$ are vectors.

Public Keys: Two quadratic maps $V_1 := T \circ \psi \circ U_1 \circ \phi^{-1} \circ S$ and $V_\delta := T \circ \psi \circ U_\delta \circ B \circ \phi^{-1} \circ S$.

$$V_1 : k^n \xrightarrow{S} k^n \xrightarrow{\phi^{-1}} M_r(k) \xrightarrow{U_1} SM_r(k) \xrightarrow{\psi} k^m \xrightarrow{T} k^m$$

$$V_\delta : k^n \xrightarrow{S} k^n \xrightarrow{\phi^{-1}} M_r(k) \xrightarrow{B} M_r(k) \xrightarrow{U_\delta} SM_r(k) \xrightarrow{\psi} k^m \xrightarrow{T} k^m$$

Signature generation: For a message $y \in k^m$, the signature is generated as follows.

Step 1. Compute $z := T^{-1}(y)$ and put $Z := \psi^{-1}(z)$.

Step 2. Find $X \in M_r(k)$ satisfying either

$$U_1(X) = Z \qquad \text{or} \qquad U_\delta(BX) = Z,$$

and put $x := \phi(X)$.

Step 3. Compute $w := S^{-1}(x)$. The signature for $y \in k^m$ is w.

Signature verification: Check whether $V_1(w) = y$ or $V_\delta(w) = y$ holds.

For Step 2 of the signature generation, the following lemma is known.

Lemma 1. *([28,30]) For any $Y \in SM_r(k)$, there exists $X \in M_r(k)$ satisfying either*

$$U_1(X) = Y \qquad \text{or} \qquad U_\delta(X) = Y.$$

Furthermore, such a matrix X can be found in time $O(r^4)$. □

See [30] for the detail algorithm finding X. Due to the lemma above, one can compute X in time $O(n^2)$.

3.2 Quadratic Forms in YTS

In this subsection, we explain the structure of quadratic forms in V_1.

For $X = (x_{ij})_{1 \leq i,j \leq r} \in M_r(k)$, let

$$x_j := (x_{1j}, \ldots, x_{rj})^t \in k^r,$$
$$x := \phi(X) = (x_{11}, \ldots, x_{r1}, x_{12}, \ldots, \ldots, x_{rr})^t \in k^n.$$

By the definition of U_1, we have

$$U_1(X) = X^t X = \begin{pmatrix} x_1^t x_1 & \cdots & x_1^t x_r \\ \vdots & \ddots & \vdots \\ x_r^t x_1 & \cdots & x_r^t x_r \end{pmatrix},$$

namely the entries in $U_1(X)$ are as follows.

$(1,1)$-entry: $x_{11}x_{11} + x_{21}x_{21} + \cdots + x_{r1}x_{r1} = x^t \begin{pmatrix} I_r & \\ & \end{pmatrix} x,$

$(1,2)$-entry: $x_{11}x_{12} + x_{21}x_{22} + \cdots + x_{r1}x_{r2} = x^t \begin{pmatrix} & \frac{1}{2}I_r \\ \frac{1}{2}I_r & \end{pmatrix} x,$

$\vdots$

(r,r)-entry: $x_{1r}x_{1r} + x_{2r}x_{2r} + \cdots + x_{rr}x_{rr} = x^t \begin{pmatrix} & \\ & I_r \end{pmatrix} x,$

Then the (i,j)-entry of $U_{ij}(x)$ is given by

$$U_{ij}(x) = \begin{cases} x^t(E_{ij} \otimes I_r)x, & (i = j), \\ \dfrac{1}{2}x^t(E_{ij} \otimes I_r)x, & (i \neq j). \end{cases} \tag{2}$$

Thus, by the construction of the public key, the quadratic map

$$V_1(x) = (V_{11}(x), \ldots, V_{rr}(x))^t$$

is described as follows.

$$\begin{aligned} V_{ij}(x) =\; & x^t S_0^t(T_{ij} \otimes I_r)S_0 x + s^t(T_{ij} \otimes I_r)S_0 x + x^t S_0^t(T_{ij} \otimes I_r)s \\ & + s^t(T_{ij} \otimes I_r)s + t_{ij}, \end{aligned} \tag{3}$$

where S_0, s are given in (1) and $T_{ij} \in SM_r(k)$, $t_{ij} \in k$ are respectively derived from T_0, t.

3.3   Efficiency and Security of YTS

Based on the results in [30], we list the number of operations for signature generation/verification, the size of keys and the security against known attacks.

Signature Generation: $O(n^2 \cdot \log q)$.

Signature Verification: Almost same to other schemes in MPKC with the same q, m, n.

Key Size: $O(n^3 \cdot \log q)$.

Security against Min-Rank Attack: $O(q^{\sqrt{n}} \cdot n^3)$ for recovering T (see also [29]).

Security against IP Attack: $O(q^{2n/3})$ for recovering S, T (see also [26]).

Security against Gröbner Basis Attack: $O(2^{m(3.31-3.62/\log_2 q)})$ for generating a dummy signature under the assumption that $\log_2 q \ll m$ and the quadratic forms in $V_1(x) - y$ or $V_\delta(x) - y$ with the public keys V_1, V_δ and a given message $y \in k^m$ is "semi-regular" (see [9,10,2,3]).

4   Proposed Attack on YTS

In this section, we propose a new attack on YTS. We first show how to recover the contributions of the vectors $s \in k^n, t \in k^m$ in the secret keys S, T (see (1)).

4.1   Recovering s and t

─────────────────────── Algorithm 1 ───────────────────────

Input: The public key $V_1(x)$.

Output: Vectors $s' \in k^n, t' \in k^m$ such that all quadratic forms in $V_1(x + s') - t'$ are homogeneous.

Step 1. Find $\hat{s} \in k^n$ such that all coefficients of the linear terms of the quadratic forms in $V_1(x + \hat{s})$ are zero by the Gaussian elimination.

Step 2. Put $\hat{t} \in k^m$ the set of constant terms in $V_1(x + \hat{s})$.

Step 3. Output $s' = \hat{s}$ and $t' = \hat{t}$.

Due to (3), we have

$$
\begin{aligned}
V_{ij}(x + \hat{s}) =\; & x^t S_0^t (T_{ij} \otimes I_r) S_0 x + (s + S_0 \hat{s})^t (T_{ij} \otimes I_r) S_0 x \\
& + x^t S_0^t (T_{ij} \otimes I_r)(s + S_0 \hat{s}) + (s + S_0 \hat{s})^t (T_{ij} \otimes I_r)(s + S_0 \hat{s}) + t_{ij}.
\end{aligned}
\tag{4}
$$

Since S_0 is invertible and the linear terms of $V_{ij}(x + \hat{s})$ are given by the second and the third terms in the right hand side of (4), all linear terms of $V_{ij}(x + \hat{s})$

vanish for any i, j if and only if

$$s + S_0 \hat{s} \in \bigcap_{1 \leq i, j \leq r} \mathrm{Ker}(T_{ij} \otimes I_r).$$

Such a vector $\hat{s}$ can be found by the Gaussian elimination, and once such $\hat{s}$ is recovered, we have

$$V_{ij}(x + \hat{s}) = x^t S_0^t (T_{ij} \otimes I_r) S_0 x + t_{ij}.$$

Then $\hat{t} = t$.   □

Complexity. This algorithm uses the Gaussian elimination for linear equations of n variables. Then the complexity is $\ll n^3 = r^6$.

Thanks to the algorithm above, we can suppose, without loss of generality, that both S and T are linear maps. In such cases, $V_{ij}(x)$ is a homogeneous quadratic form. Then, in the discussions later, we interpret V_{ij} as the $n \times n$ symmetric matrix with

$$V_{ij}(x) = x^t V_{ij} x.$$

4.2   Weak Keys

In this subsection, we show that, when

$$S = (Q \otimes I_r)(L_1 \oplus \cdots \oplus L_r) = \begin{pmatrix} q_{11} I_r & \cdots & q_{1r} I_r \\ \vdots & \ddots & \vdots \\ q_{r1} I_r & \cdots & q_{rr} I_r \end{pmatrix} \begin{pmatrix} L_1 & & \\ & \ddots & \\ & & L_r \end{pmatrix} \qquad (5)$$

for some invertible $r \times r$ matrices $Q = \begin{pmatrix} q_{11} & \cdots & q_{1r} \\ \vdots & \ddots & \vdots \\ q_{r1} & \cdots & q_{rr} \end{pmatrix}$, $L_1, \ldots, L_r \in \mathrm{M}_r(k)$, the

attacker can recover matrices $S' \in \mathrm{M}_n(k)$ and $T' \in \mathrm{M}_m(k)$ with

$$T'(V_1(S'(x))) = (U_1 \circ \phi^{-1})(x) = \begin{pmatrix} x^t (E_{11} \otimes I_r) x \\ \vdots \\ x^t (E_{rr} \otimes I_r) x \end{pmatrix}. \qquad (6)$$

It is obvious that, once such S', T' are recovered, the attacker can generate dummy signatures.

The algorithm to recover S', T' is as follows.

Algorithm 2

Input: The public key $V_1(x)$ when

$$S = (Q \otimes I_r)(L_1 \oplus \cdots \oplus L_r)$$

for some invertible matrices $Q, L_1, \ldots, L_r \in M_r(k)$.

Output: Invertible matrices $S' \in M_n(k)$ and $T' \in M_m(k)$ such that

$$T'(V_1(S'x)) = (U_1 \circ \phi^{-1})(x).$$

Step 1. Choose (i, j) arbitrary and denote $V_{ij} = \begin{pmatrix} M_{11} & \cdots & M_{1r} \\ \vdots & \ddots & \vdots \\ M_{r1} & \cdots & M_{rr} \end{pmatrix}$ with

$M_{11}, \ldots, M_{rr} \in M_r(k)$. For $2 \leq u \leq r$, choose $1 \leq l_u \leq r$ such that both $M_{l_u 1}, M_{l_u u}$ are invertible and put

$$R_u := M_{l_u u}^{-1} M_{l_u 1}.$$

If there are no such pair $(M_{l_u 1}, M_{l_u u})$, try it again for another (i, j).

Step 2. Calculate

$$\hat{V}_{ij} := (I_r \oplus R_2 \oplus \cdots \oplus R_r)^t V_{ij}(I_r \oplus R_2 \oplus \cdots \oplus R_r).$$

Step 3. Find $L \in M_r(k)$ such that

$$(L^{\oplus r})^t \hat{V}_{ij} L^{\oplus r} = D_{ij} \otimes I_r$$

for some $D_{ij} \in SM_r(k)$ by the algorithm for Lemma 1.

Step 4. Find $\hat{T} \in M_m(k)$ such that

$$\hat{T} \begin{pmatrix} D_{11} \\ \vdots \\ D_{rr} \end{pmatrix} = \begin{pmatrix} E_{11} \\ \vdots \\ E_{rr} \end{pmatrix} \tag{7}$$

by the Gaussian elimination.

Step 5. Output $S' = (I_r \oplus R_2 \oplus \cdots \oplus R_r)L^{\oplus r}$ and $T' = \hat{T}$.

When $S = (Q \otimes I_r)(L_1 \oplus \cdots \oplus L_r)$, we have

$$
\begin{aligned}
V_{ij} &= (L_1 \oplus \cdots \oplus L_r)^t((Q^t T_{ij} Q) \otimes I_r)(L_1 \oplus \cdots \oplus L_r) \\
&= \begin{pmatrix} \tilde{q}_{11} L_1^t L_1 & \cdots & \tilde{q}_{1r} L_1^t L_r \\ \vdots & \ddots & \vdots \\ \tilde{q}_{r1} L_r^t L_1 & \cdots & \tilde{q}_{rr} L_r^t L_r \end{pmatrix} =: \begin{pmatrix} M_{11} & \cdots & M_{1r} \\ \vdots & \ddots & \vdots \\ M_{r1} & \cdots & M_{rr} \end{pmatrix}
\end{aligned}
$$

where $\tilde{q}_{11}, \ldots, \tilde{q}_{rr} \in k$ are the entries of $Q^t T_{ij} Q$. Then R_u in Step 2 is a constant multiple of $L_u^{-1} L_1$ and we get

$$
\begin{aligned}
\hat{V}_{ij} &= (I_r \oplus R_2 \oplus \cdots \oplus R_r)^t V_{ij} (I_r \oplus R_2 \oplus \cdots \oplus R_r) \\
&= \left((1 \oplus \alpha_2 \oplus \cdots \oplus \alpha_r) Q^t T_{ij} Q (1 \oplus \alpha_2 \oplus \cdots \oplus \alpha_r) \right) \otimes (L_1^t L_1) \\
&=: (\hat{Q}^t T_{ij} \hat{Q}) \otimes (L_1^t L_1)
\end{aligned}
\tag{8}
$$

for some $\alpha_1, \ldots, \alpha_r \in k$. This means that any $r \times r$ block in $\hat{V}_{ij}$ for any (i, j) is a constant multiple of $L_1^t L_1$. It is easy to see that L in Step 3 can be found due to Lemma 1.

Since $L(L_1^t L_1) L = \beta I_r$ for some $\beta \in k$, we have

$$
D_{ij} = \beta \hat{Q}^t T_{ij} \hat{Q}.
\tag{9}
$$

By the definition of T_{ij}, we see that

$$
\begin{pmatrix} D_{11} \\ \vdots \\ D_{rr} \end{pmatrix} = \beta T \begin{pmatrix} \hat{Q}^t E_{11} \hat{Q} \\ \vdots \\ \hat{Q}^t E_{rr} \hat{Q} \end{pmatrix}.
$$

The entries in the right hand side are $r \times r$ symmetric matrices and any $r \times r$ symmetric matrix is expressed by a linear combination of $E_{11}, \ldots, E_{rr}$. Then there exists $\Lambda \in M_m(k)$ such that

$$
\begin{pmatrix} \hat{Q}^t E_{11} \hat{Q} \\ \vdots \\ \hat{Q}^t E_{rr} \hat{Q} \end{pmatrix} = \Lambda \begin{pmatrix} E_{11} \\ \vdots \\ E_{rr} \end{pmatrix}.
$$

The matrix Λ is known as the "symmetric square" of $\hat{Q}$ and the determinant of Λ is a power of that of $\hat{Q}$ (its proof is complicated; see the discussions in Chap. 2 of [23]). Thus, there always exists $\hat{T} = (\beta T \Lambda)^{-1}$ satisfying (7) and such $\hat{T}$ can be found by the Gaussian elimination. □

Complexity. In Step 1, we take inversions and multiplications of $r \times r$ matrices r times. Then Step 1 is in time $O(r^4)$. Step 2 is for multiplications of special type matrices $2m$ times. We see that the complexity of each multiplication is $\ll r^5$. Then Step 2 is in time $O(r^7)$. In Step 3, we use the algorithm for Lemma 1. Then Step 3 is in time $O(r^4)$. In Step 4, we use the Gaussian elimination for $m \times m$ matrices and its complexity is $\ll m^3 = r^6$. We thus conclude that the total complexity of Algorithm 2 is $\ll r^7$.

4.3 On Conjugations of Matrices

In this subsection, we give the following lemma for conjugations of matrices to explain our attack on YTS.

Lemma 2. *Let* $r, d \geq 1$ *be integers,* $G \in M_d(k)$ *and* $g(t) := \det(t \cdot I_d - G)$. *Suppose that* $g(t)$ *is square free and is factored by* $g(t) = g_1(t) \cdots g_l(t)$ *over* k. *Put* $d_1 := \deg g_1(t), \ldots, d_l := \deg g_l(t)$. *Then it holds that*
(i) there exists $P \in M_{rd}(k)$ *such that*

$$P^{-1}(G \otimes I_r)P = (C(g_1) \oplus \cdots \oplus C(g_l)) \otimes I_r, \tag{10}$$

(ii) if $P_1, P_2 \in M_{rd}(k)$ *satisfy*

$$P_1^{-1}(G \otimes I_r)P_1 = P_2^{-1}(G \otimes I_r)P_2 = (C(g_1) \oplus \cdots \oplus C(g_l)) \otimes I_r,$$

there exist $B_1 \in M_{rd_1}(k), \ldots, B_l \in M_{rd_l}(k)$ *such that*

$$P_2^{-1}P_1 = B_1 \oplus \cdots \oplus B_l. \tag{11}$$

Proof. (i) Recall that the characteristic polynomial $g(t)$ of G is square free. It is known (see e.g. [17]) that, in this case, there exists $A_1 \in M_d(k)$ such that

$$A_1^{-1}GA_1 = C(g).$$

Since $C(g_1) \oplus \cdots \oplus C(g_l)$ also has the same characteristic polynomial $g(t)$, there exists $A_2 \in M_d(k)$ such that

$$A_2^{-1}(C(g_1) \oplus \cdots \oplus C(g_l))A_2 = C(g).$$

Thus $P := (A_1 A_2^{-1}) \otimes I_r$ satisfies (10).

(ii) It is easy to see that $B := P_2^{-1}P_1$ satisfies

$$((C(g_1) \oplus \cdots \oplus C(g_l)) \otimes I_r)B = B((C(g_1) \oplus \cdots \oplus C(g_l)) \otimes I_r). \tag{12}$$

Divide B by $B = \begin{pmatrix} B_{11} & \cdots & B_{1l} \\ \vdots & \ddots & \vdots \\ B_{l1} & \cdots & B_{ll} \end{pmatrix}$, where B_{ab} is a $d_a r \times d_b r$ matrix. Then the equation (12) gives

$$(C(g_a) \otimes I_r)B_{ab} = B_{ab}(C(g_b) \otimes I_r), \qquad (1 \leq a, b \leq l). \tag{13}$$

We now describe the diagonalization of $C(g_a) \otimes I_r$ by

$$C(g_a) = D_a^{-1}(\alpha_1^{(a)} I_r \oplus \cdots \oplus \alpha_l^{(a)} I_r)D_a, \tag{14}$$

where $\alpha_1^{(a)}, \ldots, \alpha_l^{(a)}$ are elements in an extension field of k and D_a is an invertible $d_a \times d_a$ matrix over an extension field of k. Combining (13) and (14), we have

$$(\alpha_1^{(a)} I_r \oplus \cdots \oplus \alpha_{d_a}^{(a)} I_r)(D_a B_{ab} D_b) = (D_a B_{ab} D_b)(\alpha_1^{(b)} I_r \oplus \cdots \oplus \alpha_{d_b}^{(b)} I_r).$$

Since $g(t)$ is square free, the eigenvalues $\alpha_1^{(a)}, \ldots, \alpha_{d_a}^{(a)}, \alpha_1^{(b)}, \ldots, \alpha_{d_b}^{(b)}$ are distinct to each other if $a \neq b$. This means that $D_a B_{ab} D_b = 0$ and then $B_{ab} = 0$ for $a \neq b$. Thus (11) holds with $B_1 = B_{11}, \ldots, B_l = B_{ll}$. $\qquad\square$

The matrix P in (i) of Lemma 2 is computed as follows.

Algorithm 3

Input: Integers $d, r \geq 1$ and a matrix $H \in M_{dr}(k)$ given by

$$H = B^{-1}(G \otimes I_r)B$$

for some matrices $B \in M_{dr}(k)$ and $G \in M_d(k)$. Suppose that the characteristic polynomial $g(t) := \det(t \cdot I_d - G) = g_1(t) \cdots g_l(t)$ is square free.

Output: A matrix $P \in M_{dr}(k)$ such that

$$P^{-1}HP = (C(g_1) \oplus \cdots \oplus C(g_l)) \otimes I_r.$$

Step 1. Compute $g_1(H), g_2(H), \ldots, g_l(H)$.

Step 2. For $1 \leq u \leq l$, choose an $dr \times r$ matrix Y_u such that $g_u(H)Y_u = 0$.

Step 3. Put

$$\hat{P} := (Y_1, HY_1, H^2Y_1, \ldots, H^{d_1-1}Y_1, Y_2, HY_2, \ldots, H^{d_2-1}Y_2, \ldots,$$
$$\ldots, Y_l, HY_l, \ldots, H^{d_l-1}Y_l),$$

where $d_1 := \deg g_1(t), \ldots, d_l := \deg g_l(t)$. If $\hat{P}$ is invertible then $P = \hat{P}$. If not, go to Step 2 and choose other Y_u's.

Due to Lemma 2, there always exists such P. It is easy to check that $H\hat{P}$ and $\hat{P}((C(g_1) \oplus \cdots \oplus C(g_l)) \otimes I_r)$ coincides with each other.   □

Complexity. In Step 1, we compute at most d-th power of H. Then the complexity is $\ll d^4 r^3$. In Step 2, each Y_u is found in time $O(d^3 r^3)$. Then Step 2 is in time $\ll l \cdot d^3 r^3 \ll d^4 r^3$. In Step 3, we take at most d times multiplications between $dr \times dr$ matrix and $dr \times r$ matrix. Then the complexity of Step 3 is $\ll d^3 r^3$. We thus conclude that the total complexity of Algorithm 3 is $\ll d^4 r^3$.

4.4   For General S

In §4.2, we give Algorithm 2 to recover equivalent keys when S is a weak key given in the form (5). In this subsection, we study the case that S is randomly chosen and we propose algorithms to recover a matrix $\tilde{S} \in M_n(k)$ such that

$$S\tilde{S} = (Q \otimes I_r)(L_1 \oplus \cdots \oplus L_r)$$

for some $Q, L_1, \ldots, L_r \in M_r(k)$. Once such a matrix $\tilde{S}$ is recovered, the attacker can recover equivalent keys by Algorithm 2. We first give the following algorithm based on Algorithm 3 to recover $\tilde{S}$ partially.

―――――――― Algorithm 4 ――――――――

Input: Integers $r, d \geq 1$ and $m = r(r+1)/2$ matrices $F_{11}, \ldots, F_{rr} \in M_{dr}(k)$ given by
$$F_{ij} = S^t(G_{ij} \otimes I_r)S, \qquad (1 \leq i \leq j \leq r)$$
for some $G_{ij} \in SM_r(k)$ and an invertible $S \in M_{dr}(k)$.

Output: An integer $1 \leq l \leq r$, a set of positive integers $\{d_1, \ldots, d_l\}$ with $d_1 + \cdots + d_l = d$ and an invertible $P \in M_{dr}(k)$ satisfying

$$SP = (Q \otimes I_r)(S_1 \oplus \cdots \oplus S_l) \qquad (15)$$

for some invertible matrices $Q \in M_d(k)$, $S_1 \in M_{d_1 r}(k), \ldots, S_l \in M_{d_l r}(k)$.

Step 1. If $d = 1$, output $l = 1$, $d_1 = 1$ and $P = I_{dr}$. If not, go to the next step.

Step 2. Take two linear sums W_1, W_2 of $\{F_{ij}\}_{i,j}$ such that W_2 is invertible.

Step 3. Compute $W := W_2^{-1}W_1$ and its characteristic polynomial $w(t) := \det(t \cdot I_{dr} - W)$ of W.

Step 4. Factor $w(t)$ and let $w_0(t)$ be a polynomial of degree d such that $w(t) = w_0(t)^r$. If $w_0(t)$ is irreducible or has a square factor, go back to Step 2 and change W_1 and W_2. If not, let $w_0(t) = w_1(t) \cdots w_l(t)$ be the factorization of $w(t)$ and go to the next step.

Step 5. Find $P \in M_{dr}(k)$ such that

$$P^{-1}WP = (C(w_1) \oplus \cdots \oplus C(w_l)) \otimes I_r \qquad (16)$$

by Algorithm 3.

Step 6. Output $2 \leq l \leq r$, $d_1 := \deg w_1(t), \ldots, d_l := \deg w_l(t)$ and P.

Since both W_1, W_2 are in the form $S^t(G \otimes I_r)S$ for some $G \in M_r(k)$, the matrix W is given by

$$W = S^{-1}(W_0 \otimes I_r)S \qquad (17)$$

for some $W_0 \in M_d(k)$. Then there exists a polynomial $w_0(t)$ of degree d with $w(t) = w_0(t)^r$. It is known that the probability that a randomly chosen polynomial over k of degree d is irreducible is $d^{-1} + O(d^{-1}q^{-d/2})$ (see e.g. [19]) and the probability that a randomly chosen polynomial has a square factor is q^{-1} (see [25]). Then the success probability of Step 4 is considered to be about $1 - d^{-1} - O(q^{-1})$. Remark that we need more delicate discussions to conclude that the success probability is in this way since W_0 is a product of symmetric matrices and the probability that a randomly chosen such a matrix has a given characteristic polynomial is not necessarily uniformly distributed. Table 1 shows the probabilities by 1000 times experiments that the characteristic polynomials of such W_0's satisfy the conditions of Step 4 for $q = 31, 257$ and 6781. These

Table 1. Success probability (%) of Step 4 in Algorithm 4 by experiments

r	2	3	4	5	6	7	8	9	10	11	12
$q = 31$	51.3	65.3	71.9	76.7	81.0	82.4	82.6	86.4	87.1	87.8	88.3
$q = 257$	48.1	67.5	76.6	80.3	86.2	84.6	88.5	89.7	88.8	91.6	91.1
$q = 6781$	49.9	65.7	74.8	79.8	85.5	86.0	86.3	87.8	91.2	89.9	92.9

probabilities are close to $1 - d^{-1} - q^{-1}$ and we can consider that it is high enough in practice.

Due to (17), we have

$$P^{-1}WP = (SP)^{-1}(W_0 \otimes I_r)(SP).$$

Thus, thanks to (ii) of Lemma 3, we see that there exists $P \in M_{dr}(k)$ with (16) and such a matrix P satisfies the property (15). □

Complexity. Step 2 is for summations of matrices and checking invertibility, and Step 3 is for inversion/multiplication of matrices and calculating the characteristic polynomial. Then the complexities of Step 2 and 3 are $\ll d^3 r^3$. Step 4 is for factoring a polynomial. It is roughly estimated by $\ll d^3 r^3$ (see e.g. [15]). According to Table 1, we see that the probability that $w_0(t)$ passes Step 4 is $\geq 1/3$ in practice. Then Step 4 is repeated less than three times on average. Step 5 uses Algorithm 3 and then its complexity is $\ll d^4 r^3$. Thus we conclude that the total complexity of Algorithm 4 is $\ll d^4 r^3$.

Repeating Algorithm 4 in several times, we can recover $\tilde{S}$ as follows.

───────── Algorithm 5 ─────────

Input: An integer $r \geq 1$ and the public key $V_1(x) = \{x^t V_{ij} x\}$.

Output: An invertible matrix $\tilde{S} \in M_n(k)$ such that

$$S\tilde{S} = (Q \otimes I_r)(L_1 \oplus \cdots L_r)$$

for some invertible matrices $Q, L_1, \ldots, L_r \in M_r(k)$.

Step 1. Use Algorithm 4 for an input

$$\{r; d = r; V_{11}, \ldots, V_{rr}\}$$

and get its output

$$\{l; d_1, \ldots, d_l; P\}.$$

Let

$$F_{ij} := P^t V_{ij} P.$$

Step 2. If $l = r$ then output $\tilde{S} = P$ and finish. If not, go to the next step.

Step 3. Let $F_{ij}^{(1)} \in M_{rd_1}(k), \ldots, F_{ij}^{(l)} \in M_{rd_l}(k)$ be matrices given by

$$F_{ij} = \begin{pmatrix} F_{ij}^{(1)} & & * \\ & \ddots & \\ * & & F_{ij}^{(l)} \end{pmatrix}.$$

Use Algorithm 4 for inputs

$$\{r; d_1; F_{11}^{(1)}, \ldots, F_{rr}^{(1)}\}, \quad \ldots, \quad \{r; d_l; F_{11}^{(l)}, \ldots, F_{rr}^{(l)}\}$$

and get their outputs

$$\{l_1; d_{1,1}, \ldots, d_{1,l_1}; P_1\}, \quad \ldots, \quad \{l_l; d_{l,l}, \ldots, d_{l,l_l}; P_l\}.$$

Step 4. Replace l with $l_1 + \cdots + l_l$, $\{d_1, \ldots, d_l\}$ with $\{d_{1,1}, \ldots, d_{1,l_1}, d_{2,1}, \ldots, \ldots, d_{l,l_l}\}$, F_{ij} with $(P_1 \oplus \cdots \oplus P_l)^t F_{ij}(P_1 \oplus \cdots \oplus P_l)$ and P with $P(P_1 \oplus \cdots \oplus P_l)$. Go to Step 2.

Due to (16), the matrix P satisfies

$$SP = (Q \otimes I_r)(S_1 \oplus \cdots \oplus S_l)$$

for some $Q \in M_r(k), S_1 \in M_{rd_1}(k), \ldots, S_l \in M_{rd_l}(k)$. Then the matrix $F_{ij}^{(u)}$ $(1 \leq u \leq l)$ is given by

$$F_{ij}^{(u)} = S_u^t(G_{ij}^{(u)} \otimes I_r)S_u$$

for some $G_{ij}^{(u)} \in SM_{d_u}(k)$. Thus Algorithm 4 works for an input $\{r; d_u; F_{11}^{(u)}, \ldots, F_{rr}^{(u)}\}$.

If its output is $\{l_u; d_{u,1}, \ldots, d_{u,l_u}; P_u\}$, it holds

$$S_u P_u = (Q_u \otimes I_r)(S_{u,1} \oplus \cdots \oplus S_{u,l_u})$$

for some $Q_u \in M_{d_u}(k), S_{u,1} \in M_{rd_{u,1}}(k), \ldots, S_{u,l_u} \in M_{rd_{u,l_u}}(k)$, and then

$$\begin{aligned}
&(P_1 \oplus \cdots \oplus P_l)^t F_{ij}(P_1 \oplus \cdots \oplus P_l) \\
=&(S_1 P_1 \oplus \cdots \oplus S_l P_l)^t((Q^t G_{ij}Q) \otimes I_r)(S_1 P_1 \oplus \cdots \oplus S_l P_l) \\
=&(S_{1,1} \oplus \cdots \oplus S_{1,l_1} \oplus S_{2,1} \oplus \cdots \cdots \oplus S_{l,l_l})^t \\
&\cdot \left(((Q_1 \oplus \cdots \oplus Q_l)^t Q^t G_{ij}Q(Q_1 \oplus \cdots \oplus Q_l)) \otimes I_r\right) \\
&\cdot (S_{1,1} \oplus \cdots \oplus S_{1,l_1} \oplus S_{2,1} \oplus \cdots \cdots \oplus S_{l,l_l})
\end{aligned}$$

Thus, changing $l, \{d_1, \ldots, d_l\}, F_{ij}, P$ as in Step 4, we can take Step 2-4 again. Since $l_1 + \cdots + l_l$ is greater than l unless $l = r$ (equivalently $\{d_1, \ldots, d_l\} = \{1, \ldots, 1\}$), this algorithm finishes after at most $r - 1$ times repeats. $\square$

Complexity. Step 1 is Algorithm 4 for $d = r$. Then Step 1 is in time $\ll r^7$. In Step 3, we use Algorithm 4 for $d = d_1, \ldots, d = d_l$. Then the complexity of Step

3 is $\ll d_1^4 r^3 + \cdots d_l^4 r^3 \ll (d_1 + \cdots + d_l)^4 r^3 = r^7$. Since Step 2-4 are repeated at most $r - 1$ times, the total complexity of Algorithm 5 is $\ll r^8$.

4.5 Summary of the Proposed Attack

We summarize our attack on YTS in this subsection.

─────────────── Proposed attack on YTS ───────────────

Input: The public key $V_1(x)$ of YTS.

Output: Affine maps $S' : k^n \to k^n$ and $T' : k^m \to k^m$ such that

$$T'(V_1(S'(x))) = (U_1 \circ \phi^{-1})(x).$$

Step 1. Find vectors $\tilde{s} \in k^n$ and $\tilde{t} \in k^m$ such that $V_1(x + \tilde{s}) - \tilde{t}$ is homogeneous by Algorithm 1.

Step 2. Find $\tilde{S} \in M_n(k)$ such that

$$S_0 \tilde{S} = (Q \otimes I_r)(L_1 \oplus \cdots L_r)$$

for some $Q, L_1, \ldots, L_r \in M_r(k)$ by Algorithm 5.

Step 3. Find $S_1 \in M_n(k)$ and $T_1 \in M_m(k)$ such that

$$T_1(V_1(\hat{S}S_1(x + \tilde{s})) - \tilde{t}) = (U_1 \circ \phi)(x)$$

by Algorithm 2. Output affine maps S', T' given by

$$S'(x) = \tilde{S}S_1(x + \tilde{s}), \qquad T'(y) = T_1(y - \tilde{t}).$$

Note that Algorithm 4 is included in Algorithm 5 and Algorithm 3 is in Algorithm 4.

Summing up the complexities of Algorithm 1,5 and 2 estimated in §4.1, 4.4 and 4.2 respectively, we can claim that our attack recovers equivalent secret keys in time $O(r^8) = O(n^4)$. Once affine maps S', T' are recovered by our attack, the attacker can generate dummy signatures for arbitrary messages. Thus we conclude that the scheme YTS is insecure.

5 Experiments

We made experiments of our attack in 20 times for YTS of $(q, r) = (6781, 11)$, which has at least 140-bits security against the min-rank attack [30]. These experiments are carried out under Windows 7, Core-i7 2.67GHz and Magma ver.2.15-10 [4]. For every experiments, we succeeded to recover equivalent secret keys S', T' and to generate dummy signatures. The running times to recover equivalent secret keys are 240 $\sim$ 450 seconds. Note that, in our experiments, the running times mainly depend on how many times one tries Step 4 in Algorithm 4 for large d. We pick up the following three cases to show the relation between the running times and how $\{d_i\}$ changes in Algorithm 5.

Case 1

$$\{d_i\} : \{11\} \rightarrow \{1, 2, 8\} \rightarrow \underbrace{\{1, \ldots, 1, 2, 4\}}_{5} \rightarrow \underbrace{\{1, \ldots, 1, 3\}}_{8} \rightarrow \underbrace{\{1, \ldots, 1\}}_{11}.$$

Running time: about 301 seconds.

Case 2

$$\{d_i\} : \{11\} \rightarrow \{1, 1, 1, 2, 3, 3\} \rightarrow \underbrace{\{1, \ldots, 1, 2, 2\}}_{7} \rightarrow \underbrace{\{1, \ldots, 1\}}_{11}.$$

Running time: about 240 seconds.

Case 3

$$\{d_i\} : \{11\} \rightarrow \{2, 2, 3, 4\} \rightarrow \underbrace{\{1, \ldots, 1, 3\}}_{8} \rightarrow \underbrace{\{1, \ldots, 1, 2\}}_{9} \rightarrow \underbrace{\{1, \ldots, 1\}}_{11}.$$

Running time: about 443 seconds.

In Case 1 and Case 2, we passed Step 4 in Algorithm 4 for $d = 11$ at the first trial, but in Case 3, we passed it at the second trial. Then the running time of Case 3 is largest in these three cases. In Case 1, "8" appears in the second $\{d_i\}$. Then the running time of Case 1 is a little larger than that of Case 2.

The results of our experiments show that YTS of $(q, r) := (6781, 11)$ which had been considered to be secure in [30] can be broken in several minutes and then it is not secure at all.

6   Conclusion

In PQCrypto 2013, a new multivariate signature scheme YTS [30] was presented. Its signature generation is fast enough and its structure is quite different to other known MPKCs. Then YTS had been expected as a new idea to build secure and efficient MPKCs. However, the present paper shows that YTS is not secure at all. YTS must be repaired for practical use.

Acknowledgment. The author is partially supported by JSPS Grant-in-Aid for Young Scientists (B) no. 26800020. He would like to thank the shepherd and anonymous reviewers for giving helpful comments to improve this paper.

References

1. Akkar, M.L., Courtois, N., Goubin, L., Duteuil, R.: A fast and secure implementation of Sflash. In: Desmedt, Y.G. (ed.) PKC 2003. LNCS, vol. 2567, pp. 267–278. Springer, Heidelberg (2002)
2. Bardet, M., Faugère, J.C., Salvy, B., Yang, B.Y.: Asymptotic Expansion of the Degree of Regularity for Semi-Regular Systems of Equations. In: MEGA 2005 (2005)
3. Bettale, L., Faugère, J.C., Perret, L.: Solving Polynomial Systems over Finite Fields: Improved Analysis of the Hybrid Approach. In: ISSAC 2012, pp. 67–74 (2012)

4. Bosma, W., Cannon, J., Playoust, C.: The Magma algebra system. I. The user language. J. Symbolic Comput. 24, 235–265 (1997)
5. Chen, A.I.-T., Chen, M.-S., Chen, T.-R., Cheng, C.-M., Ding, J., Kuo, E.L.-H., Lee, F.Y.-S., Yang, B.-Y.: SSE Implementation of Multivariate PKCs on Modern x86 CPUs. In: Clavier, C., Gaj, K. (eds.) CHES 2009. LNCS, vol. 5747, pp. 33–48. Springer, Heidelberg (2009)
6. Coppersmith, D., Stern, J., Vaudenay, S.: Attacks on the birational permutation signature schemes. In: Stinson, D.R. (ed.) CRYPTO 1993. LNCS, vol. 773, pp. 435–443. Springer, Heidelberg (1994)
7. Ding, J., Schmidt, D.: Rainbow, a new multivariable polynomial signature scheme. In: Ioannidis, J., Keromytis, A.D., Yung, M. (eds.) ACNS 2005. LNCS, vol. 3531, pp. 164–175. Springer, Heidelberg (2005)
8. Dubois, V., Fouque, P.-A., Shamir, A., Stern, J.: Practical cryptanalysis of SFLASH. In: Menezes, A. (ed.) CRYPTO 2007. LNCS, vol. 4622, pp. 1–12. Springer, Heidelberg (2007)
9. Faugère, J.C.: A new efficient algorithm for computing Grobner bases (F_4). J. Pure and Applied Algebra 139, 61–88 (1999)
10. Faugère, J.-C., Joux, A.: Algebraic Cryptanalysis of Hidden Field Equation (HFE) Cryptosystems Using Gröbner Bases. In: Boneh, D. (ed.) CRYPTO 2003. LNCS, vol. 2729, pp. 44–60. Springer, Heidelberg (2003)
11. Faugère, J.-C., Levy-dit-Vehel, F., Perret, L.: Cryptanalysis of MinRank. In: Wagner, D. (ed.) CRYPTO 2008. LNCS, vol. 5157, pp. 280–296. Springer, Heidelberg (2008)
12. Fouque, P.-A., Granboulan, L., Stern, J.: Differential cryptanalysis for multivariate schemes. In: Cramer, R. (ed.) EUROCRYPT 2005. LNCS, vol. 3494, pp. 341–353. Springer, Heidelberg (2005)
13. Fouque, P.-A., Macario-Rat, G., Perret, L., Stern, J.: Total break of the ℓ-IC signature scheme. In: Cramer, R. (ed.) PKC 2008. LNCS, vol. 4939, pp. 1–17. Springer, Heidelberg (2008)
14. Garey, M.R., Johnson, D.S.: Computers and Intractability, A Guide to the Theory of NP-completeness. W.H. Freeman (1979)
15. Gathen, J., Panario, D.: Factoring Polynomials Over Finite Fields: A Survey, J. Symbolic Computation 31, 3–17 (2001)
16. Hasegawa, S., Kaneko, T.: An attacking method for a public-key cryptosystem based on the difficulty of solving a system of non-linear equations (in Japanese). In: Proc. 10th SITA, vol. JA5-3 (1987)
17. Horn, R., Johnson, C.: Matrix Analysis. Cambridge University Press, Cambridge (1985)
18. Jiang, X., Hu, L., Ding, J., Sun, S.: On the Kipnis-Shamir method solving the MinRank problem. In: Proc. IWSEC 2010 (Short Papers), pp. 1–13 (2010)
19. Lidl, R., Niederreiter, H.: Finite Fields. Addison-Wesley (1983)
20. Kipnis, A., Patarin, J., Goubin, L.: Unbalanced Oil and Vinegar Signature Schemes. In: Stern, J. (ed.) EUROCRYPT 1999. LNCS, vol. 1592, pp. 206–2006. Springer, Heidelberg (1999), extended in citeseer/231623.html, 2003-06-11
21. Kipnis, A., Shamir, A.: Cryptanalysis of the HFE public key cryptosystem by relinearization. In: Wiener, M. (ed.) CRYPTO 1999. LNCS, vol. 1666, pp. 19–30. Springer, Heidelberg (1999)
22. Kipnis, A., Shamir, A.: Cryptanalysis of the Oil & Vinegar Signature Scheme. In: Krawczyk, H. (ed.) CRYPTO 1998. LNCS, vol. 1462, pp. 257–267. Springer, Heidelberg (1998)

23. Marcus, M.: Finite Dimensional Multilinear Algebra, Pure and Applied Mathematics, vol. 23. Marcel Dekker, Inc., New York (1973)
24. Matsumoto, T., Imai, H.: Public quadratic polynomial-tuples for efficient signature-verification and message-encryption. In: Günther, C.G. (ed.) EUROCRYPT 1988. LNCS, vol. 330, pp. 419–453. Springer, Heidelberg (1988)
25. Morrison: Random polynomials over finite fields (1999)
26. Patarin, J.: Cryptanalysis of the Matsumoto and Imai Public Key Scheme of Eurocrypt '88. In: Coppersmith, D. (ed.) CRYPTO 1995. LNCS, vol. 963, pp. 248–261. Springer, Heidelberg (1995)
27. Patarin, J.: Hidden fields equations (HFE) and isomorphisms of polynomials (IP): Two new families of asymmetric algorithms. In: Maurer, U.M. (ed.) EUROCRYPT 1996. LNCS, vol. 1070, pp. 33–48. Springer, Heidelberg (1996)
28. Scharlau, W.: Quadratic and Hermitian Forms. Springer (1987)
29. Yang, B.-Y., Chen, J.-M.: Building secure tame-like multivariate public-key cryptosystems: The new TTS. In: Boyd, C., González Nieto, J.M. (eds.) ACISP 2005. LNCS, vol. 3574, pp. 518–531. Springer, Heidelberg (2005)
30. Yasuda, T., Takagi, T., Sakurai, K.: Multivariate signature scheme using quadratic forms. In: Gaborit, P. (ed.) PQCrypto 2013. LNCS, vol. 7932, pp. 243–258. Springer, Heidelberg (2013)

Attacking Code-Based Cryptosystems with Information Set Decoding Using Special-Purpose Hardware

Stefan Heyse, Ralf Zimmermann, and Christof Paar

Horst Görtz Institute for IT-Security (HGI)
Ruhr-University Bochum, Germany

Abstract. In this work, we describe the first implementation of an information set decoding (ISD) attack against code-based cryptosystems like McEliece or Niederreiter using special-purpose hardware. We show that in contrast to other ISD attacks due to Lee and Brickel [7], Leon [8], Stern [15] and recently [9] (May *et al.*) and [2] (Becket *et al.*), reconfigurable hardware requires a different implementation and optimization approach: Proposed time-memory trade-off techniques are not possible in the desired parameter sets. We thus derive new parameter sets from all steps involved in the ISD attack, taking a near cycle-accurate runtime estimation as well as the communication overhead into account.

Finally, we present the implementation of a hardware/software co-design – based on the Stern's attack –, evaluate it against the challenges from the Wild-McEliece website[5], discuss its shortcomings and possible enhancements.

Keywords: Special-purpose hardware, Implementation, McEliece, Niederreiter, Challenge, Information Set Decoding.

1 Introduction

The majority of the currently deployed asymmetric cryptosystems work on the basis of either the discrete logarithm or the integer factorization problem as the underlying mathematical problem. Shor's Algorithm [14] in combinination with upcoming advances in quantum computing pose a severe threat to these primitives.

The McEliece cryptosystem – introduced by McEliece in 1978 [10] – is one of the alternative code-based cryptosystems unaffected by the known weaknesses against quantum computers. Like most other systems, its key size needs to be doubled to withstand Grovers algorithms [6,12]. The same holds for Niederreiter's variant [11], proposed in 1986. The best know attacks on these promising code-based cryptosystems are decoding-attacks based on information set decoding (ISD) [13,7,8,15,9,2].

So far, all proposed ISD-variants and the single public implementation we are aware of [3] optimize the parameters for CPU-based software implementations. As code-based systems mature over time, it is important to know if and how

M. Mosca (Ed.): PQCrypto 2014, LNCS 8772, pp. 126–141, 2014.

these attacks scale when using not only CPUs, but incorporating also dedicated hardware accelerators. This allows a more realistic estimation of the true attacking costs and attack efficiency than the analysis of an algorithm's asymptotic behaviour.

The base field of most proposed code-based systems is $GF(2)$, which is favourable for hardware implementations. The authors of [4] published a wide range of challenges [5] – including binary codes, which we target in this work with a hardware attack.

Contribution of This Work: In this paper, we describe the first hardware accelerated ISD-attack using special-purpose hardware. Starting with Stern's variant [15], analyze the possibilities and restrictions of dedicated hardware, present a way of mapping collision search techniques to hardware and derive parameter sets for binary codes. We also present a nearly cycle-accurate runtime estimation targeting different FPGA families for a wide range of parameter sets from [5] and discuss the drawbacks of the attack and possible ways to build upon these results.

Outline: In Section 2, we give the necessary background regarding code-based cryptosystems and describe the basic ISD-variants. We explain the different optimization strategies and hardware restrictions in Section 3. Then, we present our implementation of the hardware optimized attack in Section 4 and finish with a discussion of the results and conclusions in Sections 5 and 6.

2 Background

In this section, we briefly discuss the background required for the remainder of this work. We start with a very short introduction into code-base cryptography including McEliece, Niederreiter and Information Set Decoding, followed by a short overview on reprogrammable hardware.

2.1 Code-Based Cryptography

Definition 1. *Let $\mathbb{F}_q$ denote a finite field of q elements and $\mathbb{F}_q^n$ a vector space of n tuples over $\mathbb{F}_q$. An [n,k]-linear code $\mathcal{C}$ is a k-dimensional vector subspace of $\mathbb{F}_q^n$. The vectors $(a_1, a_2, \ldots, a_{q^k}) \in \mathcal{C}$ are called* codewords *of $\mathcal{C}$.*

Definition 2. *The* Hamming *distance $d(x, y)$ between two vectors $x, y \in \mathbb{F}_q^n$ is defined to be the number of positions at which corresponding symbols x_i, y_i, $\forall 1 \leq i \leq n$ are different. The* Hamming *weight $wt(x)$ of a vector $x \in \mathbb{F}_q^n$ is defined as Hamming distance $d(x, 0)$ between x and the zero-vector.*

Definition 3. *A matrix $G \in \mathbb{F}_q^{k \times n}$ is called* generator *matrix for an [n,k]-code $\mathcal{C}$ if its rows form a basis for $\mathcal{C}$ such that $\mathcal{C} = \{x \cdot G \mid x \in \mathbb{F}_q^k\}$. In general there are many generator matrices for a code. An* information set *of $\mathcal{C}$ is a set of coordinates corresponding to any k linearly independent columns of G while the remaining $n - k$ columns of G form the* redundancy set *of $\mathcal{C}$.*

If G is of the form $[I_k|Q]$, where I_k is the $k \times k$ identity matrix, then the first k columns of G form an information set for $\mathcal{C}$. Such a generator matrix G is said to be in standard (systematic) form.

Definition 4. *For any [n,k]-code $\mathcal{C}$ there exists a matrix $H \in \mathbb{F}_q^{n-k \times n}$ with $(n-k)$ independent rows such that $\mathcal{C} = \{y \in \mathbb{F}_q^n \mid H \cdot y^T = 0\}$. Such a matrix H is called* parity-check matrix *for $\mathcal{C}$. In general, there are several possible parity-check matrices for $\mathcal{C}$.*

McEliece. The secret key of the McEliece cryptosystem consists of a linear code $\mathcal{C}$ over $\mathbb{F}_q$ of length n and dimension k capable of correction w errors. A *generator matrix G*, an $n \times n$ permutation P and an invertible $k \times k$ matrix S are randomly generated and form the secret key. The public key consists of the $k \times n$ matrix $\hat{G} = SGP$ and the error weight w. A message m of length k is encrypted as $y = m\hat{G} + e$, where e has Hamming weight w. The decryption works by computing $yP^{-1} = mSG + eP^{-1}$ and using a decoding algorithm for $\mathcal{C}$ to find mS and finally m.

Niederreiter. The secret key of the Niederreiter cryptosystem consists of a linear code $\mathcal{C}$ over $\mathbb{F}_q$ of length n and dimension k capable of correction w errors. A *parity check matrix H*, an $n \times n$ permutation P and an invertible $n - k \times n - k$ matrix S are randomly generated and form the secret key. The public key is the $n \times n - k$ matrix $\hat{H} = SHP$ and the error weight w. To encrypt, the message m of length n and Hamming weight w is encrypted as $y = \hat{H}m^{\mathrm{T}}$. To decrypt, compute $S^{-1}y = HPm^{\mathrm{T}}$ and use a decoding algorithm for $\mathcal{C}$ to find Pm^{T} and finally m.

Information Set Decoding. Attacks based on information set decoding were introduced by Prange in [13]. They are the best known algorithms, which do not rely on any specific structure in the code, which is the case for code-based cryptography, i.e., an attacker deals with a random-looking code without a known structure. In its simplest form, an attacker tries to find a subset of generator matrix columns that is error-free and where the submatrix composed by this subset is invertible. The message can then be recovered by multiplying the codeword by the inverse of this submatrix. Several improvements of the attack were published, including [7] (Lee and Brickel), [8] (Leon), [15] (Stern) and recently [9] (May et al.) and [2] (Becket et al.).

The latest and – to the best of our knowledge – only publicly available implementation is [3]. The authors present an improved attack based on Stern's variant that broke the originally proposed parameters (a binary (1024,524) Goppa code with 50 errors added) of the McEliece system. The attack ran for 1400 days on a single 2.4 GHz Core2 Quad CPU or 7 days on a cluster of 200 CPUs.

We now give a short introduction into the classical ISD-variants based on [12]. Given a word $y = c + e$ with $c \in \mathcal{C}$, the basic idea is to find a word e with Hamming weight of $e \leq w$. The ISD-algorithms differ in the assumption on the distribution of 1s in e. If a given matrix G does not successfully find a solution,

---

Algorithm 1. Information set decoding for parameter p

Input: $k \times n$ matrix G, Integer w
Output: a non-zero codeword c of weight $\leq w$
1: **repeat**
2:    pick a $n \times n$ permutation P.
3:    compute $G' = UGP = (ID|R)$ (w.l.o.g we assume the first k positions from an information set).
4:    compute all the sums s of $\leq p$ rows of G'
5: **until** Hamming weight of $s \leq w$
6: **return** s

Table 1. Weight profile of the codewords searched for by the different algorithms. Numbers in boxes are Hamming weight of the tuples. Derived from [12].

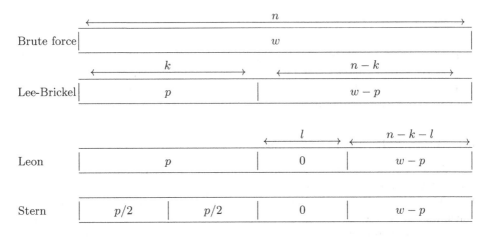

the matrix is randomized, swapping columns and converting the result back into reduced row-echelon form by Gauss-Jordan elimination. As each of these column swaps also transforms the positions of the error vector e, there is a chance that it now matches the assumed distribution. The trade-off is between the success probability of one iteration of Algorithm 1 (or, in other words, the number of required randomizations) and the cost of a single iteration of this algorithm. Stern's algorithm is special as it allows a collision search in the two $p/2$ sized windows by a birthday attack technique.

The latest improvements from [9] and [2] extend this technique, but are out of scope of this work because they introduce large tables highly unsuitable for hardware implementations. For the sake of completeness, Table 1 on page 4 in [9] shows the time and memory complexities of the different ISD-variants.

2.2   Reprogrammable Hardware

Compared to general-purpose CPUs (and also GPUs as a many-core architecture), application-specific integrated circuits (ASICs) – chips designed for exactly one task – are much more efficient in terms of area- and power consumption. There are none of the architectural limitations like fixed register-width or data-busses: you have full control over the design and data paths, e. g., if you need to store matrix columns of 139 bits, you may operate natively on them. The full power and potential of ASICs comes at a price: once produces, the chip can be used for one tasks only, e. g., reusing it for 141-bit columns is not possible.

An effort to balance the two approaches leads to reconfigurable hardware, i. e., Field-Programmable Gate Arrays (FPGAs), allowing rapid hardware prototyping at the cost of a reconfiguration overhead. These chips provide a large number of lookup-tables (LUTs) and storage elements (FF) and combine them with dedicated hardware cores, e. g., fast dual-port memory or digital signal processing (DSP) cores. The designer builds upon these resources and creates a chip with an application-specific architecture, but can reprogram it on demand.

3   Modified Hardware Attack

In this section, we will describe the modified algorithms for the hardware-based attack. We will highlight the main differences to a pure software attack, the limitations posed by the hardware and the solutions to circumvent these restrictions. We will end with the parameters generated for selected challenges.

3.1   From Software to Hardware

As this is the first hardware implementation of the attacks, we need to figure out the best basis and tweak the parameters for the underlying hardware platforms. It is important to keep in mind that we are mostly restricted by the memory consumption of the matrices and that this is a hard limitation on FPGAs. Thus, we cannot precompute collision tables of several gigabytes to speed up the attack.

We evaluated the choices of parameters of the attacks for hardware suitability. As starting point, we chose Stern's ISD variant without the requirement of splitting the p-sized windows into two equal sized halves. The main problem we identified in this process were the l-bit collision-search proposed in [15] and the different choices for splitting p into p_1 and p_2 to gain the most from this search. To take advantage of the birthday-like attack strategy, while at the same time reducing memory consumption to a hardware friendly level, we developed a hash-table like memory structure called collision memory ($CMEM$). Please note that this construction fixes $p_1 = 1$ and thus $p_2 = p - 1$.

Before we explain the different hardware modules required for an ISD-attack, we need to define the parts of the matrix we use in each step. Figure 1 shows the full matrix including the identity part and the notation we use: The last k_2 columns of the matrix of $n - k$ bits each form the submatrix HK_2, where the enumerator computes all sums of $p_2 = p - 1$ columns. In the middle, k_1 columns form HK_1 of $n - k - l$ bits each. $CMEM$ contains all information about the integer representation of the remaining lower l bits of these k_1 columns.

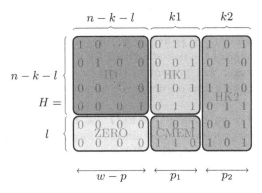

Fig. 1. Splitting of the public key into memory segments. Values under the arrows denote the assumed Hamming weight distribution of the error e.

3.2   Enumerator

The most expensive step in the attacks is the computation of the $\binom{k_2}{p_2}$ sums of p_2 columns each. As $n - k$ bits per column usually do not match the register sizes of CPUs [3], we may need even more operations for each addition to update all registers involved. To reduce the costs, only the sum of the lower l bits is computed. In case of a collision with the p_1-sums from the first part of the columns, more bits are used for the sum and checked for the final Hamming weight, where usually early-abort techniques reduce the number of times the full check is done.

Please note that – as long as we store the full matrix on the FPGA – we can perform the full $n - k$ bit addition of two columns in one clock cycle in hardware, regardless of the parameters. This allows us to perform the full iteration on the FPGA without further post-computations, e. g., to sum up remaining bits.

This has another advantage: instead of computing the sums from scratch for each intermediate step, we can modify the previous sum (of p_2 columns) by utilizing a gray-code approach: we add one new column and remove one old column in one step. That way, we keep the number of p_2 columns in the sum constant and minimize the effort - given that this enumeration process is fast enough.

3.3   Collision Search

As we outlined before, collision search is tricky in hardware. The approach of a large precomputed memory is not possible within the restricted device. We use a $CMEM$ construction, consisting of of $2^l \times (\lceil \log_2(k_1) \rceil + 1)$ bits, which prepares the relevant information for fast access in hardware: for a given l-bit integer, we can find out (a) if at least one of the k_1 columns contains this bit sequence in the last l positions, (b) how many matches exist and (c) the position in the memory of these columns – all in one clock cycle.

In order to remove additional wait cycles and minimize the memory consumption, we generate the part denoted as $CMEM$ in Figure 1 in two steps during the matrix generation. First, we sort the k_1 columns according to the integer representation of the last l bits. Please note that the cost for the column swaps are negligible, as the matrix is stored in column representation. Afterwards, we generate the 2^l elements of the new structure: for index i, the MSB of $CMEM[i]$ is set only if the integer was present in the k_1 columns. The remaining l bits contain the position of its first occurrence.

Example: In the following example, we use $l = 3, k_1 = 6$. Each line represents a step in the generation process: (1) contains the integer representation of the last $l = 3$ bits of the $k_1 = 6$ columns, while (2) consists of the sorted column list and (2) of the (larger) memory content of $CMEM$.

```
1 [   0,   1,   0,   4,   3,   6 ]
2 [   0,   0,   1,   3,   4,   6 ]
3 [ 1|0, 1|2, 0|3, 1|3, 1|4, 0|5, 1|5, 0|6 ]
```

When checking for a collision with i, we simply check the MSB of $CMEM[i]$. As we are able to use two ports simultaneously, we can directly derive the number of collisions from the subtraction of $CMEM[i + 1] - CMEM[i]$ and only need one multiplexer for the special case $i = k_1 - 1$. The base address is provided by the last l bits of $CMEM[i]$.

3.4   Determining Hamming Weight

For all collisions found by the collision search, a column from HK_1 is added to the current sum computed from the HK_2 columns and the Hamming weight of the result is checked against $w - p$.

The Hamming weight check in hardware needs to be a fully pipelined adder-tree, automatically generated for the target FPGA: the size of the internal look-up tables are used as a parameter during this process. More recent FPGAs with 6-input LUTs can benefit from this.

4   Implementation

In this section, we will present our hardware-implementation of the modified attack and start from a algorithmic description of the attack before we describe the software and hardware parts in more detail.

The hardware design was carefully build to work on different types of FPGAs – in this case the Xilinx Spartan-3, Spartan-6 and Virtex-6 Familiy – and integrate well into the RIVYERA FPGA cluster. Algorithm 2 describes the combination of the FPGA and the host-CPU for pre- and post-processing: the iteration on the FPGAs is computed in parallel to the generation step (CPU) and the CPU may utilize multiple parallel cores for the matrix randomization.

Algorithm 2. Modified HW/SW algorithm

Input: Challenge Parameters and the optimal attack configuration
    Challenge Parameters: n, k, w, public key matrix, ciphertext
    Attack Parameters: FPGA bitstream, #FPGAs, #cores, p, l, k_1
Output: Valid solution to the challenge
 1: Program all available FPGAs with the provided bitstream
 2: **repeat**
 3:    **for** all cores **do**
 4:       Randomize matrix
 5:       Generate collision memory
 6:       Store $HK_1, HK_2, CMEM$ in datastream
 7:       Store permutation
 8:    **end for**
 9:    Evaluate FPGA success flag of previous iteration
10:    **if** success **then**
11:       Read columns of successful FPGA
12:    **else**
13:       Burst-Transfer datastream to FPGAs
14:       *FPGAs: compute iteration on all datasets in parallel*
15:    **end if**
16: **until** success flag is set
17: Recover solution on challenge

4.1 Software Part

As mentioned in Section 3, the complete randomization step is done in software. After the challenge file and actual attack parameter are read in, as many data sets as cores available are generated. The data sets are generated using the OpenMP library in parallel. Each thread takes the original public key matrix and processes as described in Algorithm 3.

Algorithm 3. Randomization Step

Input: Public key matrix, r=#columns to swap
Output: Randomized matrix in reduced row echelon form
 1: **while** less than r columns swapped **do**
 2:    Choose a column i from the identity part at random
 3:    Choose a random column j from the redundant part, but ensure that the bit at position (i, j) is one.
 4:    Swap columns i and j
 5:    Eliminate by optimized Gauss-Jordan
 6: **end while**
 7: Construct the collision memory($CMEM$)
 8: Store HK_1, HK_2 and $CMEM$ in memory.

As the FPGA expects the data in columns, the matrix is also organized in columns in memory. Thus, pointer swaps reflect the column swaps. The Gauss-Jordan elimination is optimized taking advantage of the following facts: Only one column in the identity part has changed and the pivot bit in this column is one by definition, therefore only this column is important during elimination. Thus, only the $k + l$ rightmost bits of each row (which are in the redundant part) must be added to other rows, as the leftmost $n - k - l$ bits (except the pivot column) remain unchanged.

The performed column swaps during randomization and $CMEM$ construction are stored in a separate memory. This is necessary to recover the actual matrix the successful FPGA core was working on, as the randomized matrices are not stored. Once an FPGA sends back the $p1 = 1$ column from $CMEM$ and the $p2$ columns from the enumerator, the low weight word is recomputed locally after applying all previous permutations to the original matrix, followed by a Gauss-Jordan elimination. In a final step, the remaining $w - p$ 1s in the plaintext are recovered.

4.2   Hardware Part

As it is not possible to generate an optimized design inherently suitable for all matrices, the ISD attack requires a flexible hardware design, where we traded some hand-optimizations for a more generic design. This allows us to generate custom configurations for every parameter set with a close to optimal configuration in terms of area utilization and the number of parallel cores. These parameters are included into the source code as a configuration package and define constants used throughout the design. Thus, we can adjust the parameters very easily and automatically create valid bitstreams for the challenges.

The basic layout is the same for all FPGAs types. We use a fast interface to read incoming data, distribute it to multiple ISD-cores and initialize the local memory cores. After this initialization, all ISD-cores compute the iteration steps in parallel.

The iteration step consists of three major parts: the gray-code enumeration, the collision search and the Hamming weight computation.

Algorithm 4 describes the iteration process of each core on the FPGA. First, the different memories are initialized from the transferred data. Afterwards, the columns from the enumeration step provide the intermediate sum, which is used in the collision check step. If a collision is found on the lower l bits, the corresponding column from HK_1 is added to the sum and the Hamming weight is computed.

Enumeration Step. For the enumeration process, we implemented a generic, optimized, constant-weight gray-code enumerator as described in Section 3.2. It starts with the initial state of $[0, 1, \ldots, p_2 - 1]$ and keeps track of the columns used to build the current column-sum. Aside from the internal state necessary to recover the solutions, it provides the memory core with two addresses to modify the sum. With this setup, we can compute a new valid sum of p_2 columns in exactly one clock cycle. The timing is independent of the parameters, even though the area consumption is determined by the p_2 registers of $\log_2 k_2$ bits. The enumerator is automatically adjusted to these parameters and always provides the optimal implementation for the given FPGA and Challenge.

Algorithm 4. Iteration Step in Hardware

Input: Memory content for $HK_1, HK_2, CMEM$, Parameters $n, k, l, w, p_2, k_1, k_2$
Output: On success: 1 column index from HK_1, p_2 column indices from HK_2
 1: Initialize HK_1: ($k_1 \times (n - k - l)$)-bit memory (BRAM)
 2: Initialize HK_2: ($k_2 \times (n - k)$)-bit memory (BRAM)
 3: Initialize $CMEM$: ($2^l \times (\lceil \log_2 k_1 \rceil + 1)$)-bit memory (BRAM or LUT)
 4: **while** (not enumeration_done) **and** (not successful) **do**
 5:     Enumerate columns in HK_2 and update **sum**
 6:     **for** all collisions of **sum** (last l-bit) in $CMEM$ **do**
 7:         Update **sum** (upper part) with column from HK_1
 8:         **if** HammingWeight(sum) $= w$ **then**
 9:             Set success flag and column indices
10:             Set done flag and terminate
11:         **end if**
12:     **end for**
13: **end while**

Collision Search. After the enumerator provides a sum of p_2 columns from HK_2, we check the lower l bits for collisions with $CMEM$ for valid candidates. Due to the memory restrictions on FPGAs, we keep the parameter l smaller than in software-oriented attacks. If storage in distributed memory (in constrast to a BRAM memory core) requires only small area, we automatically evaluate if an additional core may be placed when using LUTs instead of BRAMs and configure the design accordingly.

The additional logic surrounding the memory triggers the Hamming weight check in case a match was found and provides the column addresses to access HK_1.

Hamming Weight Computation. The final part of the implementation is the computation of the Hamming weight. To speed up the process at a minimal delay, we split the resulting $(n - k - l)$-bit word into an adder-tree of depth $log_2(n - k - l) - 1$ and compute the Hamming weight of the different parts in parallel. These intermediate results are merged afterwards with a delay equal to the depth of the tree. The circuit is automatically generated from the parameters and uses multiple registers as pipeline steps, i.e., we can start a new Hamming weight computation in each clock cycle.

4.3   Pipeline and Routing

To maximize the effect of the hardware attack, the design is build as a fully pipelined implementation: All modules work independently and store the intermediate values in registers.

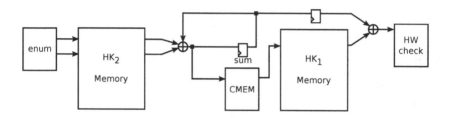

Fig. 2. Overview of the different modules inside one iteration core

Figure 2 illustrates this pipeline structure. Every memory provides an implicit stage and the HW check is automatically pipelined. In addition, the figure shows that the single most important resource for the attack is the on-chip memory.

Due to the large amount of free area in terms of logic, i.e., not memory hardcores, the routing is usually unproblematic. In theory, we could also use parts of the free logic resources as memory and add to the dedicated memory cores. This complicates the automated generation process and does not guarantee a successful build for all parameters. Thus, we did not utilize these resources and used them to relax the routing process.

5   Results

In this section, we present the results of our analysis. The hardware results are based on Xilinx ISE Foundation 14 for synthesis and place and route. We compiled the software part using GCC 4.1.2[1] and the OpenMP library for multithreading and ran the tests on the i7 CPU integrated in the RIVYERA cluster.

5.1   Runtime Analysis

Based on the partition of the public key matrix (see Figure 1) and the distribution of errors necessary for a successful attack, the number of expected iterations is

$$\#it = \left\lceil \frac{\binom{n}{w}}{\binom{k_1}{p_1} \times \binom{k_2}{p_2} \times \binom{n-k-l}{w-p}} \right\rceil.$$

---

[1] Please note that the version is due to the LTS system and mentioned only for completeness. While better compiler optimizations may increase software speed, the speed-up for the overall hardware attack is negligible.

As the hardware layout is very straight-forward and is fully pipelined, we can determine the amount of cycles per iteration as

$$\#c = c_{enum} + c_{pipe} + c_{popcount} + c_{collision}$$

with

$$
\begin{aligned}
c_{enum} &= \binom{k_2}{p_2} \\
c_{pipe} &= 4 \\
c_{popcount} &= \log_2 (n - k - l) - 1 \\
c_{collision} &= \frac{c_{enum}}{2^l} \times \frac{1}{\#mcols}
\end{aligned}
$$

All operations of the iteration are computed in exactly one clock cycle. After a constant pipeline delay, every clock cycle generates an iteration result. Thus, we have an almost equal running time for all iterations with one exception: The only part, which may vary from iteration to iteration is the collision search. If we find more than one candidate using $CMEM$, we need to process them before continuing with the next enumeration step. Thus, we need to add the number of multiple column candidates to the total number of clock cycles.

We can estimate the expected number of collisions inside $CMEM$ - which is the amount of multiple column candidates to test - as

$$\#mcols = k_1 \times (1 - (1 - \frac{1}{2^l})^{k_1 - 1}).$$

5.2   Optimal Parameters

We will now derive the optimal parameter sets for selected challenges taken from [5] and provide the expected number of iterations on different FPGA families: the Xilinx Spartan-3, Spartan-6 and Virtex-6. The first two are integrated into the RIVYERA framework, which features 128 Spartan-3 5000 (RIVYERA-S3) and 64 Spartan-6 LX150 (RIVYERA-S6) FPGAs, respectively. During the tests with the RIVYERA framework we noticed that the transfer time of the randomized data exceeds the generation time.

To measure the impact of the transfer speed on the overall performance, we added a single Virtex-6 LX240T evaluation board offering PCIe interface including DMA transfer. The PCIe engine based on [16,1,17,18] is, depending on the data block size, capable of transferring at 0.014Mbps, 181Mbps, 792Mbps, 1412Mbps, 2791Mbps for block sizes of 128 byte, 100 Kbyte, 500 Kbyte, 1 Mbyte, 4 Mbyte, respectively.[2]

---

[2] As only a single device was available and a completely different interface must be used, the actual attack is not performed using these device.

We use a Sage script to generate the optimal parameters for all challenge and provide the script and the output online[3]. Table 4 in the Appendix contains the results for the selected challenges. Given the bottleneck of the data transfer time, the script optimizes the parameters l, p and k_1 in such a way that the iteration step requires approximately as much time as transferring the data for all cores. The number of cores per FPGA depends on the challenge and the available memory and takes the area and memory consumption of the data transfer interface into account.

As the challenges from [5] are sorted according to there public key size, we selected four challenges as examples. These are the binary field challenges with public key sizes of 5Kbyte, 20KByte, 62Kbyte and 168Kbyte. The last two correspond roughly to 80 and 128 bit symmetric security, respectively[3]. All solved challenges will be send to the authors of [5] and hopefully published on their site after verification. The related parameters of the challenges C_1 to C_4 are given in Table 2 and the implementation related data in Table 3.

Table 2. Parameters of C_1 to C_4

	C_1	C_2	C_3	C_4
n	414	848	1572	2752
k	270	558	1132	2104
w	16	29	40	54

Table 3. HW settings of $C_1 to C_4$

	RIV-S3	RIV-S6	V6 LX240T
clk (MHz)	75	125	250
data rate (Mbps)	240	640	up to 2791

5.3 Discussion

We also implemented the complete algorithm in software to generate testvectors and to compare the runtime of the FPGA version against the CPU implementation – for small challenges – on a CPU cluster. As the algorithm operates on the full columns, the software version was extremely slow compared to both the FPGA implementation and other software implementations. Usually, only small parts of the columns (fitting into native register sizes) are added up before the collision search. Afterwards – for the candidates found in the previous step – more the sum on more register-sized parts is updates and the Hamming weight is checked, making additional use of early-abort techniques to increase the speed as well. This makes a comparison of the algorithm difficult, as neither the parameters nor the assumptions on the distribution target asymptotic behaviour.

The FPGA implementation is very fast on small challenges. Please note that one hardware iteration includes the iteration step for all cores on all FPGAs in parallel, as the parameters take the full transfer time into account. Nevertheless, for larger challenges, the implementation performs less well: the memory requirements for the matrices then reduce the number of parallel cores drastically and thus remove the advantage of the dedicated hardware. This makes a

---

[3] http://fs.crypto.rub.de/isd

software attack with a large amount of memory the better choice, as it also has the advantage of larger collision tables.

To circumvent these problems, we can also implement trade-offs in hardware as described for software implementations. To increase the number of parallel cores, we can store smaller parts of the columns, which fit the BRAM cores better and utilize the early-abort techniques. The drawback is that this approach further increases the I/O communication, as a post-processing step per iteration is necessary to check all candidates off-chip. As the communication was the bottleneck in our implementation, we did not implement this approach.

A different approach and a way to minimize the I/O communication up the process might be to generate the randomization on-chip. While the column swaps are easy to implement in one clock cycle, we need more algorithms on the device: We need both a pseudo-random number generator to identify the columns to swap and also a dedicated Gauss-Jordan elimination and also add control logic to the design so that we may reuse them by sequentially updating the cores. In addition, this approach will enforce the storage of the full matrix on the FPGA.

These restrictions and drawbacks lead to another interesting platform for ISD attacks: recent GPUs combine a large amount of parallel cores at high clock frequency and large memory. Even though the memory structure imposes restrictions, an optimized GPU implementation may prove superior to both CPUs and FPGAs. This is especially true when attacking non-binary codes, which are not optimal for FPGAs.

6 Conclusions

We presented the first hardware implementation of ISD-attacks on binary Wild McEliece challenges. Our results show that it is possible to create optimized hardware, mapping the ideas from previously available software approaches into the hardware domain and derived hardware-optimized parameters. We verified the results first in simulation and ran an unoptimized version on the FPGA cluster.

While software attacks benefit from the huge amount of available memory, CPUs are not inherently suited for the underlying operations, e. g., as the columns exceed the register sizes or as the precomputed lookup tables exceed the CPU cache. Nevertheless, a lot of effort was already invested into improvements of these software attacks.

We showed that the strength of a fully pipelined hardware implementation - the computation of all operations including memory access per iteration in exactly one clock cycle - does not lead to the expected massive parallelism, e. g., as hardware clusters have done in case of DES, and does not weaken the security of code-based cryptography dramatically: the benefit is restricted not only by the data bus latency but - far more importantly - by the memory requirements of the attacks.

These results should be considered as a proof-of-concept and the basis for upcoming hardware/software attacks trying different implementation approaches and evaluating other algorithmic choices. We discussed the benefits and draw-backs of potential techniques for on-chip implementation of the ISD-attacks and stressed the need of an optimized GPU implementation for a better security analysis.

References

1. Ayer, J.J.: Using the Memory Endpoint Test Driver (MET) with the Programmed Input/Output Example Design for PCI Express Endpoint Cores. Xilinx, xapp1022 v2.0 edition (November 2009)
2. Becker, A., Joux, A., May, A., Meurer, A.: Decoding Random Binary Linear Codes in $2^n/20$: How $1 + 1 = 0$ Improves Information Set Decoding. In: Pointcheval, D., Johansson, T. (eds.) EUROCRYPT 2012. LNCS, vol. 7237, pp. 520–536. Springer, Heidelberg (2012)
3. Bernstein, D.J., Lange, T., Peters, C.: Attacking and Defending the McEliece Cryptosystem. In: Buchmann, J., Ding, J. (eds.) PQCrypto 2008. LNCS, vol. 5299, pp. 31–46. Springer, Heidelberg (2008)
4. Bernstein, D.J., Lange, T., Peters, C.: Wild mcEliece. In: Biryukov, A., Gong, G., Stinson, D.R. (eds.) SAC 2010. LNCS, vol. 6544, pp. 143–158. Springer, Heidelberg (2011)
5. Bernstein, D.J., Lange, T., Peters, C.: Cryptanalytic challenges for wild McEliece (June 2013), http://pqcrypto.org/wild-challenges.html
6. Hallgren, S., Vollmer, U.: Quantum Computing. In: Post-Quantum Cryptography, pp. 15–34 (2008)
7. Lee, P.J., Brickell, E.F.: An Observation on the Security of McEliece's Public-Key Cryptosystem. In: Günther, C.G. (ed.) EUROCRYPT 1988. LNCS, vol. 330, pp. 275–280. Springer, Heidelberg (1988)
8. Leon, J.S.: A Probabilistic Algorithm for Computing Minimum Weights of Large Error-correcting Codes. IEEE Transactions on Information Theory 34(5), 1354–1359 (1988)
9. May, A., Meurer, A., Thomae, E.: Decoding Random Linear Codes in $\mathcal{O}(2^{0.054n})$. In: Lee, D.H., Wang, X. (eds.) ASIACRYPT 2011. LNCS, vol. 7073, pp. 107–124. Springer, Heidelberg (2011)
10. McEliece, R.J.: A Public-key Cryptosystem Based on Algebraic Coding Theory. Technical report, Jet Propulsion Lab Deep Space Network Progress report (1978)
11. Niederreiter, H.: Knapsack-type Cryptosystems and Algebraic Coding Theory. Problems Control Inform. Theory/Problemy Upravlen. Teor. Inform. 15(2), 159–166 (1986)
12. Overbeck, R., Sendrier, N.: Code-based Cryptogrpahy. In: Post-Quantum Cryptography, pp. 95–145 (2008)
13. Prange, E.: The Use of Information Sets in Decoding Cyclic Codes. IRE Transactions on Information Theory 8(5), 5–9 (1962)
14. Shor, P.W.: Polynomial-time algorithms for prime factorization and discrete logarithms on a quantum computer. SIAM J. Comput. 26(5), 1484–1509 (1997)
15. Stern, J.: A Method for Finding Codewords of Small Weight. In: Cohen, G., Wolfmann, J. (eds.) Coding Theory 1988. LNCS, vol. 388, pp. 106–113. Springer, Heidelberg (1989)
16. Wiltgen, J., Ayer, J.: Bus Master DMA Performance Demonstration Reference Design for the Xilinx Endpoint PCI Express Solutions. Xilinx, xapp1052 edition (September 2010)

17. Xilinx. Bus Master DMA Performance Demonstration Reference Design for the Xilinx Endpoint PCI Virtex-6, Virtex-5, Spartan-6 and Spartan-3 FPGA Families Bus Master DMA Performance Demonstration Reference Design for the Xilinx Endpoint PCI (2010)
18. Xilinx. Virtex-6 FPGA Integrated Block for PCI Express, ug517 v5.0 edition (April 2010)

A   Appendix

Table 4. Optimal Parameter Set for selected Challenges

		C_1	C_2	C_3	C_4
Rivyera-S3	cores/FPGA	12	5	2	1
	p	5	4	4	4
	l	7	7	9	11
	k_1	113	127	511	1424
	k_2	164	438	630	691
	#cycles / iterations (log_2)[1]	24.79	23.73	25.31	25.71
	#expected iterations (log_2)	10.58	29.53	55.76	94.32
Rivyera-S6	cores/FPGA	32	15	7	2
	p	5	4	4	4
	l	7	7	9	11
	k_1	126	127	502	1525
	k_2	151	438	639	590
	#cycles / iterations (log_2)[1]	24.31	23.73	25.37	25.02
	#expected iterations (log_2)	10.9	29.53	55.72	94.90
Virtex-6[2]	cores/FPGA	43	21	14	6
	p	3	3	3	3
	l	6	8	10	11
	k_1	63	204	642	1578
	k_2	213	362	500	537
	#cycles / iterations (log_2)[1]	17.72	16.55	18.58	19.50
	#expected iterations (log_2)	13.82	33.40	59.95	94.96

[1] Please note that the amount of cycles is the total cycle count to perform $\#cores \times \#FPGAs$ iterations, as they start after receiving data and finish all iterations within the transfer time frame of the other FPGAs.

[2] As the data transfer rate is significantly higher for the Virtex-6 device, the sage script does not optimize correctly as it neglects the - in this case - relevant pre-processing time in software and assumes zero delay.

Transcript Secure Signatures Based on Modular Lattices

Jeff Hoffstein[1], Jill Pipher[1], John M. Schanck[2,3], Joseph H. Silverman[1],
and William Whyte[3]

[1] Brown University, Providence, USA
{jhoff,jpipher,jhs}@math.brown.edu
[2] University of Waterloo, Waterloo, Canada
[3] Security Innovation, Wilmington, USA
{jschanck,wwhyte}@securityinnovation.com

Abstract. We introduce a class of lattice-based digital signature schemes based on modular properties of the coordinates of lattice vectors. We also suggest a method of making such schemes transcript secure via a rejection sampling technique of Lyubashevsky (2009). A particular instantiation of this approach is given, using NTRU lattices. Although the scheme is not supported by a formal security reduction, we present arguments for its security and derive concrete parameters based on the performance of state-of-the-art lattice reduction and enumeration techniques.

1 Introduction

In the GGH and NTRUSign signature schemes [4, Sections 7.4,7.5] a document to be signed is thought of as a point m in $\mathbb{Z}^n$. A lattice L has a private basis, known only to the signer, that is reasonably short and close to orthogonal. The signer uses the private basis to solve a CVP and locate a point $s \in L$ that lies reasonably close to m. A verifier of the signature checks that s is indeed a point in the lattice L, and that the Euclidean distance between s and m is shorter than some pre-specified bound. The security assumption underlying the acceptance of the signature is that it is hard to find a point in L that is close to m unless one knows the private short basis for L.

A major difficulty with these signature schemes is the fact that when the private basis is used to locate s, the difference $s - m$ has the form

$$s - m = \sum_{i=1}^{n} \epsilon_i v_i,$$

where $v_1, \ldots, v_n$ is the private basis and where each $|\epsilon_i| \leq 1/2$. Thus $s - m$ is a point in the interior of the fundamental parallelepiped associated to the private basis. If the signature is obtained by, say, Babai's rounding approach, the ϵ_i will be randomly and uniformly distributed in the interval $(-1/2, 1/2)$. A long transcript of signatures then corresponds to a large collection of points randomly and uniformly distributed inside the parallelepiped, and a sufficiently

M. Mosca (Ed.): PQCrypto 2014, LNCS 8772, pp. 142–159, 2014.

long transcript eventually reveals the vertices of the parallelepiped, and the secret basis. This was demonstrated successfully in [11, 12, 1].

It has been proposed that such an attack could be thwarted by carefully signing in such a way that the distribution of the ϵ_i was controlled, and it was proved that using such methods it is possible to construct signing protocols where the transcript contains no information pertaining to the private basis [2]. While effective at preventing information leakage, this process of controlling the distribution of the ϵ_i is computationally expensive.

The present work introduces a similar technique which does not require sampling complicated distributions.

Very roughly, the idea is as follows. Fix a public small prime p, and, rather than taking $\boldsymbol{m}$ to be a point in $\mathbb{Z}^n$, consider it instead to be a point $\boldsymbol{m}_p \in (\mathbb{Z}/p\mathbb{Z})^n$. Fix also a specific public region $\mathcal{R}$ in $\mathbb{Z}^n$. The region $\mathcal{R}$ should be sufficiently large that the volume of $\mathcal{R}$, which we denote by $|\mathcal{R}|$, satisfies

$$\frac{|\mathcal{R}|}{p^n} > C^n,$$

for a sufficiently large C. Precise examples will be given below. A signature on $\boldsymbol{m}_p$ is a point $\boldsymbol{s} \in L \cap \mathcal{R}$, with $\boldsymbol{s} \equiv \boldsymbol{m}_p \pmod{p}$.

Signing is accomplished as follows. To sign $\boldsymbol{m}_p \in (\mathbb{Z}/p\mathbb{Z})^n$, a random point $\boldsymbol{s}_0 \in L \cap \mathcal{R}$ is chosen. Let M be a matrix whose rows are the private basis, and let M_p be the reduction of this basis modulo p. Use M_p to find $\boldsymbol{v}_p \in (\mathbb{Z}/p\mathbb{Z})^n$ such that

$$\boldsymbol{s}_0 + \boldsymbol{v}_p \cdot M_p \equiv \boldsymbol{m}_p \pmod{p}.$$

Let $\boldsymbol{v}$ be the lift of $\boldsymbol{v}_p$ to $\mathbb{Z}^n$ with coefficients chosen from the interval $(-p/2, p/2)$. Then as M is a short basis and p is small, the vector $\boldsymbol{v} \cdot M$ will also be short, and $\boldsymbol{s} = \boldsymbol{s}_0 + \boldsymbol{v} \cdot M$ will satisfy $\boldsymbol{s} \equiv \boldsymbol{m}_p \pmod{p}$. Also, as $\boldsymbol{s}_0$ was chosen to lie in $L \cap \mathcal{R}$, and $\boldsymbol{v} \cdot M$ is short, there is a reasonable chance that $\boldsymbol{s}$ will also lie in $L \cap \mathcal{R}$. The algorithm of choosing $\boldsymbol{s}_0$ and solving for $\boldsymbol{s}$ is repeated until $\boldsymbol{s} \in L \cap \mathcal{R}$.

Any lattice point $\boldsymbol{s}$ satisfying $\boldsymbol{s} \equiv \boldsymbol{m}_p \pmod{p}$ is a valid signature, and such points will be well distributed throughout $\mathcal{R}$. Anyone can use a public basis to find a point in L with the desired properties modulo p, and if $\mathcal{R}$ is sufficiently large it is easy, using a short basis, to find points of $L \cap \mathcal{R}$, but if one does not know a short basis, then it is hard to satisfy both criteria simultaneously.

To create a collection of $\boldsymbol{s} - \boldsymbol{s}_0$, an attacker must also locate the nearby lattice point $\boldsymbol{s}_0$, However, for any $\boldsymbol{s} \in L \cap \mathcal{R}$, there will be many potential $\boldsymbol{s}_0'$ that are close to $\boldsymbol{s}$. In fact, if it is not only required that $\boldsymbol{s} \in L \cap \mathcal{R}$, but also that $\boldsymbol{s}$ lies at least a certain distance inside the boundary of $\mathcal{R}$, then it can be shown that with equal probability any s_0' within a fixed radius of $\boldsymbol{s}$ could have been the actual $\boldsymbol{s}_0$ used in the signing process. This idea can be used to give a proof that the transcript contains no information about the private basis. This aspect of the approach is inspired by a rejection sampling technique of Lyubashevsky [7–9].

Another contribution of this paper is a particular, efficient, instantiation of this idea using NTRU lattices. We make this choice for two reasons. First, there is a natural dimension doubling: the dimension is $n = 2N$, where N is the number of coordinates needed to determine a point. Second, the lattice can be sufficiently well described using only half of a complete basis, and this half can be made quite short and sufficiently orthogonal. We will refer to this new signature scheme as an *NTRU Modular Lattice Signature Scheme*, or NTRUMLS for short.

2   Description of NTRUMLS

2.1   Notation

We work in the ring

$$\mathcal{R} = \mathcal{R}_N = \frac{\mathbb{Z}[x]}{\langle x^N - 1 \rangle}.$$

We implicitly identify each element of $\mathcal{R}$ with the unique polynomial of degree less than N in its congruence class. Having done this, we identify a polynomial with its vector of coefficients in $\mathbb{Z}^N$. Writing an element $f \in \mathcal{R}$ as

$$f = \sum_{i=0}^{N-1} a_i x^i,$$

we set

$$\|f\| = \max_{0 \leq i < N} |a_i|,$$

and we define the restriction of $\mathcal{R}$ to the max-norm ball of radius k as

$$\mathcal{R}(k) = \{f \in \mathcal{R} : \|f\| \leq k\}.$$

So that, for example, $\mathcal{R}(3/2)$ is the set of trinary polynomials.

We will frequently work in the quotient ring $\mathcal{R}/q\mathcal{R}$ with $q \in \mathbb{Z}$. We set the convention that when lifting an element of $\mathcal{R}/q\mathcal{R}$ to $\mathcal{R}(q/2)$ the lifted coefficients are chosen to satisfy $-q/2 \leq a_i < q/2$ when q is even, and $-\lfloor q/2 \rfloor \leq a_i \leq \lfloor q/2 \rfloor$ when q is odd.

2.2   System Parameters

N	dimension parameter
p	a small odd prime
q	an integer larger, and relatively prime to, p
B_s, B_t	norm constraints

The B_s and B_t parameters serve primarily to fine tune the balance between security and performance. Reducing B_s and B_t may, for instance, allow one to choose a smaller q, but this may come at the expense of making it difficult for an honest party to compute a signature. Typical values of B_s and B_t satisfy $B_s = pB_t$, and

$$\|a * b\| \leq B_t \quad \text{for all } a, b \in \mathcal{R}\left(\frac{p}{2}\right).$$

Smaller B_s and B_t may be used provided that the signer performs an additional check during signature generation.

There will be further conditions on (N, p, q) to prevent search and lattice attacks, while still making it possible to find valid signatures; see Sections 4 and 5 for details.

2.3 Private Key

Choose polynomials

$$f \xleftarrow{\$} p\mathcal{R}(3/2) \qquad \text{and} \qquad g \xleftarrow{\$} \mathcal{R}(p/2).$$

Writing $f = pF$, so F is trinary, check that both g and F are invertible modulo q and modulo p. Sample a new pair if they are not. (We remark that the probability of g and F being invertible is quite high if $(x^N - 1)/(x - 1)$ does not have low degree factors when reduced modulo p and q.)

The private signing key is the pair (f, g).

2.4 Public Key

The public verification key is the polynomial

$$h \equiv f^{-1} * g \pmod{q}.$$

Also let

$$L_h = \{(s, t) \in \mathcal{R}^2 : t \equiv h * s \pmod{q}\}$$

be the usual NTRU lattice associated to h.

We will often consider subsets of L_h consisting of vectors of bounded norm. This will be denoted by

$$L_h(k_1, k_2) = L_h \cap \left(\mathcal{R}(k_1) \times \mathcal{R}(k_2)\right).$$

2.5 Document Hashes and Valid Signatures

A document hash is a $2N$-vector

$$(s_p, t_p) \in \mathcal{R}(p/2) \times \mathcal{R}(p/2),$$

i.e.,

$$\|(s_p, t_p)\| = \max\{\|s_p\|, \|t_p\|\} \leq p/2.$$

We fix a hash function

$$\mathsf{Hash} : \mathcal{R}(q/2) \times \{0, 1\}^* \longrightarrow \mathcal{R}(p/2) \times \mathcal{R}(p/2).$$

A valid signature on the document hash (s_p, t_p) for the signing key h is a $2N$-vector $(s, t) \in \mathcal{R}^2$ satisfying:

(a) $(s, t) \in L_h\left(\frac{q}{2} - B_s, \frac{q}{2} - B_t\right).$
(b) $(s, t) \equiv (s_p, t_p) \pmod{p}.$

2.6   Algorithms

Algorithm 1. NTRUMLS Signature Algorithm

Input: $(\boldsymbol{f}, \boldsymbol{g}, \boldsymbol{h}, \mu)$, where $(\boldsymbol{f}, \boldsymbol{g})$ is a private key, $\boldsymbol{h}$ is the corresponding public key, and $\mu \in \{0,1\}^*$ is a document to be signed.

1: $(\boldsymbol{s}_p, \boldsymbol{t}_p) \longleftarrow \mathsf{Hash}(\boldsymbol{h}, \mu)$

2: **repeat**

3: $\quad \boldsymbol{r} \xleftarrow{\$} \mathcal{R}\left(\left\lfloor \frac{q}{2p} + \frac{1}{2} \right\rfloor\right)$

4: $\quad \boldsymbol{s}_0 \longleftarrow \boldsymbol{s}_p + p\boldsymbol{r}$

5: $\quad \boldsymbol{t}_0 \longleftarrow \boldsymbol{h} * \boldsymbol{s}_0 \pmod{q}$ with $\boldsymbol{t}_0 \in \mathcal{R}(q/2)$

6: $\quad \boldsymbol{a} \longleftarrow \boldsymbol{g}^{-1} * (\boldsymbol{t}_p - \boldsymbol{t}_0) \pmod{p}$ with $\boldsymbol{a} \in \mathcal{R}(p/2)$

7: $\quad (\boldsymbol{s}, \boldsymbol{t}) \longleftarrow (\boldsymbol{s}_0, \boldsymbol{t}_0) + (\boldsymbol{a} * \boldsymbol{f}, \boldsymbol{a} * \boldsymbol{g})$

8: **until** $\|\boldsymbol{a} * \boldsymbol{f}\| \leq B_s$ and $\|\boldsymbol{a} * \boldsymbol{g}\| \leq B_t$ and $\|\boldsymbol{s}\| \leq \frac{q}{2} - B_s$ and $\|\boldsymbol{t}\| \leq \frac{q}{2} - B_t$

Output: $(\boldsymbol{s}, \boldsymbol{t}, \mu)$

Remark 1. Notice the rejection criterion in Step 8 of the signing algorithm. We compute a potential signature $(\boldsymbol{s}, \boldsymbol{t})$, but then we reject it if it, or the correction $(\boldsymbol{a} * \boldsymbol{f}, \boldsymbol{a} * \boldsymbol{g})$, is too big; specifically, we reject $(\boldsymbol{s}, \boldsymbol{t})$ if it falls outside of $L_{\boldsymbol{h}}\left(\frac{q}{2} - B_s, \frac{q}{2} - B_t\right)$, or if $(\boldsymbol{a} * \boldsymbol{f}, \boldsymbol{a} * \boldsymbol{g})$ falls outside $L_{\boldsymbol{h}}(B_s, B_t)$.

Remark 2. Since $\boldsymbol{t} \equiv \boldsymbol{h} * \boldsymbol{s} \pmod{q}$ it does not need to be published explicitly. Furthermore since $\boldsymbol{s} \equiv \boldsymbol{s}_p \pmod{p}$ and $\boldsymbol{s}_p$ can be obtained by hashing $\boldsymbol{h}$ with the message, the signer can simply publish $(\boldsymbol{s} - \boldsymbol{s}_p)/p$ as the signature. The resulting signature is of length $N\lceil \log_2 q/p \rceil$ bits.

Algorithm 2. NTRUMLS Verification Algorithm

Input: $(\boldsymbol{s}, \boldsymbol{t}, \mu, \boldsymbol{h})$

1: *valid* $\longleftarrow$ yes

2: $(\boldsymbol{s}_p, \boldsymbol{t}_p) \longleftarrow \mathsf{Hash}(\boldsymbol{h}, \mu)$

3: **if** $\boldsymbol{t} \not\equiv \boldsymbol{h} * \boldsymbol{s} \pmod{q}$ **then**

4: $\quad$ *valid* $\longleftarrow$ no

5: **end if**

6: **if** $\|\boldsymbol{s}\| > \frac{q}{2} - B_s$ or $\|\boldsymbol{t}\| > \frac{q}{2} - B_t$ **then**

7: $\quad$ *valid* $\longleftarrow$ no

8: **end if**

9: **if** $(\boldsymbol{s}, \boldsymbol{t}) \not\equiv (\boldsymbol{s}_p, \boldsymbol{t}_p) \pmod{p}$ **then**

10: $\quad$ *valid* $\longleftarrow$ no

11: **end if**

Output: *valid*

Proposition 1. *The Signing Algorithm produces signatures that are verified as valid by the Verification Algorithm.*

Proof. This is an easy exercise.

3 Transcript Security

In this section we prove that, under a reasonable assumption, a transcript of signatures created using the signing algorithm contains no information that is not already available to someone who knows the public verification key h. We do this by showing that an honest signer produces signatures that are uniformly distributed on $L_h \left(\frac{q}{2} - B_s, \frac{q}{2} - B_t \right)$. We are able to show that for any document hash, (s_p, t_p), the signer's distribution is precisely the uniform distribution on the subset of signature points in $(s_p, t_p) + p\mathbb{Z}^{2N}$ (proposition 2). For uniformity on the entire signature region we must assume that each coset of $p\mathbb{Z}^{2N}$ contains roughly the same number of signature points (assumption 1).

We further show that a party who knows h alone can produce a transcript of pairs

$$(\text{Valid Signature}_i, \text{Document Hash}_i)_{i=1,2,3,\ldots}$$

that is statistically indistinguishable from an analogous transcript produced using the signing algorithm and the private key (f, g). Specifically, the signature points produced by such a party are uniform on $L_h \left(\frac{q}{2} - B_s, \frac{q}{2} - B_t \right)$, and the document hashes (obtained by reducing the signature coefficients modulo p), are uniform on $\mathcal{R}(p/2)$.

We start by analyzing the transcript created using the signing algorithm and (f, g). We note that the rejection sampling condition is what allows us to prove that the resulting signatures are uniformly distributed in a certain space of allowable signatures.

We assume that our hash function outputs document hashes

$$(s_p, t_p) \in \mathcal{R}(p/2)^2$$

that are uniformly distributed on $\mathcal{R}(p/2)^2$. We use Steps 3 through 7 of the Signing Algorithm to define a signing function

$$(s, t) = \sigma'(f, g, s_p, t_p, r).$$

Thus σ' is a map

$$\sigma' : \overbrace{p\mathcal{R}\left(\frac{3}{2}\right) \times \mathcal{R}\left(\frac{p}{2}\right)}^{\text{private key } (f, g)} \times \overbrace{\mathcal{R}\left(\frac{p}{2}\right) \times \mathcal{R}\left(\frac{p}{2}\right)}^{\text{document hash } (s_p, t_p)} \times \overbrace{\mathcal{R}\left(\left\lfloor \frac{q}{2p} - \frac{1}{2} \right\rfloor \right)}^{\text{random element } r}$$

$$\longrightarrow \underbrace{L_h \left(\frac{q}{2} + B_s, \frac{q}{2} + B_t \right)}_{\text{potential signature } (s, t)}$$

given explicitly by

$$\sigma'(f, g, s_p, t_p, r) = (s_0 + a * f, t_0 + a * g), \tag{1}$$

where

$$s_0 = s_p + pr, \tag{2}$$

$$t_0 \equiv h * s_0 \pmod{q} \quad \text{with } t_0 \in \mathcal{R}(q/2), \tag{3}$$

$$a \equiv g^{-1} * (t_p - t_0) \pmod{p} \quad \text{with } a \in \mathcal{R}(p/2). \tag{4}$$

We will write

$$\Omega' = p\mathcal{R}\left(\frac{3}{2}\right) \times \mathcal{R}\left(\frac{p}{2}\right) \times \mathcal{R}\left(\frac{p}{2}\right) \times \mathcal{R}\left(\frac{p}{2}\right) \times \mathcal{R}\left(\left\lfloor \frac{q}{2p} - \frac{1}{2} \right\rfloor\right)$$

for the domain of σ'.

We now introduce rejection sampling by defining

$$\Omega_{B_s, B_t} = \left\{ (f, g, s_p, t_p, r) \in \Omega' : \begin{array}{l} (s, t) := \sigma'(f, g, s_p, t_p, r) \\ \quad = (s_0 + a * f, t_0 + a * g), \\ \|s\| \leq \frac{q}{2} - B_s, \|t\| \leq \frac{q}{2} - B_t, \\ \|a * f\| \leq B_s, \|a * g\| \leq B_t \end{array} \right\}.$$

The restriction of σ' to Ω_{B_s, B_t}, which we denote by σ, is then a map

$$\sigma : \Omega_{B_s, B_t} \longrightarrow L_h\left(\frac{q}{2} - B_s, \frac{q}{2} - B_t\right).$$

To ease notation, we let

$$A = \left\lfloor \frac{q}{2p} + \frac{1}{2} \right\rfloor,$$

so by Step 3 of the Signing Algorithm, the random element r used to generate a signature is chosen uniformly from the set $\mathcal{R}(A)$. The following proposition says that every signature that is valid for the document hash (s_p, t_p) has the same number of preimages in $\mathcal{R}(A)$.

Proposition 2. *The signature function σ has the following property: For a given*

$$\text{private key} \quad (f, g) \in p\mathcal{R} \times \mathcal{R},$$

$$\text{document hash} \quad (s_p, t_p) \in \mathcal{R}\left(\frac{p}{2}\right) \times \mathcal{R}\left(\frac{p}{2}\right),$$

the output of σ, when queried on uniformly random $r \in \mathcal{R}(A)$, is uniformly distributed over the set

$$\left\{ (s, t) \in L_h\left(\frac{q}{2} - B_s, \frac{q}{2} - B_t\right) : (s, t) \equiv (s_p, t_p) \pmod{p} \right\}.$$

of valid signatures for (s_p, t_p). Equivalently, the size of the set

$$\{ r \in \mathcal{R}(A) : \sigma(f, g, s_p, t_p, r) = (s, t) \}$$

is the same for all

$$(s, t) \in L_h\left(\frac{q}{2} - B_s, \frac{q}{2} - B_t\right) \quad \text{satisfying} \quad (s, t) \equiv (s_p, t_p) \pmod{p}.$$

Proof. Since we know from Proposition 1 that $\sigma(\boldsymbol{f}, \boldsymbol{g}, \boldsymbol{s}_p, \boldsymbol{t}_p, \boldsymbol{r})$ is congruent to $(\boldsymbol{s}_p, \boldsymbol{t}_p)$ modulo p, it is clear that there is zero probability of generating the signature $(\boldsymbol{s}, \boldsymbol{t})$ if $(\boldsymbol{s}, \boldsymbol{t}) \not\equiv (\boldsymbol{s}_p, \boldsymbol{t}_p) \pmod{p}$. So we assume henceforth that

$$(\boldsymbol{s}, \boldsymbol{t}) \equiv (\boldsymbol{s}_p, \boldsymbol{t}_p) \pmod{p}. \tag{5}$$

The random element $\boldsymbol{r}$ used to generate a signature is chosen uniformly from the set $\mathcal{R}(A)$, so there are $(2A+1)^N$ possible choices for $\boldsymbol{r}$. Hence the probability of obtaining $(\boldsymbol{s}, \boldsymbol{t})$ as a signature on $(\boldsymbol{s}_p, \boldsymbol{t}_p)$ is equal to $(2A+1)^{-N}$ times the number of elements in the set

$$\Sigma(\boldsymbol{f}, \boldsymbol{g}, \boldsymbol{s}, \boldsymbol{t}) = \{\boldsymbol{r} \in \mathcal{R}(A) : \sigma(\boldsymbol{f}, \boldsymbol{g}, \boldsymbol{s}_p, \boldsymbol{t}_p, \boldsymbol{r}) = (\boldsymbol{s}, \boldsymbol{t})\}. \tag{6}$$

The key to counting the size of the set $\Sigma(\boldsymbol{f}, \boldsymbol{g}, \boldsymbol{s}, \boldsymbol{t})$ is the bijection described in the following lemma.

Lemma 1. *Let*

$$\mathcal{C} = \left\{ \boldsymbol{b} \in \mathcal{R}\left(\frac{p}{2}\right) : \|\boldsymbol{b} * \boldsymbol{f}\| \leq B_s \text{ and } \|\boldsymbol{b} * \boldsymbol{g}\| \leq B_t \right\},$$

and let

$$(\boldsymbol{s}, \boldsymbol{t}) \in L_h\left(\frac{q}{2} - B_s, \frac{q}{2} - B_t\right) \quad \text{satisfy} \quad (\boldsymbol{s}, \boldsymbol{t}) \equiv (\boldsymbol{s}_p, \boldsymbol{t}_p) \pmod{p}.$$

Then there is a well-defined bijection of sets

$$\phi : \mathcal{C} \longrightarrow \Sigma(\boldsymbol{f}, \boldsymbol{g}, \boldsymbol{s}, \boldsymbol{t}),$$
$$\boldsymbol{b} \longmapsto \frac{\boldsymbol{s} - \boldsymbol{s}_p}{p} - \boldsymbol{b} * \frac{\boldsymbol{f}}{p}. \tag{7}$$

Proof. First, since the coefficients of $\boldsymbol{s} - \boldsymbol{s}_p$ are multiples of p, and similarly $\boldsymbol{f} \in p\mathcal{R}(3/2)$ has coefficients divisible by p, we see that the polynomial on the right-hand side of (7) has coefficients in $\mathbb{Z}$.

We next need to show that $\phi(\boldsymbol{b}) \in \Sigma(\boldsymbol{f}, \boldsymbol{g}, \boldsymbol{s}, \boldsymbol{t})$, which by the definition of $\Sigma(\boldsymbol{f}, \boldsymbol{g}, \boldsymbol{s}, \boldsymbol{t})$ means showing that $\phi(\boldsymbol{b}) \in \mathcal{R}(A)$ and

$$\sigma(\boldsymbol{f}, \boldsymbol{g}, \boldsymbol{s}_p, \boldsymbol{t}_p, \phi(\boldsymbol{b})) = (\boldsymbol{s}, \boldsymbol{t}).$$

First note that because $\boldsymbol{s} \in \mathcal{R}\left(\frac{q}{2} - B_s\right)$, $\boldsymbol{s}_p \in \mathcal{R}\left(\frac{p}{2}\right)$, and $\boldsymbol{b} \in \mathcal{C}$, the triangle inequality gives

$$\|\phi(\boldsymbol{b})\| = \left\| \frac{1}{p}(\boldsymbol{s} - \boldsymbol{s}_p - \boldsymbol{b} * \boldsymbol{f}) \right\| \leq \left\lfloor \frac{\frac{q}{2} - B_s + \frac{p}{2} + B_s}{p} \right\rfloor = A.$$

The use of the floor function is justified by noting that $\phi(\boldsymbol{b})$ has integer coefficients. This establishes that $\phi(\boldsymbol{b}) \in \mathcal{R}(A)$.

Next we use the four formulas (1)–(4) to compute the signature $\sigma(f, g, s_p, t_p, \phi(b))$:

$$s_0 = s_p + p\phi(b)$$
$$= s_p + p\left(\frac{s - s_p}{p} - b * \frac{f}{p}\right)$$
$$= s - b * f, \tag{8}$$
$$t_0 \equiv h * s_0 \pmod{q}$$
$$\equiv h * (s - b * f) \pmod{q}$$
$$\equiv h * s - b * g \pmod{q} \quad \text{since } h \equiv f^{-1} * g \pmod{q},$$
$$\equiv t - b * g \pmod{q} \quad \text{since } (s, t) \in L_h. \tag{9}$$

Since $(s, t) \in L_h \left(\frac{q}{2} - B_s, \frac{q}{2} - B_t\right)$ and $b \in \mathcal{C}$, we have

$$\|s_0\| \leq \|s\| + \|b * f\| = \frac{q}{2} - B_s + B_s = \frac{q}{2},$$
$$\|t_0\| \leq \|t\| + \|b * g\| = \frac{q}{2} - B_t + B_t = \frac{q}{2},$$

i.e. (9), similar to (8), is an equality, not just a congruence. Continuing with the computation of $\sigma(f, g, s_p, t_p, \phi(b))$, we use (5) to compute

$$a \equiv g^{-1} * (t_p - t_0) \equiv b \pmod{p}.$$

(Note that $t \equiv t_p \pmod{p}$ from (4).) Since both a and b are in $\mathcal{R}(p/2)$, this tells us that $a = b$.

We now use (1) to compute the signature

$$\sigma(f, g, s_p, t_p, \phi(b)) = (s_0 + a * f, t_0 + a * g) \quad \text{definition of } \sigma,$$
$$= (s - b * f + a * f, t - b * g + a * g)$$
$$\text{from (8) and (9),}$$
$$= (s, t) \quad \text{since } a = b.$$

Hence directly from the definition (6) of the set $\Sigma(f, g, s, t)$, we see that

$$\phi(b) \in \Sigma(f, g, s, t).$$

We next fix an $r \in \Sigma(f, g, s, t)$ and compute how many $b \in \mathcal{C}$ satisfy $\phi(b) = r$. Since all coefficients of the polyomials $s - s_p$ and f are divisible by p, to ease notation we write

$$s - s_p = pS \quad \text{and} \quad f = pF.$$

We recall that by assumption, the polynomial F is invertible modulo p. We have

$$\phi(b) = r \iff S - b * F = r$$
$$\iff b \equiv F^{-1} * (S - r) \pmod{p} \quad \text{and} \quad \|b\| \leq \frac{p}{2}.$$

There is thus exactly one value of b in C satisfying $\phi(b) = r$, namely the unique element of C that is congruent modulo p to $F^{-1} * (S - r)$. This shows that ϕ is bijective, which concludes the proof of Lemma 1.

Resuming the proof of Proposition 2, we have, for all $(s, t) \equiv (s_p, t_p) \pmod{p}$,

$$\text{Prob}_{r \leftarrow \mathcal{R}(A)} \begin{pmatrix} \text{signature} & | & \text{private key is } (f, g) \text{ and} \\ \text{is } (s, t) & | & \text{document hash is } (s_p, t_p) \end{pmatrix}$$

$$= \frac{\#\Sigma(f, g, s, t)}{\#\mathcal{R}(A)} = \frac{\#C}{\#\mathcal{R}(A)},$$

where the penultimate equality follows from Lemma 1. This completes the proof of Proposition 2.

To give a complete proof of transcript security we need a slightly stronger version of Proposition 2 to be true:

Proposition 3. *The distribution of signatures produced by querying σ on uniformly random $(s_p, t_p) \in R(p/2)^2$ and uniformly random $r \in \mathcal{R}(A)$ is indistinguishable from the uniform distribution on $L_h \left(\frac{q}{2} - B_s, \frac{q}{2} - B_t\right)$.*

Proposition 3 is an immediate consequence of proposition 2 under the assumption that, for any given h, the number of lattice vectors of bounded norm in each coset of $p\mathbb{Z}^{2N}$ is essentially constant. This certainly fails to be the case for some lattices, for instance $h = 1$ has vectors in only p^N distinct cosets. However, it seems likely that assumption 1 holds for the lattices used in NTRUMLS.

Assumption 1. *There are constants C, ϵ such that $\epsilon = 1/\text{poly}(N)$ and for all $(s_p, t_p) \in \mathcal{R}(p/2)$*

$$(1 - \epsilon)C \leq \left| L_h \left(\frac{q}{2} - B_s, \frac{q}{2} - B_t\right) \cap ((s_p, t_p) + p\mathbb{Z}^{2N})) \right| \leq (1 + \epsilon)C.$$

We conclude this section by noting that any party with access to h can sample the uniform distribution on $L_h \left(\frac{q}{2} - B_s, \frac{q}{2} - B_t\right)$. One simply generates random $s \in \mathcal{R}(\frac{q}{2} - B_s)$ until $h * s \in \mathcal{R}(\frac{q}{2} - B_t)$. Since the signing region contains a large fraction of $L_h \left(\frac{q}{2}, \frac{q}{2}\right)$ (at least 30% for the parameter sets we consider), this suceeds after a small number of iterations. A transcript of

$$((s, t)_i, (s_p, t_p)_i)_{i=1,2,3,\dots}$$

where $(s, t)_i$ is produced in this manner and $(s_p, t_p)_i = (s, t)_i \pmod{p}$ is uniformly distributed on $L_h \left(\frac{q}{2} - B_s, \frac{q}{2} - B_t\right) \times \mathcal{R}(p/2)$ by assumption 1. By proposition 3, and the assumption that the output of Hash is uniform on $\mathcal{R}(p/2)^2$, this transcript is indistinguishable from one produced by an honest signer. The only difference between the two transcripts is that the party who used h alone does not know messages, μ_i, such that $\text{Hash}(h, \mu_i) = (s_p, t_p)_i$.

4   Probability of Generating a Valid Signature

To simplify our analysis we let $B = \lceil p^2 N/4 \rceil$ and take

$$B_s = B_t = B.$$

With this assumption there is zero probability of rejecting a candidate signature due to $\|a * s\| > B_s$ or $\|a * t\| > B_t$, but the probability of rejection due to non-inclusion in $\mathcal{R}(q/2 - B) \times \mathcal{R}(q/2 - B)$ is significant. Regardless, we can show that the probability of generating a valid signature is approximately $e^{-8/k}$, which is still practical. Further, the probability of rejection can be made significantly lower by fine-tuning B_s and B_t; our proposed parameters in section 6 reflect this optimization.

For this section we assume that the various parameters satisfy the conditions given in Table 1.

Table 1. Parameter guidelines

N	a moderate sized prime, say $200 < N < 5000$
p	a small prime chosen so that $N \log_2(p)$ is greater than the desired bit security
B	$\leq \lceil p^2 N/4 \rceil$
k	a small constant, say $2 \leq k \leq 50$
q	an integer coprime with p and satisfying $q \approx kNB \approx kp^2N^2/4$

The rejection criterion says that we only accept signatures whose norm is smaller than $q/2 - B$, so we want q to be a lot larger than B, or it will be too hard to find an acceptable signature. We consider the sup norm of a potential signature

$$(s, t) = (s_0, t_0) + (a * f, a * g)$$

produced in Step 7 of the signing algorithm. The coefficients of s_0 and t_0 are in $\mathcal{R}(q/2)$, the coefficents of $a * f$ are in $\mathcal{R}(p^2 N/4)$, and the coefficients of $a * g$ are in $\mathcal{R}(pN/2)$. Hence the coefficients of an (s, t) pair produced by Step 7 satisfy

$$\|(s, t)\| \leq \frac{q}{2} + B. \tag{10}$$

We will make the simplifying assumption[1] that the coefficients of s and t are equally likely to take on each of the values in the interval (10). The rejection criterion says that we only accept signatures whose coefficents are at most $q/2 - B$.

---

[1] In actuality, the coefficients of the products $a * f$ and $a * g$ tend to cluster more towards 0, since they are more-or-less hypergeometrically distributed.

Since we need all $2N$ of the coefficients of (s, t) to satisfy this condition, we find that

$$\text{Prob}\big((s, t) \text{ is accepted}\big) \approx \left(\frac{q/2 - B}{q/2 + B}\right)^{2N}.$$

Using the chosen value

$$q \approx \frac{kp^2 N^2}{4} \approx kNB$$

from Table 1, we find that

$$\text{Prob}\big((s, t) \text{ is accepted}\big) \approx \left(\frac{1 - 2B/q}{1 + 2B/q}\right)^{2N}$$

$$\approx \left(\frac{1 - 2/kN}{1 + 2/kN}\right)^{2N}$$

$$\approx e^{-8/k},$$

where for the last equality we use the estimate $(1 + t/n)^n \approx e^t$, valid when t is small and n is large.

5   Lattice Problems Associated to NTRUMLS

In this section we consider the lattice problems underlying signature keys and signature forgery. We note that shortest and closest vector problems (SVP and CVP) are analyzed using the L^2-norm, not the L^∞-norm. We write

$$\|v\|_2 = \sqrt{v_1^2 + v_2^2 + \cdots}$$

for the L^2-norm of the vector $v = (v_1, v_2, \ldots)$.

We will use the following elementary lattice result, whose proof we defer to Section A of the appendix.

Proposition 4. *Let $L_1 \subset \mathbb{Z}^r$ and $L_2 \subset \mathbb{Z}^r$ be lattices of rank r, let $t_1, t_2 \in \mathbb{Z}^r$ be arbitrary vectors, and let*

$$M = (L_1 + t_1) \cap (L_2 + t_2)$$

be the intersection of the indicated translations of L_1 and L_2. We make the following assumptions:

(i) *$\gcd\big(\det(L_1), \det(L_2)\big) = 1$.*
(ii) *Either $t_1 \notin L_1$ or $t_2 \notin L_2$ (or both), so in particular $M \neq L_1 \cap L_2$.*

Then the following are true:

(a) *$\det(L_1 \cap L_2) = \det(L_1) \cdot \det(L_2)$.*
(b) *$M \neq \emptyset$.*

(c) *For every $\boldsymbol{w}_0 \in M$, the map*

$$L_1 \cap L_2 \longrightarrow M, \qquad \boldsymbol{v} \longmapsto \boldsymbol{v} + \boldsymbol{w}_0 \qquad (11)$$

is a bijection.

(d) *Let $\boldsymbol{w}_0 \in M$, and let $\boldsymbol{w}' \in M$ be a shortest non-zero vector in M. Then $\boldsymbol{w}_0 - \boldsymbol{w}'$ solves the the closest vector problem in $L_1 \cap L_2$ for the vector $\boldsymbol{w}_0$. (This is true for any norm on $\mathbb{Z}^r$, so in particular it is true for both the L^∞ norm and the L^2 norm.)*

We recall two key quantities associated to lattice problems.

Heuristic 1. *The Gaussian heuristic says that the likely L^2-size of a solution to SVP or CVP in a "random" lattice L of reasonably large dimension is approximately*

$$\gamma(L) = \sqrt{\frac{\dim L}{2\pi e}} \cdot \det(L)^{1/\dim(L)}.$$

In other words, for "most" lattices L and "most" target vectors $\boldsymbol{v}_0$,

$$\min_{\boldsymbol{v} \in L \smallsetminus \boldsymbol{0}} \|\boldsymbol{v}\|_2 \approx \gamma(L) \quad and \quad \min_{\boldsymbol{v} \in L} \|\boldsymbol{v} - \boldsymbol{v}_0\|_2 \approx \gamma(L).$$

Heuristic 2. *Let $L \subset \mathbb{Z}^n$ be a lattice for which we want to solve either τ-appr-SVP or τ-appr-CVP. In other words, let $\boldsymbol{v}_0 \in \mathbb{Z}^n$, and suppose that we want to find a vector $\boldsymbol{v} \in L$ satisfying either*

$$0 < \|\boldsymbol{v}\|_2 \leq \tau \quad or \quad \|\boldsymbol{v} - \boldsymbol{v}_0\|_2 \leq \tau.$$

We call τ the target length *of the problem. The Gaussian defect of the problem is the ratio*

$$\rho(L, \tau) = \frac{\tau}{\gamma(L)}.$$

Let $0 < \delta < 2$. The δ-LLL heuristic, which has been confirmed in numerous experiments, says that solving the τ-appr-SVP or τ-appr-CVP problem is (exponentially) hard as a function of $\dim(L)$, provided that the Gaussian defect $\rho(L, \tau)$ is no more than a small multiple of $\dim(L)^\delta$.

We consider the problem of forging a signature. The forger needs to find a vector $(\boldsymbol{s}, \boldsymbol{t}) \in L_h$ satisfying:

Congruence Condition :	$(\boldsymbol{s}, \boldsymbol{t}) = (\boldsymbol{s}_p, \boldsymbol{t}_p) \pmod{p}$.	(12)
Norm Condition :	$\|\boldsymbol{s}\| \leq \dfrac{q}{2} - B_s$	(13)
	$\|\boldsymbol{t}\| \leq \dfrac{q}{2} - B_t$.	(14)

N.B. The norm condition (13) is an L^∞-norm condition.

The vectors $\boldsymbol{s}_p, \boldsymbol{t}_p \in R(p/2)$ are given, so the congruence condition (12) may be rephrased as saying that the target vector $(\boldsymbol{s}, \boldsymbol{t})$ is in the translation of the lattice $p\mathbb{Z}^{2N}$ by the vector (s_p, t_p). Thus the forger is looking for an L^∞-short vector in the intersection

$$(s, t) \in L_h \cap (p\mathbb{Z}^{2N} + (s_p, t_p)).$$

The determinants

$$\det(L_h) = q^N \quad \text{and} \quad \det(p\mathbb{Z}^{2N}) = p^{2N}$$

are relatively prime, so we can use Proposition 4(a) to conclude that

$$\det(L_h \cap p\mathbb{Z}^{2N}) = p^{2N} q^N.$$

Then Proposition 4(d) tells us that finding a short vector in the intersection $L_h \cap (p\mathbb{Z}^{2N} + (s_p, t_p))$ is equivalent to solving an appr-CVP problem in the lattice $L_h \cap p\mathbb{Z}^{2N}$. Since the Gaussian heuristic of $L_h \cap p\mathbb{Z}^{2N}$ is

$$\gamma(L_h \cap p\mathbb{Z}^{2N}) = \sqrt{\frac{N}{\pi e}} (p^{2N} q^N)^{1/2N} = \sqrt{\frac{p^2 q^N}{\pi e}},$$

it only remains to estimate the target length.

The rejection criterion in the signature algorithm says that a valid signature (s, t) has sup norm at most $q/2 - \min(B_s, B_t)$. Hence in particular a valid signature satisfies the L^2-norm bound

$$\|(s, t)\|_2 \le \left(\frac{q}{2} - \min(B_s, B_t)\right) \sqrt{2N}, \tag{15}$$

but not every vector in L_h satisfying the L^2-norm condition (15) and the congruence condition (12) will be a valid signature. We are going to simplify the life of a potential forger and assume that she only needs to satisfy the L^2-norm condition (15), rather than the more stringent L^∞-norm condition (13). Furthermore we will assume, again in the forger's favor, that $B_s = B_t = 0$, so that the she need only find a vector in $\mathcal{R}(\frac{q}{2}) \times \mathcal{R}(\frac{q}{2})$. This gives a target length

$$\tau = q\sqrt{N/2}.$$

Hence the Gaussian defect for our appr-CVP problem is

$$\rho = \frac{q\sqrt{N/2}}{\sqrt{p^2 q N/2\pi e}},$$

and using the relations in Table 1 between the various parameters, a little bit of algebra yields

$$\rho = N\sqrt{\frac{k\pi e}{8}}.$$

Thus ρ is a small multiple of $\dim(L_h \cap p\mathbb{Z}^{2N})$, so the LLL-heuristic says that solving the associated appr-CVP is a hard problem provided that the dimension is chosen appropriately. Of course, in practice one needs to do experiments with current LLL technology to obtain extrapolated estimates for the actual running time when N is moderately large, say in the range from 500 to 5000.

We next briefly consider the problem of finding the private key $(\boldsymbol{f}, \boldsymbol{g})$ from the public key $\boldsymbol{h}$. The attacker knows that $\boldsymbol{f} = p\boldsymbol{F}$, and standard methods allow him to reduce to the problem of finding the shorter vector $(\boldsymbol{F}, \boldsymbol{g})$. Then, since on average we have

$$\|\boldsymbol{F}\|_2 \approx \sqrt{N} \quad \text{and} \quad \|\boldsymbol{g}\|_2 \approx \frac{1}{2}p\sqrt{N},$$

the corresponding lattice problem needs to be balanced, also a well-known procedure. See for example [3, 5, 10] for details. For all of the proposed parameter sets in Section 6, the parameters have been chosen so that the difficulty of the private key lattice problem is roughly equal to that of the lattice forgery problem, taking into account the heuristic fact that solving unique-SVP tends to be a bit easier in practice than it is in theory.

6   Proposed Parameter Sets and Implementation

We have implemented NTRUMLS and made it available at https://github.com/NTRUOpenSourceProject/NTRUMLS. The parameter sets we have implemented are listed in Tables 2 and 3.

The only feature of our implementation not documented above is the use of product form polynomials for $\boldsymbol{f}$ and $\boldsymbol{g}$. Precisely we specify three small integers d_1, d_2, and d_3 and take

$$\boldsymbol{f} = p(\boldsymbol{F}_1 * \boldsymbol{F}_2 + \boldsymbol{F}_3 + 1), \text{and}$$
$$\boldsymbol{g} = \boldsymbol{G}_1 * \boldsymbol{G}_2 + \boldsymbol{G}_3 + 1$$

Table 2. Sample NTRUMLS Parameters

	Set #1	Set #2	Set #3	Set #4
N	401	439	593	743
p	3	3	3	3
$\log_2 q$	18	19	19	20
B_s	240	264	300	336
B_t	80	88	100	112
d_1, d_2, d_3	8,8,6	9, 8, 5	10, 10, 8	11, 11, 15
Key & signature size (bytes)	853	988	1335	1765
$\approx \text{Prob[accept]}$	38%	55%	41%	53%
$\approx$ bit security	112	128	192	256

Table 3. Performance results. Average time for each operation, in microseconds, over 10000 iterations. Code was run on an Intel Core i7-2640M. More extensive benchmarks on a variety of machines are available at http://bench.cr.yp.to/.

	Set #1	Set #2	Set #3	Set #4
KeyGen (μs)	2431	2928	5183	7855
Sign (μs)	575	436	1033	1000
Verify (μs)	92	102	179	231

where the polynomials F_i and G_i have exactly d_i coefficients equal to $+1$ and d_i coefficients equal to -1. The extra constant terms are to ensure that $f(1) \neq 0$ and $g(1) \neq 0$. Product form keys were introduced to NTRUEncrypt in [6].

References

1. Ducas, L., Nguyen, P.Q.: Learning a zonotope and more: Cryptanalysis of NTRUSign countermeasures. In: Wang, X., Sako, K. (eds.) ASIACRYPT 2012. LNCS, vol. 7658, pp. 433–450. Springer, Heidelberg (2012)
2. Gentry, C., Peikert, C., Vaikuntanathan, V.: Trapdoors for hard lattices and new cryptographic constructions. In: Proceedings of the 40th Annual ACM Symposium on Theory of Computing, STOC 2008, pp. 197–206. ACM, New York (2008)
3. Hoffstein, J., Pipher, J., Silverman, J.H.: NTRU: a ring-based public key cryptosystem. In: Buhler, J.P. (ed.) ANTS 1998. LNCS, vol. 1423, pp. 267–288. Springer, Heidelberg (1998)
4. Hoffstein, J., Pipher, J., Silverman, J.H.: An Introduction to Mathematical Cryptography. Undergraduate Texts in Mathematics. Springer, New York (2008)
5. Hoffstein, J., Silverman, J.: Optimizations for NTRU. In: Public-Key Cryptography and Computational Number Theory, Warsaw, pp. 77–88. de Gruyter, Berlin (2001)
6. Hoffstein, J., Silverman, J.H.: Random small Hamming weight products with applications to cryptography. Discrete Applied Mathematics 130(1), 37–49 (2003)
7. Lyubashevsky, V.: Lattice-based identification schemes secure under active attacks. In: Cramer, R. (ed.) PKC 2008. LNCS, vol. 4939, pp. 162–179. Springer, Heidelberg (2008)
8. Lyubashevsky, V.: Fiat-Shamir with aborts: applications to lattice and factoring-based signatures. In: Matsui, M. (ed.) ASIACRYPT 2009. LNCS, vol. 5912, pp. 598–616. Springer, Heidelberg (2009)
9. Lyubashevsky, V.: Lattice signatures without trapdoors. In: Pointcheval, D., Johansson, T. (eds.) EUROCRYPT 2012. LNCS, vol. 7237, pp. 738–755. Springer, Heidelberg (2012)
10. May, A., Silverman, J.H.: Dimension reduction methods for convolution modular lattices. In: Silverman, J.H. (ed.) CaLC 2001. LNCS, vol. 2146, pp. 110–125. Springer, Heidelberg (2001)
11. Nguyen, P.Q., Regev, O.: Learning a parallelepiped: cryptanalysis of GGH and NTRU signatures. In: Vaudenay, S. (ed.) EUROCRYPT 2006. LNCS, vol. 4004, pp. 271–288. Springer, Heidelberg (2006)
12. Nguyen, P.Q., Regev, O.: Learning a parallelepiped: cryptanalysis of GGH and NTRU signatures. J. Cryptology 22(2), 139–160 (2009)

A   Short Vectors in Intersections of Translated Lattices

In this appendix we prove Proposition 4, which relates the problem of finding short vectors in intersections of translated lattices to the problem of finding close vectors in the associated intersection of lattices. We applied this result in Section 5 to the intersection of an NTRU lattice L_h and the lattice $p\mathbb{Z}^{2N}$.

Proof (Proof of Propostion 4). (a) The fact that the determinants multiply is a standard fact from the theory of lattices.
(b) We let $D_i = \det(L_i)$ for $i = 1, 2$. We use the fact that for any lattice $L \subset \mathbb{Z}^r$ of determinant D, we have $D\mathbb{Z}^r \subset L$. The assumption that $\gcd(D_1, D_2) = 1$ means that we can find $(x, y) \in \mathbb{Z}$ such that

$$xD_1 + yD_2 = 1.$$

We let

$$e_1 = yD_2 = 1 - xD_1, \qquad e_2 = xD_1 = 1 - yD_2.$$

We now consider the vector

$$t = e_1 t_1 + e_2 t_2.$$

Then

$$t - t_1 = (e_1 - 1)t_1 + e_2 t_2 = -xD_1 t_1 + xD_1 t_2 \in D_1 \mathbb{Z}^r \subset L_1,$$

and similarly,

$$t - t_2 = e_1 t_1 + (e_2 - 1)t_2 = yD_2 t_1 - yD_2 t_2 \in D_2 \mathbb{Z}^r \subset L_2.$$

Hence t is in M, so $M \neq \emptyset$.
(c) In order to prove that (11) is a bijection, we will show that

$$v \in L_1 \cap L_2 \quad \Longrightarrow \quad v + w_0 \in M \tag{16}$$

and

$$w \in M \quad \Longrightarrow \quad w - w_0 \in L_1 \cap L_2. \tag{17}$$

For (16), we know that $w_0 \in M$, so by definition of M,

$$w_0 = v_1 + t_1 = v_2 + t_2 \quad \text{with } v_i \in L_1 \text{ and } v_2 \in L_2.$$

Then

$$v + w_0 = \underbrace{(v + v_1)}_{\text{in } L_1} + t_1 = \underbrace{(v + v_2)}_{\text{in } L_2} + t_2,$$

so $v + w_0 \in M$. For (17), we write the given $w \in M$ as

$$w = v_1' + t_1 = v_2' + t_2 \quad \text{with } v_i' \in L_1 \text{ and } v_2' \in L_2.$$

Then

$$w - w_0 = \underbrace{v_1' - v_1}_{\text{in } L_1} = \underbrace{v_2' - v_2}_{\text{in } L_2},$$

so $w - w_0 \in L_1 \cap L_2$.

(d) We are given that $w_0, w' \in M$ and that

$$\|w'\|_2 = \min_{w \in M \setminus 0} \|w\|_2.$$

To ease notation, we set

$$v' = w_0 - w'.$$

We know from (c) that $w' - w_0 \in L_1 \cap L_2$, and $L_1 \cap L_2$ is a lattice, so $v' \in L_1 \cap L_2$. We estimate

$$
\begin{aligned}
\|v' &- w_0\|_2 \\
&= \|w'\|_2 \quad \text{by definition of } v', \\
&= \min_{w \in M \setminus 0} \|w\|_2 \quad \text{by definition of } w', \\
&= \min_{v \in (L_1 \cap L_2) \setminus w_0} \| - v + w_0\|_2 \quad \text{since (c) says } M = (L_1 \cap L_2) + w_0.
\end{aligned}
$$

Hence if $w_0 \notin L_1 \cap L_2$, then we have shown that

$$\|v' - w_0\|_2 = \min_{v \in (L_1 \cap L_2)} \|v - w_0\|_2,$$

which is the desired result.

Finally, suppose that $w_0 \in L_1 \cap L_2$. Since also

$$w_0 \in M = (L_1 + t_1) + (L_2 + t_2),$$

we can write

$$w_0 = v_1 + t_1 \quad \text{and} \quad w_0 = v_2 + t_2 \quad \text{with } v_1 \in L_1 \text{ and } v_2 \in L_2.$$

But then $t_1 = w_0 - v_1 \in L_1$ and $t_2 = w_0 - v_2 \in L_2$, contradicting the initial assumption on t_1 and t_2. Hence $w_0 \notin L_1 \cap L_2$, which completes the proof of Proposition 4.

Isogeny-Based Quantum-Resistant Undeniable Signatures

David Jao[1] and Vladimir Soukharev[2]

[1] Department of Combinatorics and Optimization
[2] David R. Cheriton School of Computer Science
University of Waterloo, Waterloo, Ontario, N2L 3G1, Canada
{djao,vsoukhar}@uwaterloo.ca

Abstract. We propose an undeniable signature scheme based on elliptic curve isogenies, and prove its security under certain reasonable number-theoretic computational assumptions for which no efficient quantum algorithms are known. Our proposal represents only the second known quantum-resistant undeniable signature scheme, and the first such scheme secure under a number-theoretic complexity assumption.

Keywords: undeniable signatures, elliptic curves, isogenies.

1 Introduction

Many current cryptographic schemes are based on mathematical problems that are considered difficult with classical computers, but can easily be solved using quantum algorithms. To prepare for the emergence of quantum computers, we aim to design cryptographic primitives for common operations such as encryption and authentication which resist quantum attacks. One family of such primitives, proposed by De Feo, Jao, and Plût [13,20], uses isogenies between supersingular elliptic curves to construct cryptographic protocols for public-key encryption, key exchange, and entity authentication which are believed to be quantum-resistant. To date, however, this protocol family lacks comprehensive techniques for achieving data authentication, although certain limited capabilities, such as isogeny-based strong designated verifier signatures, are available [30].

In this article, we present a new construction of quantum-resistant undeniable signatures based on the difficulty of computing isogenies between supersingular elliptic curves. Few such constructions are known, and indeed the only other proposed quantum-resistant undeniable signature scheme in the literature is the code-based scheme of Aguilar-Melchor et al. [1]. Our scheme uses a completely different approach and is based on completely different assumptions, making it a useful alternative in the event that some breakthrough arises in the cryptanalysis of code-based systems.

1.1 Related Work

Mainstream post-quantum cryptosystems can be categorized into several broad families: lattice-based systems [17,25] and learning with errors [26], code-based

M. Mosca (Ed.): PQCrypto 2014, LNCS 8772, pp. 160–179, 2014.
© Springer International Publishing Switzerland 2014

systems [2,7,24], hash-based signatures [6,11], and systems based on multivariate polynomials [3,34]. Isogeny-based cryptosystems represent an interesting alternative to the above because they are based on a (relatively) naturally occurring number-theoretic computational problem, namely, the problem of computing isogenies between elliptic curves. These systems thus constitute one of the only families of quantum-resistant cryptosystems based on a number-theoretic assumption (depending on whether one counts solutions to multivariate polynomials as a number-theoretic problem).

Generally speaking, lattice-based systems are more naturally suited to encryption, with lattice-based signature schemes being less mature than the corresponding encryption schemes, whereas hash functions and multivariate polynomials more readily yield signature schemes compared to encryption schemes. Isogeny-based cryptosystems to date have dealt primarily with encryption, with the exception of the entity authentication protocol of [13, §3.1]. We remark that, although entity authentication in the classical setting enables data authentication via the Fiat-Shamir transformation [14], the Fiat-Shamir transformation fails against a quantum adversary [10]. This work, together with Sun et al.'s construction of strong designated verifier signatures [30], provides some evidence that isogenies can also be used as the basis for signatures and data authentication in the post-quantum setting.

We emphasize again that quantum-safe undeniable signatures seem to be difficult to construct by any means. The only known prior quantum-resistant undeniable signature scheme is by Aguilar-Melchor et al. [1], using linear codes.

2   Background

Due to space constraints, we cannot provide here a full treatment of the necessary background information. For further details on the mathematical foundations of isogenies, we refer the reader to [13,20,28].

Given two elliptic curves E_1 and E_2 over some finite field $\mathbb{F}_q$ of cardinality q, an *isogeny* ϕ is an algebraic morphism from E_1 to E_2 of the form

$$\phi(x,y) = \left(\frac{f_1(x,y)}{g_1(x,y)}, \frac{f_2(x,y)}{g_2(x,y)} \right),$$

such that $\phi(\infty) = \infty$ (here f_1, f_2, g_1, g_2 are polynomials in two variables, and ∞ denotes the identity element on an elliptic curve). Equivalently, an isogeny is an algebraic morphism which is a group homomorphism. The degree of ϕ, denoted $\deg(\phi)$, is its degree as an algebraic morphism. Two elliptic curves are *isogenous* if there exists an isogeny between them.

Given an isogeny $\phi\colon E_1 \to E_2$ of degree n, there exists another isogeny $\hat{\phi}\colon E_2 \to E_1$ of degree n satisfying $\phi \circ \hat{\phi} = \hat{\phi} \circ \phi = [n]$ (where $[n]$ is the multiplication by n map). It follows that the relation of being isogenous is an equivalence relation. The isogeny $\hat{\phi}$ is called the *dual isogeny* of ϕ. Section 6 (Remark 6.1) describes how to compute dual isogenies in our application.

For any natural number n, we define $E[n]$ to be the subgroup

$$E[n] = \{P \in E(\bar{\mathbb{F}}_q) : nP = \infty\}.$$

In other words, $E[n]$ is the kernel of the multiplication by n map over the algebraic closure $\bar{\mathbb{F}}_q$ of $\mathbb{F}_q$. The group $E[n]$ is isomorphic to $(\mathbb{Z}/n\mathbb{Z})^2$ as a group whenever n and q are relatively prime [28]. We define the *endomorphism ring* $\text{End}(E)$ to be the set of all isogenies from E to itself defined over the algebraic closure $\bar{\mathbb{F}}_q$ of $\mathbb{F}_q$. The endomorphism ring is a ring under the operations of pointwise addition and functional composition. If $\dim_{\mathbb{Z}}(\text{End}(E)) = 2$, then we say that E is *ordinary*; otherwise $\dim_{\mathbb{Z}}(\text{End}(E)) = 4$ and we say that E is *supersingular*. Two isogenous curves are either both ordinary or both supersingular. All elliptic curves used in this work are supersingular.

The isogeny $\phi\colon E_1 \to E_2$ is defined to be *separable* if the function field extension $\mathbb{F}_q(E_1)/\phi^*(\mathbb{F}_q(E_2))$ is separable. In this work, we will only consider separable isogenies. An important property of a separable isogeny is that the size of the kernel of that isogeny is equal to the degree of that isogeny (as an algebraic map) [28, III.4.10(c)]. The kernel K of ϕ uniquely defines the isogeny ϕ up to isomorphism [28, III.4.12]; for this reason, we use the notation E_1/K to denote the codomain E_2 of the isogeny ϕ. Methods for computing and evaluating isogenies are given in [5,13,20,21,32]. All the isogenies that we use have the property that the kernels are cyclic groups, and knowledge of the kernel, or any single generator of the kernel, allows for efficient evaluation of the isogeny (up to isomorphism); conversely, the ability to evaluate the isogeny via a black box allows for efficient determination of the kernel (cf. Remark 3.1). Thus, in our application, the following are equivalent: knowledge of the isogeny, knowledge of the kernel, or knowledge of any generator of the kernel.

3   Quantum-Resistant Elliptic Curve Cryptography

The term "elliptic curve cryptography" typically encompasses cryptographic primitives and protocols whose security is based on the hardness of the discrete logarithm problem on elliptic curves. Against quantum computers, this hardness assumption is invalid [27]. Hence, traditional elliptic curve cryptography is not a viable foundation for constructing quantum-resistant cryptosystems. As a result, alternative elliptic curve cryptosystems based on hardness assumptions other than discrete logarithms have been proposed for use in settings where quantum resistance is desired. One early proposal by Stolbunov [29], based on isogenies between ordinary elliptic curves, was subsequently shown by Childs et al. [8] to offer only subexponential difficulty against quantum computers.[1]

Following these developments, De Feo et al. [13,20] proposed a new collection of quantum-resistant public-key cryptographic protocols for entity authentication, key exchange, and public-key cryptography, based on the difficulty of

---

[1] An essentially identical scheme had also been proposed earlier by Couveignes in an unpublished manuscript [9], although not with quantum resistance as a motivation.

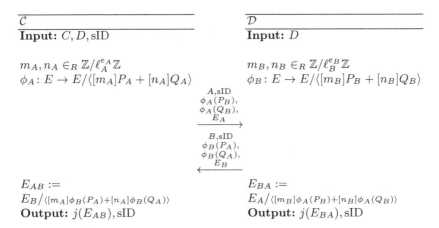

Fig. 1. Key-exchange protocol using isogenies on supersingular curves

computing isogenies between supersingular elliptic curves. We review here the operation of the most fundamental protocol in the collection, the key exchange protocol, since it contains several critical ideas upon which our undeniable signature scheme is based.

3.1 Parameter Generation

Fix a prime p of the form $\ell_A^{e_A} \ell_B^{e_B} \cdot f \pm 1$ where ℓ_A and ℓ_B are small primes, e_A and e_B are positive integers, and f some (typically very small) cofactor. Also, fix a supersingular curve E defined over $\mathbb{F}_{p^2}$ such that $\#E(\mathbb{F}_{p^2})$ has order divisible by $(\ell_A^{e_A} \ell_B^{e_B})^2$, and bases $\{P_A, Q_A\}$ and $\{P_B, Q_B\}$ which generate $E[\ell_A^{e_A}]$ and $E[\ell_B^{e_B}]$ respectively, so that $\langle P_A, Q_A \rangle = E[\ell_A^{e_A}]$ and $\langle P_B, Q_B \rangle = E[\ell_B^{e_B}]$. Methods for performing these computations are given in [13, Section 4.1].

3.2 Key Exchange

Suppose Carol and Dave wish to establish a secret key. Carol chooses two random elements $m_A, n_A \in_R \mathbb{Z}/\ell_A^{e_A}\mathbb{Z}$, not both divisible by ℓ_A. The values of m_A and n_A constitute Carol's secret information. (Since Carol and Dave's roles might be reversed in another session, in practice each user requires two sets of values, one for ℓ_A and one for ℓ_B.) On input E and $m_A \cdot P_A + n_A \cdot Q_A$, Carol computes using the method of [13, Section 4.2.2] a curve E_A and an isogeny $\phi_A \colon E \to E_A$ whose kernel K_A is equal to $\langle [m_A]P_A + [n_A]Q_A \rangle$ (the cyclic subgroup of E generated by $m_A \cdot P_A + n_A \cdot Q_A$). Carol also computes the auxiliary points $\{\phi_A(P_B), \phi_A(Q_B)\} \subset E_A$ obtained by applying her secret isogeny ϕ_A to the basis $\{P_B, Q_B\}$ for $E[\ell_B^{e_B}]$, and sends these points to Dave together with E_A. Similarly, Dave selects random elements $m_B, n_B \in_R \mathbb{Z}/\ell_B^{e_B}\mathbb{Z}$ and computes an isogeny $\phi_B \colon E \to E_B$ having kernel $K_B := \langle [m_B]P_B + [n_B]Q_B \rangle$, along with the auxiliary points $\{\phi_B(P_A), \phi_B(Q_A)\}$. Upon receipt of E_B and $\phi_B(P_A), \phi_B(Q_A) \in E_B$ from Dave, Carol computes an isogeny $\phi'_A \colon E_B \to E_{AB}$ having kernel equal to $\langle [m_A]\phi_B(P_A) + [n_A]\phi_B(Q_A) \rangle$; Dave proceeds *mutatis mutandis*. Carol and Dave can then use the common j-invariant of

$$E_{AB} = \phi'_B(\phi_A(E)) = \phi'_A(\phi_B(E)) = E/\langle [m_A]P_A + [n_A]Q_A, [m_B]P_B + [n_B]Q_B \rangle$$

to form a secret shared key.

The full protocol is given in Figure 1. We denote by A and B the identifiers of Carol and Dave, and use sID to denote the unique session identifier.

Remark 3.1. Carol's auxiliary points $\{\phi_A(P_B), \phi_A(Q_B)\}$ allow Dave (or any eavesdropper) to compute Carol's isogeny ϕ_A on any point in $E[\ell_B^{e_B}]$. This ability is necessary in order for the scheme to function, since Dave needs to compute $\phi_A(K_B)$ as part of the scheme. However, Carol must never disclose $\phi_A(P_A)$ or $\phi_A(Q_A)$ (or more generally any information that allows an adversary to evaluate ϕ_A on $E[\ell_A^{e_A}]$), since disclosing this information would allow the adversary to solve a system of discrete logarithms in $E[\ell_A^{e_A}]$ (which are easy since $E[\ell_A^{e_A}]$ has smooth order) to recover K_A.

4   Undeniable Signatures from Isogenies

In this section, we present a new construction of an undeniable signature scheme from isogenies. An undeniable signature can be verified by any party, but verification requires interaction with the signer. To distinguish between invalid (forged) signatures and valid signatures that the verifier refuses to verify, an undeniable signature scheme also includes a mechanism for the signer to prove (interactively) that an invalid signature is forged. Our construction uses a three-prime variant of the original two-prime protocol given in Section 3.2. As a consequence, the resulting commutative diagrams for zero-knowledge proofs become 3-dimensional rather than 2-dimensional.

4.1   Definition

We were unable to find any prior publications containing a definition and security model for undeniable signatures incorporating quantum computation. For this reason, we make a first attempt at addressing this gap in this section. Our definition of an undeniable signature scheme is the same as that of Kurosawa and Furukawa [22], except for those changes necessary for achieving security in the quantum setting. We caution that our proposed security model is preliminary and may not represent a perfect resolution for this issue.

An undeniable signature scheme [22] consists of a key generation algorithm, a signing algorithm, a validity check, a signature simulator, a confirmation protocol π_{con} and a disavowal protocol π_{dis}. The role of the confirmation protocol π_{con} is for the signer to prove to the verifier that the signature is valid. The role of the disavowal protocol π_{dis} is for a valid signer to be able to prove to the verifier that the signature that the verifier has received is not valid. Quantum (entangled) information may be transmitted between any two parties which are both capable of quantum computation, or within a single quantum computation, but not between two classical-only parties, or a classical-only party and a quantum-capable party.

In what follows, we make the simplifying assumption that all parties except possibly the adversary are limited to classical computation only; the adversary is permitted to perform quantum computation. This assumption is not part of our security definition; rather, it is merely a simplifying assumption to make our task of analyzing our scheme easier.

Unforgeability is defined using the following game between a challenger and an adversary A.

1. The challenger generates a key pair (vk, sk) randomly, and gives the verification key vk to A.
2. For $i = 1, 2, \ldots, q_s$ for some q_s, A queries the signing oracle adaptively with a message m_i and receives a signature σ_i.
3. Eventually, A outputs a forgery (m^*, σ^*).

We allow the adversary A to submit pairs (m_j, σ_j) to the confirmation/disavowal oracle adaptively in step 2, where the confirmation/disavowal oracle responds as follows:

- If (m_j, σ_j) is a valid pair, then the oracle returns a bit $\mu = 1$ and proceeds with the execution of the confirmation protocol π_{con} with A.
- Otherwise, the oracle returns a bit $\mu = 0$ and proceeds with the execution of the disavowal protocol π_{dis} with A.

We say that A succeeds in producing a strong forgery if (m^*, σ^*) is valid and (m^*, σ^*) is not among the pairs (m_i, σ_i) generated during the signing queries. The signature scheme is *strongly unforgeable* if the probability that A succeeds in producing a strong forgery is negligible for any PPT adversary A in the above game.

Invisibility is defined using the following game between a challenger and an adversary A.

1. The challenger generates a key pair (vk, sk) randomly, and gives the verification key vk to A.
2. A is permitted to issue a series of signing queries m_i to the signing oracle adaptively and receive a signature σ_i.
3. At some point, A chooses a message m^* and sends it to the challenger.
4. The challenger chooses a random bit b. If $b = 1$, then he computes the real signature for m^* using sk and sets it to be σ^*. Otherwise he computes a fake signature m^* using vk and sets it to be σ^*. He sends σ^* to A.
5. A performs some signing queries again.
6. At the end of this game, A outputs a guess b'.

We allow the adversary A to submit pairs (m_j, σ_j) to the confirmation/disavowal oracle adaptively in step 2 and in step 5. However, A is not allowed to submit the challenge (m^*, σ^*) to the confirmation/disavowal oracle in step 5. Also, A is not allowed to submit m^* to the signing oracle. We say that the signature scheme is *invisible* if no PPT adversary A has non-negligible advantage in this game.

For an undeniable signature scheme to be secure, it must satisfy unforgeability and invisibility. In addition, the confirmation π_{con} and disavowal π_{dis} protocols must be complete, sound, and zero-knowledge.

4.2   Protocol

Let p be a prime of the form $\ell_A^{e_A} \ell_M^{e_M} \ell_C^{e_C} \cdot f \pm 1$, and fix a supersingular curve E over $\mathbb{F}_{p^2}$ such that $\#E(\mathbb{F}_{p^2})$ is divisible by $(\ell_A^{e_A} \ell_M^{e_M} \ell_C^{e_C})^2$, together with bases $\{P_A, Q_A\}$, $\{P_M, Q_M\}$ and $\{P_C, Q_C\}$ of $E[\ell_A^{e_A}]$, $E[\ell_M^{e_M}]$ and $E[\ell_C^{e_C}]$ respectively. The design of the protocol is such that, generally speaking, points in $\langle P_A, Q_A \rangle$ are used for key material, points in $\langle P_M, Q_M \rangle$ are used for message data, and points in $\langle P_C, Q_C \rangle$ correspond to commitment data.

To generate such primes p, fix a choice of $\ell_A^{e_A}$, $\ell_M^{e_M}$, and $\ell_C^{e_C}$, and test random values of f until a value is found for which $\ell_A^{e_A} \ell_M^{e_M} \ell_C^{e_C} \cdot f \pm 1$ is prime. The prime number theorem in arithmetic progressions (specifically, the effective version of Lagarias and Odlyzko [23]) guarantees that only $O(\log p)$ trials are needed in expectation before a suitable prime is found. For any prime p, Bröker's algorithm for constructing supersingular curves [4] can efficiently produce a supersingular curve E over $\mathbb{F}_{p^2}$ having any admissible cardinality, namely any cardinality of the form $p^2 + 1 - t$ where t satisfies the Hasse-Weil bound $t \leq 2p$ and the supersingularity condition $t \equiv 0 \pmod{p}$. If we take the admissible value $t = \pm 2p$ in Bröker's algorithm, then we obtain a supersingular elliptic curve of cardinality $(p \mp 1)^2 = (\ell_A^{e_A} \ell_M^{e_M} \ell_C^{e_C} \cdot f)^2$, as desired. We remark that in the event E happens to be defined over $\mathbb{F}_p$, the cardinality of E over $\mathbb{F}_{p^2}$ is necessarily $(p + 1)^2$.

The signer generates two secret random integers $m_A, n_A \in \mathbb{Z}/\ell_A^{e_A}\mathbb{Z}$, obtains $K_A = [m_A]P_A + [n_A]Q_A$ and computes $E_A = E/\langle K_A \rangle$. Let ϕ_A be an isogeny from E to E_A.

Public Parameters: $p, E, \{P_A, Q_A\}, \{P_M, Q_M\}, \{P_C, Q_C\}$, and a hash function $H: \{0,1\}^* \to \mathbb{Z}$.
Public Key: E_A, $\phi_A(P_C)$, $\phi_A(Q_C)$.
Private Key: m_A, n_A.

To sign a message M, we compute the hash $h = H(M)$. Let $K_M = P_M + [h]Q_M$. Then the signer computes the isogenies

- $\phi_M \colon E \to E_M = E/\langle K_M \rangle$
- $\phi_{M,AM} \colon E_M \to E_{AM} = E_M/\langle \phi_M(K_A) \rangle$
- $\phi_{A,AM} \colon E_A \to E_{AM} = E_A/\langle \phi_A(K_M) \rangle$

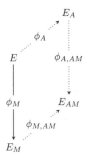

Fig. 2. Signature generation

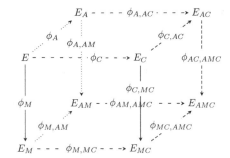

Fig. 3. Confirmation protocol

along with the auxiliary points $\phi_{M,AM}(\phi_M(P_C))$ and $\phi_{M,AM}(\phi_M(Q_C))$. The signer then presents these two auxiliary points along with E_{AM} as the signature. (See Figure 2.)

The *confirmation protocol* proceeds as follows. We must confirm E_{AM} without revealing the isogenies used to produce it. We do so by "blinding" E_{AM} using ϕ_C and disclosing the blinded isogenies (see Figure 3).

1. The signer secretly selects random integers $m_C, n_C \in \mathbb{Z}/\ell_C^{e_C}\mathbb{Z}$, and computes the point $K_C = [m_C]P_C + [n_C]Q_C$ together with the curves and isogenies in Figure 3. Here $E_C = E/\langle K_C \rangle$, $E_{MC} = E_M/\langle \phi_M(K_C) \rangle = E_C/\langle \phi_C(K_M) \rangle$, $E_{AC} = E_A/\langle \phi_A(K_C) \rangle = E_C/\langle \phi_C(K_A) \rangle$, and $E_{AMC} = E_{MC}/\langle \phi_{C,MC}(K_A) \rangle$.
2. The signer outputs E_C, E_{AC}, E_{MC}, E_{AMC}, and $\ker(\phi_{C,MC})$ as the commitment.
3. The verifier randomly selects $b \in \{0, 1\}$.
4. If $b = 0$, the signer outputs $\ker(\phi_C)$. Using the signer's public key, the verifier computes $\ker(\phi_{A,AC})$. Using knowledge of $\ker(\phi_M)$, the verifier computes $\phi_{M,MC}$. Using the auxiliary points given as part of the signature, the verifier can compute $\phi_{AM,AMC}$. The verifier checks that each isogeny maps between the corresponding two curves specified in the commitment. Using knowledge of $\ker(\phi_C)$, the verifier also independently re-computes $\phi_{C,MC}$ and checks that it matches the commitment.
5. If $b = 1$, the signer outputs $\ker(\phi_{C,AC})$. The verifier computes $\phi_{MC,AMC}$ and $\phi_{AC,AMC}$, and checks that each of $\phi_{C,AC}$, $\phi_{MC,AMC}$, and $\phi_{AC,AMC}$ maps between the corresponding two curves specified in the commitment.

We now describe the *disavowal protocol*. Suppose the signer is presented with a falsified signature (E_F, F_P, F_Q) for a message M, where E_F is the falsified E_{AM}, and $\{F_P, F_Q\}$ are the falsified auxiliary points corresponding to $\phi_{M,AM}(\phi_M(P_C))$ and $\phi_{M,AM}(\phi_M(Q_C))$ respectively. We must disavow E_F without disclosing E_{AM}. To do this, we blind E_{AM} as before to obtain E_{AMC}, and disclose enough information to allow the verifier to compute E_{FC} and check that $E_{FC} \neq E_{AMC}$.

1. The signer secretly selects random integers $m_C, n_C \in \mathbb{Z}/\ell_C^{e_C}\mathbb{Z}$, and computes $K_C = [m_C]P_C + [n_C]Q_C$ along with all the curves and isogenies in Figure 4.

2. The signer outputs E_C, E_{AC}, E_{MC}, E_{AMC}, and $\ker(\phi_{C,MC})$ as the commitment.
3. The verifier randomly selects $b \in \{0, 1\}$.
4. If $b = 0$, the signer outputs $\ker(\phi_C)$. The verifier computes ϕ_C, $\phi_{M,MC}$, $\phi_{A,AC}$, and $\phi_F \colon E_F \to E_{FC} = E_F/\langle[m_C]F_P + [n_C]F_Q\rangle$, and checks that each isogeny maps between the corresponding two curves specified in the commitment. The verifier independently re-computes $\phi_{C,MC}$ and checks that it matches the commitment. The verifier also checks that $E_{FC} \neq E_{AMC}$.
5. If $b = 1$, the signer outputs $\ker(\phi_{C,AC})$. The verifier computes $\phi_{AC,AMC}$ and $\phi_{MC,AMC}$, and checks that these isogenies map to E_{AMC}.

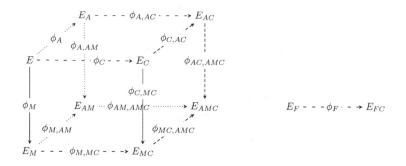

Fig. 4. Disavowal protocol

5   Complexity Assumptions

As before, let p be a prime of the form $\ell_A^{e_A} \ell_B^{e_B} \ell_C^{e_C} \cdot f \pm 1$, and fix a supersingular curve E over $\mathbb{F}_{p^2}$ together with bases $\{P_A, Q_A\}$, $\{P_B, Q_B\}$, and $\{P_C, Q_C\}$ of $E[\ell_A^{e_A}]$, $E[\ell_B^{e_B}]$, and $E[\ell_B^{e_B}]$ respectively. In analogy with [13,20], we define the following computational problems, which we assume are quantum-infeasible:

Problem 5.1 (Decisional Supersingular Isogeny (DSSI) problem).
Let E_A be another supersingular curve defined over $\mathbb{F}_{p^2}$. Decide whether E_A is $\ell_A^{e_A}$-isogenous to E.

Problem 5.2 (Computational Supersingular Isogeny (CSSI) problem).
Let $\phi_A \colon E \to E_A$ be an isogeny whose kernel is $\langle[m_A]P_A + [n_A]Q_A\rangle$, where m_A and n_A are chosen at random from $\mathbb{Z}/\ell_A^{e_A}\mathbb{Z}$ and not both divisible by ℓ_A. Given E_A and the values $\phi_A(P_B)$, $\phi_A(Q_B)$, find a generator R_A of $\langle[m_A]P_A + [n_A]Q_A\rangle$.

We remark that given a generator $R_A = [m_A]P_A + [n_A]Q_A$, it is easy to solve for (m_A, n_A), since E has smooth order and thus extended discrete logarithms are easy in E [31].

Problem 5.3 (Supersingular Computational Diffie-Hellman (SSCDH) problem).
Let $\phi_A \colon E \to E_A$ be an isogeny whose kernel is equal to $\langle[m_A]P_A + [n_A]Q_A\rangle$,

and let $\phi_B : E \to E_B$ be an isogeny whose kernel is $\langle [m_B]P_B + [n_B]Q_B \rangle$, where m_A, n_A (respectively m_B, n_B) are chosen at random from $\mathbb{Z}/\ell_A^{e_A}\mathbb{Z}$ (respectively $\mathbb{Z}/\ell_B^{e_B}\mathbb{Z}$) and not both divisible by ℓ_A (respectively ℓ_B). Given the curves E_A, E_B and the points $\phi_A(P_B)$, $\phi_A(Q_B)$, $\phi_B(P_A)$, $\phi_B(Q_A)$, find the j-invariant of

$$E/\langle [m_A]P_A + [n_A]Q_A, [m_B]P_B + [n_B]Q_B \rangle.$$

Problem 5.4 (Supersingular Decision Diffie-Hellman (SSDDH) problem).
Given a tuple sampled with probability $1/2$ from one of the following two distributions:

- $(E_A, E_B, \phi_A(P_B), \phi_A(Q_B), \phi_B(P_A), \phi_B(Q_A), E_{AB})$, where E_A, E_B, $\phi_A(P_B)$, $\phi_A(Q_B)$, $\phi_B(P_A)$, and $\phi_B(Q_A)$ are as in the SSCDH problem and

$$E_{AB} \cong E/\langle [m_A]P_A + [n_A]Q_A, [m_B]P_B + [n_B]Q_B \rangle,$$

- $(E_A, E_B, \phi_A(P_B), \phi_A(Q_B), \phi_B(P_A), \phi_B(Q_A), E_C)$, where E_A, E_B, $\phi_A(P_B)$, $\phi_A(Q_B)$, $\phi_B(P_A)$, and $\phi_B(Q_A)$ are as in the SSCDH problem and

$$E_C \cong E/\langle [m_A']P_A + [n_A']Q_A, [m_B']P_B + [n_B']Q_B \rangle,$$

where m_A', n_A' (respectively m_B', n_B') are chosen at random from $\mathbb{Z}/\ell_A^{e_A}\mathbb{Z}$ (respectively $\mathbb{Z}/\ell_B^{e_B}\mathbb{Z}$) and not both divisible by ℓ_A (respectively ℓ_B),

determine from which distribution the tuple is sampled.

Problem 5.5 (Decisional Supersingular Product (DSSP) problem).
Given an isogeny $\phi : E \to E_3$ of degree $\ell_A^{e_A}$ and a tuple sampled with probability $1/2$ from one of the following two distributions:

- (E_1, E_2, ϕ'), where the product $E_1 \times E_2$ is chosen at random among those $\ell_B^{e_B}$-isogenous to $E \times E_3$, and where $\phi' : E_1 \to E_2$ is an isogeny of degree $\ell_A^{e_A}$, and
- (E_1, E_2, ϕ'), where E_1 is chosen at random among the curves having the same cardinality as E, and $\phi' : E_1 \to E_2$ is a random isogeny of degree $\ell_A^{e_A}$,

determine from which distribution the tuple is sampled.

Our security proofs also make use of the following additional modified assumptions not stated in [13,20].

Problem 5.6 (Modified Supersingular Computational Diffie-Hellman (MSSCDH) problem). With notation as in the SSDDH problem, given E_A, E_B, and $\ker(\phi_B)$, determine E_{AB}. Note that no auxiliary points for ϕ_A are given.

An equivalent formulation of the MSSCDH problem is: Given E_A, m_B, and n_B, determine E_{AB}.

Problem 5.7 (Modified Supersingular Decision Diffie-Hellman (MSSDDH) problem). With notation as in the SSDDH problem, given E_A, E_B, E_C, and $\ker(\phi_B)$, determine whether $E_C = E_{AB}$. Note that no auxiliary points for ϕ_A are given.

Problem 5.8 (One-sided Modified Supersingular Computational Diffie-Hellman problem (OMSSCDH)). For fixed E_A and E_B, given an oracle to solve MSSCDH for any E_A, $E_{B'}$, $\ker(\phi_{B'})$ where $E_{B'} \not\cong E_B$, solve MSSCDH for E_A, E_B, and $\ker(\phi_B)$.

Problem 5.9 (One-sided Modified Supersingular Decision Diffie-Hellman problem (OMSSDDH)). For fixed E_A, E_B, and E_C, given an oracle to solve MSSCDH for any E_A, $E_{B'}$, $\ker(\phi_{B'})$ where $E_{B'} \not\cong E_B$, solve MSSDDH for E_A, E_B, E_C, and $\ker(\phi_B)$.

We conjecture that these problems are computationally infeasible, in the sense that for any polynomial-time solver algorithm, the advantage of the algorithm is a negligible function of the security parameter $\log p$. The resulting security assumptions are referred to as the DSSI assumption, CSSI assumption, etc.

We also need a heuristic assumption concerning the distribution of blinded false signatures:

Assumption 5.10. *Fix a supersingular elliptic curve E, an $\ell_A^{e_A}$-isogeny ϕ_A, an $\ell_B^{e_B}$-isogeny ϕ_B, and a curve E_F, not isomorphic to E_{AB}. For any pair of points $\{F_P, F_Q\}$ in E_F, only a negligibly small fraction of integer pairs m_C, n_C satisfy $E_F / \langle m_C F_P + n_C F_Q \rangle = E_{AB} / \langle \phi_{B,AB}(\phi_B(m_C P_C + n_C Q_C)) \rangle$.*

5.1 Hardness of the Underlying Assumptions

All of our unmodified complexity assumptions (those not containing "Modified" in the name) are identical to the corresponding assumptions from [13,20], except that our assumptions are formulated using primes of the form $p = \ell_A^{e_A} \ell_B^{e_B} \ell_C^{e_C} \cdot f \pm 1$, rather than primes of the form $p = \ell_A^{e_A} \ell_B^{e_B} \cdot f \pm 1$. We have no reason to believe that this alteration would affect the validity of these assumptions. A close analogy to this situation is the comparison between three-prime RSA and two-prime RSA.

Our modified assumptions are needed in order to prove the security of our undeniable signature scheme. The MSSCDH and MSSDDH assumptions are complementary to the SSCDH and SSDDH assumptions, with the main difference being that the input consists of a kernel but not two pairs of auxiliary points (rather than the other way around). The standard algorithm for computing the commuting isogeny from E_B to E_{AB} requires knowing both the values of the kernel of ϕ_B and the auxiliary points for ϕ_A. Similarly, the standard algorithm for computing the commuting isogeny from E_A to E_{AB} requires knowing both the values of the kernel of ϕ_A and the auxiliary points for ϕ_B. In SSCDH (say), the two sets of auxiliary points are known, but the kernels are not known. In MSSCDH, we break the symmetry, giving the attacker the kernel (and hence also the auxiliary points) for ϕ_B, but no secret information about ϕ_A. This kind of asymmetry is unavoidably necessary for any sort of isogeny-based signature scheme, since one isogeny somewhere will invariably be message-based, and this

isogeny can have no secrets. Nevertheless, it is clear that the standard algorithm is not able to solve the modified problems, and we are not aware of any
alternative algorithm which would be able to solve the modified problems using
only the information given. Indeed, despite extensive study of these problems,
we have not managed to devise any plausible approach to these problems other
than the claw-finding attack against CSSI originally proposed in [13, Section
5.1]. This attack does not utilize the auxiliary points, and hence works equally
well against our modified assumptions, with a running time of $\sqrt[4]{p}$ (respectively
$\sqrt[6]{p}$) on a classical (respectively quantum) computer. Other potential strategies
discussed in [13, Section 5.1], such as algebraic approaches based on ideal classes
in the endomorphism rings, fail in this setting for the same reasons as in [13].
Based on these considerations, we feel that some confidence can be ascribed
to the MSSCDH and MSSDDH assumptions. The OMSSCDH and OMSSDDH
assumptions are somewhat more artificial, and more study will be needed to justify confidence in them. They arise naturally in the analysis of our undeniable
signature scheme.

Our heuristic assumption (Assumption 5.10) seems quite natural, and we
have conducted numerous empirical experiments for random choices of triplets
(E_F, F_P, F_Q) without finding any violations at cryptographic parameter sizes.
For artificially small parameter sizes, our experiments found that for any fixed
choice of $(E, \phi_A, \phi_B, E_F, F_P, F_Q)$, equality occurs with probability around $1/N$
over all pairs of integers (m_C, n_C), where $N = \frac{p+1}{12} + O(1)$ is the number of
isomorphism classes of supersingular curves in characteristic p. Based on these
experiments, we have no reason to suspect that the assumption would fail to
hold. However, we have not yet succeeded in finding a proof of the assumption.

6   Security Proofs

To prove the security of our scheme, we must show that the confirmation and
disavowal protocols are complete, sound and zero-knowledge, and that the overall scheme satisfies the unforgeability and invisibility properties. In this section
we consider a **classical** adversary; the case of quantum adversaries will be considered in Section 7.

The basic principle behind the proofs is that, as was the case in the basic key-
exchange protocol (Section 3.2), knowledge of (the kernels of) any two opposite-
side isogenies lying in a given cube face reveals no information about the other
edges in the cube, by the DSSI and DSSP assumptions. On the other hand,
knowledge of any two adjacent isogenies in a given commutative square yields
full information about all the isogenies in the square. It does not matter which
direction the arrows point, since one can reverse the direction of any arrow using
dual isogenies (Section 2).

Remark 6.1. To compute the dual isogeny of an isogeny $\phi\colon E \to E_A = E/\langle A \rangle$
whose kernel is generated by a point A, pick any point $B \in E \setminus \langle A \rangle$, and compute $\phi(B)$. Then $\phi(B)$ generates a kernel subgroup whose corresponding isogeny

$\phi' : E_A \to E = E_A/\langle\phi(B)\rangle$ is isomorphic to the dual isogeny $\hat{\phi}$. In general, $E_A/\langle\phi(B)\rangle$ is isomorphic but not equal to E, so we also need to compute the appropriate isomorphism, but computing isomorphisms in general is known to be easy [16].

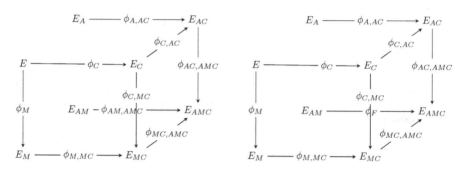

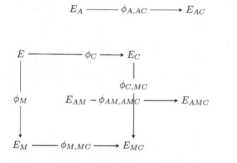
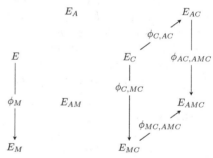

Fig. 5. Proof of soundness (confirmation)   **Fig. 6.** Proof of soundness (disavowal)

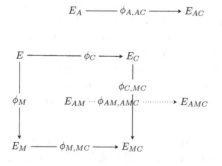
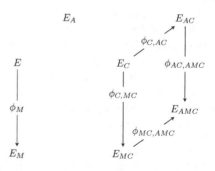

Fig. 7. Confirmation ($b = 0$ case)   **Fig. 8.** Confirmation ($b = 1$ case)

Fig. 9. Disavowal ($b = 0$ case)   **Fig. 10.** Disavowal ($b = 1$ case)

6.1   Confirmation Protocol

We need to prove three things: *completeness*, *soundness* and *zero-knowledge*. We apply classical techniques from [12,18].

Proof (Proof of completeness). Completeness for this protocol is obvious. Using the algorithm presented in Section 4.2, the signer can always compute the diagram in Figure 3 and make the verifier accept.

Proof (Proof of soundness). Let Charles be a cheating prover that is able to convince the verifier to accept an invalid signature with non-negligible probability. In order for Charles to be able to provide correct answers to both possible challenges in the confirmation protocol, there must exist a commutative diagram as in Figure 5 with all the edges filled in with actual isogenies. However, the existence of even a single such diagram implies that the signature must actually have been valid, since any three edges of a cube face determine the fourth edge. It follows that isogenies exist between E, E_A, E_M, and E_{AM} to fill in the left face of the cube, rendering the signature valid. Hence soundness holds even against an infinitely powerful malicious prover.

Proof (Proof of zero-knowledge). To prove that this scheme is zero knowledge we construct a simulator. Our simulator S makes uniformly random guesses about what the verifier's challenge will be. Regardless of the guess, S chooses random integers $m_C, n_C \in \mathbb{Z}/\ell_C^{e_C}\mathbb{Z}$ and computes

$$\phi_C \colon E \to E_C = E/\langle m_C P_C + n_C Q_C \rangle.$$

If S guesses $b = 0$, it computes the diagram given in Figure 7. The simulator can now answer any cheating verifier's challenge in the case $b = 0$. The simulator's response is indistinguishable from, and indeed identical to, that of the real prover.

If S guesses $b = 1$, it chooses some random isogeny $\phi_{C,AC} \colon E_C \to E_{AC}$, and computes the diagram given in Figure 8. The simulator uses this diagram to answer the cheating verifier's challenge in the case $b = 1$. In this diagram, the curves E_C and E_{MC} are genuine, and the curves E_{AC} and E_{AMC} are fake. However, the cheating verifier cannot tell that these curves are fake, or else one would be able to solve DSSP for the top face of the cube. Hence the simulator's response is indistinguishable from that of the real prover.

Remark 6.2. The indistinguishability portion of the above proof of the zero-knowledge property holds in the quantum setting as well as in the classical setting. Specifically, if we presume the existence of some quantum cheating verifier (CV) which can perform some quantum computation to distinguish the real transcript from the simulated transcript, then one could use this quantum cheating verifier to obtain a quantum algorithm for solving DSSP simply by alternately supplying the CV with either real curves E_{AC} and E_{AMC} (i.e. the real transcript), or with falsified curves E_{AC} and E_{AMC} (i.e. the simulated transcript), and seeing whether the CV's desired computation performs differently in the two cases.

6.2 Disavowal Protocol

As before, we prove *completeness*, *soundness* and *zero-knowledge*.

Proof (Proof of completeness). Suppose first that E_F is not equal to E_{AM}. Using the algorithm presented in Section 4.2, the signer can always compute the diagram in Figure 3 and make the verifier accept. Assumption 5.10 guarantees that the verifier will always accept except with negligible probability. Note that the assumption is formulated without regard to whether the putative auxiliary points F_P and F_Q are compatible with E_F or not.

Now suppose that E_F is equal to E_{AM}. In this case, completeness can only fail if $E_F = E_{AM}$ contains two distinct cyclic subgroups $K_1 = \langle m_C P + n_C Q \rangle$ and $K_2 = \langle \phi_{B,AB}(\phi_B(m_C P_C + n_C Q_C)) \rangle$ of cardinality $\ell_C^{e_C}$ in $E_{AB}[\ell_C^{e_C}]$ such that $E_{AM}/K_1 = E_{AM}/K_2$. But then E_{AM} would be a branch point in the covering space of the modular curve $X_0(\ell_C^{e_C})$ over the upper half plane, and the only such non-cusp branch points are the elliptic curves of j-invariant equal to 0 or 1728. The chance of E_{AM} being equal to such a curve is negligibly small. Indeed, there are only two problematic j-invariants, and there are cryptographically many (e.g. 2^{768}) non-problematic j-invariants. A failure probability of 2 in 2^{768} represents no cause for concern, since an adversary could simply guess the private key by brute force with higher success probability. Note that the j-invariant of E_{AM} is determined by a combination of A's public key and the value of the hash $h = H(M)$ of the message M, and this value is never at any point under the control of an adversary. Likewise, the honest user has no control over E_{AM}—its value is completely determined from the user's public key and the message.

Proof (Proof of soundness). Let Charles be a cheating prover that is able to convince the verifier with non-negligible probability that a valid signature is invalid. In order for Charles to be able to provide correct answers to both possible challenges in the confirmation protocol, there must exist a commutative diagram as in Figure 6 with all the edges filled in with actual isogenies. However, in this case, the forged isogeny ϕ_F is computed using exactly the same inputs as the corresponding isogeny $\phi_{AM,AMC}$ for the valid signature in the confirmation protocol, and hence necessarily has codomain E_F equal to E_{AMC}. Equality of E_F and E_{AMC} causes the disavowal protocol to fail. Hence soundness holds even against an infinitely powerful malicious prover.

Proof (Proof of zero-knowledge). To prove that this scheme is zero knowledge we construct a simulator. The simulator S makes uniformly random guesses about what the verifier's challenge will be. The simulator S first chooses random integers $m_C, n_C \in \mathbb{Z}/\ell_C^{e_C}\mathbb{Z}$ and computes

$$\phi_{M,MC} \colon E_M \to E_{MC} = E_M/\langle m_C \phi_M(P_C) + n_C \phi_M(Q_C) \rangle.$$

If S guesses $b = 0$, it computes the diagram given in Figure 9. Here the curves E_C, E_{MC}, and E_{AC} are genuine, and the curves E_{AM} and E_{AMC} are fake. The simulator uses the diagram to answer the cheating verifier's challenge in the case

$b = 0$. The simulator's response is indistinguishable from the real prover, since otherwise one could solve DSSP for the bottom face of the cube.

If S guesses $b = 1$, it chooses some random isogeny $\phi_{C,AC} \colon E_C \to E_{AC}$, and computes the diagram given in Figure 10. The simulator uses this diagram to answer the cheating verifier's challenge in the case $b = 1$. In this diagram, the curves E_C and E_{MC} are genuine, and the curves E_{AC} and E_{AMC} are fake. However, the cheating verifier cannot tell that these curves are fake, or else one would be able to solve DSSP for the top face of the cube. Hence the simulator's response is indistinguishable from that of the real prover.

Remark 6.3. The indistinguishability portion of the above proof of the zero-knowledge property holds in the quantum setting as well as in the classical setting. Specifically, if we presume the existence of some quantum cheating verifier (CV) which can perform some quantum computation to distinguish the real transcript from the simulated transcript, then one could use this quantum cheating verifier to obtain a quantum algorithm for solving DSSP simply by alternately supplying the CV with either real curves E_{AC} and E_{AMC} (i.e. the real transcript), or with falsified curves E_{AC} and E_{AMC} (i.e. the simulated transcript), and seeing whether the CV's desired computation performs differently in the two cases.

6.3   Unforgeability and Invisibility

Finally, we prove that the protocol satisfies the unforgeability and invisibility properties from Section 4.1.

Proof (Proof of unforgeability). To prove unforgeability, we must show that after making a polynomial number of queries to a signing oracle, an adversary is still unable to generate a valid signature. Note that we have shown that the confirmation and disavowal protocols are zero-knowledge. Forging signatures is then equivalent to solving OMSSCDH.

Proof (Proof of invisibility). To prove invisibility, we must show that after making a polynomial number of queries to a signing oracle, an adversary will still be unable to decide whether a given signature is valid. This problem is equivalent to OMSSDDH.

7   Quantum-Resistant Undeniable Signatures

Under our simplifying assumption from Section 4.1, all parties except possibly the adversary are restricted to classical computation only. In this setting, all the security proofs in Section 6 other than those for the zero-knowledge proofs hold without modification, since none of these proofs ever at any point involves two quantum parties, and hence we do not need to consider quantum interactions.

By contrast, for zero-knowledge proofs, a classical security proof is not always automatically valid against quantum attacks, since there is the possibility of a nontrivial quantum interaction: a quantum cheating verifier could conceivably perform some quantum computation on an auxiliary input containing entangled state which is not accessible to the verifier or simulator [33]. Nevertheless, by Hallgren et al. [19], any classical zero-knowledge proof secure against classical honest verifiers can be transformed into a classical zero knowledge proof secure against quantum cheating verifiers at the cost of doubling the number of messages, under the mild condition that the real message transcripts are quantum computationally indistinguishable from the simulated message transcripts. By Remarks 6.2 and 6.3, the real message transcripts are quantum computationally indistinguishable from the simulated message transcripts, for both the confirmation and disavowal protocols, under the assumption that the various computational problems of Section 5 are infeasible on a quantum computer. Therefore the Hallgren et al. transformation can be applied to our confirmation and disavowal protocols to obtain protocols which are zero-knowledge against quantum cheating verifiers. We remark that the prior work of Aguilar-Melchor et al. [1] does not specifically discuss the case of quantum adversaries, and may also require this transformation in order to achieve security against quantum adversaries.

8   Parameter Sizes

As stated in [13,20], the fastest known quantum isogeny finding algorithms in our setting require $O(n^{1/3})$ running time, where n is the size of the kernel. Based on this figure, we obtain the following parameter sizes and signature sizes for various levels of security:

Security level	$\log_2 p$	Signature size
80 bits	720	5760 bits
112 bits	1008	8064 bits
128 bits	1152	9216 bits

These numbers compare favorably with those of the only other prior quantum-resistant undeniable signature scheme, that of Aguilar-Melchor et al. [1]. For example, at the 128-bit security level, the scheme of [1] requires a signature size of 5000 bits for the code-based portion plus an additional "roughly 40k Bytes" [1, p. 116] for the conventional digital signature portion.

Regarding performance, a comparison is difficult because [1] does not provide any performance numbers. For isogeny computations, recent implementation work of De Feo et al. [13, Table 3] and Fishbein [15, Figure 4.1] demonstrates that a single 1024-bit isogeny computation can be performed in 120 ms on a desktop PC, and in under 1 second on an Android device. Our protocol requires three such computations for signing, up to eight for confirmation, and up to nine for disavowal.

9 Conclusion

In this paper we present a quantum-resistant undeniable signature scheme based on the hardness of computing isogenies between supersingular elliptic curves. Our scheme represents the first quantum-resistant undeniable signature scheme based on a number-theoretic computational assumption, and compares well with the only prior undeniable quantum-resistant signature scheme (a code-based scheme) in terms of performance and bandwidth. Future work may entail developing new protocols such as digital signature schemes or more efficient schemes based on weaker assumptions.

Acknowledgments. We thank the anonymous referees for providing extensive feedback and assistance in improving our article and our presentation. We also thank Andrew M. Childs, Douglas R. Stinson, Vijay M. Patankar, and Srinath Seshadri for helpful comments and suggestions. This work was supported in part by the Natural Sciences and Engineering Research Council of Canada Collaborative Research and Development Grant CRDPJ 405857-10, and an Ontario Ministry of Research and Innovation Early Researcher Award.

References

1. Aguilar-Melchor, C., Bettaieb, S., Gaborit, P., Schrek, J.: A code-based undeniable signature scheme. In: Stam, M. (ed.) IMACC 2013. LNCS, vol. 8308, pp. 99–119. Springer, Heidelberg (2013)
2. Baldi, M., Bianchi, M., Chiaraluce, F., Rosenthal, J., Schipani, D.: Using LDGM codes and sparse syndromes to achieve digital signatures. In: Gaborit, P. (ed.) PQCrypto 2013. LNCS, vol. 7932, pp. 1–15. Springer, Heidelberg (2013)
3. Boucher, D., Gaborit, P., Geiselmann, W., Ruatta, O., Ulmer, F.: Key exchange and encryption schemes based on non-commutative skew polynomials. In: Sendrier, N. (ed.) PQCrypto 2010. LNCS, vol. 6061, pp. 126–141. Springer, Heidelberg (2010)
4. Bröker, R.: Constructing supersingular elliptic curves. J. Comb. Number Theory 1(3), 269–273 (2009)
5. Bröker, R., Charles, D., Lauter, K.: Evaluating large degree isogenies and applications to pairing based cryptography. In: Galbraith, S.D., Paterson, K.G. (eds.) Pairing 2008. LNCS, vol. 5209, pp. 100–112. Springer, Heidelberg (2008)
6. Buchmann, J., Dahmen, E., Hülsing, A.: XMSS - A practical forward secure signature scheme based on minimal security assumptions. In: Yang, B.-Y. (ed.) PQCrypto 2011. LNCS, vol. 7071, pp. 117–129. Springer, Heidelberg (2011)
7. Cayrel, P.-L., Meziani, M.: Post-quantum cryptography: Code-based signatures. In: Kim, T.-H., Adeli, H. (eds.) AST/UCMA/ISA/ACN 2010. LNCS, vol. 6059, pp. 82–99. Springer, Heidelberg (2010)
8. Childs, A., Jao, D., Soukharev, V.: Constructing elliptic curve isogenies in quantum subexponential time. J. Math. Cryptol. 8(1), 1–29 (2014)
9. Couveignes, J.-M.: Hard homogeneous spaces (2006), http://eprint.iacr.org/2006/291/
10. Dagdelen, Ö., Fischlin, M., Gagliardoni, T.: The Fiat–Shamir Transformation in a Quantum World. In: Sako, K., Sarkar, P. (eds.) ASIACRYPT 2013, Part II. LNCS, vol. 8270, pp. 62–81. Springer, Heidelberg (2013)

11. Dahmen, E., Okeya, K., Takagi, T., Vuillaume, C.: Digital signatures out of second-preimage resistant hash functions. In: Buchmann, J., Ding, J. (eds.) PQCrypto 2008. LNCS, vol. 5299, pp. 109–123. Springer, Heidelberg (2008)
12. Feige, U., Fiat, A., Shamir, A.: Zero-knowledge proofs of identity. Journal of Cryptology 1(2), 77–94 (1988)
13. De Feo, L., Jao, D., Plût, J.: Towards quantum-resistant cryptosystems from supersingular elliptic curve isogenies. J. Math. Cryptol. (to appear), http://eprint.iacr.org/2011/506
14. Fiat, A., Shamir, A.: How to prove yourself: Practical solutions to identification and signature problems. In: Odlyzko, A.M. (ed.) CRYPTO 1986. LNCS, vol. 263, pp. 186–194. Springer, Heidelberg (1987)
15. Fishbein, D.: Machine-level software optimization of cryptographic protocols. Master's thesis, University of Waterloo (2014), http://hdl.handle.net/10012/8400
16. Galbraith, S.D.: Constructing isogenies between elliptic curves over finite fields. LMS J. Comput. Math. 2, 118–138 (electronic) (1999)
17. Gentry, C., Peikert, C., Vaikuntanathan, V.: Trapdoors for hard lattices and new cryptographic constructions. In: Proceedings of the Fortieth Annual ACM Symposium on Theory of Computing, STOC 2008, pp. 197–206. ACM, New York (2008)
18. Goldreich, O., Micali, S., Wigderson, A.: Proofs that yield nothing but their validity or all languages in NP have zero-knowledge proof systems. Journal of the Association for Computing Machinery 38(3), 690–728 (1991)
19. Hallgren, S., Kolla, A., Sen, P., Zhang, S.: Making classical honest verifier zero knowledge protocols secure against quantum attacks. In: Aceto, L., Damgård, I., Goldberg, L.A., Halldórsson, M.M., Ingólfsdóttir, A., Walukiewicz, I. (eds.) ICALP 2008, Part II. LNCS, vol. 5126, pp. 592–603. Springer, Heidelberg (2008)
20. Jao, D., De Feo, L.: Towards quantum-resistant cryptosystems from supersingular elliptic curve isogenies. In: Yang, B.-Y. (ed.) PQCrypto 2011. LNCS, vol. 7071, pp. 19–34. Springer, Heidelberg (2011)
21. Jao, D., Soukharev, V.: A subexponential algorithm for evaluating large degree isogenies. In: Hanrot, G., Morain, F., Thomé, E. (eds.) ANTS-IX. LNCS, vol. 6197, pp. 219–233. Springer, Heidelberg (2010)
22. Kurosawa, K., Furukawa, J.: Universally composable undeniable signature. In: Aceto, L., Damgård, I., Goldberg, L.A., Halldórsson, M.M., Ingólfsdóttir, A., Walukiewicz, I. (eds.) ICALP 2008, Part II. LNCS, vol. 5126, pp. 524–535. Springer, Heidelberg (2008)
23. J.C. Lagarias, A.M. Odlyzko. Effective versions of the Chebotarev density theorem. In *Algebraic number fields: L-functions and Galois properties (Proc. Sympos., Univ. Durham, Durham, 1975)*, pages 409–464. Academic Press, London, 1977.
24. McEliece, R.J.: A Public-Key Cryptosystem Based On Algebraic Coding Theory. Deep Space Network Progress Report 44, 114–116 (1978)
25. Micciancio, D., Regev, O.: Lattice-based cryptography. In: Bernstein, D.J., Buchmann, J., Dahmen, E. (eds.) Post-Quantum Cryptography, pp. 147–191. Springer, Heidelberg (2009)
26. Regev, O.: On lattices, learning with errors, random linear codes, and cryptography. In: Proceedings of the Thirty-seventh Annual ACM Symposium on Theory of Computing, STOC 2005, pp. 84–93. ACM, New York (2005)
27. Shor, P.W.: Polynomial-time algorithms for prime factorization and discrete logarithms on a quantum computer. SIAM J. Comput. 26(5), 1484–1509 (1997), Preliminary version in FOCS 1994. arXiv:quant-ph/9508027v2
28. Silverman, J.H.: The arithmetic of elliptic curves. Graduate Texts in Mathematics, vol. 106. Springer, New York (1992) (Corrected reprint of the 1986 original)

29. Stolbunov, A.: Constructing public-key cryptographic schemes based on class group action on a set of isogenous elliptic curves. Adv. Math. Commun. 4(2), 215–235 (2010)

30. Sun, X., Tian, H., Wang, Y.: Toward quantum-resistant strong designated verifier signature from isogenies. In: 4th International Conference on Intelligent Networking and Collaborative Systems (INCoS), pp. 292–296 (2012)

31. Teske, E.: The Pohlig-Hellman method generalized for group structure computation. Journal of Symbolic Computation 27(6), 521–534 (1999)

32. Vélu, J.: Isogénies entre courbes elliptiques. C. R. Acad. Sci. Paris Sér. A-B 273, A238–A241 (1971)

33. Watrous, J.: Zero-knowledge against quantum attacks. In: Kleinberg, J.M. (ed.) STOC, pp. 296–305. ACM (2006)

34. Yasuda, T., Takagi, T., Sakurai, K.: Multivariate signature scheme using quadratic forms. In: Gaborit, P. (ed.) PQCrypto 2013. LNCS, vol. 7932, pp. 243–258. Springer, Heidelberg (2013)

An Asymptotically Optimal Structural Attack on the ABC Multivariate Encryption Scheme

Dustin Moody[1], Ray Perlner[1], and Daniel Smith-Tone[1,2]

[1] National Institute of Standards and Technology,
Gaithersburg, Maryland, USA
[2] Department of Mathematics, University of Louisville,
Louisville, Kentucky, USA
{dustin.moody,ray.perlner,daniel.smith}@nist.gov

Abstract. Historically, multivariate public key cryptography has been less than successful at offering encryption schemes which are both secure and efficient. At PQCRYPTO '13 in Limoges, Tao, Diene, Tang, and Ding introduced a promising new multivariate encryption algorithm based on a fundamentally new idea: hiding the structure of a large matrix algebra over a finite field. We present an attack based on subspace differential invariants inherent to this methodology. The attack is a structural key recovery attack which is asymptotically optimal among all known attacks (including algebraic attacks) on the original scheme and its generalizations.

Keywords: multivariate public key cryptography, differential, invariant, encryption.

1 Introduction

In the mid 1990s, Peter Shor developed efficient algorithms for factoring and computing discrete logarithms with quantum computers [1]. Since that time, the state-of-the-art of quantum computing has changed significantly, indicating that large scale quantum computing may become an eventual reality. In the years since Shor's discovery, there has emerged a rapidly growing community dedicated to the task of constructing algorithms resistant to cryptanalysis with quantum computers.

Multivariate Public Key Cryptography(MPKC) is one among a few serious candidates to have risen to prominence as post-quantum options. The appeal of MPKC is due to several factors. The fundamental problem of solving a system of quadratic equations is known to be NP-hard, and so in the worst case, solving a system of generic quadratic equations is unfeasible for a classical computer; neither is there any indication that the task is easier in the quantum computing paradigm. Furthermore, experience indicates that this problem is hard even in the average case; thus multivariate cryptosystems at least have a chance of being difficult to break. Secondly, multivariate cryptosystems are often very efficient,

M. Mosca (Ed.): PQCrypto 2014, LNCS 8772, pp. 180–196, 2014.

see [2–4]. Finally, such cryptosystems can be very amenable to the user demands, with multiple parameters hidden within the system which can be altered by the user to achieve different performance goals.

Though MPKC has a turbulent history with many schemes failing against only a few attack techniques, there are still some entirely usable and trustworthy quantum-resistant multivariate signature schemes. Specifically, UOV [5], HFE- [6], and HFEv- [7] are noteworthy in this regard. Moreover, some of these schemes have optimizations which have strong theoretical support or have stood unbroken in the literature for some time. Specifically, UOV has a cyclic variant [8] which reduces the key size dramatically, and QUARTZ, an HFEv- scheme, has had its parameters tweaked [9] due to greater confidence in the complexity of algebraically solving the underlying system of equations [10].

Where MPKC has failed more directly has been encryption. There is a striking lack of reliable multivariate encryption schemes in the literature. Many attempts, see [11, 12] for example, have been shown to be weak based on rank or differential weaknesses. The most recent and promising attempt, by Tao et al., see [13], uses a fundamentally new structure for the derivation of an encryption system. Specifically, the scheme masks matrix multiplication to generate a system of structured quadratic equations.

In this article, we present a structural attack which is the asymptotically optimal attack on this matrix encryption scheme, having a complexity on the order of q^{s+4}, where s is the dimension of the matrices in the scheme. This technique uses a differential invariant property of the core map to perform a key recovery attack. We reevaluate some of the security analysis from the original ABC specification and conclude that this attack is asymptotically optimal among structural attacks. In fact, the attack uses a property which uniquely distinguishes the isomorphism class of the core map from that of a random collection of formulae. This attack asymptotically defeats algebraic attacks as well, though falling short of the benchmark established by generic algebraic attacks for the original parameters. This result supports the security claims of the designers (modulo decryption failure).

The paper is organized as follows. In the next section, we present the structure of the original ABC encryption scheme. The following section reviews some of the previous cryptanalyses of the scheme, and clarifies some of the previous attacks. In the subsequent section, we recall differential invariants. The differential invariant structure of the ABC scheme is then presented and the effect of this structure on minrank calculations is derived. In the following section, the complexity of the full attack is calculated and compared to the complexity of other valid structural attacks. Finally, we review these results and discuss the implications for the practical security of the ABC scheme.

2   The ABC Matrix Encryption Scheme

In [13], Tao et al. introduce the ABC Matrix encryption scheme. For the simplicity of the exposition, we will analyze the original scheme noting that all results carry over exactly as stated to the updated version, see [14].

The scheme depends on an initial parameter $s \in \mathbb{N}$. The public key consists of $n = s^2$, variables taking values in a fixed finite field $k = \mathbb{F}_q$, and $m = 2s^2$ equations. The system utilizes the butterfly construction, creating a private collection of formulae Q, and deriving a public key P by composing two invertible linear transformations $U \in GL_n(k)$ and $T \in GL_m(k)$, so that $P = T \circ Q \circ U$. What makes the system unique is the derivation of the map Q. For ease of analysis later, we will denote plaintext by $\bar{x} = (x_1, \ldots, x_n) \in k^n$, ciphertext by $\bar{y} = (y_1, \ldots, y_m) \in k^m$, and the input and output of Q by $\bar{u} = (u_1, \ldots, u_n) = U(x_1, \ldots, x_n) \in k^n$ and $\bar{v} = (v_1, \ldots, v_m) = T^{-1}(y_1, \ldots, y_m) \in k^m$, respectively. The construction begins by defining three $s \times s$ matrices A, B, and C. Specifically, we have:

$$A = \begin{bmatrix} u_1 & u_2 & \cdots & u_s \\ u_{s+1} & u_{s+2} & \cdots & u_{2s} \\ \vdots & \vdots & \ddots & \vdots \\ u_{s^2-s+1} & u_{s^2-s+2} & \cdots & u_{s^2} \end{bmatrix}, B = \begin{bmatrix} b_1 & b_2 & \cdots & b_s \\ b_{s+1} & b_{s+2} & \cdots & b_{2s} \\ \vdots & \vdots & \ddots & \vdots \\ b_{s^2-s+1} & b_{s^2-s+2} & \cdots & b_{s^2} \end{bmatrix},$$

and

$$C = \begin{bmatrix} c_1 & c_2 & \cdots & c_s \\ c_{s+1} & c_{s+2} & \cdots & c_{2s} \\ \vdots & \vdots & \ddots & \vdots \\ c_{s^2-s+1} & c_{s^2-s+2} & \cdots & c_{s^2} \end{bmatrix}.$$

Here the b_i and c_i are linear combinations of the u_i chosen independently and uniformly at random from the collection of all possible k-linear combinations of the u_i.

Next, the $s \times s$ matrices $E_1 = AB$ and $E_2 = AC$ are constructed. Since all of A, B, and C are linear in u_i, E_1 and E_2 are quadratic in the u_i. Finally, setting $Q_{(l-1)s^2+(i-1)s+j}$ to be the (i, j)th element of E_l, we have the private key T, Q, U and the public key $P = T \circ Q \circ U$.

Encryption with this system is standard: given a plaintext $(x_1, \ldots, x_n)$, compute $(y_1, \ldots, y_m) = P(x_1, \ldots, x_n)$. Decryption is somewhat more complicated.

To decrypt, one inverts each of the private maps in turn: apply T^{-1}, invert Q, and apply U^{-1}. To "invert" Q, one assumes that A is invertible, and forms a matrix

$$A^{-1} = \begin{bmatrix} w_1 & w_2 & \cdots & w_s \\ w_{s+1} & w_{s+2} & \cdots & w_{2s} \\ \vdots & \vdots & \ddots & \vdots \\ w_{s^2-s+1} & w_{s^2-s+2} & \cdots & w_{s^2} \end{bmatrix},$$

where the w_i are indeterminants. Then using the relations $A^{-1}E_1 = B$ and $A^{-1}E_2 = C$, we have $m = 2s^2$ linear equations in $2n = 2s^2$ unknowns w_i and u_i.

(We note here that it would be more correct to say $A^{-1}(\bar{u})E_1(\bar{u}) = B(\bar{u})$ and $A^{-1}(\bar{u})E_2(\bar{u}) = C(\bar{u})$, since the values of these matrices depend on $\bar{u}$.) Using, for example, Gaussian elimination one can eliminate all of the variables w_i and most of the u_i. The resulting relations can be substituted back into $E_1(\bar{u})$ and $E_2(\bar{u})$ to obtain a large system of equations in very few variables which can be solved efficiently in a variety of ways.

In [14], the scheme is revised, replacing the square matrices A, B, and C with matrices of dimension $s \times r$, $r \times u$, and $r \times v$, respectively, where $r < s$. In addition, the matrix A consists of random linear forms just as B and C in the improved scheme. The public key is constructed in the exact same way, and encryption is performed by evaluating the public polynomials at the plaintext. Decryption is analogous to the original scheme, except now, since A is $s \times r$, only a left inverse of A on k^r is needed, so the matrix W, a left inverse, is $r \times s$ such that $WA = I_r$, the $r \times r$ identity matrix. Such a W plays the role of A^{-1} in the decryption, and decryption proceeds as above.

3 Security Claims, Revisions, and Corrections

3.1 Decryption Failure

In [13], it was claimed in error that the probability of decryption failure in the ABC scheme is very small, depending specifically on the probability that $dim(ker(A)) \leq 2$. This mistake was corrected in [14], revealing that the probability is approximately q^{-1}, where $|k| = q$. Also in [14], the scheme was generalized so that decryption can be accomplished as long as A (reparametrized as an $s \times r$ matrix) merely has a left inverse as a function on k^r, which occurs with high probability, roughly $1 - q^{r-s-1}$ when $s > r$.

3.2 HOLEs Attack

In [13], HOLEs attack analysis against the scheme was presented. Consider the equation

$$BE_1^{-1}E_2 = C. \tag{1}$$

For $B, C, E_1, E_2 \in M_s(k)$, we can consider the characteristic polynomial $f(x) = x^s + a_{s-1}x^{s-1} + \cdots + a_1x + a_0$ of E_1, and then we have that $E_1(-E_1^{s-1} - a_{s-1}E_1^{s-2} + \cdots - a_1I) = det(E_1)I$ by the Cayley-Hamilton theorem. In fact, the set of all polynomials evaluating to this scalar matrix at E_1 is $a_0 + \langle min_k(E_1) \rangle$, where $min_k(E_1)$ is the minimal polynomial of E_1. Let $xg(x) \in a_0 + \langle min_k(E_1) \rangle$ be a polynomial of smallest degree with constant coefficient zero. Since $det(E_1)I$ is a scalar matrix, it is in the center of $GL_s(k)$, and so multiplying equation (1) on the left by $-E_1g(E_1) = det(E_1)I$, we obtain

$$Bg(E_1)E_2 = det(E_1)C. \tag{2}$$

In this equation, g clearly depends on E_1, which for the purposes of the HOLEs attack is a function of $\bar{y}$. Thus to create a similar relation for plaintext/ciphertext pairs requires us to consider $B(\bar{x}), C(\bar{x}) \in M_s(k[x_1, \ldots, x_n])$ & $E_1(\bar{y}), E_2(\bar{y}) \in M_s(k[y_1, \ldots, y_m])$, where $k[\cdot, \ldots, \cdot]$ is a polynomial ring in the indeterminants $x_1, \ldots, x_n$ and $y_1, \ldots, y_m$, respectively. Then by the invertibility of T we have that the minimal polynomial of $E_1(\bar{y})$ is equal to the characteristic polynomial. Thus there is a polynomial $g(z) \in k(y_1 \ldots, y_m)[z]$ of degree $s - 1$ (specifically $(-min_{k(y_1,\ldots,y_m)}(E_1(\bar{y})) + det(E_1(\bar{y})))/z$) such that $zg(z) = det(E_1(\bar{y}))$. Clearly, if $E_1(\bar{y})$ is singular then equation (1) is invalid; however, equation (2) still holds since

$$Bg(E_1)E_2 = Bg(AB)AC = BAg(BA)C = 0,$$

with the last equality due to the fact that the characteristic polynomials of AB and BA are identical. We may then obtain the relation (2). Notice that if U and T are linear as in the original description of the scheme then this equation is homogeneous of degree $s + 1$, specifically:

$$\sum_{i=1}^{n} \sum_{j_1,\ldots,j_s=1}^{m} \alpha_{i,j_1,\ldots,j_s} x_i y_{j_1} \cdots y_{j_s} = 0. \tag{3}$$

Even in this more manageable situation, the complexity of finding a nontrivial solution is immense. First, the adversary must generate $O(n\binom{m}{s}) = O(s^2\binom{2s^2}{s})$ plaintext/ciphertext pairs, and then solve a system of roughly $s^2\binom{2s^2}{s}$ equations in $s^2\binom{2s^2}{s}$ variables. The complexity of this operation is roughly $(s^2\binom{2s^2}{s})^\omega$ where $\omega = 2.3766$ operations. In the more realistic scenario of having a nonhomogeneous system, the analysis in [13] indicates that the complexity of the HOLEs attack is $O((s^2\binom{2s^s+s}{s} + 2s^2 + 1)^\omega)$.

Remark 1. It is important to note that the HOLEs attack fails in the generalization [14] because the matrices are no longer square.

3.3 Rank Attacks

Rank attacks use linear maps associated with the public key to detect abnormal behavior. In the context of the ABC scheme, we may look at the associated quadratic forms of the public and private keys, or more or less equivalently, at the differentials of these maps. The MinRank attack searches for maps of low rank when viewed as matrices. We will discuss the MinRank attack in greater detail as well as a variant of the high rank attack not considered in [13] in Sections 5 and 6. The dual rank attack searches for a small subspace of the plaintext space which is in the kernel of a large subspace of the span of the maps.

In [13], it was stated that the task of finding a subspace of dimension $n - 2s$ of the associated quadratic forms which share a common nonzero element in their kernels is of complexity $O(n^6 q^{2s})$. This claim is overcautious. Given an element Q_0 in the first row of either $E_1(\bar{u})$ or $E_2(\bar{u})$, the formula is derived from the product of the first row of $A(\bar{u})$ and some column of $B(\bar{u})$ or $C(\bar{u})$ respectively. Since these columns are independent of one another and follow the uniform distribution on the set of all column vectors (the joint distribution is inherited from the i.i.d. entries of B and C), Q_0 has rank $2s$ with near certainty. Since Q_0 has a matrix representation in the block form:

$$
Q_0 = \begin{bmatrix} \begin{array}{c|ccc} R_1 & R_2 \cdots R_s \\ \hline R_{s+1} & \\ \vdots & 0 \\ R_{2s-1} & \end{array} \end{bmatrix},
$$

where each R_i is an $s \times s$ matrix, any element $\bar{z}$ in the kernel of Q_0 has an s-dimensional leading block of zeros with probability $\prod_{j=0}^{s-1} \frac{q^{s^2}-q^j}{q^{s^2}}$ which is extremely close to one. The first s rows of Q_0 put a further s constraints on $\bar{z}$. Given that the condition of being in the kernel of s such maps of the same structure results in an expected solution space of dimension 0, it is clear that there is no nontrivial element in the kernel of any large subspace of the span of the associated matrices. Thus the dual rank attack is nonexistent for the ABC scheme.

3.4   Algebraic Attacks

Based on an analysis of the degree of regularity for the ABC scheme the designers computed a degree of regularity $d_{reg} = 9$, and given the formula from [15] they estimated the complexity of the algebraic attack to be approximately

$$
\binom{n + d_{reg}}{d_{reg}}^{2.3766} = \binom{73}{9}^{2.3766} \approx 2^{86}.
$$

4   Subspace Differential Invariants

Let $f : k^n \to k^m$ be an arbitrary fixed function on k^n. Consider the differential $Df(a, x) = f(a + x) - f(a) - f(x) + f(0)$. We can express the differential as an n-tuple of differential coordinate forms in the following way: $[Df(a, x)]_i = a^T Df_i x$, where Df_i is a symmetric matrix representation of the action on the ith coordinate of the bilinear differential.

In [16], the following definition of a differential invariant was provided:

Definition 1. *A differential invariant of a map $f : k^n \to k^m$ is a subspace $V \subseteq k^n$ with the property that there exists a $W \subseteq k^n$ of dimension at most $\dim(V)$ for which simultaneously $AV \subseteq W$ for all $A \in Span_i(Df_i)$.*

The motivation for the definition is to capture the behaviour of a nonlinear function which acts linearly on a subspace.

We note that any simultaneous invariant of all $Span_i(Df_i)$ satisfies the above definition, as well as invariants in the balanced oil and vinegar primitive, which are found in the product of an element and the inverse of another element in

$Span_i(Df_i)$. A differential invariant is thus a more general construct than a simultaneous invariant among all differential coordinate forms.

A natural generalization of the notion of a differential invariant is a subspace differential invariant.

Definition 2. *A* subspace differential invariant *of a map* $f : k^n \rightarrow k^m$ *with respect to a subspace* $X \subseteq k^m$ *is a subspace* $V \subseteq k^n$ *with the property that there exists a* $W \subseteq k^n$ *of dimension at most* $dim(V)$ *such that simultaneously* $AV \subseteq W$ *for all* $A = \sum_{i=1}^{m} x_i Df_i$ *where* $(x_1, \ldots, x_m) \in X$, *i.e.* $A \in Span_X(Df_i)$.

While the motivation for the differential invariant is to detect the linear action of a function on a subspace, the motivation for the subspace differential invariant is to detect the linear action of a subspace of the span of the public polynomials on a subspace of the plaintext space.

5   The Differential Invariant Structure of the ABC scheme

5.1   Prototypical Band-Spaces

Each component of the central $Q(\bar{u}) = E_1(\bar{u}) \| E_2(\bar{u})$ map may be written as:

$$Q_{(i-1)s+j} = \sum_{l=1}^{s} u_{(i-1)s+l} b_{(l-1)s+j}, \tag{4}$$

for the E_1 equations, and likewise, for the E_2 equations:

$$Q_{s^2+(i-1)s+j} = \sum_{l=1}^{s} u_{(i-1)s+l} c_{(l-1)s+j} \tag{5}$$

where i and j run from 1 to s.

Note that these $2s^2$ component equations may be grouped into s sets, indexed by i, of $2s$ equations. In particular note that the only quadratic monomials contained in $Q_{(i-1)s+j}$ and $Q_{s^2+(i-1)s+j}$ are those involving at least one factor of the variables $u_{(i-1)s+1}, \ldots, u_{(i-1)s+s}$. Moreover, since the coefficients of the linear polynomials $b_r(u)$ and $c_r(u)$ are uniformly random and independent, the nonzero coefficents are uniformly random and independent within each set of $2s$ equations.

Definition 3. *The* ith band-space of maps $\mathcal{B}_i$ *is the* $2s$-dimensional space of quadratic forms given by

$$\mathcal{B}_i = Span\{Q_{(i-1)s+1}, Q_{(i-1)s+2}, \cdots, Q_{is}, Q_{s^2+(i-1)s+1}, Q_{s^2+(i-1)s+2}, \cdots, Q_{s^2+is}\}.$$

In particular, the ith band-space is the span of the maps in the private key derived from the product of the* ith row of A with the columns of B and C.

Any map Q_0 in the ith band-space has a differential in block form:

$$
DQ_0 = \left[
\begin{array}{c|c|c}
0 & R_1 & 0 \\
\hline
R_1^T & R_2 & R_3 \\
\hline
0 & R_3^T & 0
\end{array}
\right]
\tag{6}
$$

having a band of nonzero values restricted to the ith s-dimensional block column and ith S-dimensional block row, hence the name. Notice that any vector $\bar{u}$ of the form:

$$(u_1, \ldots, u_{(i-1)s}, 0, \ldots, 0, u_{is+1}, \ldots, u_{s2})^T$$

is mapped to a vector $\bar{v}$ of the form:

$$(0, \ldots, 0, v_{(i-1)s+1}, \ldots, v_{is-1}, 0, \ldots, 0)^T$$

by the differential of any map in $\mathcal{B}_i$. Therefore, the space of all such $\bar{u}$ is a subspace differential invariant of Q with respect to $\mathcal{B}_i$.

5.2   Generalized Band-Spaces

A critical observation is that the band-spaces associated with the rows of A are not the only band-spaces corresponding to a subspace differential invariant.

Definition 4. *Fix an arbitrary vector v in the rowspace of A, i.e. $v = \sum_{d=1}^{s} \lambda_d A_d$ where A_d is the dth row of A. The $2s$-dimensional space of quadratic forms $\mathcal{B}_v$ given by the span of the columns of vB and vC is called the* generalized band-space *generated by v.*

Theorem 1. *There is a subspace $V \subseteq k^n$ which is a subspace differential invariant with respect to $\mathcal{B}_v$ for all v in the rowspace of A. Moreover, $\text{rank}(DQ) \leq 2s$ for all $Q \in \mathcal{B}_v$.*

Proof. We prove the result for $v = \lambda_1 A_1 + \lambda_2 A_2$, an arbitrary linear combination of the first two rows of A. The general result follows from an analogous argument.

Any quadratic form in $\mathcal{B}_v$ is a linear combination of the columns of vB and vC, $Q_0 = \sum_{l=1}^{s} \gamma_l vB_l + \sum_{l=1}^{s} \delta_l vC_l$. This quantity can be rewritten as $Q_0 = v(\sum_{l=1}^{s} \gamma_l B_l + \sum_{l=1}^{s} \delta_l C_l)$. Since each of the entries of B and C are independent and random linear combinations in the coefficients of $\bar{u}$, each entry of the linear combination of the column vectors is itself a fixed but arbitrary such linear combination. Expressing the ith entry in this column vector as $\sum_{j=1}^{s^2} \zeta_{i,j} u_j$, and using the fact that $v = [\lambda_1 u_1 + \lambda_2 u_{s+1}, \lambda_1 u_2 + \lambda_2 u_{s+2}, \ldots, \lambda_1 u_s + \lambda_2 u_{2s}]$ we obtain:

$$Q_0 = v(\sum_{l=1}^{s} \gamma_l B_l + \sum_{l=1}^{s} \delta_l C_l)$$

$$= \sum_{i=1}^{s}(\lambda_1 u_i + \lambda_2 u_{s+i}) \sum_{j=1}^{s^2} \zeta_{i,j} u_j \qquad (7)$$

$$= \sum_{i=1}^{s}\sum_{j=1}^{s^2}(\lambda_1 \zeta_{i,j} u_i u_j + \lambda_2 \zeta_{i,j} u_{s+i} u_j).$$

Let M be the $s^2 \times s^2$ matrix obtained from this sum by setting the (i,j)th entry equal to the coefficient of $u_i u_j$, the $(s+i,j)$th entry equal to the coefficient of $u_{s+i} u_j$, and all other entries zero:

$$M = \begin{bmatrix} \lambda_1 \zeta_{1,1} & \lambda_1 \zeta_{1,2} & \cdots & \lambda_1 \zeta_{1,s^2} \\ \vdots & \vdots & \ddots & \vdots \\ \lambda_1 \zeta_{s,1} & \lambda_1 \zeta_{s,2} & \cdots & \lambda_1 \zeta_{s,s^2} \\ \lambda_2 \zeta_{1,1} & \lambda_2 \zeta_{1,2} & \cdots & \lambda_2 \zeta_{1,s^2} \\ \vdots & \vdots & \ddots & \vdots \\ \lambda_2 \zeta_{s,1} & \lambda_2 \zeta_{s,2} & \cdots & \lambda_2 \zeta_{s,s^2} \\ 0 & 0 & \cdots & 0 \\ \vdots & \vdots & \ddots & \vdots \\ 0 & 0 & \cdots & 0 \end{bmatrix}$$

Notice that the differential of Q_0 is exactly the sum of M and M^T: $DQ_0 = M + M^T$. Since M has rank at most s, M^T has rank at most s. Thus by the subadditivity of rank, the rank of DQ_0 is at most $2s$. By the randomness of the coefficients of B and C the rank of DQ_0 is $2s$ with overwhelming probability (roughly q^{s-s^2-1}).

Consider performing column operations on M^T. In particular, consider operations such as subtracting $\lambda_2 \lambda_1^{-1}$ times column 1 from column $s+1$. It is clear that these operations can be used to eliminate the entries in columns $s+1$ through $2s$ of M^T. Let R be the matrix representing these column operations. Then $M^T R$ only has nonzero entries in the first s columns. Similarly, $R^T M$ only has nonzero entries in the first s rows.

Finally, consider the action $R^T DQ_0 R$. By distributivity we have $R^T DQ_0 R = R^T M R + R^T M^T R$, and by associativity, we have $(R^T M)R + R^T(M^T R)$. In the first summand column operations are performed on a matrix with nonzero entries in only the first s rows, resulting in a matrix with entries in only the top s rows. The second summand is the transpose of the first. Therefore, we see that $R^T DQ_0 R$ has the form:

$$R^T D Q_0 R = \left[\begin{array}{c|c} D_1 & D_2 \\ \hline D_2^T & 0 \end{array} \right],$$

where D_1 is $s \times s$ and D_2 is $s \times s^2 - s$. Thus $R^T D Q_0 R$ maps the subspace V' consisting of column vectors with the first s entries zero to its orthogonal complement. Consequently $D Q_0$ maps $R V'$ to an s dimensional space. Further, notice that the row and column operations depend only on v, and not on the fixed but arbitrary $Q_0 \in \mathcal{B}_v$. Therefore DQ maps RV' to an s dimensional space for all $Q \in \mathcal{B}_v$. Thus RV' is a subspace differential invariant with respect to $\mathcal{B}_v$.

Remark 2. *We note that a subspace differential invariant V with respect to a generalized band-space $\mathcal{B}_v$ is special in that V, of dimension $s^2 - s$, is mapped to a subspace W of dimension s by any differential of a band-space map. Thus, given two such subspace differential invariants, V and V' with respect to $\mathcal{B}_v$ and $\mathcal{B}_{v'}$, we can find another subspace differential invariant $V \cap V'$ with respect to $Span(\mathcal{B}_v, \mathcal{B}_{v'})$. In this manner we can generate subspace differential invariants with respect to spaces containing differentials of even full rank. In particular, if one manages to find a linear combination of the public differentials which is of rank $s^2 - 2s$, the kernel reveals some information about the structure of the scheme. Given the invariant structure of the ABC scheme, this task amounts to finding a linear combination that avoids any equation derived from a $\frac{s+2}{2}$ dimensional subspace of the rowspace of A.*

This technique forms the foundation of a high rank version of a differential invariant attack. The complexity of recovering such a map is on the order of $q^{3s/2}$, and more information is still needed to constitute a full attack; therefore, we conclude that the ABC scheme is safe from the high rank side.

6 The Effect of Invariant Structure on the Complexity of MinRank

The Minrank attack searches for a low rank linear combination of m $n \times n$ bilinear forms over $k = \mathbb{F}_q$, $B_1, \ldots, B_m$. In the case of Ding's ABC scheme, $m = 2s^2$, $n = s^2$, and the B_i maps are the public differentials DP_i. The attack proceeds by randomly choosing $\lceil \frac{m}{n} \rceil$ vectors, x_k, setting

$$\left(\sum_{i=1}^{m} \bar{t}_i D P_i \right) x_k = 0 \tag{8}$$

and solving for the $\bar{t}_i$. The attack succeeds when all of the x_k are in the kernel of the target map. Simple rank analysis suggests that the probability of success per iteration is $q^{-r \lceil \frac{m}{n} \rceil}$ where r is the rank of the target map. In the case of the

ABC scheme, the target maps are those within a band space, which typically have rank $2s$. Therefore, if we consider the rank of the target maps alone, we should expect a complexity on the order of q^{4s}. A more careful rank analysis reveals that the kernels of the band-space maps are interlinked in the sense given in [17]. Computing via a crawling process as described in [17], we see that the best estimate from a rank perspective has expected complexity roughly q^{2s}, since there are roughly sq^{2s} such kernels. However, the actual complexity of this process is on the order of q^s, due to the subspace differential invariant structure, as will be demonstrated in this section. To emphasize the advantage the differential invariant structure provides, we note that the recovery of maps of rank $r = 2s$ is accomplished with this attack in time roughly $q^{r/2}$.

This demonstation proceeds by defining the "band kernel", an $s^2 - s$ dimensional subspace of k^{s^2}, corresponding to each generalized band-space, $\mathcal{B}_v$. We then show that with probability q^{-1}, if x_1 and x_2 fall within band kernel j, then they are both in the kernel of some band-space differential

$$DQ = \sum_{Q_i \in \mathcal{A}_j} \tau_i DQ_i,$$

where the Q_i in the sum form a basis $\mathcal{A}_v$ of the band-space generated by v, $\mathcal{B}_v$.

Definition 5. *Let $u_1 \ldots u_{s^2}$ be the components of $U\bar{x}$ and fix an arbitrary vector v in the rowspace of A, i.e. $v = \sum_{d=1}^{s} \lambda_d A_d$ where A_d is the dth row of A. An s^2 dimensional vector, $\bar{x}$ is in the band kernel generated by v iff $\sum_{d=1}^{s} \lambda_d u_{ds+k} = 0$ for $k = 1 \ldots s$.*

Theorem 2. *If x_1 and x_2 fall within band kernel generated by v, then they are both in the kernel of some generalized band-space differential $DQ = \sum_{Q_i \in \mathcal{B}_v} \tau_i DQ_i$ with probability approximately q^{-1}.*

Proof. A DQ meeting the above condition exists iff there is a nontrivial solution to the following system of equations

$$\sum_{Q_i \in \mathcal{B}_v} \tau_i DQ_i {x_1}^T = 0$$

$$\sum_{Q_i \in \mathcal{B}_v} \tau_i DQ_i {x_2}^T = 0 \tag{9}$$

Expressed in a basis where the first s basis vectors are chosen to be outside the band kernel, and the remaining $s^2 - s$ basis vectors are chosen from within the band kernel, the band-space differentials take the form:

$$DQ_i = \begin{bmatrix} S_i & R_i \\ \hline R_i^T & 0 \end{bmatrix} \tag{10}$$

where R_i is a random $s \times s^2 - s$ matrix and S_i is a random symmetric $s \times s$ matrix. Likewise x_1 and x_2 take the form $(0|\ x_k\ )$. Thus removing the redundant degrees of freedom we have the system of $2s$ equations in $2s$ variables:

$$\sum_{i=1}^{2s} \tau_i R_i x_1{}^T = 0$$

$$\sum_{i=1}^{2s} \tau_i R_i x_2{}^T = 0 \tag{11}$$

This has a nontrivial solution precicely when the following matrix is singular:

$$\left[\begin{array}{ccc} | & | & | \\ R_1 x_1{}^T & R_2 x_1{}^T & \ldots R_{2s} x_1{}^T \\ | & | & | \\ \hline | & | & | \\ R_1 x_2{}^T & R_2 x_2{}^T & \ldots R_{2s} x_2{}^T \\ | & | & | \end{array}\right] \tag{12}$$

As the R_i are random and independent, this is simply a random matrix over $k = \mathbb{F}_q$, which is singular with probability approximately q^{-1}, for practical parameters.

The band space differentials DQ_i for the private maps $Q_i \in \mathcal{B}_v$ generate a subspace of the space generated by public differentials DP_i, the solutions $\sum_{Q_i \in \mathcal{B}_v} \tau_i DQ_i$ of equation (9) form a subspace of the solutions $\sum_{i=1}^{2s^2} \bar{t}_i DP_i$ of equation (8). The condition on x_1 for membership in the band kernel of $\mathcal{B}_v$ for some v is that the matrix A, formed as in equation (13) from the components $u_1 \ldots u_{s^2}$ of Ux_1, is singular.

$$A = \begin{bmatrix} u_1 & u_2 & \cdots & u_s \\ u_{s+1} & u_{s+2} & \cdots & u_{2s} \\ \vdots & \vdots & \ddots & \vdots \\ u_{s^2-s+1} & u_{s^2-s+2} & \cdots & u_{s^2} \end{bmatrix} \tag{13}$$

This occurs with probability approximately q^{-1}. Given x_1 is in some band kernel, x_2 has a probability of q^{-s} of being chosen within the same band kernel. Given that x_1 and x_2 are in the same band kernel, the probability that they are in the kernel of the same band-space map is q^{-1}. Thus, a generalized band space map may be found among the solutions of equation (8) with probability $q^{-(s+2)}$.

Equation (8) is a system of $2s^2$ equations in $2s^2$ variables, one might expect it to generally have a 0-dimensional space of solutions. There are, however, linear dependencies among the equations, due to the fact that the DQ_i are symmetric matrices. In odd characteristic, the only linear dependency is $x_1 DQ_i x_2{}^T - x_2 DQ_i x_1{}^T = 0$, thus we should expect a 1-dimensional space of solutions. However, in even characteristic there are two more linear dependencies:

$x_1 DQ_i x_1{}^T = 0$ and $x_2 DQ_i x_2{}^T = 0$. Thus, in even characteristic, we expect a 3-dimensional solution space for equation (8). Finding the expected 1-dimensional space of band-space solutions in this 3-dimensional space costs q^2+q+1 rank operations, which in turn cost $(s^2)^3$ field operations. Thus the total cost of finding a band-space map using MinRank is approximately $q^{s+4}s^6$ for even characteristic and $q^{s+2}s^6$ for odd characteristic.

We ran a series of experiments to determine the number of trials required for randomly selected x_1 and x_2 to lie in the kernel of a differential of rank $2s$. The experiments were performed using toy examples of the scheme with $q = 3, 5$ and $s = 4, 5, 6, 7, 8$. In each of these cases the data support the theoretical complexity of $O(q^{s+2})$.

7   Complexity of Invariant Attack

While the detection of a low rank map in the space generated by the public differentials already constitutes a distinguisher from a random system of equations, it still falls short of a full key extraction. However, once two low rank differentials, DQ_1 and DQ_2, from the same generalized band space are found, the attacker can use similar methods to those used to attack balanced oil and vinegar. Recall that oil and vinegar can be broken by computing a product matrix $M = M_1^{-1}M_2$ and searching for large invariant subspaces. One complication arises, however which is that neither DQ_1 nor DQ_2 will be invertible, only having rank $2s$. This can be overcome by simply restricting DQ_1 and DQ_2 to act on random $2s$ dimensional subspace, W, of k^n. As long as the restrictions $DQ_1(W), DQ_2(W)$ are full rank in W, then $DQ_1(W)^{-1}DQ_2(W)$ will have an s dimensional invariant subspace, whose generators are also generators of the band kernel associated with DQ_1 and DQ_2.

Note that once we've found DQ_1 in $\mathcal{B}_v$, finding DQ_2 is approximately q times less costly. Since DQ_1 is known to contain in its kernel two vectors x_1 and x_2 from the band kernel generated by v, we simply need to find a rank $2s$ map, DQ_2, in the space of public differentials, whose kernel contains x_1 and another vector x_3. With overwhelming probability the only way this will occur is if x_3 is in the band kernel generated by v and DQ_2 is in $\mathcal{B}_v$.

Given bases for s independent band kernels generated by $v_1, \ldots, v_s$ we can reconstruct a private key of the same structure as that of the original ABC scheme, which has the same public differentials as the instance we are attacking. To see this, first note that there exists a U' for which the generalized band spaces $\mathcal{B}_{v_1} \ldots \mathcal{B}_{v_s}$ take the form of ordinary band spaces (i.e. for which $(U'^{-1})^T DQU'^{-1}$ takes the form given in equation (6) when DQ is in $\mathcal{B}_{v_i}$.) U' is simply given by $U' = VU$, where V obeys

$$A(Vu) = \begin{bmatrix} v_1(u) \\ v_2(u) \\ \vdots \\ v_s(u) \end{bmatrix}.$$

Moreover there exists a B' C' and T' corresponding to U', that will give the same public key as U, B, C and T. These are given by:

$$B'(Vu) = B(u) \; i.e. \; B'(u') = B(V^{-1}u')$$
$$C'(Vu) = C(u) \; i.e. \; C'(u') = C(V^{-1}u')$$
$$T'(e_1', e_2') = T(V^{-1}e_1', V^{-1}e_2').$$

Thus, there exists an ABC private key, whose prototypical band spaces are equal to the generalized band spaces found by our attack. The task then remains to find it, or something equivalent. First note that the elements of row j of $A(U'x)$, which we will denote as $\bar{A}_j(U'x)$, are are in the band kernel generated by v_i for all $i \neq j$. The intersection of the band kernels generated by $v_1, \ldots, v_{j-1}, v_{j+1}, \ldots, v_s$ is readily computable, given what we already have, and it has dimension s, and is therefore identical to the space generated by the elements of $\bar{A}_j(U'x)$.

This allows us to compute a map U'' which mostly mimics the action of U'. Specifically U'' only differs from U' by mixing the elements within the rows of the matrix A. i.e. $\bar{A}_j(U''x) = \Omega_j \bar{A}_j(U'x)$, where Ω_j is a nonsingular linear operator on s variables. U'' may also be extended into a full private key, U'', B'', C'', T'' for the target public key. The choice of B'' and C'' is straightforward:

$$B''(u'') = B'(U'U''^{-1}u'')$$
$$C''(u'') = C'(U'U''^{-1}u'')$$

All that remains is the choice of T''. To demonstrate that a choice is possible note that

$$\bar{A}_j(U''x)B''(U''x) = [\Omega_j \bar{A}_j(U'x)]B''(U''x)$$
$$= \Omega_j[\bar{A}_j(U'x)B''(U''x)]$$
$$= \Omega_j(\bar{A}_j(U'x)B'(U'x))$$

And similarly:

$$\bar{A}_j(U''x)C''(U''x) = \Omega_j(\bar{A}_j(U'x)C'(U'x)).$$

Thus, the components of $E'(U'x) = (A(U'x)B'(U'x), A(U'x)C'(U'x))$ are linearly related to the components of $E''(U''x) = (A(U''x)B''(U''x), A(U''x)C''(U''x))$ by the invertible maps Ω_j. There therefore exists an invertible T'' such that $T''E''(U''x) = T'E'(U'x) = TE(Ux)$.

All that remains is to solve for T'', B'', and C'', given our U''. This can be done by solving linear equations in the coefficients of B'', C'' and T''^{-1}:

$$D_k(A(x)B''(x), A(x)C''(x)) = \sum_l T''^{-1}_{kl}(U''^{-1})^T Dy_l(x)U''^{-1}$$

where the y_l are the components of the public map $TE(Ux)$.

The primary cost of the attack involves finding the s independent band kernels. Thus, the cost of a full private key extraction is $q^{s+4}s^7$ for even characteristic and $q^{s+2}s^7$ for odd characteristic.

Remark 3. The full key recovery attack for the improved ABC scheme of [14] (using an $s \times r$ A and n variables) requires $sq^{r+4}n^3$ operations for even characteristic and $sq^{r+2}n^3$ operations for odd characteristic.

8   Conclusion

The ABC scheme offers a promising new idea for the development of multivariate encryption schemes. Although the original presentation of the scheme contained errors— most significantly in the estimated probability of decryption failure— the scheme is easily generalized to nonsquare matrices and these anomalies are inconsequential in this context. In particular, the HOLEs attack is nonexistent when A, B, and C are replaced with rectangular matrices.

The attack outlined in this article exploits the subspace differential invariant structure inherent to the ABC methodology. The attack method works both for the original scheme and when applied to the updated scheme. With the original parameters, the attack is asymptotically the most efficient structural attack, with bit complexity scaling linearly with s, the square root of the number of variables. In the improved scheme, the attack scales in bit complexity in proportion to the parameter r which is less than the square root of the number of variables. This analysis is tighter than any relevant rank analysis in the literature, with the most appropriate technique in [17] scaling in bit complexity linearly with $2s$. In comparison, even the bit complexity of algebraic attacks scale superlinearly in s, though the break-even point for the two attacks is slightly beyond the 120-bit security threshold. Taking both time and memory into consideration, however, the differential invariant attack may be the more practical.

A remarkable fact about the attack outlined in this article is that it exploits characteristics which uniquely distinguish the public polynomials in the ABC scheme or its improvement from random formulae, namely, the existence of the s subspace differential invariants. The existence of the differential invariants relative to the band spaces is *equivalent* to the property of being isomorphic to a product of matrices of linear forms as in the central map of the ABC scheme; indeed, the attack produces such an isomorphism. In this sense, it is hard to imagine any key recovery attack on such a scheme designed for 80-bit security which is significantly more efficient in terms of time than the algebraic attack, directly solving the system via Gröbner Bases, or an XL variant such as the Mutant XL algorithms, see [18–20].

On the other hand, it is worthwhile mentioning Gröbner basis techniques for solving MinRank problems using minors modeling as in [21], and perhaps most notably exemplified in [22]. Assuming no additional structure in the MinRank instances arising from the cryptanalysis of the ABC scheme generic, the degree of regularity of the resulting MinRank polynomial systems is $2s+1$ for small values of s, and so the complexity of this approach is immense. The actual MinRank instances arising from the ABC scheme, however, hold some of the structure of the central map and so there is some hope for improvement in this area, though this remains an open problem.

While it is clear that the decryption failure issue of the ABC scheme can be fixed by inflating the field size and/or by making the core matrices rectangular, the scalability of the scheme is an issue. The public key size of the original scheme scales with the *sixth* power of s. If we take into consideration security requirements beyond 80 bits, the ABC scheme becomes problematic; increasing s by one more than doubles the key size. While the evidence seems to suggest that the enhanced ABC scheme, despite having such a distinct differential structure, may ironically be secure, the task of turning the scheme into a more finely tuneable technology is still an open question.

References

1. Shor, P.W.: Polynomial-time algorithms for prime factorization and discrete logarithms on a quantum computer. SIAM J. Sci. Stat. Comp. 26, 1484 (1997)
2. Chen, A.I.-T., Chen, M.-S., Chen, T.-R., Cheng, C.-M., Ding, J., Kuo, E.L.-H., Lee, F.Y.-S., Yang, B.-Y.: SSE implementation of multivariate PKCs on modern x86 CPUs. In: Clavier, C., Gaj, K. (eds.) CHES 2009. LNCS, vol. 5747, pp. 33–48. Springer, Heidelberg (2009)
3. Chen, A.I.-T., Chen, C.-H.O., Chen, M.-S., Cheng, C.-M., Yang, B.-Y.: Practical-sized instances of multivariate PKCs: Rainbow, TTS, and ℓIC-derivatives. In: Buchmann, J., Ding, J. (eds.) PQCrypto 2008. LNCS, vol. 5299, pp. 95–108. Springer, Heidelberg (2008)
4. Yang, B.-Y., Cheng, C.-M., Chen, B.-R., Chen, J.-M.: Implementing minimized multivariate PKC on low-resource embedded systems. In: Clark, J.A., Paige, R.F., Polack, F.A.C., Brooke, P.J. (eds.) SPC 2006. LNCS, vol. 3934, pp. 73–88. Springer, Heidelberg (2006)
5. Kipnis, A., Patarin, J., Goubin, L.: Unbalanced oil and vinegar signature schemes. In: Stern, J. (ed.) EUROCRYPT 1999. LNCS, vol. 1592, pp. 206–222. Springer, Heidelberg (1999)
6. Patarin, J., Goubin, L., Courtois, N.T.: C_-+^* and HM: Variations around two schemes of T. Matsumoto and H. Imai. In: Ohta, K., Pei, D. (eds.) ASIACRYPT 1998. LNCS, vol. 1514, pp. 35–50. Springer, Heidelberg (1998)
7. Patarin, J., Courtois, N., Goubin, L.: QUARTZ, 128-bit long digital signatures. In: Naccache, D. (ed.) CT-RSA 2001. LNCS, vol. 2020, pp. 282–297. Springer, Heidelberg (2001)
8. Petzoldt, A., Bulygin, S., Buchmann, J.: CyclicRainbow – A multivariate signature scheme with a partially cyclic public key. In: Gong, G., Gupta, K.C. (eds.) INDOCRYPT 2010. LNCS, vol. 6498, pp. 33–48. Springer, Heidelberg (2010)
9. Anonymous: New parameters for quartz. Private Communication (2013)
10. Ding, J., Yang, B.Y.: Degree of regularity for hfev and hfev-. In: [23], pp. 52–66
11. Goubin, L., Courtois, N.T.: Cryptanalysis of the TTM cryptosystem. In: Okamoto, T. (ed.) ASIACRYPT 2000. LNCS, vol. 1976, pp. 44–57. Springer, Heidelberg (2000)
12. Tsujii, S., Gotaishi, M., Tadaki, K., Fujita, R.: Proposal of a signature scheme based on STS trapdoor. In: Sendrier, N. (ed.) PQCrypto 2010. LNCS, vol. 6061, pp. 201–217. Springer, Heidelberg (2010)

13. Tao, C., Diene, A., Tang, S., Ding, J.: Simple matrix scheme for encryption. In: [23], pp. 231–242
14. Tao, C., Diene, A., Tang, S., Ding, J.: Improvement of simple matrix scheme for encryption. Personally Communicated (2013), Corresponding Author: Ding, J.
15. Bardet, M., Faugere, J.C., Salvy, B.: On the complexity of gröbner basis computation of semi-regular overdetermined algebraic equations. In: Proceedings of the International Conference on Polynomial System Solving (2004)
16. Perlner, R.A., Smith-Tone, D.: A classification of differential invariants for multivariate post-quantum cryptosystems. In: [23], pp. 165–173
17. Yang, B.-Y., Chen, J.-M.: Building secure tame-like multivariate public-key cryptosystems: The new TTS. In: Boyd, C., González Nieto, J.M. (eds.) ACISP 2005. LNCS, vol. 3574, pp. 518–531. Springer, Heidelberg (2005)
18. Ding, J., Buchmann, J., Mohamed, M., Mohamed, W., Weinmann, R.: Mutant xl. In: SCC 2008, LMIB, pp. 16–22 (2008)
19. Mohamed, M.S.E., Mohamed, W.S.A.E., Ding, J., Buchmann, J.: *MXL2*: Solving polynomial equations over GF(2) using an improved mutant strategy. In: Buchmann, J., Ding, J. (eds.) PQCrypto 2008. LNCS, vol. 5299, pp. 203–215. Springer, Heidelberg (2008)
20. Mohamed, M.S.E., Cabarcas, D., Ding, J., Buchmann, J., Bulygin, S.: MXL3: An efficient algorithm for computing gröbner bases of zero-dimensional ideals. In: Lee, D., Hong, S. (eds.) ICISC 2009. LNCS, vol. 5984, pp. 87–100. Springer, Heidelberg (2010)
21. Faugère, J.C., Din, M.S.E., Spaenlehauer, P.J.: Computing loci of rank defects of linear matrices using gröbner bases and applications to cryptology. In: Koepf, W. (ed.) ISSAC, pp. 257–264. ACM (2010)
22. Bettale, L., Faugère, J.C., Perret, L.: Cryptanalysis of hfe, multi-hfe and variants for odd and even characteristic. Des. Codes Cryptography 69, 1–52 (2013)
23. Gaborit, P. (ed.): PQCrypto 2013. LNCS, vol. 7932. Springer, Heidelberg (2013)

Lattice Cryptography for the Internet

Chris Peikert⋆

School of Computer Science
Georgia Institute of Technology

Abstract. In recent years, *lattice-based* cryptography has been recognized for its many attractive properties, such as strong provable security guarantees and apparent resistance to quantum attacks, flexibility for realizing powerful tools like fully homomorphic encryption, and high asymptotic efficiency. Indeed, several works have demonstrated that for basic tasks like encryption and authentication, lattice-based primitives can have performance competitive with (or even surpassing) those based on classical mechanisms like RSA or Diffie-Hellman. However, there still has been relatively little work on developing lattice cryptography for deployment in *real-world* cryptosystems and protocols.

In this work we take a step toward that goal, by giving efficient and practical lattice-based protocols for key transport, encryption, and authenticated key exchange that are suitable as "drop-in" components for proposed Internet standards and other open protocols. The security of all our proposals is provably based (sometimes in the random-oracle model) on the well-studied "learning with errors over rings" problem, and hence on the conjectured worst-case hardness of problems on ideal lattices (against quantum algorithms).

One of our main technical innovations (which may be of independent interest) is a simple, low-bandwidth *reconciliation* technique that allows two parties who "approximately agree" on a secret value to reach *exact* agreement, a setting common to essentially all lattice-based encryption schemes. Our technique reduces the ciphertext length of prior (already compact) encryption schemes nearly twofold, at essentially no cost.

1   Introduction

Recent progress in lattice cryptography, especially the development of efficient *ring-based* primitives, puts it in excellent position for use in practice. In particular, the *short integer solution over rings* (ring-SIS) problem [49,55,44] (which

---

⋆ This material is based upon work supported by the National Science Foundation under CAREER Award CCF-1054495, by DARPA under agreement number FA8750-11-C-0096, and by the Alfred P. Sloan Foundation. Any opinions, findings, and conclusions or recommendations expressed in this material are those of the author(s) and do not necessarily reflect the views of the National Science Foundation, DARPA or the U.S. Government, or the Sloan Foundation. The U.S. Government is authorized to reproduce and distribute reprints for Governmental purposes notwithstanding any copyright notation thereon.

M. Mosca (Ed.): PQCrypto 2014, LNCS 8772, pp. 197–219, 2014.

was originally inspired by the NTRU cryptosystem [31]) has served as a foundation for practical collision-resistant hash functions [46,3] and signature schemes [45,29,43,50,26], while the *learning with errors over rings* (ring-LWE) problem [47,48] is at the heart of many kinds of encryption schemes. Much like their less efficient integer-based counterparts SIS [2,52,29] and LWE [58,54,13], both ring-SIS and ring-LWE enjoy strong provable hardness guarantees: they are hard on the average as long as the Shortest Vector Problem is hard to approximate (by quantum computers, in the case of ring-LWE) on so-called *ideal* lattices in the corresponding ring, *in the worst case.* These results provide good theoretical evidence that ring-SIS and ring-LWE are a solid foundation on which to design cryptosystems, which is reinforced by concrete cryptanalytic efforts (e.g., [19,41,42]). (We refer the reader to [49,55,44,47,48] for further details on these problems' attractive efficiency and security properties.)

By now there is a great deal of theoretical work constructing a broad range of powerful cryptographic objects from (ring-)SIS and (ring-)LWE. However, far less attention has been paid to lower-level, "workhorse" primitives like key exchange and key transport protocols, which are widely used on real-world networks like the Internet. Indeed, almost all asymmetric cryptography standards are still designed around traditional mechanisms like Diffie-Hellman [22] and RSA [59].

1.1   Our Contributions

Toward the eventual goal of broader adoption and standardization of efficient lattice-based cryptography, in this work we give efficient and practical lattice-based protocols for central asymmetric tasks like encryption, key encapsulation/transport, and authenticated key exchange (AKE). Our proposals can all be proved secure (in some cases, in the random oracle model [8]) in strong, commonly accepted attack models, based on the presumed hardness of the ring-LWE problem plus other generic assumptions (e.g., signatures and message authentication codes).

Because our goal is to obtain primitives that are suitable for *real-world* networks like the Internet, we seek designs that adhere *as closely as possible* to the abstract protocols underlying existing proposed standards, e.g., IETF RFCs like [32,57,30,33,34]. This is so that working code and other time-tested solutions to engineering challenges can be reused as much as possible. Existing proposals are built around classical mechanisms like Diffie-Hellman and RSA, and ideally we would just be able to substitute those mechanisms with lattice-based ones without affecting the protocols' surrounding structure. However, lattice problems have very different mathematical properties than RSA and Diffie-Hellman, and many protocols are not easily adapted to use lattice-based mechanisms, or can even become *insecure* if one does so. Fortunately, we are able to show that in certain cases, existing protocols can be generalized so as to yield secure lattice-based instantiations, without substantially affecting their overall form or security analysis.

In the rest of this introduction we give an overview of our proposals.

Encryption and key transport. We first consider the task of asymmetric *key encapsulation* (also known as key transport), where the goal is for a sender to transmit a random cryptographic key K using the receiver's public key, so that K can be recovered only by the intended receiver. This task is central to the use of "hybrid" encryption, in which the parties later encrypt and/or authenticate bulk data under K using symmetric algorithms. Of course, one way to accomplish this goal is for the sender to choose K and simply encrypt it under the receiver's public encryption key. However, it is conceptually more natural (and can offer better efficiency and security bounds) to use a *key encapsulation mechanism* (KEM), in which the key K is produced as an *output* of the sender's "encapsulation" algorithm, which is run on the receiver's public key alone.

Our first technical contribution is a new ring-LWE-based KEM that has better bandwidth (i.e., ciphertext length) than prior compact encryption/KEM schemes [47,48] by nearly a factor of two, at essentially no cost in security or other efficiency measures. The improvement comes from our new, simple "reconciliation" technique that allows the sender and receiver to (noninteractively) reach *exact* agreement from their *approximate* or "noisy" agreement on a ring element. (See Section 3 for details.) Compared to the encryption schemes of [47,48], this technique allows us to replace one of the two ring elements modulo $q = \text{poly}(n)$ in the ciphertext with a *binary* string of the same dimension n, thus nearly halving the ciphertext length. (See Section 4 for details.) We mention that going back at least to the public-key cryptosystem of [54], it has been known that one can improve ciphertext length by simply "rounding," i.e., dropping less-significant bits. However, the resulting modulus must still remain larger than the norm of the secret key—in particular, polynomial in n—whereas our technique is able to "round" (in a certain way) all the way to a modulus of two. We also remark that approximate agreement is common to essentially all lattice-based encryption and key-agreement protocols, and our reconciliation technique is general enough to apply to all of them.

The KEM described above is *passively* secure, i.e., secure against passive eavesdroppers that see the public keys and ciphertexts, but do not create any of their own. Many applications require a much stronger form of security against *active* attackers, or more formally, security against adaptive chosen-ciphertext attacks. The literature contains several actively secure encryption/KEM schemes (sometimes in the random oracle model), obtained either via generic or semi-generic transformations from simpler objects (e.g., [24,9,61,27,28]), or more directly from particular algebraic structures and assumptions (e.g., [21,20,12,56]). For various reasons, most of these construction paradigms turn out to be unsuitable for obtaining highly efficient, actively secure lattice-based KEM/encryption schemes (see Section 5.3 for discussion). One method that does work well, however, is the Fujisaki-Okamoto transformation [28]. In Section 5 we apply it to obtain an actively secure encryption and KEM scheme that is essentially as efficient as our passively secure KEM. This can be used as an alternative to, e.g., RSA-based actively secure key encapsulation as in the proposed standard [57].

Authenticated key exchange (AKE). An AKE protocol allows two parties to generate a fresh, mutually authenticated secret key, e.g., for use in setting up a secure point-to-point channel. Formal attack models, security definitions, and protocols for AKE have been developed and refined in several works, e.g., [7,10,37,5,60,16,18,17,40,39]. In this work we focus on the strong notion of "SK-security" [16] in the "post-specified peer" model [17]. This model is particularly relevant to the Internet because it allows the identity of the peering party to be discovered during the protocol, rather than specified in advance. It also ensures other desirable properties like perfect forward secrecy.

We give a generalization of an AKE protocol of Canetti and Krawczyk [17], which inherits from Krawczyk's SIGMA family of protocols [38], and which underlies the Internet Key Exchange (IKE) proposed standard [30,33,34]. All these protocols are built specifically around the (unauthenticated) Diffie-Hellman key-exchange mechanism. We show that the Canetti-Krawczyk protocol can be generalized to instead use *any* passively secure KEM—in particular, our lattice-based one—with only minor changes to the proof of SK-security in the post-specified peer model. Again, we view the relative lack of novelty in our protocol and its analysis as a practical advantage, since it should eventually allow for the reuse of existing code and specialized knowledge concerning the real-world implementation of these protocols.

2   Preliminaries

For $x \in \mathbb{R}$, define $\lfloor x \rceil = \lfloor x + \frac{1}{2} \rfloor \in \mathbb{Z}$. For an integer $q \geq 1$, let $\mathbb{Z}_q$ denote the quotient ring $\mathbb{Z}/q\mathbb{Z}$, i.e., the ring of cosets $x + q\mathbb{Z}$ with the induced addition and multiplication operations. For any two subsets X, Y of some additive group, define $-X = \{-x : x \in X\}$ and $X + Y = \{x + y : x \in X, y \in Y\}$.

Due to space constraints, we assume familiarity with the syntax and standard security notions for public-key cryptosystems (PKCs) and key-encapsulation mechanisms (KEMs), and we give only the minimal mathematical background related to subgaussian random variables and cyclotomic rings. This will be sufficient to describe how our schemes operate, but their analysis requires many more details; these are given in the full version.

2.1   Subgaussian Random Variables

We define and analyze "error" distributions using the standard notion of *subgaussian* random variables, relaxed slightly as in [50]. For any $\delta \geq 0$, a random variable X (or its distribution) over $\mathbb{R}$ is δ-*subgaussian* with parameter $r > 0$ if for all $t \in \mathbb{R}$, we have

$$\mathbb{E}[\exp(2\pi t X)] \leq \exp(\delta) \cdot \exp(\pi r^2 t^2).$$

A standard fact is that any B-bounded centered random variable X (i.e., $\mathbb{E}[X] = 0$ and $|X| \leq B$ always) is 0-subgaussian with parameter $B\sqrt{2\pi}$.

Extending to vectors, a random real vector X is δ-subgaussian with parameter r if for all real unit vectors $\mathbf{u}$, the random variable $\langle \mathbf{u}, X \rangle \in \mathbb{R}$ is δ-subgaussian with parameter r. More generally, X and $\mathbf{u}$ may be taken from any real inner product space, such as $\mathbb{C}^n$.

2.2   Cyclotomic Rings

For a positive integer index m, let $K = \mathbb{Q}(\zeta_m)$ and $R = \mathbb{Z}[\zeta_m] \subset K$ denote the mth cyclotomic number field and ring (respectively), where ζ_m denotes an abstract element having order m. Then K has degree $n = \varphi(m)$ as a field extension of $\mathbb{Q}$, and similarly for R over $\mathbb{Z}$. In this work we are largely agnostic to how K and R are represented, except when analyzing "error" terms, in which case we use the *decoding basis* of R, described below. For any integer modulus $q \geq 1$, let R_q denote the quotient ring R/qR.

For any $p|m$, let $\zeta_p = \zeta_m^{m/p} \in R$ (which has order p), and define

$$g = \prod_{\text{odd prime } p|m} (1 - \zeta_p) \in R.$$

Also define $\hat{m} = m/2$ if m is even, and $\hat{m} = m$ otherwise. We recall a standard fact about these elements (see, e.g., [48, Section 2.5.4]).

Fact 1. *The element g divides $\hat{m}$ in R, and is coprime in R with all integer primes* except *the odd primes p dividing m.*

The *canonical embedding* σ from K (and hence also $R \subset K$) into $\mathbb{C}^n$ yields a natural geometry on cyclotomic fields/rings. We extend geometric notions, such as norms and subgaussianity, to K by identifying its elements with their canonical embeddings. In particular, the ℓ_2 (Euclidean) and ℓ_∞ norms on K are defined by $\|e\|_p := \|\sigma(e)\|_p$ for $p \in \{2, \infty\}$. Similarly, we say that $e \in K$ is δ-subgaussian with parameter r if $\sigma(e) \in \mathbb{C}^n$ is.

Decoding Basis. A central object in the definition and usage of ring-LWE is the fractional "codifferent" ideal $R^\vee = (\hat{m}/g)^{-1}R \subset K$. In [48, Section 6] it is shown that a certain $\mathbb{Z}$-basis of $R^\vee$ (and hence $\mathbb{Q}$-basis of K), called the *decoding basis*, has essentially optimal error tolerance (e.g., for decryption) and admits fast sampling of error terms from appropriate distributions.

In this work, for convenience we avoid the codifferent ideal $R^\vee = (\hat{m}/g)^{-1}R$, and instead give an alternative (but equivalent) definition of the decoding basis, by multiplying by $\hat{m}/g \in R$ to map $R^\vee$ to R. In particular, we define the decoding basis of R to be $\hat{m}/g$ times the elements of the decoding basis of $R^\vee$. Then by linearity, the coefficient vector of any $e^\vee \in K$ with respect to the "true" decoding basis (of $R^\vee$) is identical to that of $e = (\hat{m}/g)e^\vee$ with respect to the decoding basis of R.

We note that multiplying by $\hat{m}/g$ can significantly distort an element's canonical embedding. However, multiplying by $g \in R$ undoes this distortion, because $\sigma(g \cdot e) = \hat{m} \cdot \sigma(e^{\vee})$. So, we typically deal with error terms $e \in R$ where $g \cdot e$ is subgaussian, and analyze the coefficients of e itself with respect to the decoding basis of R. The following is a reformulation of [48, Lemma 6.6] to our definition of decoding basis.

Lemma 1. *Let $e \in K$ be such that $g \cdot e$ is δ-subgaussian with parameter $\hat{m} \cdot r$, and let $e' \in K$ be arbitrary. Then every decoding-basis coefficient of $e \cdot e'$ is δ-subgaussian with parameter $r \cdot \|e'\|_2$.*

Error Distributions. In the context of ring-LWE we work with certain Gaussian-like error distributions over the number field K, and discretized to R. For $r > 0$, the Gaussian distribution D_r over $\mathbb{R}$ with parameter r has probability distribution function $\exp(-\pi x^2/r^2)/r$. For convenience, but with a slight abuse of formality, we also define the Gaussian distribution D_r over the number field K to output an element $a \in K$ for which $\langle \sigma(a), \mathbf{u} \rangle$ has distribution D_r for all unit vectors $\mathbf{u}$ in the span of $\sigma(K) \subset \mathbb{C}^n$.[1]

In our applications we use error distributions of the form $\psi = (\hat{m}/g) \cdot D_r$ over K; the extra $\hat{m}/g$ factor corresponds to the translation from $R^{\vee}$ to R as described above in Section 2.2. We also *discretize* such distributions to the ring R, denoting the resulting distribution by $\chi = \lfloor \psi \rceil$, by sampling an element $a \in K$ from ψ and then rounding each of its rational decoding-basis coefficients to their nearest integers. We rely on the following facts from [48].

Fact 2. *Let $e \leftarrow \chi$ where $\chi = \lfloor \psi \rceil$ for $\psi = (\hat{m}/g) \cdot D_r$. Then:*

1. *$g \cdot e$ is δ-subgaussian with parameter $\hat{m} \cdot \sqrt{r^2 + 2\pi \operatorname{rad}(m)/m}$ for some $\delta \leq 2^{-n}$.*
2. *$\|g \cdot e\|_2 \leq \hat{m} \cdot (r + \sqrt{\operatorname{rad}(m)/m}) \cdot \sqrt{n}$ except with probability at most 2^{-n}.*

2.3   Ring-LWE

We now recall the ring-LWE probability distribution and (decisional) computational problem. For simplicity and convenience for our applications, we present the problem in its discretized, "normal" form, where all quantities are from R or $R_q = R/qR$, and the secret is drawn from the (discretized) error distribution. (See [47] for a more general form.)

Definition 1 (Ring-LWE Distribution). *For an $s \in R$ and a distribution χ over R, a sample from the ring-LWE distribution $A_{s,\chi}$ over $R_q \times R_q$ is generated by choosing $a \leftarrow R_q$ uniformly at random, choosing $e \leftarrow \chi$, and outputting $(a, b = a \cdot s + e)$.*

---

[1] This is an abuse because $\sigma(K)$ is not equal to H, but is merely dense in it. Since in practice Gaussians can only be sampled with finite precision, in this work we ignore such subtleties.

Definition 2 (Ring-LWE, Decision). *The* decision *version of the ring-LWE problem, denoted* R-DLWE$_{q,\chi}$*, is to distinguish with non-negligible advantage between independent samples from* $A_{s,\chi}$*, where* $s \leftarrow \chi$ *is chosen once and for all, and the same number of* uniformly random *and independent samples from* $R_q \times R_q$*.*

Theorem 3 ([47]). *Let* R *be the* mth *cyclotomic ring, having dimension* $n = \varphi(m)$*. Let* $\alpha = \alpha(n) < \sqrt{\log n/n}$*, and let* $q = q(n)$*,* $q = 1 \bmod m$ *be a* poly(n)*-bounded prime such that* $\alpha q \geq \omega(\sqrt{\log n})$*. There is a* poly$(n)$*-time quantum reduction from* $\tilde{O}(\sqrt{n}/\alpha)$*-approximate* SIVP *(or* SVP*) on ideal lattices in* R *to solving* R-DLWE$_{q,\chi}$ *given only* $\ell - 1$ *samples, where* $\chi = \lfloor \psi \rceil$ *and* ψ *is the Gaussian distribution* $(\hat{m}/g) \cdot D_{\xi q}$ *for* $\xi = \alpha \cdot (n\ell/\log(n\ell))^{1/4}$*.*

Note that the above worst-case hardness result deteriorates with the number of samples ℓ; fortunately, all our applications require only a small number of samples.

In addition to the above theorem, a plausible conjecture is that the *search* version of ring-LWE is hard for the fixed error distribution $\psi = (\hat{m}/g) \cdot D_{\alpha q}$, where $\alpha q \geq \omega(\sqrt{\log n})$.[2] (Informally, the search problem is to *find* the secret s given arbitrarily many ring-LWE samples; see [47] for a precise definition.) Unfortunately, for technical reasons it is not known whether this is implied by the worst-case hardness of ideal lattice problems in R, except for impractically large q and small α. However, it is proved in [47, Theorem 5.3] that the decision version with error distribution ψ (or its discretization $\lfloor \psi \rceil$) is at least as hard as the search version. Note that unlike Theorem 3, this results avoids the extra $(n/\log n)^{1/4}$ factor in the error distribution for the decision version, which leads to better parameters in applications.

3   New Reconciliation Mechanism

As mentioned in the introduction, one of our contributions is a more bandwidth-efficient method for two parties to agree on a secret bit, assuming they "approximately agree" on a (pseudo)random value modulo q. This is based on a new reconciliation mechanism that we describe in this section.

We remark that a work of Ding *et al.* [23] proposes a different reconciliation method for lower-bandwidth "approximate agreement," in the context of a key exchange against a passive adversary. However, we observe that the agreed-upon bit produced by their protocol is necessarily *biased*, not uniform, so it should not be used directly as a secret key (and the protocol as described does not satisfy the standard definition of passive security for key exchange). A nearly uniform key can be obtained via some post-processing, e.g., by applying an extractor, but this reduces the length of the usable key. By contrast, our method directly produces an unbiased key.

---

[2] The conjecture seems plausible even for the weaker bound $\alpha q \geq 1$. However, when $\alpha q = o(1)$, the search problem can be solved in subexponential $2^{o(n)}$ time, given a sufficiently large number of samples [4].

For an integer p that divides q (where typically $p = 2$), we define the modular rounding function $\lfloor \cdot \rceil_p \colon \mathbb{Z}_q \to \mathbb{Z}_p$ as $\lfloor x \rceil_p := \lfloor \frac{p}{q} \cdot x \rceil$, and similarly for $\lfloor \cdot \rfloor_p$. Note that the function is well-defined on the quotient rings because $\frac{p}{q} \cdot q\mathbb{Z} = p\mathbb{Z}$. For now we have restricted to the case $p|q$ so that the rounding function is unbiased. In Section 3.2 below we lift this restriction, using randomness to avoid introducing bias.

3.1   Even Modulus

Here we define the reconciliation mechanism where $p = 2$ and the modulus $q \geq 2$ is even. The mechanism is depicted in Figure 1 at the end of this subsection.

Define disjoint intervals $I_0 := \{0, 1, \ldots, \lfloor \frac{q}{4} \rceil - 1\}$, $I_1 := \{-\lfloor \frac{q}{4} \rfloor, \ldots, -1\} \bmod q$ consisting of $\lfloor \frac{q}{4} \rceil$ and $\lfloor \frac{q}{4} \rfloor$ (respectively) cosets in $\mathbb{Z}_q$. Observe that these intervals form a partition of all the elements $v \in \mathbb{Z}_q$ such that $\lfloor v \rceil_2 = 0$ (where we identify 0 and 1 with their residue classes modulo two). Similarly, $\frac{q}{2} + I_0$ and $\frac{q}{2} + I_1$ partition all the v such that $\lfloor v \rceil_2 = 1$.

Now define the *cross-rounding* function $\langle \cdot \rangle_2 \colon \mathbb{Z}_q \to \mathbb{Z}_2$ as

$$\langle v \rangle_2 := \lfloor \tfrac{4}{q} \cdot v \rfloor \bmod 2.$$

Equivalently, $\langle v \rangle_2$ is the $b \in \{0, 1\}$ such that v belongs to the disjoint union $I_b \cup (\frac{q}{2} + I_b)$; hence the name "cross-rounding." If v is uniformly random, then $\langle v \rangle_2$ is uniformly random if and only if $q/2$ is even; otherwise, $\langle v \rangle_2$ is biased toward zero. Regardless of this potential bias, however, the next claim shows that $\langle v \rangle_2$ hides $\lfloor v \rceil_2$ perfectly.

Claim 1. *For even q, if $v \in \mathbb{Z}_q$ is uniformly random, then $\lfloor v \rceil_2$ is uniformly random given $\langle v \rangle_2$.*

Proof. For any $b \in \{0, 1\}$, if we condition on $\langle v \rangle_2 = b$, then v is uniform over $I_b \cup (\frac{q}{2} + I_b)$. As already observed, if $v \in I_b$ then $\lfloor v \rceil_2 = 0$, whereas if $v \in (\frac{q}{2} + I_b)$ then $\lfloor v \rceil_2 = 1$, so $\lfloor v \rceil_2$ is uniformly random given $\langle v \rangle_2$. ∎

We now show that if $v, w \in \mathbb{Z}_q$ are sufficiently close, then we can recover $\lfloor v \rceil_2$ given w and $\langle v \rangle_2$. Define the set $E := [-\frac{q}{8}, \frac{q}{8}) \cap \mathbb{Z}$, and define the *reconciliation* function $\mathrm{rec} \colon \mathbb{Z}_q \times \mathbb{Z}_2 \to \mathbb{Z}_2$ as

$$\mathrm{rec}(w, b) := \begin{cases} 0 & \text{if } w \in I_b + E \ (\bmod \ q) \\ 1 & \text{otherwise.} \end{cases}$$

Claim 2. *For even q, if $w = v + e \bmod q$ for some $v \in \mathbb{Z}_q$ and $e \in E$, then $\mathrm{rec}(w, \langle v \rangle_2) = \lfloor v \rceil_2$.*

Proof. Let $b = \langle v \rangle_2 \in \{0, 1\}$, so $v \in I_b \cup (\frac{q}{2} + I_b)$. Then $\lfloor v \rceil_2 = 0$ if and only if $v \in I_b$. This in turn holds if and only if $w \in I_b + E$, because $((I_b + E) - E) \subseteq I_b + (-\frac{q}{4}, \frac{q}{4})$ and $(\frac{q}{2} + I_b)$ are disjoint (modulo q). The claim follows. ∎

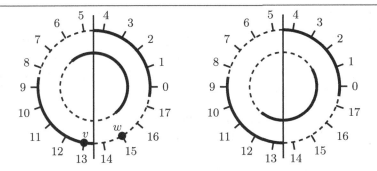

Fig. 1. (Cross-)rounding and reconciliation intervals for $q = 18$; solid arcs denote 0, while dashed arcs denote 1. The rounding function $\lfloor \cdot \rceil_2$ simply partitions each circle into its left and right halves. The outermost circles show the values of the cross-rounding function $\langle \cdot \rangle_2$. The innermost circles on the left and right show the values of the reconciliation functions $\mathrm{rec}(\cdot, 0)$ and $\mathrm{rec}(\cdot, 1)$, respectively. On the left, the example values v, w show how the reconciliation function ensures $\mathrm{rec}(w, 0) = \lfloor v \rceil_2 = 1$ even though $\lfloor w \rceil_2 = 0$.

3.2 Odd Modulus

All of the above applies when q is even, but in applications of ring-LWE this is often not the case. (For instance, it is often desirable to let q be a sufficiently large prime, for efficiency and security reasons.) When q is odd, while it is possible to use the above methods to agree on a bit derived by rounding a uniform $v \in \mathbb{Z}_q$, the bit will be *biased*, and hence not wholly suitable as key material. Here we show how to avoid such bias by temporarily "scaling up" to work modulo $2q$, and introducing a small amount of extra randomness.

Define the randomized function $\mathrm{dbl} \colon \mathbb{Z}_q \to \mathbb{Z}_{2q}$ that, given a $v \in \mathbb{Z}_q$, outputs $\bar{v} = 2v - \bar{e} \in \mathbb{Z}_{2q}$ for some random $\bar{e} \in \mathbb{Z}$ that is uniformly random modulo two and independent of v, and small in magnitude (e.g., bounded by one).[3] The first of these properties imply that if v is uniformly random in $\mathbb{Z}_q$, then so is $\bar{v}$ in $\mathbb{Z}_{2q}$, and hence the following extension of Claim 1 holds:

Claim 3. *For odd q, if $v \in \mathbb{Z}_q$ is uniformly random and $\bar{v} \leftarrow \mathrm{dbl}(v) \in \mathbb{Z}_{2q}$, then $\lfloor \bar{v} \rceil_2$ is uniformly random given $\langle \bar{v} \rangle_2$.*

Moreover, if $w, v \in \mathbb{Z}_q$ are close, then so are $2w, \mathrm{dbl}(v) \in \mathbb{Z}_{2q}$, i.e., if $w = v + e \pmod{q}$ for some (small) e, then $2w = \bar{v} + (2e + \bar{e}) \pmod{2q}$. Therefore, to (cross-)round from $\mathbb{Z}_q$ to $\mathbb{Z}_2$, we simply apply dbl to the argument and then apply the appropriate rounding function from $\mathbb{Z}_{2q}$ to $\mathbb{Z}_2$. Similarly, to reconcile some $w \in \mathbb{Z}_q$ we apply rec to $2w \in \mathbb{Z}_{2q}$; note that this process is still deterministic.

---

[3] For example, we could simply take $\bar{e}$ to be uniform over $\{0, 1\}$. However, it is often more analytically convenient for $\bar{e}$ to be zero-centered and hence subgaussian. To achieve this we can take $\bar{e} = 0$ with probability $1/2$, and $\bar{e} = \pm 1$ each with probability $1/4$.

3.3 Extending to Cyclotomic Rings

We extend (cross-)rounding and reconciliation to cyclotomic rings R using the decoding basis. For even q, the rounding functions $\lfloor \cdot \rceil_2, \langle \cdot \rangle_2 \colon R_q \to R_2$ are obtained by applying their integer versions (from $\mathbb{Z}_q$ to $\mathbb{Z}_2$) coordinate-wise to the input's decoding-basis $\mathbb{Z}_q$-coefficients. Formally, if $D = \{d_j\} \subset R$ denotes the decoding basis and $v = \sum_j v_j \cdot d_j \in R_q$ for coefficients $v_j \in \mathbb{Z}_q$, then $\lfloor v \rceil_2 := \sum_j \lfloor v_j \rceil_2 \cdot d_j \in R_2$, and similarly for $\langle \cdot \rangle_2$. The reconciliation function $\mathrm{rec} \colon R_q \times R_2 \to R_2$ is obtained from its integer version as $\mathrm{rec}(w, b) = \sum_j \mathrm{rec}(w_j, b_j) \cdot d_j$, where $w = \sum_j w_j \cdot d_j$ and $b = \sum_j b_j \cdot d_j$.

For odd q, we define the randomized function $\mathrm{dbl} \colon R_q \to R_{2q}$ which applies its (randomized) integer version *independently* to each of the input's decoding-basis coefficients. The (cross-)rounding functions from R_q to R_2 are defined to first apply dbl to the argument, then (cross-)round the result from R_{2q} to R_2. To reconcile $w \in R_q$ we simply reconcile $2w \in R_{2q}$.

4 Passively Secure KEM

In this section we construct, based on ring-LWE, an efficient key encapsulation mechanism (KEM) that is secure against *passive* (i.e., eavesdropping) attacks. In later sections this will be used as a component of actively secure constructions. Specifically, we use the KEM as part of an authenticated key exchange protocol, and we use the induced passively secure encryption scheme to obtain actively secure encryption/KEM schemes via the Fujisaki-Okamoto transformation.

Our KEM is closely related to the compact ring-LWE cryptosystem from [48, Section 8.2] (which generalizes the one sketched in [47] to arbitrary cyclotomics), with two main changes: first, we avoid using the "codifferent" ideal $R^\vee$ using the approach described in Section 2.2; second, we use the reconciliation mechanism from Section 3 to improve ciphertext length. A third minor difference is that the system is constructed explicitly as a KEM (not a cryptosystem), i.e., the encapsulated key is not explicitly chosen by either party. Instead, the sender and receiver "approximately agree" on a pseudorandom value in R_q using ring-LWE, and use the reconciliation technique from Section 3 to derive the ephemeral key from it.

As compared with the previous most efficient ring-LWE cryptosystems and KEMs, the new reconciliation mechanism reduces the ciphertext length by nearly a factor of two, because it replaces one of the ciphertext's two R_q elements with an R_2 element. So the ciphertext length is reduced from $2n \log q$ bits to $n(1 + \log q)$ bits, where n is both the dimension of R and the length of the agreed-upon key. In terms of security, the reconciliation technique requires a ring-LWE error rate that is half as large as in prior schemes, but this weakens the concrete security only very slightly. (The reason for the smaller error rate is that we need the error term's decoding-basis coefficients to be bounded by $q/8$ instead of by $q/4$; see Claim 2.) Of course, if necessary we can compensate for this security loss by increasing the parameters (and hence the key size) very slightly. For practical purposes, the improvement in ciphertext length seems to outweigh the small loss in security or key size.

4.1 Construction

The KEM is parameterized by:

- A positive integer m specifying the mth cyclotomic ring R of degree $n = \varphi(m)$.
- A positive integer modulus q which is coprime with every odd prime dividing m, so that $g \in R$ is coprime with q (see Fact 1). For efficiency and provable security, we typically take q to be prime and 1 modulo m (or if necessary, a product of such primes), which implies the coprimality condition.
- A discretized error distribution $\chi = \lfloor \psi \rceil$ over R, where $\psi = (\hat{m}/g) \cdot D_r$ is over K (see Section 2.2), for some parameter $r > 0$.

The ciphertext space is $\mathcal{C} = R_q \times R_2$, and the key space is $\mathcal{K} = R_2$. We can identify elements in $\mathcal{K} = R_2$ with bit strings in $\{0,1\}^n = \mathbb{Z}_2^n$ in some canonical way, e.g., the jth bit of the string is the jth decoding-basis coefficient of the element in R_2.

In what follows we assume that q is odd (since this will typically be the case in practice), and use the randomized function dbl: $\mathbb{Z}_q \to \mathbb{Z}_{2q}$ and (deterministic) reconciliation function rec: $\mathbb{Z}_q \times \mathbb{Z}_2 \to \mathbb{Z}_2$ from Section 3.[4] In dbl we take the random term $\bar{e}$ to be 0 with probability $1/2$, and ± 1 each with probability $1/4$, so that $\bar{e}$ is uniform modulo two (as needed for security) and 0-subgaussian with parameter $\sqrt{2\pi}$. We also extend dbl and rec to cyclotomic rings as described in Section 3.3.

The algorithms of the KEM are as follows.

- KEM1.Setup(): choose $a \leftarrow R_q$ and output $pp = a$.
- KEM1.Gen($pp = a$): choose $s_0, s_1 \leftarrow \chi$, let $b = a \cdot s_1 + s_0 \in R_q$, and output public key $pk = b$ and secret key $sk = s_1$.
- KEM1.Encaps($pp = a, pk = b$): choose independent $e_0, e_1, e_2 \leftarrow \chi$. Let $u = e_0 \cdot a + e_1 \in R_q$ and $v = g \cdot e_0 \cdot b + e_2 \in R_q$. Let $\bar{v} \leftarrow$ dbl(v) and output the encapsulation $c = (u, v' = \langle \bar{v} \rangle_2) \in R_q \times R_2$ and key $\mu = \lfloor \bar{v} \rceil_2 \in R_2$.
- KEM1.Decaps($sk = s_1, c = (u, v')$): compute $w = g \cdot u \cdot s_1 \in R_q$ and output $\mu = \text{rec}(w, v') \in R_2$.

The proofs of the following lemmas can be found in the full version.

Lemma 2 (Security). *KEM1 is IND-CPA secure, assuming the hardness of $R\text{-DLWE}_{q,\chi}$ given two samples.*

---

[4] If q is even, then the Encaps and Decaps algorithms can be simplified by using the deterministic (cross-)rounding and associated reconciliation functions from Section 3.1. Lemmas 2 and 3 then remain true as stated, with essentially the same (but somewhat simpler) proofs.

Lemma 3 (Correctness). *Suppose* $\|g \cdot s_i\|_2 \leq \ell$ *for* $i = 0, 1$ *(where s_i are the secret values chosen by KEM1.Gen), and*

$$(q/8)^2 \geq (r'^2 \cdot (2\ell^2 + n) + \pi/2) \cdot \omega^2$$

for some $\omega > 0$, where $r'^2 = r^2 + 2\pi \operatorname{rad}(m)/m$. Then KEM1.Decaps decrypts correctly except with probability at most $2n \exp(3\delta - \pi\omega^2)$ over the random choices of KEM1.Encaps, for some $\delta \leq 2^{-n}$.

4.2 Instantiating the Parameters

We now instantiate the parameters to analyze their asymptotic behavior and the underlying (worst-case) hardness guarantees. These calculations work for arbitrary choices of m and error parameter $r \geq 1$, and can therefore be slightly loose by small constant factors. Very sharp bounds can easily be obtained for particular choices of m and r using Lemma 3.

Since $\operatorname{rad}(m)/m \leq 1$, by Item 2 of Fact 2 we have that each $\|g \cdot s_i\|_2 \leq \hat{m} \cdot (r + 1) \cdot \sqrt{n}$ except with probability at most 2^{-n}. Similarly, $r'^2 \leq r^2 + 2\pi$. Therefore, by taking $\omega = \sqrt{\ln(2n/\varepsilon)/\pi}$ and

$$q \geq 8\sqrt{(r^2 + 2\pi)(2\hat{m}^2 \cdot (r + 1)^2 + 1) \cdot n} \cdot \omega = O(\hat{m} \cdot r^2 \cdot \sqrt{n}) \cdot \omega,$$

we obtain a probability of decryption failure bounded by $\approx \varepsilon$. Thus we may take $q = O(r^2 \cdot n^{3/2} \log n)$ in the typical case where $\hat{m} = O(n)$ and, say, $\varepsilon = 2^{-128}$.

To apply Theorem 3 for $\ell = 2$ samples, we let $r = \xi q$ and $\xi = \alpha \cdot (3n/\log(3n))^{1/4}$, where

- $r = (3n/\log(3n))^{1/4} \cdot \omega(\sqrt{\log n})$ to guarantee $\alpha q \geq \omega(\sqrt{\log n})$, and
- $q = O(r^2 \cdot n^{3/2} \log n) = \tilde{O}(n^2)$ is a sufficiently large prime congruent to one modulo m.

Then we obtain that $R\text{-DLWE}_{q,\chi}$ is hard (and hence the KEM is IND-CPA secure, by Lemma 2) assuming that SVP on ideal lattices in R is hard to approximate to within $\tilde{O}(\sqrt{n}/\alpha) = \tilde{O}(\sqrt{n} \cdot q) = \tilde{O}(n^{5/2})$ factors for quantum algorithms.

Alternatively, we may conjecture that the search version of ring-LWE with error distribution $\psi = D_r$ is hard for $r \geq \omega(\sqrt{\log n})$ (or even $r \geq 1$), which by [47, Theorem 5.3] implies that $R\text{-DLWE}_{q,\chi}$ is hard as well. This lets us use a modulus as small as $q = \tilde{O}(n^{3/2})$, and implies a smaller modulus-to-noise ratio of $q/r = \tilde{O}(n^{3/2})$, rather than $\tilde{O}(n^{7/4})$ as when invoking Theorem 3 above. A smaller modulus-to-noise ratio provides stronger concrete security against known attacks, so this parameterization may be preferred in practice.

5 Actively Secure KEM

In this section we construct an actively secure (i.e., secure under chosen-ciphertext attack) encryption scheme, using the passively secure encryption derived from

KEM1 as a component. As noted in the preliminaries, actively secure encryption immediately yields an actively secure KEM or *key transport* protocol. Our construction may be seen as an alternative to proposed Internet standards for RSA-based key transport, such as [32,57].

5.1 Overview

The literature contains many constructions of actively secure encryption, both in the standard and random-oracle models, and from both general assumptions and specific algebraic or structural ones (including lattices and LWE), e.g., [24,8,9,11,27,28,53,1,21,20,12,56,54,50]. Since our focus here is on efficiency, we allow for the use of the random-oracle heuristic as well as potentially strong (but plausible) non-standard assumptions. However, even with this permissive approach, it turns out that most known approaches for obtaining active security are either *insecure* when applied to our KEM (and other lattice-based encryption schemes more generally), or are unsuitable for other reasons. See Section 5.3 for further discussion on this point.

Considering all the options from the existing literature, we conclude that the best choice appears to be the second Fujisaki-Okamoto transformation [28], which converts any passively secure encryption scheme into one which is provably actively secure, in the random-oracle model. (Note that the transformation requires an *encryption* scheme, and cannot be applied directly to a KEM.) Among the reasons for our choice are that the original passively secure scheme can have a minimally small plaintext space, and the resulting scheme is a "hybrid" one, i.e., it *symmetrically* encrypts a plaintext of arbitrary length. However, the transformation does have one important efficiency and implementation disadvantage in our setting: the random oracle's output is used as the *randomness* for asymmetric encryption, and the decryption algorithm re-runs the encryption algorithm with the same randomness to check ciphertext validity. This is somewhat unnatural in the (ring-)LWE setting, where encryption uses many random bits to generate high-precision Gaussians.[5] We therefore slightly modify the construction so that the random oracle's output is used as the seed of a cryptographic pseudorandom generator (sometimes also called a stream cipher), which produces the randomness for asymmetric encryption.

We remark that another approach is to use a different transformation, such as one like OAEP [9,61] or REACT [53], in which the asymmetric encryption randomness is "freely chosen." In our context, these transformations require the use of an injective trapdoor function. Such functions can be constructed reasonably efficiently based on (ring-)LWE [56,29,50], but it is not clear whether they can offer efficiency and bandwidth comparable to that of our passively

---

[5] This disadvantage could be mitigated by using *uniformly random* error terms from a small interval, rather than Gaussians. When appropriately parameterized, the (ring-)LWE problem does appear to be hard with such errors, and there is some theoretical evidence of hardness as well [25,51]. However, the theoretical bounds are rather weak, and more investigation of concrete security is certainly needed.

secure KEM. An interesting open problem is to devise a passive-to-active security transformation that does not suffer any of the above-discussed drawbacks.

5.2   Construction

Our (actively secure) encryption scheme PKC2 is parameterized by:

- an integer N, the bit length of the messages that PKC2 will encrypt, such that 2^{-N} is negligible in λ;
- an asymmetric encryption scheme PKC with message space $\{0,1\}^n$, where PKC.Enc uses at most L uniformly random bits (i.e., PKC.Enc$(pp, pk, \cdot ; r)$ is a deterministic function on $\{0,1\}^n$ for any fixed pp, pk, and coins $r \in \{0,1\}^L$), e.g., the encryption scheme induced by KEM1;
- a cryptographic pseudorandom generator PRG: $\{0,1\}^\ell \to \{0,1\}^L$, for some seed length ℓ;
- hash functions $G: \{0,1\}^n \to \{0,1\}^N$ and $H: \{0,1\}^{n+N} \to \{0,1\}^\ell$, modelled as independent random oracles.

PKC2 is defined as follows:

- PKC2.Setup(): let $pp \leftarrow$ PKC.Setup() and output pp.
- PKC2.Gen(pp): let $(pk, sk) \leftarrow$ PKC.Gen(pp) and output public key pk and secret key sk.
- PKC2.Enc(pp, pk, μ): choose $\sigma \leftarrow \{0,1\}^n$, let $c =$ PKC.Enc$(pp, pk, \sigma; \mathsf{PRG}(H(\sigma\|\mu)))$ and $w = G(\sigma) \oplus \mu$, and output the ciphertext $c\|w$.
- PKC2.Dec$(sk, (c, w))$: compute $\sigma =$ PKC.Dec(sk, c) and $\mu = G(\sigma) \oplus w$, and check whether $c \overset{?}{=}$ PKC.Enc$(pp, pk, \sigma; \mathsf{PRG}(H(\sigma\|\mu)))$. If so, output μ, otherwise output $\bot$.

Theorem 4. *PKC2 is IND-CCA secure, assuming that PKC is IND-CPA secure, PRG is a secure pseudorandom generator, and G and H are modeled as random oracles.*

A few remarks on the above security theorem are in order.

- The only difference between our construction and the one from [28] (specialized to use the one-time pad as symmetric encryption) is in the use of the pseudorandom generator; the corresponding modification to the security proof is standard and straightforward.
- Fujisaki and Okamoto actually prove, under the weaker assumption that PKC is *one-way* secure and "γ-uniform" for some negligible γ, that PKC2 is both IND-CPA secure and "plaintext aware" (PA), which implies (but is not necessarily implied by) IND-CCA security by the results of [6]. The PA property is proved in [28, Lemma 11] by demonstrating a suitable "knowledge extractor."
- The proof of the PA property implicitly assumes that the underlying cryptosystem PKC has *zero* probability of decryption error on *honestly generated*

ciphertexts. However, in our setting PKC may only be *statistically* correct, i.e., there may be a nonzero but negligible probability of decrypting to a different message than the encrypted one. This has only a minor effect on the proof, namely, it merely decreases the knowledge extractor's success probability by at most the probability of decryption error.

- Concrete bounds relating the PA and IND-CCA security of PKC2 to the security of PKC are given in [28, Section 5]. In our setting they need only be modified slightly to account for the use of the pseudorandom generator and the probability of decryption error.

5.3   Alternatives

We considered several other known methods for obtaining active security. Unfortunately, most of them are either *insecure* when instantiated with our KEM1, or suffer from other costly drawbacks. For example:

- Constructions in the spirit of "hashed ElGamal," such as DHIES [11,1] or variants [21, Section 10], in which the key from the passively secure KEM (and possibly ciphertext as well) are hashed by a random oracle to derive the final output key, are *not* actively secure when instantiated with our KEM1 or others like it. Briefly, the reason is related to the search/decision equivalence for (ring-)LWE: the adversary can query the decryption oracle on specially crafted ciphertexts for which the random oracle input is one of only a small number of possibilities (and depends on only a small portion of the secret key), and can thereby learn the entire secret key very easily.
- For similar reasons, applying the REACT transformation [53] to our KEM does not yield an actively secure scheme, because the KEM is not one-way under a "plaintext checking attack" (OW-PCA) due to the search/decision equivalence.
- The Bellare-Rogaway [8] and OAEP transformations [9,61] cannot be applied to our KEM, because they require a trapdoor permutation (or an injective trapdoor function). We remark that injective trapdoor functions can be constructed from (ring-)LWE [56,29,50], and the most recent constructions are even reasonably efficient. However, it is not clear whether they can compete with the efficiency and bandwidth of our KEM.
- The first Fujisaki-Okamoto transformation [27] *does* yield actively secure encryption when instantiated with our KEM's associated encryption scheme. However, it has the big disadvantage that the message length of the resulting scheme is substantially shorter than that of the original one, by (say) at least 128 bits for reasonable security bounds. Since our KEM's plaintext-to-ciphertext expansion is somewhat large, it is important to keep the size of the plaintext as small as possible.

6   Authenticated Key Exchange

In this section we give a protocol for authenticated key exchange which may be instantiated using our passively secure KEM from Section 4, together with other generic cryptographic primitives like signatures, which may also be instantiated with efficient ring-based constructions, e.g., [29,50,43,26].

6.1   Overview

Informally, a key-exchange protocol allows two parties to establish a common secret key over a public network. The first such protocol was given by Diffie and Hellman [22]. However, it is well-known that this protocol can only be secure against a *passive* adversary who only reads the network traffic, but does not modify it or introduce messages of its own. An *authenticated key exchange* (AKE) protocol authenticates the parties' identities to each other, and provides a "consistent view" of the completed protocol to the peers, even in the presence of an active adversary who may control the network entirely (e.g., it may delete, delay, inject, or modify messages at will). Moreover, an AKE protocol may provide various security properties even if the adversary compromises some of the protocol participants and learns their local secrets. For example, "perfect forward secrecy" ensures the security of secret keys established by prior executions of the protocol, even if the long-term secrets of one or both parties are exposed later on. An excellent in-depth (yet still informal) discussion of these issues, and of the design considerations for AKE protocols, may be found in [38].

Formal attack models, security definitions, and abstract protocols for AKE have been developed and refined in several works, e.g., [7,10,37,5,60,16,18,17,40,39]. Of particular relevance to this work is the notion of "SK-security" due to Canetti and Krawczyk [16], which was shown to be sufficient for the prototypical application of constructing secure point-to-point channels. However, this model is not entirely appropriate for networks like the Internet, where peer identities are not necessarily known at the start of the protocol execution, and where identity concealment may be an explicit security goal. With this motivation in mind, Canetti and Krawczyk then gave an alternative formalization of SK-security which is more appropriate in such settings, called the "post-specified peer" model [17], and gave a formal analysis of an instance of the "SIGn-and-MAc" (SIGMA) family of protocols due to Krawczyk [38]. (In [18] they also investigated the relationship between SK-security, key exchange, and secure channels in Canetti's "universal composability" model [15,14].) The formal definitions of SK-security and the post-specified peer models are somewhat lengthy and we will not need them here, so we refer the reader to [16,17] for the details.

Regarding real-world protocols, the Internet Key Exchange (IKE) protocols [30,33,34] define an open standard for authenticated key exchange as part of the Internet Protocol Security (IPsec) suite [35,36]. IKE's signature-based authentication mode follows the design of the SIGMA protocols from [38] that were formally analyzed in [17].

Our Contribution. In the next subsection we give a protocol, called Σ_0', which is a slight generalization of the Σ_0 protocol from [17], which itself follows the SIGMA design [38] underlying the IKE protocol. The only difference between Σ_0' and Σ_0 is that we replace the (unauthenticated) Diffie-Hellman key-agreement steps in

Σ_0 with an abstract IND-CPA-secure KEM (which can be instantiated by our lattice-based KEM1 from Section 4). Such a replacement is possible because the Diffie-Hellman steps in Σ_0 are used only to establish the common secret key (whereas the other steps provide authentication), and because the protocol has designated "initiator" and "responder" roles. In particular, the responder gets the initiator's start message before having to prepare its response, so the start message can contain a (fresh) KEM public key and the responder can run the encapsulation algorithm using this key. The security proof for Σ_0' is also just a slight variant of the one for Σ_0, because the latter proof uses only the KEM-like features of Diffie-Hellman, and not any of its other algebraic properties.

As mentioned in the introduction, from a practical perspective we believe the relatively minor differences between Σ_0' and Σ_0 (and their security proofs) to be an advantage: it should lessen the engineering burden required to implement the protocol correctly and securely, and may facilitate migration from, and co-existence with, existing Diffie-Hellman-based implementations.

6.2   The Protocol

The protocol Σ_0' is parameterized by an (IND-CPA-secure) a digital signature scheme SIG, a key-encapsulation mechanism KEM with key space $\mathcal{K}$, a pseudorandom function $F\colon \mathcal{K} \times \{0,1\} \to \mathcal{K}'$, and a message authentication code MAC with key space $\mathcal{K}'$ and message space $\{0,1\}^*$. A successful execution of the protocol outputs a secret key in $\mathcal{K}'$.

As in [17], we assume that each party has a long-term signing key for SIG whose corresponding verification key is registered and bound to its identity ID, and is accessible to all other parties. This may be achieved in a standard way using certificate authorities. We also assume that trusted public parameters pp for KEM have been generated by a trusted party using KEM.Setup, and are available to all parties. As noted in the preliminaries, if no trusted party is available then KEM.Setup can be folded into KEM.Gen.

1. **Start message.** $(I \to R)$: (sid, pk_I).
   The protocol is activated by the initiator ID_I with a session identifier sid, which must be distinct from all those of prior sessions initiated by ID_I. The initiator generates a fresh keypair $(pk_I, sk_I) \leftarrow \mathsf{KEM.Gen}(pp)$, stores it as the state of the session $(\mathsf{ID}_I, \mathsf{sid})$, and sends the above message to the responder.
2. **Response message.** $(R \to I)$: $(\mathsf{sid}, c, \mathsf{ID}_R, \mathsf{SIG.Sign}_R(1, \mathsf{sid}, pk_I, c), \mathsf{MAC}.\mathsf{Tag}_{k_1}(1, \mathsf{sid}, \mathsf{ID}_R))$.
   When a party ID_R receives a start message (sid, pk_I), if the session identifier sid was never used before at ID_R, the party activates session sid as responder. It generates an encapsulation and key $(c, k) \leftarrow \mathsf{KEM.Encaps}(pp, pk_I)$, derives $k_0 = F_k(0)$ and $k_1 = F_k(1)$, and erases the values pk_I and k from its memory, storing (k_0, k_1) as the state of the session. It generates and sends the above response message, where $\mathsf{SIG.Sign}_R$ is computed using its long-term signing key, and $\mathsf{MAC.Tag}$ is computed using key k_1.

3. **Finish message.** $(I \rightarrow R)$: $(\mathsf{sid}, \mathsf{ID}_I, \mathsf{SIG.Sign}_I(0, \mathsf{sid}, c, pk_I), \mathsf{MAC.Tag}_{k_1}$ $(0, \mathsf{sid}, \mathsf{ID}_I))$.

   When party ID_I receives the (first) response message $(\mathsf{sid}, c, \mathsf{ID}_R, \sigma_R, \tau_R)$ having session identifier sid, it looks up the state (pk_I, sk_I) associated with session sid and computes $k = \mathsf{KEM.Decaps}(sk_I, c)$ and $k_0 = F_k(0), k_1 = F_k(1)$. It then retrieves the signature verification key of ID_R and uses that key to verify the signature σ_R on the message tuple $(1, \mathsf{sid}, pk_I, c)$, and also verifies the MAC tag τ_R on the message tuple $(1, \mathsf{sid}, \mathsf{ID}_R)$ under key k_1. If either verification fails, the session is aborted, its state is erased, and the session output is $(\mathsf{abort}, \mathsf{ID}_I, \mathsf{sid})$. If both verifications succeed, then ID_I completes the session as follows: it generates and sends the above finish message where $\mathsf{SIG.Sign}_I$ is computed using its long-term signing key, and $\mathsf{MAC.Tag}$ is computed using key k_1. It then produces public session output $(\mathsf{ID}_I, \mathsf{sid}, \mathsf{ID}_R)$ and session secret output k_0, and erases the session state.

4. **Responder completion.** when party ID_R receives the (first) finish message $(\mathsf{sid}, \mathsf{ID}_I, \sigma_I, \tau_I)$ having session identifier sid, it looks up the state (k_0, k_1) associated with session sid. It then retrieves the signature verification key of ID_I and uses that key to verify the signature σ_I on the message tuple $(0, \mathsf{sid}, c, pk_I)$, and also verifies the MAC tag τ_I on the message tuple $(0, \mathsf{sid}, \mathsf{ID}_I)$ under key k_1. If either verification fails, the session is aborted, its state is erased, and the session output is $(\mathsf{abort}, \mathsf{ID}_r, \mathsf{sid})$. If both verifications succeed, then ID_R completes the session with public session output $(\mathsf{ID}_R, \mathsf{sid}, \mathsf{ID}_I)$ and secret session output k_0, and erases the session state.

6.3   Security

Theorem 5. *The Σ'_0 protocol is SK-secure in the post-specified peer model of [17], assuming that SIG and MAC are existentially unforgeable under chosen-message attack, that KEM is IND-CPA secure, and that F is a secure pseudorandom function.*

The proof of Theorem 5 follows by straightforwardly adapting the one from [17]. Because the changes are simple and affect only small parts of the proof, we do not duplicate the whole proof here, but only describe the differences.

According to the definition of SK-security in the post-specified peer model from [17], we need to show two properties: property P1 is essentially "correctness," or more precisely, equality of the secret outputs when two uncorrupted parties $\mathsf{ID}_I, \mathsf{ID}_R$ complete matching sessions with respective public outputs $(\mathsf{ID}_I, \mathsf{sid}, \mathsf{ID}_R), (\mathsf{ID}_R, \mathsf{sid}, \mathsf{ID}_I)$. Property P2 is essentially "secrecy," or more precisely, that no efficient attacker (in the post-specified peer model) can distinguish a real response to a test-session query from a uniformly random response, with non-negligible advantage.

Property P1 follows by adapting the proof in [17, Section 4.2, full version]. It suffices to show that both parties compute the same decapsulation key k. This is guaranteed by the correctness of KEM and the security of the signature scheme, which ensures that the key k is obtained by decapsulating the appropriate ciphertext. (Security of MAC or the PRF is not needed for this property.)

Property P2 follows by adapting the proof in [17, Section 4.3, full version]. While the proof is several pages long, very little of it is specific to the Diffie-Hellman mechanism or the DDH assumption. For example, the proof does not use any algebraic properties of the Diffie-Hellman problem beyond its assumed pseudorandomness. In the proof from [17], a distinguisher for the DDH problem is constructed, i.e., it gets as input a tuple (g, g^x, g^y, g^z) where either $z = xy$ or z is uniformly random modulo the order of the group generated by g. In our setting, we instead construct a distinguisher for the IND-CPA security of KEM, i.e., it gets as input a tuple (pp, pk, c, k) where either k is the decapsulation of ciphertext c, or is uniformly random in the key space $\mathcal{K}$. To modify the proof from [17], throughout it we syntactically replace the components of the DDH tuple with the corresponding ones of the KEM tuple (replacing g^{xy} by the real decapsulation key k, and g^z for uniform and independent z by a uniformly random and independent key $k^* \in \mathcal{K}$). With these and corresponding other syntactic changes to the component lemmas, the proof from [17] remains valid.

6.4   Variants and IKE

As in [17], we can consider variants of Σ_0' that extend its functionality or security properties, and also some important differences in the real IKE protocol that affect the analysis.

Perhaps most importantly, the signatures modes of the IKE protocol do not actually include the special distinguishing values 0,1 in the signed/MAC-tagged response and finish messages. (These values were included in Σ_0 for "symmetry breaking," to ease the analysis.) The Σ_0 protocol remains secure even without these values, as shown in [17, Section 5.1, full version] via a more involved analysis. The analysis also carries over to the corresponding Σ_0' variant, based on the negligible "collision" probabilities of two uncorrupted parties generating the same KEM public key pk, or an equal public key and KEM ciphertext. Passive security immediately implies that such collision probabilities are negligible.

Another important difference with the IKE signature mode is that in the response and finish messages of the latter, the MAC tag is not sent separately, but instead is treated as the message to be signed. (Because of this, the MAC tag is computed on a tuple of *all* the values that are either signed or tagged in Σ_0.) In order to handle this, we need the MAC.Tag algorithm to be deterministic, which is standard. Then the analysis in [17, Section 5.2, full version] goes through unchanged, as it relies only on the security of the MAC and signature schemes. The resulting protocol (also without the 0,1 values) essentially corresponds to IKE's "aggressive mode of signature authentication."

Other changes include offering identity concealment via encryption; a protocol corresponding to IKE's "main mode with signature authentication;" and more. These are all analyzed in [17, Sections 5.3-5.4], and that analysis also goes through essentially unchanged for Σ_0'.

Acknowledgments. I thank Keita Xagawa for helpful comments on the Fujisaki-Okamoto transformation, and the anonymous PQC reviewers for useful suggestions.

References

1. Abdalla, M., Bellare, M., Rogaway, P.: The oracle Diffie-Hellman assumptions and an analysis of DHIES. In: Naccache, D. (ed.) CT-RSA 2001. LNCS, vol. 2020, pp. 143–158. Springer, Heidelberg (2001)
2. Ajtai, M.: Generating hard instances of lattice problems. Quaderni di Matematica 13, 1–32 (2004), Preliminary version in STOC 1996
3. Arbitman, Y., Dogon, G., Lyubashevsky, V., Micciancio, D., Peikert, C., Rosen, A.: SWIFFTX: A proposal for the SHA-3 standard. Submitted to NIST SHA-3 competition (2008)
4. Arora, S., Ge, R.: New algorithms for learning in presence of errors. In: Aceto, L., Henzinger, M., Sgall, J. (eds.) ICALP 2011, Part I. LNCS, vol. 6755, pp. 403–415. Springer, Heidelberg (2011)
5. Bellare, M., Canetti, R., Krawczyk, H.: A modular approach to the design and analysis of authentication and key exchange protocols (extended abstract). In: STOC, pp. 419–428 (1998)
6. Bellare, M., Desai, A., Pointcheval, D., Rogaway, P.: Relations among notions of security for public-key encryption schemes. In: Krawczyk, H. (ed.) CRYPTO 1998. LNCS, vol. 1462, pp. 26–45. Springer, Heidelberg (1998)
7. Bellare, M., Rogaway, P.: Entity authentication and key distribution. In: Stinson, D.R. (ed.) CRYPTO 1993. LNCS, vol. 773, pp. 232–249. Springer, Heidelberg (1994)
8. Bellare, M., Rogaway, P.: Random oracles are practical: A paradigm for designing efficient protocols. In: ACM Conference on Computer and Communications Security, pp. 62–73 (1993)
9. Bellare, M., Rogaway, P.: Optimal asymmetric encryption. In: De Santis, A. (ed.) EUROCRYPT 1994. LNCS, vol. 950, pp. 92–111. Springer, Heidelberg (1995)
10. Bellare, M., Rogaway, P.: Provably secure session key distribution: the three party case. In: STOC, pp. 57–66 (1995)
11. Bellare, M., Rogaway, P.: Minimizing the use of random oracles in authenticated encryption schemes. In: ICICS, pp. 1–16 (1997)
12. Boneh, D., Canetti, R., Halevi, S., Katz, J.: Chosen-ciphertext security from identity-based encryption. SIAM J. Comput. 36(5), 1301–1328 (2007)
13. Brakerski, Z., Langlois, A., Peikert, C., Regev, O., Stehlé, D.: Classical hardness of learning with errors. In: STOC, pp. 575–584 (2013)
14. Canetti, R.: Universally composable security: A new paradigm for cryptographic protocols. Cryptology ePrint Archive, Report 2000/067 (2000), http://eprint.iacr.org/
15. Canetti, R.: Universally composable security: A new paradigm for cryptographic protocols. In: FOCS, pp. 136–145 (2001)
16. Canetti, R., Krawczyk, H.: Analysis of key-exchange protocols and their use for building secure channels. In: Pfitzmann, B. (ed.) EUROCRYPT 2001. LNCS, vol. 2045, pp. 453–474. Springer, Heidelberg (2001), Full version at http://eprint.iacr.org/2001/040

17. Canetti, R., Krawczyk, H.: Security analysis of IKE's signature-based key-exchange protocol. In: Yung, M. (ed.) CRYPTO 2002. LNCS, vol. 2442, pp. 143–161. Springer, Heidelberg (2002), Full version at http://eprint.iacr.org/2002/120

18. Canetti, R., Krawczyk, H.: Universally composable notions of key exchange and secure channels. In: Knudsen, L.R. (ed.) EUROCRYPT 2002. LNCS, vol. 2332, pp. 337–351. Springer, Heidelberg (2002), Full version at http://eprint.iacr.org/2002/059

19. Chen, Y., Nguyen, P.Q.: BKZ 2.0: Better lattice security estimates. In: Lee, D.H., Wang, X. (eds.) ASIACRYPT 2011. LNCS, vol. 7073, pp. 1–20. Springer, Heidelberg (2011)

20. Cramer, R., Shoup, V.: Universal hash proofs and a paradigm for adaptive chosen ciphertext secure public-key encryption. In: Knudsen, L.R. (ed.) EUROCRYPT 2002. LNCS, vol. 2332, pp. 45–64. Springer, Heidelberg (2002)

21. Cramer, R., Shoup, V.: Design and analysis of practical public-key encryption schemes secure against adaptive chosen ciphertext attack. SIAM J. Comput. 33(1), 167–226 (2003), Preliminary version in CRYPTO 1998

22. Diffie, W., Hellman, M.E.: New directions in cryptography. IEEE Transactions on Information Theory IT-22(6), 644–654 (1976)

23. Ding, J., Xie, X., Lin, X.: A simple provably secure key exchange scheme based on the learning with errors problem. Cryptology ePrint Archive, Report 2012/688 (2014), http://eprint.iacr.org/

24. Dolev, D., Dwork, C., Naor, M.: Nonmalleable cryptography. SIAM J. Comput. 30(2), 391–437 (1991), Preliminary version in STOC 1991

25. Döttling, N., Müller-Quade, J.: Lossy codes and a new variant of the learning-with-errors problem. In: Johansson, T., Nguyen, P.Q. (eds.) EUROCRYPT 2013. LNCS, vol. 7881, pp. 18–34. Springer, Heidelberg (2013)

26. Ducas, L., Durmus, A., Lepoint, T., Lyubashevsky, V.: Lattice signatures and bimodal gaussians. In: Canetti, R., Garay, J.A. (eds.) CRYPTO 2013, Part I. LNCS, vol. 8042, pp. 40–56. Springer, Heidelberg (2013)

27. Fujisaki, E., Okamoto, T.: How to enhance the security of public-key encryption at minimum cost. In: Imai, H., Zheng, Y. (eds.) PKC 1999. LNCS, vol. 1560, pp. 53–68. Springer, Heidelberg (1999)

28. Fujisaki, E., Okamoto, T.: Secure integration of asymmetric and symmetric encryption schemes. In: Wiener, M. (ed.) CRYPTO 1999. LNCS, vol. 1666, pp. 537–554. Springer, Heidelberg (1999)

29. Gentry, C., Peikert, C., Vaikuntanathan, V.: Trapdoors for hard lattices and new cryptographic constructions. In: STOC, pp. 197–206 (2008)

30. Harkins, D., Carrel, D.: The Internet Key Exchange (IKE). RFC 2409 (Proposed Standard) (November 1998). Obsoleted by RFC 4306, updated by RFC 4109

31. Hoffstein, J., Pipher, J., Silverman, J.H.: NTRU: A ring-based public key cryptosystem. In: Buhler, J.P. (ed.) ANTS 1998. LNCS, vol. 1423, pp. 267–288. Springer, Heidelberg (1998)

32. Housley, R.: Use of the RSAES-OAEP Key Transport Algorithm in Cryptographic Message Syntax (CMS). RFC 3560 (Proposed Standard) (July 2003)

33. Kaufman, C.: Internet Key Exchange (IKEv2) Protocol. RFC 4306 (Proposed Standard) (December 2005), Obsoleted by RFC 5996, updated by RFC 5282

34. Kaufman, C., Hoffman, P., Nir, Y., Eronen, P.: Internet Key Exchange Protocol Version 2 (IKEv2). RFC 5996 (Proposed Standard) (September 2010), Updated by RFCs 5998, 6989

35. Kent, S., Atkinson, R.: Security Architecture for the Internet Protocol. RFC 2401 (Proposed Standard) (November 1998), Obsoleted by RFC 4301, updated by RFC 3168

36. Kent, S., Seo, K.: Security Architecture for the Internet Protocol. RFC 4301 (Proposed Standard) (December 2005), Updated by RFC 6040

37. Krawczyk, H.: SKEME: a versatile secure key exchange mechanism for Internet. In: NDSS, pp. 114–127 (1996)

38. Krawczyk, H.: SIGMA: The 'SIGn-and-MAc' approach to authenticated Diffie-Hellman and its use in the IKE-protocols. In: Boneh, D. (ed.) CRYPTO 2003. LNCS, vol. 2729, pp. 400–425. Springer, Heidelberg (2003), Full version at http://webee.technion.ac.il/~hugo/sigma.html

39. Krawczyk, H.: HMQV: A high-performance secure Diffie-Hellman protocol. In: Shoup, V. (ed.) CRYPTO 2005. LNCS, vol. 3621, pp. 546–566. Springer, Heidelberg (2005)

40. Law, L., Menezes, A., Qu, M., Solinas, J.A., Vanstone, S.A.: An efficient protocol for authenticated key agreement. Des. Codes Cryptography 28(2), 119–134 (2003)

41. Lindner, R., Peikert, C.: Better key sizes (and attacks) for LWE-based encryption. In: Kiayias, A. (ed.) CT-RSA 2011. LNCS, vol. 6558, pp. 319–339. Springer, Heidelberg (2011)

42. Liu, M., Nguyen, P.Q.: Solving BDD by enumeration: An update. In: Dawson, E. (ed.) CT-RSA 2013. LNCS, vol. 7779, pp. 293–309. Springer, Heidelberg (2013)

43. Lyubashevsky, V.: Lattice signatures without trapdoors. In: Pointcheval, D., Johansson, T. (eds.) EUROCRYPT 2012. LNCS, vol. 7237, pp. 738–755. Springer, Heidelberg (2012)

44. Lyubashevsky, V., Micciancio, D.: Generalized compact knapsacks are collision resistant. In: Bugliesi, M., Preneel, B., Sassone, V., Wegener, I. (eds.) ICALP 2006, Part II. LNCS, vol. 4052, pp. 144–155. Springer, Heidelberg (2006)

45. Lyubashevsky, V., Micciancio, D.: Asymptotically efficient lattice-based digital signatures. In: Canetti, R. (ed.) TCC 2008. LNCS, vol. 4948, pp. 37–54. Springer, Heidelberg (2008)

46. Lyubashevsky, V., Micciancio, D., Peikert, C., Rosen, A.: SWIFFT: A modest proposal for FFT hashing. In: Nyberg, K. (ed.) FSE 2008. LNCS, vol. 5086, pp. 54–72. Springer, Heidelberg (2008)

47. Lyubashevsky, V., Peikert, C., Regev, O.: On ideal lattices and learning with errors over rings. Journal of the ACM 60(6), 43:1–43:35 (2013). Preliminary version in Gilbert, H. (ed.) EUROCRYPT 2010. LNCS, vol. 6110, pp. 1–23. Springer, Heidelberg (2010)

48. Lyubashevsky, V., Peikert, C., Regev, O.: A toolkit for ring-LWE cryptography. In: Johansson, T., Nguyen, P.Q. (eds.) EUROCRYPT 2013. LNCS, vol. 7881, pp. 35–54. Springer, Heidelberg (2013)

49. Micciancio, D.: Generalized compact knapsacks, cyclic lattices, and efficient one-way functions. Computational Complexity 16(4), 365–411 (2007), Preliminary version in FOCS 2002

50. Micciancio, D., Peikert, C.: Trapdoors for lattices: Simpler, tighter, faster, smaller. In: Pointcheval, D., Johansson, T. (eds.) EUROCRYPT 2012. LNCS, vol. 7237, pp. 700–718. Springer, Heidelberg (2012)

51. Micciancio, D., Peikert, C.: Hardness of SIS and LWE with small parameters. In: Canetti, R., Garay, J.A. (eds.) CRYPTO 2013, Part I. LNCS, vol. 8042, pp. 21–39. Springer, Heidelberg (2013)

52. Micciancio, D., Regev, O.: Worst-case to average-case reductions based on Gaussian measures. SIAM J. Comput. 37(1), 267–302 (2004), Preliminary version in FOCS 2004
53. Okamoto, T., Pointcheval, D.: REACT: Rapid enhanced-security asymmetric cryptosystem transform. In: Naccache, D. (ed.) CT-RSA 2001. LNCS, vol. 2020, pp. 159–175. Springer, Heidelberg (2001)
54. Peikert, C.: Public-key cryptosystems from the worst-case shortest vector problem. In: STOC, pp. 333–342 (2009)
55. Peikert, C., Rosen, A.: Efficient collision-resistant hashing from worst-case assumptions on cyclic lattices. In: Halevi, S., Rabin, T. (eds.) TCC 2006. LNCS, vol. 3876, pp. 145–166. Springer, Heidelberg (2006)
56. Peikert, C., Waters, B.: Lossy trapdoor functions and their applications. SIAM J. Comput. 40(6), 1803–1844 (2011), Preliminary version in STOC 2008
57. Randall, J., Kaliski, B., Brainard, J., Turner, S.: Use of the RSA-KEM Key Transport Algorithm in the Cryptographic Message Syntax (CMS). RFC 5990 (Proposed Standard) (September 2010)
58. Regev, O.: On lattices, learning with errors, random linear codes, and cryptography. J. ACM 56(6), 1–40 (2009), Preliminary version in STOC 2005
59. Rivest, R.L., Shamir, A., Adleman, L.M.: A method for obtaining digital signatures and public-key cryptosystems. Commun. ACM 21(2), 120–126 (1978)
60. Shoup, V.: On formal models for secure key exchange. Cryptology ePrint Archive, Report 1999/012 (1999), http://eprint.iacr.org/
61. Shoup, V.: OAEP reconsidered. J. Cryptology 15(4), 223–249 (2002). Preliminary version in Kilian, J. (ed.) CRYPTO 2001. LNCS, vol. 2139, pp. 223–249. Springer, Heidelberg (2001)

Optimizing Information Set Decoding Algorithms to Attack Cyclosymmetric MDPC Codes

Ray Perlner

National Institute of Standards and Technology,
Gaithersburg, Maryland, USA
ray.perlner@nist.gov

Abstract. Recently, several promising approaches have been proposed
to reduce keysizes for code based cryptography using structured, but
non-algebraic codes, such as quasi-cyclic (QC) Moderate Density Parity
Check (MDPC) codes. Biasi et al. propose further reducing the keysizes
of code-based schemes using cyclosymmetric (CS) codes. While Biasi
et al. analyze the complexity of attacking their scheme using standard
information-set-decoding algorithms, the research presented here shows
that information set decoding algorithms can be improved, by choosing
the columns of the information set in a way that takes advantage of the
added symmetry. The result is an attack that significantly reduces the
security of the proposed CS-MDPC schemes to the point that they no
longer offer an advantage in keysize over QC-MDPC schemes of the same
security level. QC-MDPC schemes are not affected by this paper's result.

Keywords: information set decoding, code-based cryptography, moderate density parity check (MDPC) codes, cyclosymmetric.

1 Introduction

The McEliece cryptosystem [1] is one of the oldest and most studied candidates
for a postquantum cryptosystem. However, its keysizes, on the order of a million
bits, are a major drawback. The most aggressive approaches to keysize reduction
have focused on imposing structure on the public generator and parity check
matrices such that they consist of cyclic [2] or dyadic [3] blocks, each of which
can be represented using only the top row of the block.

However, these matrices have significant algebraic structure, and when the
private code is itself an algebraic code, like the Goppa codes used in the original
McEliece cryptosystem, such schemes tend to be open to algebraic attack[4]. A
promising solution to this problem is to use nonalgebraic codes. In particular
Misoczki et al. proposed [5] using moderate density parity check (MDPC) codes
with quasicyclic structure (QC-MDPC).

A typical approach to attacking a scheme based on MDPC codes is to use
information set decoding techniques to find low weight codewords in the dual

M. Mosca (Ed.): PQCrypto 2014, LNCS 8772, pp. 220–228, 2014.

code space (i.e. the row space of the public parity check matrix.) The concept of information set decoding originates with Prange [6]. Further optimizations were subsequently proposed by Lee and Brickell [7], Leon [8] and Stern [9].

Biasi et al. [10] attempt further keysize reduction by replacing blockwise cyclic structure with blockwise cyclosymmetric (CS) structure. The advantage of such matrices is that they can be represented by only half of the elements of their top rows. Indeed, a cyclosymmetric matrix consisting of smaller cyclosymmetric blocks can be represented using only a quarter of the elements in its top row, which would seem to provide significant opportunities for keysize reduction above and beyond what can be achieved using cyclic matrices. This further optimization was suggested by Biasi et al. in earlier versions of their paper[11],[12], but not in the published version, for reasons discussed in Section 4.

This paper demonstrates that information set decoding techniques can be improved by restricting the selection of information set columns to take advantage of CS symmetry. The complexity of the resulting attacks on a blockwise cyclosymmetric code is almost identical to the complexity of attacking a similar blockwise cyclic code with half the dimension, and half the row weight.

2   Cyclosymmetric Matrices

Ordinary cyclic matrices are those of the form:

$$A = \begin{bmatrix} a_0 & a_1 & \dots & a_{r-1} \\ a_{r-1} & a_0 & \dots & a_{r-2} \\ \vdots & \vdots & \ddots & \vdots \\ a_1 & a_2 & \dots & a_0 \end{bmatrix}. \tag{1}$$

Each row is the right-cyclic rotation of the row above it. When their entries are elements of a field $\mathbb{F}$, cyclic matrices form a commutative ring under matrix multiplication and addition, isomorphic to the polynomial ring $\mathbb{F}[x]/(x^r - 1)$. (In most code-based-cryptography applications, including the scheme attacked in this paper, $\mathbb{F}$ is $\mathbb{F}_2$.)

Cyclosymmetric matrices are further restricted to be symmetric matrices, i.e. equal to their transpose. Using the commutativity of the ring of cyclic matrices we can show that the cyclosymmetric matrices are closed under multiplication and therefore form a subring of the cyclic matrices:

$$(AB)^T = B^T A^T = BA = AB. \tag{2}$$

A relevant fact about cyclosymmetric matrices is that $\lfloor \frac{r-1}{2} \rfloor$ pairs of entries in the top row of a cyclosymmetric matrix are constrained by symmetry to be equal:

$$\forall x | 1 \leq x < \frac{r-1}{2} : a_x = a_{r-x}. \tag{3}$$

3   MDPC Cryptosystems

The scheme of Biasi et al. [10] modifies an earlier proposal by Misoczki et al. [5]. Both schemes are variants of the Niederreiter[13] cryptosystem : The public key, H_{pub} is a $(n - k) \times n$ parity check matrix for a binary linear code, in systematic form $-[M|I]$. The plaintext, m, is encoded as an n-bit vector of Hamming weight at most t. The ciphertext is $H_{pub}m^T$. In the language of coding theory, the plaintext is the error vector, while the ciphertext is the syndrome. As in all variants of the Neiderreiter cryptosystem, the private key consists of trapdoor information that allows the owner to efficiently reconstruct the error vector m from the syndrome $H_{pub}m^T$

In the case of MDPC cryptosystems, the private key is a low density parity check matrix H sharing the same codespace as H_{pub}. The cryptographic scheme is described as using a moderate density parity check (MDPC) code, in contrast to the related low density parity check (LDPC) codes used for error correction in telecommunications applications. LDPC codes employ a significantly less dense parity check matrix and they correct more errors than the codes used in the proposed cryptographic scheme. The quasicyclic and cyclosymmetric variants of the MDPC encryption scheme construct the matrix H from n_0 cyclic or cyclosymmetric blocks each with row weight d_v, but otherwise randomly chosen:

$$H = \begin{bmatrix} H_0 & H_1 & \dots & H_{n_0-1} \end{bmatrix}. \tag{4}$$

Once a private parity check matrix is chosen as above, the public key is constructed from it as follows:

$$H_{pub} = H_{n_0-1}^{-1}H = \begin{bmatrix} H_{n_0-1}^{-1}H_0 \mid H_{n_0-1}^{-1}H_1 \mid \dots \mid H_{n_0-1}^{-1}H_{n_0-2} \mid I \end{bmatrix}. \tag{5}$$

4   Dimension Reduction for Cyclosymmetric Matrices

In their paper [10], Biasi et al. note that there is a more compact representation of the ring of cyclosymmetric matrices than that given in equation 1. For example, matrices of the form:

$$M(a,b,c,d) = \begin{bmatrix} a & b & c & d & c & b \\ b & a & b & c & d & c \\ c & b & a & b & c & d \\ d & c & b & a & b & c \\ c & d & c & b & a & b \\ b & c & d & c & b & a \end{bmatrix} \tag{6}$$

obey exactly the same multiplication rules as matrices of the form

$$M'(a,b,c,d) = \begin{bmatrix} a & 2b & 2c & d \\ b & a+c & b+d & c \\ c & b+d & a+c & b \\ d & 2c & 2b & a \end{bmatrix}. \tag{7}$$

The problem of finding a low weight basis for the row space of a matrix, made up of blocks of the form M, can therefore be reduced to the problem of finding a low weight basis for the row space of a smaller matrix, made up of blocks of the form M'.

This however does not completely break the scheme. While, this observation allows the attacker to reduce the dimension of the scheme being attacked by a factor of 2 for large matrices, it does so at the cost of reducing the sparsity (increasing the row weight) of the target private matrix by a factor of 2. This observation forced Biasi et al. to make their parameter choices less aggressive, but it did not force them to abandon the possibility of keysize reduction through cyclosymmetric matrices altogether.

5   Improving Information Set Decoding

The goal of the attack presented in this paper is to extract the private key H, from the public key H_{pub}. As is clear from equations 4 and 5, the rows of H are linear combinations of the rows of H_{pub}. In particular, as will become relevant later in this section, $h = h_{n_0-1}H_{pub}$, where h and h_{n_0-1} represent the top rows of the matrices H and H_{n_0-1} respectively. The rows of H are distinguished from other linear combinations of the rows of H_{pub} in that they are sparse. As it happens, finding sparse linear combinations of the rows of a binary matrix is precisely the application for which classical information set decoding algorithms were invented.

All information set decoding algorithms follow the same basic script[1]:

1. Permute the columns of H_{pub} :

$$H'_{pub} = H_{pub}P. \tag{8}$$

2. Check that the first r columns of the new matrix, H'_{pub}, form an invertible matrix A. These columns are referred to as the "information set." If A is not invertible go back to step 1.

3. Left-multiply by A^{-1}, resulting in a matrix of the form:

$$M = A^{-1}H'_{pub} = [I_r \mid Q]. \tag{9}$$

4. Search for low weight row-vectors among linear combinations involving small subsets of the rows of M. If none are found, go back to step 1. If a low weight vector $x' = vM$ is found, return $x = vMP^{-1}$. The return value x will be precisely the sought-after low-weight element of the row space of H_{pub}.

---

[1] The variable names are chosen to reflect the scheme being attacked. For example the matrix being attacked is represented as a parity check matrix H_{pub} rather than a generator matrix G, and its dimensions are given as $r \times n_0 r$ rather than $k \times n$.

Most optimizations to information set decoding algorithms, for example that of Stern [9], involve step 4. However, the special blockwise cyclosymmetric form of H_{pub} allows us to make a much larger improvement, based on the choice of the permutation P in step 1. To see how this works, we need to understand the significance of the row vector v in step 4: In particular, since the first r columns of M form an identity matrix, the first r bits of the candidate low weight row vector x' are equal to v. Moreover:

Theorem 1. *When computed by an information set decoding algorithm as outlined by steps 1-4 above, x' is the unique element of the rowspace of H'_{pub} whose first r bits equal v.*

Proof. Suppose there were another element of the rowspace of H'_{pub}, yH'_{pub} whose first r bits equalled v. Then, since yH'_{pub} expands as:

$$yH'_{pub} = yAM = yA|yAQ. \tag{10}$$

We may rewrite our requirement as

$$yA = v. \tag{11}$$

Since A is invertible, this implies $y = vA^{-1}$ and therefore, $yH'_{pub} = vA^{-1}H'_{pub} = vM = x'$.

Thus, given the existence of a low weight vector x in the rowspace of H_{pub}, v represents a guess of all the bits of x within the information set. Since the most probable value of a bit contained within a sparse vector is zero, the choice of v with the highest probability of success is the guess which contains as many zeroes as possible. (Note that v must contain at least one nonzero bit, since we're looking for a nontrivial solution.) As it happens, the best strategy involves checking multiple guesses of v for each choice of P, since checking a guess is computationally cheaper than inverting a matrix, but the point remains that our probability of success relies on the probability that we will choose an information set, such that the restriction v of x to the information set is significantly sparser than x itself.

This is where the choice of permutation helps us. We are much more likely to get x to be oversparse on the information set, if the bits we are guessing are not independent. As it happens, the top row, h of the private parity check matrix is a sparse vector, consisting of subvectors, $h_0 \ldots h_{n_0-1}$, whose bits come in pairs obeying the relation given in equation 3. $x = h$ will then be the target of our attack. If we restrict the permutation P to either leave both elements of such linked pairs outside of the information set, or to bring both elements in, then the probability of h matching one of our oversparse guesses v on the information set is significantly higher than it would be if P were chosen randomly.

An example may be given, based on the parameters [10] given by Biasi et al. for 128-bit security. The parameters are as follows: $n_0 = 3$, $r = 7232$, and the row/column weight, d_v, of the submatrices H_0, H_1, and H_2, is 98 (i.e. the row weight for the whole matrix H is 294.) For a random choice of P, the probability that the vector consisting of the first r bits of hP, (i.e. $Truncate(r, hP)$), has weight 2 is:

$$\frac{\binom{7232}{2}\binom{2\cdot7232}{292}}{\binom{3\cdot7232}{294}} = 2^{-160}.$$

However, for a choice of P restricted to bring mirrored pairs of bits into the information set together, the probability is

$$\frac{\binom{3616}{1}\binom{2\cdot3616}{146}}{\binom{3\cdot3616}{147}} = 2^{-80}.$$

Thus, a (rather poorly optimized) information set decoding algorithm, which tried all the values of v with weight 2, would require 2^{160} matrix inversions on average to succeed if P were chosen randomly. Our improvement brings the complexity down to 2^{80} matrix inversions, which, even accounting for the non-trivial complexity of the matrix inversion step, is already well below the claimed security level of the scheme.

6   Improved Stern Algorithm

In this section we present a variant of Stern's algorithm modified to find the top row, h of the private parity check matrix of the CS-MDPC scheme of Biasi et al. The other rows of H may then be trivially computed as rotations of h. The attacker is given H_{pub} generated from H as in equation 5. Both H and H_{pub} have dimensions $r \times n_0 r$, and consist of $r \times r$ cyclosymmetric blocks. H has column weight d_v and row weight $n_0 d_v$. The algorithm is parametrized by integers p and l.

1. Permute the columns of H_{pub} :

$$H'_{pub} = H_{pub}P \tag{12}$$

   choosing P with the restriction that cyclosymmetry forces:

$$(hP)_{2i} = (hP)_{2i+1} \ \ for \ i = 0 \ldots \lfloor r/2 \rfloor + l. \tag{13}$$

2. Check that the first r columns of the new matrix, H'_{pub}, form an invertible matrix A. If A is not invertible go back to step 1.

3. Left-Multiply by A^{-1}, resulting in a matrix of the form:

$$M = A^{-1}H'_{pub} = \left[I_r \mid Q\right]. \tag{14}$$

4. Search for low-weight row-vectors among linear combinations involving small subsets of the rows of M. In particular these will involve $2p$ of the first $\frac{r}{2}$ rows and $2p$ of the remaining rows. The search will succeed if hP has weight $2p$ on its first $\frac{r}{2}$ bits, weight $2p$ on the next $r/2$ bits, and weight 0 on the next l bits.

(a) Sum paired rows and compile in two equal length lists, i.e.:
for $0 \leq i < \frac{r}{4}$

$$x_i = row_{2i}(M) + row_{2i+1}(M) \tag{15}$$

and for $\frac{r}{4} \leq j < \frac{r}{2}$

$$y_i = row_{2j}(M) + row_{2j+1}(M) \tag{16}$$

(b) compute all the sums of p x_is and all the sums of p y_is and check for collisions on bits $r \dots r + 2l - 1$

$$bits_{r \dots r+2l+1}(x_{i_1} + \dots + x_{i_p}) = bits(r \dots r + 2l + 1, y_{j_1} + \dots + y_{j_p}) \tag{17}$$

(c) When such a collision is found, check the total weight of the sum w of the $2p$ colliding row vectors.

$$w = x_{i_1} + \dots + x_{i_p} + y_{j_1} + \dots + y_{j_p}. \tag{18}$$

If the weight of any such w is less than or equal to $n_0 d_v$ retrurn wP. Otherwise, go back to step 1.

7   Attack Complexity for Suggested Parameters

The major contributions to the overall complexity of each iteration of the modified Stern's algorithm above may be approximated as: $n_0 r^3$ for the matrix inversion (step 3), $2(p-1)n_0 r\binom{\frac{r}{4}}{p}$ for the construction of hash tables for collision search (step 4b), and $\frac{n_0 r \binom{\frac{r}{4}}{p}^2}{2^l}$ for testing candidate low-weight vectors, w (step 4c). However, the units for these complexity figures are single-bit addition operations. Since legitimate parties do computations on the order of $n_0 r^2$ during both public and private-key operations, it is reasonable to divide this factor out leaving a per iteration complexity estimate of:

$$r + \frac{2(p-1)}{r}\binom{\frac{r}{4}}{p} + \frac{1}{2^l r}\binom{\frac{r}{4}}{p}^2. \tag{19}$$

The expected number of iterations is the inverse probability of success per iteration, which is:

$$\left(\frac{n_0 r}{\frac{n_0 d_v}{2}}\right)\binom{\frac{r}{4}}{p}^{-2}\left(\frac{\frac{(n_0-1)r}{2} - l}{\frac{n_0 d_v}{2} - 2p}\right)^{-1}. \tag{20}$$

Note that the iteration count (equation 20) is identical to the iteration count of an unmodified Stern's algorithm applied to a code with $r' = \frac{r}{2}$ and $d'_v = \frac{d_v}{2}$, and the per iteration cost (equation 19) is identical up to polynomial factors in $r/r' = 2$ (The discrepancy is due to the fact that linear algebra operations are being performed on a larger matrix.) Thus, our attack may be thought of as reducing the security of a cyclosymmetric MDPC scheme with block dimension r and private row density $\frac{d_v}{r}$ to that of a corresponding cyclic scheme which with dimension $\frac{r}{2}$ and the same private row density.

Table 1 gives the results of our attack when applied to the parameters suggested by Biasi et al. For all parameter choices, the security level allowed by this attack is significantly lower than the claimed security level.

Table 1. Claimed security levels and the results of the modified Stern's algorithm attack for parameters given in [10]

Claimed Security (bits)	n_0	r	d_v	Attack Complexity (bits)	p	l
80	3	3072	53	46	2	20
112	3	5376	75	63	2	20
128	3	7232	97	81	2	22
160	3	19200	109	93	2	25

As our attack brings the security of Biasi et al.'s proposed 128-bit parameters down to nearly exactly 80 bits of security, it is informative to compare these parameters to the 80-bit security parameters of Misoczki et al.'s QC-MDPC scheme. Here we find that there is no longer any advantage to the cyclosymmetric scheme, either in public key size or cryptogram size:

Table 2. Comparison of proposed CS-MDPC and QC-MDPC parameters at 80 bits of security given this paper's attack.

	CS-MDPC [10]	QC-MDPC [5]
Public Key Length	7232	4801
Cryptogram Size	21696	9602

8   Conclusion

While the idea of using cyclosymmetric codes to reduce keysize beyond what is possible with blockwise cyclic codes seemed promising, the added structure appears to be as useful to the attacker as to the legitimate parties. In particular, information set decoding algorithms can be modified to take full advantage of the knowledge that the rows of the private parity check matrix of such a scheme are structured. It may be the case that cyclic MDPC codes are as far as we can go in keysize reduction for code-based cryptography.

References

1. McEliece, R.J.: A Public-Key Cryptosystem Based On Algebraic Coding Theory. Deep Space Network Progress Report 44, 114–116 (1978)
2. Berger, T.P., Cayrel, P.-L., Gaborit, P., Otmani, A.: Reducing key length of the McEliece cryptosystem. In: Preneel, B. (ed.) AFRICACRYPT 2009. LNCS, vol. 5580, pp. 77–97. Springer, Heidelberg (2009)
3. Misoczki, R., Barreto, P.S.L.M.: Compact mceliece keys from goppa codes. In: Jacobson Jr., M.J., Rijmen, V., Safavi-Naini, R. (eds.) SAC 2009. LNCS, vol. 5867, pp. 376–392. Springer, Heidelberg (2009)
4. Faugère, J.-C., Otmani, A., Perret, L., Tillich, J.-P.: Algebraic cryptanalysis of mceliece variants with compact keys. In: Gilbert, H. (ed.) EUROCRYPT 2010. LNCS, vol. 6110, pp. 279–298. Springer, Heidelberg (2010)
5. Misoczki, R., Tillich, J.P., Sendrier, N., Barreto, P.S.L.M.: Mdpc-mceliece: New mceliece variants from moderate density parity-check codes. Cryptology ePrint Archive, Report 2012/409 (2012), http://eprint.iacr.org/
6. Prange, E.: The use of information sets in decoding cyclic codes. IRE Transactions on Information Theory 8, 5–9 (1962)
7. Lee, P.J., Brickell, E.F.: An observation on the security of McEliece's public-key cryptosystem. In: Günther, C.G. (ed.) EUROCRYPT 1988. LNCS, vol. 330, pp. 275–280. Springer, Heidelberg (1988)
8. Leon, J.: A probabilistic algorithm for computing minimum weights of large error-correcting codes. IEEE Transactions on Information Theory 34, 1354–1359 (1988)
9. Stern, J.: A method for finding codewords of small weight. In: Wolfmann, J., Cohen, G. (eds.) Coding Theory 1988. LNCS, vol. 388, pp. 106–113. Springer, Heidelberg (1989)
10. Biasi, F., Barreto, P., Misoczki, R., Ruggiero, W.: Scaling efficient code-based cryptosystems for embedded platforms. Journal of Cryptographic Engineering, 1–12 (2014)
11. Barreto, P.: Can code-based keys and cryptograms get smaller than their rsa counterparts (2012)
12. Biasi, F.P., Barreto, P.S., Misoczki, R., Ruggiero, W.V.: Scaling efficient code-based cryptosystems for embedded platforms. arXiv preprint arXiv:1212.4317 (2012)
13. Neiderreiter, H.: Knapsack-type cryptosystems and algebraic coding theory. Problems of Control and Information Theory. Problemy Upravlenija i Teorii Informacii (15) 159–166

ZHFE, a New Multivariate Public Key Encryption Scheme

Jaiberth Porras[1], John Baena[1], and Jintai Ding[2,3,*]

[1] Universidad Nacional de Colombia, Calle 59A No 63-20, Medellin, Colombia
{jporras,jbbaena}@unal.edu.co
http://www.unalmed.edu.co/~escmat/
[2] University of Cincinnati, 4199 French Hall West, Cincinnati, OH 45221-0025, USA
jintai.ding@uc.edu
[3] Chinese Academy of Sciences, 52 Sanlihe Rd., Beijing, China

Abstract. In this paper we propose a new multivariate public key encryption scheme named ZHFE. The public key is constructed using as core map two high rank HFE polynomials. The inversion of the public key is performed using a low degree polynomial of Hamming weight three. This low degree polynomial is obtained from the two high rank HFE polynomials, by means of a special reduction method that uses Hamming weight three polynomials produced from the two high rank HFE polynomials. We show that ZHFE is relatively efficient and that it is secure against the main attacks that have threatened the security of HFE. We also propose parameters for a practical implementation of ZHFE.

Keywords: Multivariate cryptography, HFE polynomials, HFE cryptosystem, trapdoor functions, Zhuang-zi algorithm.

1   Introduction

Post-Quantum Cryptography stands for those cryptosystems which have the potential to resist possible future quantum computer attacks [3]. Multivariate public key cryptosystems (MPKCs) are an interesting option in Post-Quantum Cryptography [12]. Their main ideas come from algebraic geometry and usually the computations over these cryptosystems are very efficient.

The public key of an MPKC consists of a set of multivariate quadratic polynomials over a finite field. Thus, the security of an MPKC is related to the fact that solving a randomly system of multivariate quadratic polynomial equations over a finite field is an NP-hard problem [15]. Moreover, it seems that quantum computers have no advantage over the traditional computers to solve this problem.

---

* Corresponding author.

M. Mosca (Ed.): PQCrypto 2014, LNCS 8772, pp. 229–245, 2014.
© Springer International Publishing Switzerland 2014

1.1 Hidden Field Equations

One of the most important MPKCs is named Hidden Field Equations (HFE), proposed by Patarin in 1996 [18]. To describe HFE, let us fix a finite field k of size q and a positive integer n. Next, we choose a degree n irreducible polynomial $g(y) \in k[y]$, and consider the field extension $K = k[y]/(g(y))$ and the isomorphism $\varphi \colon K \to k^n$ defined by $\varphi \left(u_1 + u_2 y + \ldots + u_n y^{n-1} \right) = (u_1, u_2, \ldots, u_n)$.

We say that a polynomial has *Hamming weight* W if the maximum of the q-Hamming weights of all its exponents is W. The q-Hamming weight of a non-negative integer is the sum of the q-digits of its q-nary expansion. Let $F : K \to K$ be a Hamming weight two polynomial of the form

$$F(X) = \sum_{\substack{0 \leq j \leq i}}^{n-1} a_{ij} X^{q^i + q^j} + \sum_{i=0}^{n-1} b_i X^{q^i} + c \ ,$$

where the coefficients a_{ij}, b_i, c are chosen randomly in K. Such a polynomial F will be called an *HFE polynomial*. If in addition, we require that $\deg(F) \leq D$, where D is a fixed positive integer, we will say that F is an *HFE polynomial with bound* D.

We now randomly choose an HFE polynomial $F \colon K \to K$ with bound D. The public key of HFE is $P(x_1, \cdots, x_n) = T \circ \varphi \circ F \circ \varphi^{-1} \circ S(x_1, \cdots, x_n)$, where S and T are two invertible affine transformations over k^n. The private key consists of the core map F together with the transformations S and T. We denote by $\mathrm{HFE}(q, n, D)$ an HFE scheme with the described parameters q, n and D. The degree D of the core polynomial F cannot be too large because the decryption process would be very slow. This restriction over HFE introduces a vulnerability against certain attacks like the direct algebraic attack [14] and the KS MinRank attack [17].

1.2 Previous Work

In [19] we proposed a special reduction method to construct new candidates for multivariate trapdoor functions using HFE polynomials of high degree and high rank. The idea of the construction is inspired by the first steps of the Zhuang-Zi algorithm [11]. Given a finite field k of size q and a degree n extension field K, we consider two high degree HFE polynomials over K of the form $F(X) = \sum a_{ij} X^{q^i + q^j} + \sum b_i X^{q^i} + c$ and $\tilde{F}(X) = \sum \tilde{a}_{ij} X^{q^i + q^j} + \sum \tilde{b}_i X^{q^i} + \tilde{c}$, where the coefficients $a_{ij}, b_i, c, \tilde{a}_{ij}, \tilde{b}_i, \tilde{c} \in K$ are to be determined. The idea behind the method is to construct a low degree polynomial Ψ of Hamming weight three of the form

$$\Psi = X \left(\alpha_1 F_0 + \cdots + \alpha_n F_{n-1} + \beta_1 \tilde{F}_0 + \cdots + \beta_n \tilde{F}_{n-1} \right) +$$
$$X^q \left(\alpha_{n+1} F_0 + \cdots + \alpha_{2n} F_{n-1} + \beta_{n+1} \tilde{F}_0 + \cdots + \beta_{2n} \tilde{F}_{n-1} \right) \ ,$$

where $F_0, F_1, \cdots, F_{n-1}$ are the Frobenius powers of F, and $\tilde{F}_0, \tilde{F}_1, \cdots, \tilde{F}_{n-1}$ are the Frobenius powers of $\tilde{F}$.

To obtain such a polynomial Ψ we need to determine the coefficients of F and $\tilde{F}$, also the scalars α_i and β_i, such that the degree of Ψ is less than or equal to a fixed positive integer D_0, which is chosen such that we can easily invert Ψ using Berlekamp's algorithm. The method that we proposed in [19] consists in randomly choosing values for the scalars α_i and β_i, and producing with them a linear system whose solution provides the coefficients of F and $\tilde{F}$. Once the scalars α_i and β_i are randomly chosen, the linear system that is obtained has more variables than equations, and thus we can guarantee nontrivial solutions for it. One could be tempted to randomly choose the variables coming from the coefficients of F and $\tilde{F}$, and then try to solve the linear system for the variables coming from the scalars, with the intention of having generic core polynomials F and $\tilde{F}$. However, this approach produces a linear system with more equations than variables, and hence, in general, this system has no nontrivial solutions.

The new multivariate trapdoor function is built similarly to the way in which HFE is constructed, except that now the core map is replaced by the map $G = (F, \tilde{F})$. The most-consuming-time task during the inversion of the trapdoor function is the inversion of the core map G. But this is an easy task according to the following proposition, which is proved in [19], and the use of Berlekamp's algorithm.

Proposition 1. *Let (Y_1, Y_2) be an element in $\mathrm{Im}(G) \subseteq K \times K$. Then the set of pre-images of (Y_1, Y_2) under the map $G = (F, \tilde{F})$ is a subset of the roots of the low degree polynomial*

$$\Psi' = \Psi - \sum_{j=1}^{2} X^{q^{j-1}} \sum_{i=1}^{n} \alpha_{i+n(j-1)} Y_1^{q^{i-1}} + \beta_{i+n(j-1)} Y_2^{q^{i-1}} \ .$$

1.3   Contribution of this Paper

Some variants of HFE have been proposed as encryption schemes, but all of them have been proven to be insecure. The reason for this fact is that the polynomials used as core maps for these systems have been of low degree, and hence they have had low rank. This situation leads to the following question:

- Is there any way to enlarge the degree of an HFE polynomial used as core map for an encryption scheme, without affecting the efficiency of the decryption process?

We give here an affirmative answer to this question. We construct a new multivariate public key encryption scheme using the multivariate trapdoor function built in [19]. Since the new scheme utilizes as core map two HFE polynomials and the basic idea for the construction comes from the Zhuang-Zi algorithm [11], we call this new encryption scheme ZHFE. We give theoretical and experimental arguments to show that the encryption and decryption processes for ZHFE are relatively efficient. After performing the main known attacks that can threaten the security of these kind of schemes –the direct algebraic and the MinRank attacks–, we propose parameters for ZHFE. We also give values for the main features of ZHFE for the suggested parameters.

This paper is organized as follows. In Sect. 2 we describe the new encryption scheme ZHFE, including a toy example and a suggestion of parameters for a practical implementation. In Sect. 3 we carry out a security analysis of ZHFE with respect to the direct algebraic and MinRank attacks. In Sect. 4 we give some conclusions and in the Appendix we provide additional information about the security analysis.

2   The New Encryption Scheme ZHFE

We use the new multivariate trapdoor function constructed in [19] to build ZHFE, utilizing two HFE polynomials of high degree and high rank. The main reason for using these high degree and high rank HFE polynomials is to resist the MinRank attack. However, the use of high degree HFE polynomials makes the decryption process almost impossible, unless those polynomials are constructed in such a way that the decryption is easy, regardless of the high degree of those polynomials. To accomplish this, we produce a low degree polynomial which we will use to decrypt. In addition, since we are utilizing high degree HFE polynomials for the core map, we expect that the public key has high degree of regularity, very different from what was observed by Faugère and Joux [14] for a system of quadratic equations derived from a single HFE polynomial with low degree. We will develop this point in Sect. 3.

One drawback of ZHFE is the generation time of the private key. The complexity of the reduction method introduced in [19] to produce the private key is polynomial: $O\left(\left(n^3\right)^{\omega}\right)$. Here $2 \leq \omega \leq 3$ is a constant that depends on the elimination algorithm used to solve the sparse linear system derived from the reduction method. In this reduction method we have to deal with huge matrices to reach large values of n. On the plus side we have that these matrices are sparse, which is an advantage in terms of efficiency.

2.1   Description of ZHFE

Let k be a finite field of size q. Fix a positive integer n and choose a degree n irreducible polynomial $g(y) \in k[y]$. Consider the field extension $K = k[y]/(g(y))$ and the isomorphism $\varphi \colon K \to k^n$ defined by $\varphi\left(u_1 + u_2 y + \ldots + u_n y^{n-1}\right) = (u_1, u_2, \ldots, u_n)$. Let F, $\tilde{F}$ and Ψ be three polynomials in $K[X]/\left(X^{q^n} - X\right)$ constructed using the method described in Sect. 1.2, i.e., F and $\tilde{F}$ are two high degree HFE polynomials and Ψ is a low degree q-weight three polynomial which allows us to invert the map $G = (F, \tilde{F})$. Then we select two invertible affine transformations $S : k^n \to k^n$ and $T : k^{2n} \to k^{2n}$. The public map of ZHFE is the multivariate trapdoor function

$$P(x_1, \cdots, x_n) = T \circ (\varphi \times \varphi) \circ G \circ \varphi^{-1} \circ S(x_1, \cdots, x_n) .$$

Notice that P is a map from k^n to k^{2n} (see Fig. 1).

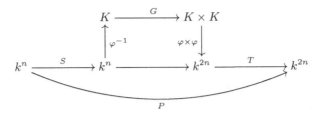

Fig. 1. Public key of ZHFE

Public Key. The public key of ZHFE includes:

- The field k and its structure.
- The trapdoor function $P(x_1, \cdots, x_n) = T \circ (\varphi \times \varphi) \circ G \circ \varphi^{-1} \circ S(x_1, \cdots, x_n)$.

Private Key. The private key of ZHFE includes:

- The low degree polynomial Ψ.
- The two invertible affine transformations S and T.
- The scalars $\alpha_1, \cdots, \alpha_{2n}, \beta_1, \cdots, \beta_{2n}$.

Encryption: To encrypt a plaintext $(x_1, \cdots, x_n) \in k^n$ we simply plug this plaintext into the public key $P = T \circ (\varphi \times \varphi) \circ G \circ \varphi^{-1} \circ S$ to obtain the ciphertext

$$(y_1, \cdots, y_{2n}) = P(x_1, \cdots, x_n) \in k^{2n} \ .$$

Decryption: To recover the plaintext from the ciphertext we must invert each part of P. We perform the following steps:

- We first compute $(w_1, \cdots, w_{2n}) = T^{-1}(y_1, \cdots, y_{2n})$.
- We next calculate $(Y_1, Y_2) = (\varphi^{-1}(w_1, \cdots, w_n), \varphi^{-1}(w_{n+1}, \cdots, w_{2n}))$.
- At this step we must invert the map $G = (F, \tilde{F})$, i.e., we have to solve the equation $G(X) = (Y_1, Y_2)$. The solutions of this equation are part of the roots of the low degree polynomial Ψ', obtained from Ψ and (Y_1, Y_2) as in Proposition 1. Let $\mathcal{Z}$ be the set

$$\mathcal{Z} = \{X \in K / \Psi'(X) = 0\} \ .$$

  We must now determine which elements of $\mathcal{Z}$ are solutions of the polynomial equation $G(X) = (Y_1, Y_2)$. In our extensive experiments we always got that only one element of $\mathcal{Z}$ was a solution for this equation.
- For each solution $X \in \mathcal{Z}$ of the equation $G(X) = (Y_1, Y_2)$, we compute the vector $\varphi(X) \in k^n$.
- Finally, we apply the transformation S^{-1} to each vector found in the previous step and these vectors are the candidates to be the plaintext. To determine which of these is the original plaintext, some redundant information must be added to the plaintext[1].

---

[1] In all our extensive experiments for each ciphertext, there was only one candidate to be the plaintext.

2.2   Toy Example

This example shows how the ZHFE scheme works. Set $q = 3$ and $n = 3$, and consider the field with three elements $k = GF(3)$. We select the irreducible polynomial $g(y) = y^3 + 2y + 1 \in k[y]$. A degree n extension field of k is $K = k[y]/(g(y))$. We can choose a generator $b \in K$ of the multiplicative group of K such that $g(b) = 0$, and we use this element to write the elements of K as powers of it. Let us take $D_0 = 5$. We now randomly choose the scalars $(\alpha_1, \cdots, \alpha_6) = (b^{23}, b^9, b^{22}, b^{16}, b^{24}, b^{22})$ and $(\beta_1, \cdots, \beta_6) = (b^5, b^{10}, b^{16}, 0, b^{17}, b^{14})$. Then, as explained in Sect. 1.2, we construct the polynomials $F(X) = b^{23}X^{18} + b^{16}X^{12} + b^{10}X^{10} + b^{23}X^9 + b^{21}X^6 + b^{24}X^4 + b^{24}X^3 + b^2X^2 + bX$, $\tilde{F}(X) = b^{15}X^{18} + b^{25}X^{12} + b^{19}X^{10} + b^{14}X^9 + bX^6 + b^2X^4 + b^{11}X^3 + b^5X^2 + b^{14}X$ and $\Psi(X) = b^{16}X^5 + b^7X^4 + b^{25}X^3 + b^9X^2$. We also select the invertible affine transformations

$$S(x_1, x_2, x_3) = \begin{pmatrix} 1 & 2 & 0 \\ 1 & 1 & 1 \\ 0 & 1 & 1 \end{pmatrix} \begin{pmatrix} x_1 \\ x_2 \\ x_3 \end{pmatrix} + \begin{pmatrix} 0 \\ 2 \\ 2 \end{pmatrix}$$

and

$$T(x_1, x_2, x_3, x_4, x_5, x_6) = \begin{pmatrix} 2 & 2 & 2 & 0 & 2 & 1 \\ 1 & 1 & 0 & 2 & 1 & 0 \\ 2 & 0 & 0 & 2 & 0 & 1 \\ 1 & 0 & 1 & 0 & 2 & 2 \\ 1 & 2 & 0 & 1 & 0 & 1 \\ 2 & 1 & 0 & 1 & 2 & 0 \end{pmatrix} \begin{pmatrix} x_1 \\ x_2 \\ x_3 \\ x_4 \\ x_5 \\ x_6 \end{pmatrix} + \begin{pmatrix} 0 \\ 2 \\ 2 \\ 0 \\ 2 \\ 1 \end{pmatrix}.$$

The core map is $G(X) = \left(F(X), \tilde{F}(X)\right)$. The composition $P(x_1, x_2, x_3) = T \circ (\varphi \times \varphi) \circ G \circ \varphi^{-1} \circ S(x_1, x_2, x_3)$ yields the public key polynomials

$$p_1(x_1, x_2, x_3) = 2x_1^2 + x_1x_2 + x_1x_3 + x_1 + x_3 + 2,$$
$$p_2(x_1, x_2, x_3) = 2x_1^2 + x_1x_2 + x_1 + x_2^2 + x_2x_3 + x_2 + 2x_3,$$
$$p_3(x_1, x_2, x_3) = x_1^2 + x_1 + x_2 + x_3^2 + 1,$$
$$p_4(x_1, x_2, x_3) = 2x_1^2 + 2x_1x_3 + x_1 + x_2^2 + 2x_2x_3 + x_2 + x_3^2 + 2,$$
$$p_5(x_1, x_2, x_3) = x_1^2 + 2x_1x_2 + 2x_1 + x_2^2 + 2x_2 + x_3 + 1,$$
$$p_6(x_1, x_2, x_3) = x_1x_2 + x_1x_3 + 2x_2^2 + x_2x_3 + x_3^2.$$

We now illustrate the encryption and decryption processes. Let $(x_1, x_2, x_3) = (0, 1, 1)$ be a plaintext. After plugging this plaintext into the public key, we obtain the ciphertext

$$(y_1, y_2, y_3, y_4, y_5, y_6) = (0, 2, 0, 1, 2, 1).$$

In order to recover the plaintext from the ciphertext we first compute

$$(w_1, \cdots, w_6) = T^{-1}(0, 2, 0, 1, 2, 1) = (0, 0, 1, 1, 1, 2).$$

We then calculate

$$\begin{aligned}(Y_1, Y_2) &= \left(\varphi^{-1}\left(w_1, w_2, w_3\right), \varphi^{-1}\left(w_4, w_5, w_6\right)\right) \\ &= \left(\varphi^{-1}\left(0, 0, 1\right), \varphi^{-1}\left(1, 1, 2\right)\right) \\ &= \left(b^2, b^{20}\right).\end{aligned}$$

As explained in Proposition 1, we now create the low degree polynomial Ψ' using the low degree polynomial Ψ, the scalars $\alpha_1, \cdots, \alpha_6, \beta_1, \cdots, \beta_6$ and the vector $(Y_1, Y_2) = \left(b^2, b^{20}\right)$:

$$\Psi' = b^{16} X^5 + b^7 X^4 + b^9 X^2 + b^{15} X \ .$$

The set of roots of Ψ' is[2] $\mathcal{Z} = \left\{0, b^{11}\right\}$. The only element of $\mathcal{Z}$ which is solution of the equation $G\left(X\right) = \left(Y_1, Y_2\right) = \left(b^2, b^{20}\right)$ is $X = b^{11}$. If we apply the isomorphism φ we get $\varphi\left(b^{11}\right) = (2, 1, 1)$. We next apply the transformation S^{-1} and then we recover the plaintext $S^{-1}(2, 1, 1) = (0, 1, 1)$.

The main part of the decryption process is the computation of roots of the polynomial Ψ'. For this task we use Berlekamp's algorithm. This algorithm has complexity $\mathcal{O}\left(nD^2 \log_q D + D^3\right)$, where D is the degree of the univariate polynomial. According to this complexity, it is expected that the degree of Ψ', which is determined by the parameter D_0, has the greatest impact on the decryption time. This fact was confirmed by our experiments. Table 1 shows some average encryption and decryption times for several choices of the parameters (q, n, D_0). For each parameter choice we encrypted and decrypted 100 messages. To perform the experiments we used the software Magma V2.20-2 on an Intel Core i5-3210M CPU 2.50 GHz × 4 with 12 GB of memory installed.

Table 1. Encryption and decryption time for ZHFE, 100 messages were tested per key

q	n	D_0	Average encryption time [s]	Average decryption time [s]
7	35	57	0.006	0.089
7	55	105	0.024	0.427
11	35	33	0.003	0.043
11	35	253	0.005	0.760

2.3   Suggestion of Parameters for a Practical Implementation

In this section we propose values for the parameters (q, n, D_0) for a realistic application of ZHFE. We base our choices on the data collected with the extensive experiments of encryption and decryption time, and with the security analysis that we perform in Sects. 3.1 and 3.2.

---

[2] These roots are found using the Magma implementation of Berlekamp's algorithm.

Our suggestion is $(q, n, D_0) = (7, 55, 105)$, and let us denote the associated scheme by ZHFE(7,55,105). This means that the finite field k has size $q = 7$, the number of variables of the public polynomials is $n = 55$, and the polynomial Ψ has degree $D_0 = 105$. The public map is $P \colon k^{55} \to k^{110}$ and then the public key has $2n = 110$ quadratic polynomials with 55 variables. To store the coefficients of these polynomials we need about 66 KB.

A plaintext is a tuple $(x_1, \cdots, x_{55}) \in k^{55}$ with 165 bits of length and a ciphertext is a tuple $(y_1, \cdots, y_{110}) \in k^{110}$ with 330 bits of length.

The private key comprises the low degree polynomial Ψ, the scalars α_i and β_i and the transformations $S \colon k^{55} \to k^{55}$ and $T \colon k^{110} \to k^{110}$. The polynomial Ψ has at most 14 terms. The coefficients of Ψ and the scalars α_i and β_i are in an extension field of k of degree 55. Thus, to store the private key we need about 11 KB.

In terms of efficiency, we now compare ZHFE to HFE Challenge 1 proposed by Patarin [18]. This system was broken in [14] by means of the direct algebraic attack. We focus on the most-consuming-time task for this kind of schemes, that is, the decryption process. Challenge 1 is the instance HFE(2,80,96). In 2008 Ding, Schmidt and Werner [13] proposed the instance HFE(11,89,132), but this was also broken by Faugère et al. [4]. Compared to Patarin's Challenge 1, HFE(11,89,132) takes about twice the time to decrypt. Decryption for ZHFE(7,55,105) is faster than HFE(11,89,132) because all the parameters are smaller. Therefore, in terms of efficiency, ZHFE(7,55,105) is comparable with Patarin's Challenge 1.

Based on the security analysis that we will explain in Sects. 3.1 and 3.2, we conclude that our choice of parameters gives a security level greater than 2^{80}.

3 Security Analysis

There are two attacks that have broken the security of HFE type schemes: the direct algebraic attack and the KS MinRank attack. Since ZHFE belongs to the HFE scheme family, we must consider these attacks against our new encryption scheme.

3.1 Direct Algebraic Attack

Let us briefly review the direct algebraic attack. Suppose that someone, who does not know the private trapdoor information, wants to invert the public key $P \colon k^n \to k^{2n}$ of the new encryption scheme ($P = (p_1, \ldots, p_{2n})$). She wants to find the pre-images of an element $(y_1, \ldots, y_{2n}) \in \mathrm{Im}(P) \subseteq k^{2n}$. This person only has access to the public key P. In order to accomplish this, she tries to solve the system of quadratic equations

$$p_1(x_1, \ldots, x_n) - y_1 = 0, \cdots, p_{2n}(x_1, \ldots, x_n) - y_{2n} = 0 \ . \tag{1}$$

Solving the system (1) directly is known as the *direct algebraic attack*. One way to solve this system is finding a Gröbner basis for the ideal of $k[x_1, \cdots, x_n]$ generated by the polynomials $p_1 - y_1, \cdots, p_{2n} - y_{2n}$.

The F_4 function of MAGMA, [5], is the most efficient implementation of the Gröbner basis F_4 algorithm that is currently available. We ran extensive experiments using the F_4 algorithm of MAGMA to perform the direct algebraic attack for several choices of the parameters (q, n, D_0). We show here the results of our experiments for $q = 7$. For each choice of the parameters we used 10 different sets of quadratic equations to run the experiments.

In Table 2 and Fig. 2 we can observe that the time needed to solve the equations coming from the public key of ZHFE has an exponential growth in n. We can also see this behaviour with the memory used by the F_4 algorithm. This situation is different from the one observed by Faugere and Joux in [14]. The difference lies on the fact that in [14] the quadratic equations are produced using a polynomial of fixed low degree as core map in the HFE cryptosystem, and in our new cryptosystem the quadratic equations are generated via two high degree polynomials. In our experiments, in general, these two high degree polynomials have full degree $D = 2q^{n-1}$, so in particular this degree increases as n increases. This is the fundamental security improvement of ZHFE, when compared to traditional HFE type schemes in which D is a fixed positive integer.

Table 2. Algebraic attack against ZHFE for $q = 7$ and $D_0 = 105$. Ten systems were tested for each choice of parameters.

n	Average time [s]	Minimum time [s]	Maximum time [s]	Memory [MB]	$\lceil \log_q D \rceil$
12	0.071	0.06	0.09	32	11
14	0.289	0.28	0.31	32	13
16	5.564	5.5	5.64	64	15
18	31.392	31.01	32.19	128	17
20	148.208	143.69	160.73	288	19
22	942.269	663.62	988.45	681	21
24	18114.05	18099.43	18128.67	8334	23

Another evidence that the complexity of the algebraic attack against ZHFE is exponential, is that the degree of regularity of the trapdoor function increases as n increases. This behaviour can be observed in Fig. 3. This trend can also be explained by the fact that $D = 2q^{n-1}$ for ZHFE.

In order to compare ZHFE to the MQ-problem, we chose systems of random quadratic equations of the same dimensions $(k^n \rightarrow k^{2n})$ and performed the algebraic attack against these systems too. For each system of random equations, we found that the time needed to solve such equations using Gröbner bases is essentially the same that the one needed to solve the quadratic equations from the public key of ZHFE. These data are shown in Table 3. Notice that the degree of regularity is the same in both cases. Figure 4 shows graphically the time comparison for the two systems. In that graph we can observe that the two curves are indistinguishable.

The reader might think that the low degree of the Hamming weight three polynomial Ψ could introduce a possible weakness to ZHFE against the direct

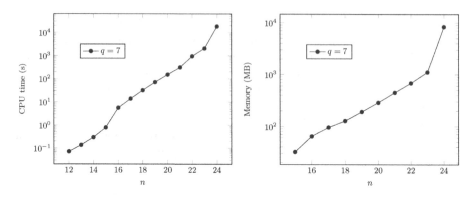

Fig. 2. Algebraic attack against ZHFE for $q = 7$ and $D_0 = 105$

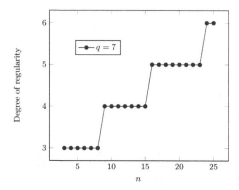

Fig. 3. Algebraic attack against ZHFE for $q = 7$ and $D_0 = 105$

algebraic attack. However, as it was shown in [13,7,8,2], the use of odd characteristic fields in HFE type schemes, provides a resistance against a Gröbner bases attack, regardless of the degree of the core polynomials used to construct the public key. The vulnerability of the schemes proposed in [13,7,8,2] is not against the direct algebraic attack, but against the MinRank attack [4]. The novelty of the present paper is that with the ZHFE cryptosystem we overcome this weakness. We will develop this idea in the next section.

3.2 Kipnis-Shamir MinRank Attack (KS Attack)

In 1999 Kipnis and Shamir [17] proposed a key-recovery attack against HFE that takes advantage of the low rank of the matrix associated to the core map. The KS attack exploits the structure behind the construction of HFE and it links the cryptanalysis of HFE with a linear algebra problem known as the MinRank Problem. Although we are using high degree and high rank polynomials

Table 3. Algebraic attack comparison between ZHFE and a system of random equations for $q = 7$ and $D_0 = 105$

(a)   ZHFE

n	Average time [s]	Memory [MB]	Dreg
16	5.564	64	5
18	31.392	128	5
20	148.208	288	5
22	942.269	681	5
24	18114.05	8334	6

(b) Random equations

n	Average time [s]	Memory [MB]	Dreg
16	5.6	64	5
18	32.19	128	5
20	144.09	288	5
22	991.72	681	5
24	18012.19	8334	6

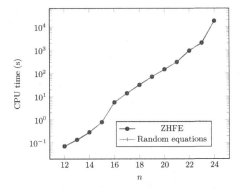

Fig. 4. Algebraic attack comparison between ZHFE and a system of random equations for $q = 7$ and $D_0 = 105$

as the core map in ZHFE, this attack could work if there was a low rank linear combination of their Frobenius powers. Because of this, we have to carefully consider this attack for our new cryptosystem.

The MinRank Problem. Let L be a finite field and consider m matrices $M_1, \cdots, M_m$ over L of size $t \times t$. Given an integer $r \leq t$, the problem is to find, if they exist, scalars $\lambda_1, \cdots, \lambda_m$, not all zero, such that

$$\text{Rank}\left(\sum_{i=1}^{m} \lambda_i M_i\right) \leq r \ .$$

This is in general an NP-hard problem [6]. However for small r, which is the case in HFE, this problem is not too hard. There exist two algebraic ways to attack this problem: the Kipnis-Shamir and the Minors Models (see Appendix).

We now test ZHFE against the KS attack, by performing extensive computer experiments for the case of odd characteristic. For characteristic 2 the attack is slightly different, and we did not perform experiments for this case. All the computations of this section were run using Magma V2.20-2 on a Sun X4440 server, with four Quad-Core AMD OpteronTM Processor 8356 CPUs and 128 GB of main memory (each CPU is running at 2.3 GHz).

The main part of the KS attack, with respect to the complexity, is to solve the MinRank problem. The original version of the KS attack was not as efficient as its authors claimed [16], because the derived MinRank problem worked with matrices with entries in the big field K. Recently, Faugère et al. [4] improved and generalized the KS attack, and were able to break HFE and its generalization Multi-HFE [7] for all practical choices of their parameters. Their main improvement was to restate the MinRank problem with the matrices associated to the public key, whose entries are in the small field k. This makes the improved KS attack significantly faster than the original version.

Let us explain how the KS attack is performed. We begin by noticing that the new trapdoor function P, which is part of the public key of ZHFE, can be seen as a particular case of the public key of an *unbounded* Multi-HFE cryptosystem as presented in [4], with $N = 2$ (for unbounded we mean that the core polynomials have no restrictions for their degrees). Because of this, in this section we perform the KS attack as it was done in [4] for a Multi-HFE scheme. For given parameters q, n and D_0, we generate the $2n$ public key polynomials $p_1, \cdots, p_{2n}$ of the new encryption scheme ZHFE ($P = (p_1, \cdots, p_{2n})$). Then, we compute the symmetric matrix M_i associated to the quadratic part of each public key polynomial p_i, $i = 1, \cdots, 2n$. Let Q-Rank(P) be the minimal rank of elements in the K-linear space generated by the matrices $M_1, \cdots, M_{2n}$. In [4] they showed that Q-Rank(P) coincides with the minimal quadratic rank of elements in the K-linear space generated by the Frobenius powers of the core polynomials F and $\tilde{F}$. The KS attack is successful against Multi-HFE when Q-Rank(P) is low (see [4]). The main purpose of this section is to show that Q-Rank(P) increases as n increases for ZHFE, and therefore the KS attack will not work against this new cryptosystem.

As it has been proved in [4] for a Multi-HFE scheme, in order to accelerate the solution of the MinRank problem, we can randomly fix $N = 2$ of the scalars $\lambda_1, \cdots, \lambda_{2n} \in K$, not all to zero. In our experiments we fixed $\lambda_{n-1} = 0$ and $\lambda_n = 1$, and we used the Kipnis-Shamir modelling for solving this MinRank problem. The reason to choose this modelling is that the minors modelling uses considerably more memory than the KS option.

We now use the MinRank problem to determine the Q-Rank(P) for different combinations of the parameters (q, n, D_0). For each n we start by taking $r = 1$ and then use the KS modelling. We utilize the Magma implementation of the F_4 algorithm to solve the equations produced by this modelling. Table 4 shows the results obtained for $q = 7$ and $D_0 = 105^3$. If for $r = 1$ the solution set of the MinRank problem is empty, then we set $r = r + 1$ and repeat this process until a solution is found. For example, in Table 4 the expression "> 3" means that for

---

[3] The instances $n = 8$ and $n = 10$ for $r = 4$ did not terminate since the processes had a 50 GB memory limitation. When this limit was reached the processes automatically stopped after more than 10 days of running time.

$r \in \{1, 2, 3\}$ the solution set obtained for the MinRank problem was empty, so Q-Rank(P) > 3 for that case.

Table 4. KS attack against ZHFE, for $q = 7$ and $D_0 = 105$

n	Q-Rank(P)	Average time	Maximum memory
2	1	0.010 s	32
4	1	0.010 s	32
6	2	1.340 s	32
8	> 3	> 10 days	> 50 GB^3
10	> 3	> 10 days	> 50 GB^3

In Table 5 we show the time and memory needed to find the solution set for the MinRank problem for $(q, n, D_0) = (7, 8, 110)$ and different values of r. The same situation is observed for other combinations of the parameters. We can see how fast those values increase as r increases. The results in Tables 4 and 5 lead us to think that the larger Q-Rank(P) is the less feasible to solve the MinRank problem is.

Table 5. Time and memory needed to find the solution set for the KS attack against ZHFE, for $q = 7$, $n = 8$ and $D_0 = 105$

r	Average Time	Maximum memory
1	0.040 s	32
2	0.510 s	32 MB
3	297.410 s	462 MB
4	> 10 days	> 50 GB^3

Now, for a fixed pair (q, n) we randomly choose a set of $2n$ quadratic equations in n variables, and perform the same process that we just used with ZHFE, in order to compare with the results that we obtained for ZHFE. The results are summarized in Table 6. We notice that we get exactly the same results for both cases. We also see that, for ZHFE, the value of Q-Rank(P) is independent of the value of D_0.

Another interesting experiment is to compare the performance of the KS attack against ZHFE with the performance of that attack against a system built in a similar way, but with low rank core polynomials F and $\tilde{F}$, i.e., a standard (bounded) Multi-HFE scheme. Table 7 shows these results for $q = 7$ and several values of n. We can observe that for the standard Multi-HFE the KS MinRank attack succeeds, while for the new encryption scheme ZHFE (Table 4) it does not. According to Tables 4, 6 and 7, we think that the quadratic rank Q-Rank(P) grows as n grows.

According to our experiments and the fact that we are using high rank core polynomials to construct the public key, we believe that ZHFE behaves as if it were a set of random equations with respect to the KS MinRank attack.

Table 6. Q-Rank(P) comparison between ZHFE and random equations for $q = 7$

(a)   ZHFE

n	$D_0 = 105$	$D_0 = 399$	$D_0 = 2751$
2	1	1	1
4	1	1	1
6	2	2	2
8	> 3	> 3	> 3
10	> 3	> 3	> 3

(b) Random equations

n	Q-Rank(P)
2	1
4	1
6	2
8	> 3
10	> 3

Table 7. KS attack against a bounded Multi-HFE scheme for $q = 7$ and $\lfloor \log_q D \rfloor = 2$

n	Q-Rank(P)	Average time [s]	Maximum Memory [MB]
2	1	0.050	32
4	1	0.100	32
6	2	1.135	32
8	2	1.190	32
10	2	6.090	32
12	2	23.080	64
14	2	67.500	138
16	2	192.850	211
18	2	479.150	363
20	2	885.720	711

4   Conclusions

We have constructed a new multivariate public key encryption scheme called ZHFE. The core map of ZHFE consists of two high rank HFE polynomials. Until now, no one had proposed any idea of how to use high degree polynomials for the core map in HFE or any of its variants, since we always had the problem of the inversion of such core polynomials. Our novel idea has allowed us to invert a map built with two high degree HFE polynomials by means of a third polynomial of low degree.

We showed that the encryption and decryption processes for ZHFE are relatively efficient. Moreover, we showed that the attacks that have threatened the security of HFE, the direct algebraic and the Kipnis-Shamir MinRank attacks, do not work against ZHFE. We gave theoretical and experimental arguments to show that ZHFE behaves as if it were a system of random quadratic equations against these attacks.

We performed numerous computer experiments to test the security and measure the encryption/decryption times for several sets of parameters of ZHFE. The data we collected guided our choices for the parameters (q, n and D_0) for plausible schemes.

What we present in this paper is the beginning of a new idea and it is necessary to explore more deeply the different features and parameters of ZHFE, in order to achieve a better understanding of its behaviour and security. For instance, in Sect. 2.3 we chose $D_0 = 105$ so that the polynomial Ψ does not have too few terms, with the intention to avoid having an extremely simple polynomial Ψ. Although this seems reasonable, we will have to study more carefully the effect of the parameter D_0 and the shape of the polynomial Ψ on the security of the new encryption scheme ZHFE.

In principle there seems to be no obvious way to recover the private polynomial Ψ (F, $\tilde{F}$ and the scalars α_i, β_i are secret) from the public key. This is an important point in the study of the security of ZHFE and we will have to consider this aspect more carefully in the future. We also want to study ways of speeding up the reduction method to construct the trapdoor functions. Speeding up the reduction method will also allow us to reach larger values of n and therefore we will be able to implement plausible schemes with smaller values of q, for example $q = 2$.

Acknowledgements. We want to thank Wael Mohamed and Daniel Cabarcas for running essential experiments for us, which helped us complete this paper. J. Ding was partially supported by the CAS/SAFEA International Partnership Program for Creative Research Teams.

References

1. Ars, G., Faugère, J.-C., Imai, H., Kawazoe, M., Sugita, M.: Comparison Between XL and Gröbner Basis Algorithms. In: Lee, P.J. (ed.) ASIACRYPT 2004. LNCS, vol. 3329, pp. 338–353. Springer, Heidelberg (2004)
2. Baena, J.B., Clough, C.L., Ding, J.: New Variants of the Square-Vinegar Signature Scheme, Revista Colombiana de Matemticas (Colombian Journal of Mathematics), Bogotá, 45(2) (2011)
3. Bernstein, D.J., Buchmann, J., Dahmen, E.: Post quantum cryptography. Springer (2009)
4. Bettale, L., Faugère, J.-C., Perret, L.: Cryptanalysis of hfe, multi-hfe and variants for odd and even characteristic. Designs, Codes and Cryptography 69(1), 1–52 (2013)
5. Bosma, W., Cannon, J., Playoust, C.: The Magma algebra system. I. The user language. J. Symbolic Comput. 24(3-4), 235–265 (1997); Computational algebra and number theory, London (1993)
6. Buss, J.F., Frandsen, G., Shallit, J.O.: The computational complexity of some problems of linear algebra. In: Reischuk, R., Morvan, M. (eds.) STACS 1997. LNCS, vol. 1200, pp. 451–462. Springer, Heidelberg (1997)
7. Chen, C.H.O., Chen, M.S., Ding, J., Werner, F., Yang, B.Y.: Odd-char multivariate hidden field equations. cryptology eprint archive (2008)
8. Clough, C., Baena, J., Ding, J., Yang, B.-Y., Chen, M.-S.: Square, a New Multivariate Encryption Scheme. In: Fischlin, M. (ed.) CT-RSA 2009. LNCS, vol. 5473, pp. 252–264. Springer, Heidelberg (2009)
9. Courtois, N.T.: The Security of Hidden Field Equations (HFE). In: Naccache, D. (ed.) CT-RSA 2001. LNCS, vol. 2020, pp. 266–281. Springer, Heidelberg (2001)

10. Courtois, N., Klimov, A., Patarin, J., Shamir, A.: Efficient Algorithms for Solving Overdefined Systems of Multivariate Polynomial Equations. In: Preneel, B. (ed.) EUROCRYPT 2000. LNCS, vol. 1807, pp. 392–407. Springer, Heidelberg (2000)
11. Ding, J., Gower, J.E., Schmidt, D.S.: Zhuang-Zi: A New Algorithm for Solving Multivariate Polynomial Equations over a Finite Field, Preprint, University of Cincinnati (2006)
12. Ding, J., Gower, J.E., Schmidt, D.S.: Multivariate public key cryptosystems. Advances in Information Security, vol. 25. Springer, New York (2006)
13. Ding, J., Schmidt, D., Werner, F.: Algebraic Attack on HFE Revisited. In: Wu, T.-C., Lei, C.-L., Rijmen, V., Lee, D.-T. (eds.) ISC 2008. LNCS, vol. 5222, pp. 215–227. Springer, Heidelberg (2008)
14. Faugère, J.-C., Joux, A.: Algebraic Cryptanalysis of Hidden Field Equation (HFE) Cryptosystems Using Gröbner Bases. In: Boneh, D. (ed.) CRYPTO 2003. LNCS, vol. 2729, pp. 44–60. Springer, Heidelberg (2003)
15. Garey, M.R., Johnson, D.S., et al.: Computers and Intractability: A Guide to the Theory of NP-completeness. WH Freeman, San Francisco (1979)
16. Jiang, X., Ding, J., Hu, L.: Kipnis-Shamir Attack on HFE Revisited. In: Pei, D., Yung, M., Lin, D., Wu, C. (eds.) Inscrypt 2007. LNCS, vol. 4990, pp. 399–411. Springer, Heidelberg (2008)
17. Kipnis, A., Shamir, A.: Cryptanalysis of the HFE public key cryptosystem by relinearization. In: Wiener, M. (ed.) CRYPTO 1999. LNCS, vol. 1666, pp. 19–30. Springer, Heidelberg (1999)
18. Patarin, J.: Hidden Field Equations (HFE) and Isomorphisms of Polynomials (IP): Two new families of asymmetric algorithms. In: Maurer, U.M. (ed.) EUROCRYPT 1996. LNCS, vol. 1070, pp. 33–48. Springer, Heidelberg (1996)
19. Porras, J., Baena, J., Ding, J.: New candidates for multivariate trapdoor functions, Cryptology ePrint Archive, Report 2014/387 (2014), http://eprint.iacr.org/2014/387.pdf
20. Shor, P.W.: Polynomial-time algorithms for prime factorization and discrete logarithms on a quantum computer. SIAM J. on Computing, 1484–1509 (1997)

Appendix: More about the KS MinRank Attack

Kipnis-Shamir Modeling. Kipnis and Shamir [17] proposed to bind the MinRank Problem to the problem of solving an algebraic quadratic system of equations. They noted that, if the matrix $M = \lambda_1 M_1 + \cdots + \lambda_m M_m$ has rank at most r, its left kernel $\{x \in L^t : xM = 0\}$ has at least $t - r$ linearly independent vectors. Therefore, solving the MinRank problem is equivalent to solving the system that comes from vanishing the entries of the matrix

$$\begin{pmatrix} 1 & & x_{1,1} & \cdots & x_{1,r} \\ & \ddots & \vdots & & \vdots \\ & & 1 & x_{t-r,1} & \cdots & x_{t-r,r} \end{pmatrix} \left(\sum_{i=1}^{m} \lambda_i M_i \right).$$

This yields an overdetermined quadratic system with $t(t - r)$ equations and $t(t - r) + m$ variables. The authors in [17] proposed a method for solving this system which they called relinearization. Later on, in [10], it has been shown that this method can be seen as a special case of the XL algorithm. In fact, the XL algorithm can be viewed as a redundant variant of the Gröbner basis algorithm F_4 [1]. Therefore, this system is usually solved using Gröbner basis tools like F_4.

Minors Modeling. Courtois proposed another way to solve the MinRank Problem [9]. Since the matrix $\lambda_1 M_1 + \cdots + \lambda_m M_m$ has rank at most r, all its minors of order $(r + 1) \times (r + 1)$ must be zero. In this way we get a system of $\binom{t}{r+1}^2$ polynomial equations in the m variables λ_i. Notice that this system has many more equations than the system coming from the Kipnis-Shamir Modeling, but the equations have degree $r + 1$.

A Note on Quantum Security for Post-Quantum Cryptography

Fang Song

Department of Combinatorics & Optimization
and Institute for Quantum Computing
University of Waterloo

Abstract. Shor's quantum factoring algorithm and a few other efficient quantum algorithms break many classical crypto-systems. In response, people proposed post-quantum cryptography based on computational problems that are believed hard even for quantum computers. However, security of these schemes against *quantum* attacks is elusive. This is because existing security analysis (almost) only deals with classical attackers and arguing security in the presence of quantum adversaries is challenging due to unique quantum features such as no-cloning.

This work proposes a general framework to study which classical security proofs can be restored in the quantum setting. Basically, we split a security proof into (a sequence of) classical security reductions, and investigate what security reductions are "quantum-friendly". We characterize sufficient conditions such that a classical reduction can be "lifted" to the quantum setting.

We then apply our lifting theorems to post-quantum signature schemes. We are able to show that the classical generic construction of hash-tree based signatures from one-way functions and and a more efficient variant proposed in [10] carry over to the quantum setting. Namely, assuming existence of (classical) one-way functions that are resistant to efficient quantum inversion algorithms, there exists a quantum-secure signature scheme. We note that the scheme in [10] is a promising (post-quantum) candidate to be implemented in practice and our result further justifies it. Actually, to obtain these result, we formalize a simple criteria, which is motivated by many classical proofs in the literature and is straightforward to check. This makes our lifting theorem easier to apply, and it should be useful elsewhere to prove quantum security of proposed post-quantum cryptographic schemes. Finally we demonstrate the generality of our framework by showing that several existing works (Full-Domain hash in the quantum random-oracle model [47] and the simple hybrid arguments framework in [23]) can be reformulated under our unified framework.

1 Introduction

Advances in quantum information processing and quantum computing have brought about fundamental challenges to cryptography. Many classical cryptographic constructions are based on computational problems that are assumed hard for efficient classical algorithms. However, some of these problems, such as factoring, discrete-logarithm and Pell's equation, can be solved efficiently on a quantum computer [39,22]. As a result,

M. Mosca (Ed.): PQCrypto 2014, LNCS 8772, pp. 246–265, 2014.

a host of crypto-systems, e.g, the RSA encryption scheme that is deployed widely over the Internet, are broken by a quantum attacker.

A natural countermeasure is to use *quantum-resistant* assumptions instead. Namely, one can switch to other computational problems which appear hard to solve even on quantum computers, and construct cryptographic schemes based on them. Examples include problems in discrete lattices [33,36] and hard coding problems [38]. We can also make generic assumptions such as the existence of one-way functions that no efficient quantum algorithms can invert. This leads to the active research area termed *post-quantum* cryptography [6]. Nonetheless, quantum-resistant assumptions alone do not immediately imply quantum security of a scheme, due to other fundamental issues that could be subtle and easily overlooked.

First of all, we sometimes fail to take into account possible attacks unique to a quantum adversary. In other words, classical definition of security may not capture the right notion of security in the presence of quantum attackers[1]. For example, many signature schemes are designed in the random-oracle (RO) model, where all users, including the attacker, can query a truly random function. This is meant to capture an idealized version of a hash function, but in practice everyone instantiate it by him/herself with a concrete hash function. As a result, when we consider quantum attacks on these schemes, there seems no reason not to allow a quantum adversary to query the random-oracle in quantum superposition. This leads to the so called quantum random-oracle model [8], in which we need to reconsider security definitions (as well as the analysis consequently) [47,46,9].

A more subtle issue concerns security proofs, which may completely fall through in the presence of quantum attacks. Roughly speaking, one needs to construct a *reduction* showing that if an efficient attacker can successfully violate the security requirements of a scheme then there exists an efficient algorithm that breaks some computational assumption. However, a classical reduction may no longer work (or make sense at all) against quantum adversaries. A key classical technique, which encounters fundamental difficulty in the presence of quantum attackers, is called *rewinding*. Loosely speaking, rewinding arguments consist of a mental experiment in which an adversary for a scheme is executed multiple times using careful variations on its input. This usually allows us to gain useful information in order to break the computational assumption. As first observed by van de Graaf [19], rewinding seems impossible with a quantum adversary since running it multiple times might modify the entanglement between its internal state and an outside reference system, thus changing the system's overall behavior. This issue is most evident in cryptographic protocols for zero-knowledge proofs and general secure computation. There has been progress in recent years that develops quantum rewinding techniques in some special cases [44,43], and a few classical protocols are proven quantum-secure [13,29,23]. Hallgren et al. [23] also formalized a family of classical security proofs against efficient adversaries that can be made go through against efficient quantum adversaries under reasonable computational

---

[1] Although our focus is security against computationally bounded attackers, this issue is also relevant in the *statistical* setting. There are classical schemes, which are proven secure against unbounded classical attackers, broken by attackers using quantum entanglement [12].

assumptions. Despite these efforts, however, still not much is known in general about how to make classical security proofs go through against quantum attackers.

This note revisits these issues for post-quantum cryptography based on computational assumptions, focusing on simple *primitives* such as signatures, encryptions and identifications, where constructions and analysis are usually not too complicated (compared to secure computation protocols for example). In this setting, the issues we have discussed seem less devastating. For instance, rewinding arguments appear only occasionally, for example in some lattice-based identification schemes [30,31]. Usually rewinding is not needed for the security proof. Nonetheless, it is still crucial to pinning down proper security definitions against quantum attacks, as illustrated in the quantum random-oracle example above. In addition, just because there are no rewinding arguments, does not mean that we can take for granted that the security reduction automatically holds against quantum attackers. Very often in the literature of post-quantum cryptography, a construction based on some quantum-resistant assumption is given together with a security proof for *classical* attackers only. The construction is then claimed to be quantum-secure without any further justification. In our opinion, this is not satisfying and quantum security of these schemes deserves a more careful treatment.

CONTRIBUTIONS. The main contribution of this note is a general framework to study which classical security proofs can be restored in the quantum setting. A security proof can be split into (a sequence of) classical security reductions, and we investigate what reductions are "quantum-friendly". Recall that informally a reduction transforms an adversary of one kind to another. We distinguish two cases, *game-preserving* and *game-updating* reductions.

A game-preserving reduction is one such that the transformation still makes sense, i.e., syntacticly well-defined, for quantum adversaries. In this case we propose the notion of *class-respectful* reductions which ensures in addition that the adversary obtained from the transformation indeed works (e.g., it is an efficient quantum algorithm and successfully solves some problem). Motivated by the structure of security reductions that occur in many post-quantum cryptographic schemes, we further characterize a simple criteria, which is straightforward to check. This makes the lifting theorem easier to apply, and should be useful to prove quantum security for many other schemes not restricted to the applications we show later in this note.

On the other hand, a game-updating reduction captures the case that the classical reduction no longer makes sense, as illustrated by the quantum random-oracle model. This is usually more difficult to analyze. We propose *translatable* reductions, which essentially reduces the problem to the game-preserving case. The basic idea is to introduce an "interpreter", so that the classical reduction becomes applicable to a quantum adversary with the translation by the interpreter. In both cases, we show in our lifting theorems that a reduction can be constructed in the quantum setting if there is a classical reduction that is respectful or translatable respectively.

We apply our framework to prove quantum security of some hash-based signature schemes. Specifically, we show that the classical generic construction of hash-tree based signature schemes from one-way functions carries over to the quantum setting, assuming the underlying one-way function is quantum-resistant. This is also true for a more efficient variant proposed in [10] assuming quantum-resistant pesudorandom functions, which in turn can be based on quantum-resistant one-way functions from known results. This scheme is a promising (post-quantum) candidate to be implemented in practice and our result further justifies it. Moreover, we give an alternative proof for the security of a general construction of signatures based on trapdoor permutations called Full-Domain hash in the quantum random-oracle model. We also show that an existing framework in the context of cryptographic protocols that characterizes a class of "quantum-friendly" classical security proofs (simple hybrid augments [23]) fits our framework. These demonstrate the generality of our framework.

REMARKS. Our framework (e.g., definitions of games and reductions) should look natural to people familiar with the provable-security paradigm. It should also be straightforward (or even obvious for experts) to verify the characterizations of "quantum-friendly" reductions in our lifting theorems. The purpose of this note, however, is to at least make people become more serious and cautious and to encourage further research, in addition to suggesting one possible formal framework to reason about the security of post-quantum cryptography against quantum attacks. Likewise, it may be just a tedious exercise to work though the classical proof for hash-based signatures and convince oneself it is indeed quantum-secure. Nonetheless, this can be done in a more abstract and rigorous way using our framework. We hope that our framework can be applied elsewhere to analyze quantum security of other post-quantum cryptographic constructions. Ideally, in some easy cases, it would serve as a tool to automate the routine parts, so that whoever designs a new scheme should be able to make some simple checks and conclude its quantum security.

OTHER RELATED WORKS. There are a few works that study systematically what classical proofs or statements can be "lifted" to the quantum setting in the context of multiparty secure computation. Unruh in [42] showed that any classical protocol that is secure in the statistical setting, i.e., against computationally *unbounded* adversaries, under a strong *universal-composable* notion is also statistically secure in an analogous quantum universal-composable model. Fehr et al. [14] considered *reducibility* between two-party cryptographic tasks in the quantum setting. For example, one can ask if there is a secure protocol for oblivious transfer assuming two parties can perform bit commitments securely. They showed that in most cases, the reducibility landscape remains unchanged in the quantum setting under the very same classical protocols. However, there are cases that classical reducibility no longer holds quantumly, and sometimes new relations can be established using quantum protocols.

The formalization of games, reductions and other terms in this note is influenced by a lot of classical literatures on game-playing proofs [17,45,27,5,40,21]. Recent developments, especially the framework of code-based game-playing proofs [21,5] have motivated automated tools for proving security [7,3,41,2]. Our treatment of computational assumptions is also inspired by the line of works classifying complexity-theoretic intractability assumptions [34,20,35,15].

2 Preliminary

BASIC NOTATIONS. For $m \in \mathbb{N}$, $[m]$ denotes the set $\{1, \ldots, m\}$. We use $n \in \mathbb{N}$ to denote a *security parameter*. The security parameter, represented in unary, is an implicit input to all cryptographic algorithms; we omit it when it is clear from the context. Quantities derived from protocols or algorithms (probabilities, running times, etc) should be thought of as functions of n, unless otherwise specified. A function $f(n)$ is said to be negligible if $f = o(n^{-c})$ for any constant c, and $\mathsf{negl}(n)$ is used to denote an unspecified function that is negligible in n. We also use $poly(n)$ to denote an unspecified function $f(n) = O(n^c)$ for some constant c. When D is a probability distribution, the notation $x \leftarrow D$ indicates that x is a sample drawn according to D. When D is a finite set, we implicitly associate with it the uniform distribution over the set. If $D(\cdot)$ is a probabilistic algorithm, $D(y)$ denotes the distribution over the output of D corresponding to input y. We will sometimes use the same symbol for a random variable and for its probability distribution when the meaning is clear from the context. Let $\mathbf{X} = \{X_n\}_{n\in\mathbb{N}}$ and $\mathbf{Y} = \{Y_n\}_{n\in\mathbb{N}}$ be two ensembles of binary random variables. We call $\mathbf{X}, \mathbf{Y}$ *indistinguishable*, denoted $\mathbf{X} \approx \mathbf{Y}$, if $|\Pr(X_n = 1) - \Pr(Y_n = 1)| \leq \mathsf{negl}(n)$.

MACHINE MODELS. We model classical parties as interactive Turing machines, which are probabilistic polynomial-time (PPT) by default. Quantum machines are modelled following that of [23]. A *quantum interactive machine* (QIM) M is an ensemble of interactive circuits $\{M_n\}_{n\in\mathbb{N}}$. For each value n of the security parameter, M_n consists of a sequence of circuits $\{M_n^{(i)}\}_{i=1,\dots,\ell(n)}$, where $M_n^{(i)}$ defines the operation of M in one round i and $\ell(n)$ is the number of rounds for which M_n operates (we assume for simplicity that $\ell(n)$ depends only on n). We omit the scripts when they are clear from the context or are not essential for the discussion. M (or rather each of the circuits that it comprises) operates on three registers: a state register S used for input and workspace; an output register O; and a network register N for communicating with other machines. The size (or running time) $t(n)$ of M_n is the sum of the sizes of the circuits $M_n^{(i)}$. We say a machine is polynomial time if $t(n) = poly(n)$ and there is a deterministic classical Turing machine that computes the description of $M_n^{(i)}$ in polynomial time on input $(1^n, 1^i)$. When two QIMs M and M' interact, their network register N is shared. The circuits $M_n^{(i)}$ and $M'^{(i)}_n$ are executed alternately for $i = 1, 2, \dots, \ell(n)$. When three or more machines interact, the machines may share different parts of their network registers (for example, a private channel consists of a register shared between only two machines; a broadcast channel is a register shared by all machines). The order in which machines are activated may be either specified in advance (as in a synchronous network) or adversarially controlled.

3   Defining Games and Reductions

This section introduces a formal definition of reductions, which captures the type of security reductions that we care mostly about. It builds upon a basic notion of games.

We use *game* G to denote a general probabilistic process between two players: the challenger $\mathcal{C}$ initiates the interaction with the other player, call it an adversary $\mathcal{A}$. After several rounds of communication, $\mathcal{C}$ outputs one bit succ or fail indicting success or failure of the game. We define the game value of G with an adversary $\mathcal{A}$ to be the probability that $\mathcal{C}$ outputs succ, and denote it $\omega_G(\mathcal{A})$. Typically in a game G, $\mathcal{C}$ is efficient, i.e., a poly-time classical or quantum machine. Very often we want to analyze the game when the adversary is restricted to a class of machines $\mathfrak{C}$ (e.g., poly-time classical machines). We write $G(\mathfrak{C})$ to indicate this case, and define $\omega_G(\mathfrak{C}) := \max\{\omega_G(\mathcal{A}) : \mathcal{A} \in \mathfrak{C}\}$. Sometimes we denote $\hat{G}$ to stress a game defined for quantum machines. We describe below as an example the standard forgery game of existentially unforgeable signatures under (adaptive) chosen-message-attacks (EU-CMA) [18,26].

Existential-Forgery Game G^{FOR}

Signature scheme: $\Pi = (\mathsf{KGen}, \mathsf{Sign}, \mathsf{Vrfy})$.

- $\mathcal{C}$ generates $(pk, sk) \leftarrow \mathsf{KGen}(1^n)$. Send pk to adversary $\mathcal{A}$.
- $\mathcal{A}$ can query signatures on messages $\{m_i\}$. $\mathcal{C}$ returns $\sigma_i := \mathsf{Sign}(sk, m_i)$. These messages can be chosen adaptively by $\mathcal{A}$.
- $\mathcal{A}$ outputs (m^*, σ^*). If $\mathsf{Vrfy}(pk, (\sigma^*, m^*)) = 1$ and $m^* \notin \{m_i\}$, $\mathcal{C}$ outputs succ. Otherwise output fail.

There are many variants of this game which will be used later in this note. For example, we denote the game in which $\mathcal{A}$ is allowed to query at most one signature $G^{\text{OT-FOR}}$. $G^{\text{RO-FOR}}$ denotes the game where a random-oracle is available to both parties, and if the random-oracle can be accessed in quantum superposition we denote the game $G^{\text{QRO-FOR}}$.

We define a reduction $\mathcal{R}$ as a 3-tuple $(G^{\text{ext}}, \mathcal{T}, G^{\text{int}})$. There are an external (explicit) game G^{ext} and an internal (implicit) game G^{int}, and an additional party $\mathcal{T}$ called the *transformer*. Loosely speaking, $\mathcal{T}$ transforms an adversary $\mathcal{A}$ in G^{int} to an adversary in G^{ext}. Specifically, $\mathcal{T}$ takes an adversary's machine $\mathcal{A}$ as input and outputs the description of an adversary in G^{ext}. We distinguish *black-box* and *non-black-box* reductions, with a focus on black-box reductions. In a black-box reduction, $\mathcal{A}$ is provided as a black-box, which means that the transformation does not look into the codes and inner workings of the adversary. Whereas in a non-black-box reduction, $\mathcal{R}$ has the explicit description of $\mathcal{A}$. We denote $\mathcal{T}(\mathcal{A})$ as the resulting adversary in G^{ext} that is "transformed" from $\mathcal{A}$ by $\mathcal{T}$. In the black-box setting, the output of $\mathcal{T}$ will always be of the form $T^{\mathcal{A}}$, i.e., an oracle machine with access to $\mathcal{A}$. Note that T is the same for all $\mathcal{A}$, and it emulates an execution of G^{int} with $\mathcal{A}$. However, in general T needs not to run the game as in a real interaction. For instance, it can stop in the middle of the game and start over (i.e., rewind).

PROPERTIES OF A REDUCTION. To make a reduction meaningful, we describe below a few properties that we may want a reduction to hold. Let $\mathfrak{A}$ and $\mathfrak{B}$ be two classes of machines.

- $\mathfrak{A}$-**compatible** reductions. We say $\mathcal{R}$ is $\mathfrak{A}$-compatible, if $\forall \mathcal{A} \in \mathfrak{A}$, $G^{\text{int}}(\mathcal{A})$ and $G^{\text{ext}}(\mathcal{T}(\mathcal{A}))$ are well defined. Namely $\mathfrak{A}$ and $\mathcal{T}(\mathcal{A})$ respect the specifications of the games.
- $(\mathfrak{A}, \mathfrak{B})$-**consistent** reductions. We say $\mathcal{R}$ is $(\mathfrak{A}, \mathfrak{B})$-consistent, if $\mathcal{R}$ is $\mathfrak{A}$-compatible and $\forall \mathcal{A} \in \mathfrak{A}$, $\mathcal{T}(\mathcal{A}) \in \mathfrak{B}$. When we write a reduction as $(G^{\text{ext}}(\mathfrak{B}), \mathcal{T}, G^{\text{int}}(\mathfrak{A}))$ or $\mathcal{R}(\mathfrak{A}, \mathfrak{B})$ in short, the reduction is assumed to be $(\mathfrak{A}, \mathfrak{B})$-consistent. Note that if $\mathcal{R}$ is black-box, it must hold that $T^{\mathfrak{A}} \subseteq \mathfrak{B}$.
- **Value-dominating**. We say $\mathcal{R}$ is value-dominating if $\omega_{G^{\text{ext}}}(\mathcal{T}(\mathcal{A})) = \omega_{G^{\text{ext}}}(\mathcal{T}(\mathcal{B}))$ whenever $\omega_{G^{\text{int}}}(\mathcal{A}) = \omega_{G^{\text{int}}}(\mathcal{B})$.

- $(\alpha_{\text{succ}}, \mathfrak{A})$-**effective** reductions. Let $\alpha_{\text{succ}} : \mathbb{R}^+ \to \mathbb{R}^+$ be some function. We say $\mathcal{R}$ is α_{succ}-effective on $\mathcal{A}$ if $\omega_{G^{\text{ext}}}(\mathcal{T}(\mathcal{A})) \geq \alpha_{\text{succ}}(\omega_{G^{\text{int}}}(\mathcal{A}))$. If this holds for any $\mathcal{A} \in \mathfrak{A}$, we call $\mathcal{R}$ $(\alpha_{\text{succ}}, \mathfrak{A})$-effective
- $(\alpha_{\text{time}}, \mathfrak{A})$-**efficient** reductions. Let $\alpha_{\text{time}} : \mathbb{R}^+ \to \mathbb{R}^+$ be some function. We say $\mathcal{R}$ is α_{time}-efficient if $\text{TIME}(\mathcal{T}(\mathcal{A})) \leq \alpha_{\text{time}}(\text{TIME}(\mathcal{A}))$ for any $\mathcal{A} \in \mathfrak{A}$.

Effective and efficient reductions are often used in combination, especially when we are concerned with tightness of a reduction. In that case, α_{succ} and α_{time} may depend on both $\text{TIME}(\mathcal{A})$ and $\omega_{G^{\text{int}}}(\mathcal{A})$. This paper will focus on effectiveness only. We often abuse notation and use α_{succ} as a scalar if this causes no confusion. We stress that these properties talk about the output machine of $\mathcal{T}$ on $\mathcal{A}$ (e.g., $\mathcal{T}(\mathcal{A})$ lies in a specific class, or it runs in time comparable to that of $\mathcal{A}$), however we do not restrict the computational power of $\mathcal{T}$, though it is typically efficient. The reason is that for our purpose, we only need to show existence of an adversary for G^{ext} with nice properties.

4   Quantum-Friendly Security Reductions: A General Framework

In this section, we attempt to propose a general framework to study which classical proofs still hold when the adversaries become quantum. Consider a classical cryptographic scheme Π. To analyze its security against efficient classical attacks (in the provable-security paradigm), one typically proceeds as follows:

1. Formalizing some security requirement by a game G^{int}. Typically we are concerned about security against a particular class of attackers (e.g., PPT machines), so we restrict the game G^{int} to a class $\mathfrak{A}$. We also associate a value $\varepsilon_{\mathfrak{A}} \in (0, 1]$ with the game, which upper bounds the success probability that any adversary in $\mathfrak{A}$ wins the game. Namely we require that $\omega_{G^{\text{int}}}(\mathfrak{A}) \leq \varepsilon_{\mathfrak{A}}$. We denote this security requirement as $(G^{\text{int}}(\mathfrak{A}), \varepsilon_{\mathfrak{A}})$.[2]
2. Formalizing some computational assumption by another game G^{ext}. Similarly the assumption is assumed to hold against a specific class of machines, so we restrict the game to a class $\mathfrak{B}$, and require that $\omega_{G^{\text{ext}}}(\mathfrak{B}) \leq \varepsilon_{\mathfrak{B}} \in (0, 1]$. Denote the computational assumption as $(G^{\text{ext}}(\mathfrak{B}), \varepsilon_{\mathfrak{B}})$.
3. Constructing an $(\mathfrak{A}, \mathfrak{B})$-consistent reduction $\mathcal{R} = (G^{\text{ext}}(\mathfrak{B}), \mathcal{T}, G^{\text{int}}(\mathfrak{A}))$. Security follows if the reduction is in addition α_{succ}-effective with $\alpha_{\text{succ}} \geq \varepsilon_{\mathfrak{B}}/\varepsilon_{\mathfrak{A}}$. This implies if there exists an $\mathcal{A} \in \mathfrak{A}$ with $\omega_{G^{\text{int}}}(\mathcal{A}) > \varepsilon_{\mathfrak{A}}$ (i.e.. $\mathcal{A}$ breaks the security requirement), there is an adversary $\mathcal{T}(\mathcal{A}) \in \mathfrak{B}$ such that $\omega_{G^{\text{ext}}}(\mathcal{T}(\mathcal{A})) \geq \alpha_{\text{succ}} \cdot \omega_{G^{\text{int}}}(\mathcal{A}) > \varepsilon_{\mathfrak{B}}$ (i.e., it breaks the computational assumption).

Now we want to know if the classical security reductions are "quantum-friendly" so that we can claim that the scheme is secure against quantum attacks. We need to reconsider each step of the classical analysis in the quantum setting (See Table 1 for a comparison between classical provable-security and quantum provable-security for a scheme.). Let $(\hat{\mathfrak{A}}, \hat{\mathfrak{B}})$ be two classes of quantum machines. We adapt G^{int} and define

---

[2] Sometime we write $(G^{\text{int}}(\mathfrak{A}), \varepsilon_{\mathfrak{A}})_{\Pi}$ to emphasize the specific scheme we are dealing with, though it is usually clear from the context.

$(\hat{G}^{int}(\hat{\mathfrak{A}}), \varepsilon_{\hat{\mathfrak{A}}})$. It is supposed to capture some security requirement against quantum attackers in $\hat{\mathfrak{A}}$, and we require that $\omega_{\hat{G}^{int}}(\hat{\mathfrak{A}}) \leq \varepsilon_{\hat{\mathfrak{A}}}$. Likewise, we adapt G^{ext} to a game $\hat{G}^{ext}$, which should formalize a reasonable computational assumption $(\hat{G}^{ext}(\hat{\mathfrak{B}}), \varepsilon_{\hat{\mathfrak{B}}})$ against quantum adversaries. Then we can ask the fundamental question (still informal):

Can we "lift" $\mathcal{R}$ to the quantum setting?
Namely, is there a reduction $\hat{\mathcal{R}}(\hat{\mathfrak{A}}, \hat{\mathfrak{B}})$ that preserves similar properties as $\mathcal{R}(\mathfrak{A}, \mathfrak{B})$?

To answer this question, we distinguish two cases. In the simpler case, $\hat{G}$ are syntactically identical to G. Namely, $\hat{G}^{ext}(\hat{\mathfrak{B}})$ (resp. $\hat{G}^{int}(\hat{\mathfrak{A}})$) is just G^{ext} (resp. G^{int}) restricted to the quantum class $\hat{\mathfrak{B}}$ (resp. $\hat{\mathfrak{A}}$). In particular, this means that G^{ext} and G^{int} are still the right games that capture a computational assumption and some security requirement. We call this case *game-preserving*. In contrast, as illustrated by the quantum random-oracle example, $\hat{G}$ may change and this leads to a more complicated case to analyze. We call it *game-updating*. In the following subsections, we investigate in each case what reductions can be lifted to the quantum setting, and hence are quantum-friendly.

Table 1. Components of classical and quantum provable-security for a classical construction

	Classical Provable-Security	Quantum Provable-Security
Security Requirement	$(G^{int}(\mathfrak{A}), \varepsilon_{\mathfrak{A}})$	$(\hat{G}^{int}(\hat{\mathfrak{A}}), \varepsilon_{\hat{\mathfrak{A}}})$
Computational Assumption	$(G^{ext}(\mathfrak{B}), \varepsilon_{\mathfrak{B}})$	$(\hat{G}^{ext}(\hat{\mathfrak{B}}), \varepsilon_{\hat{\mathfrak{B}}})$
Reduction	$\mathcal{R}(\mathfrak{A}, \mathfrak{B})$	$\overset{?}{\longrightarrow} \hat{\mathcal{R}}(\hat{\mathfrak{A}}, \hat{\mathfrak{B}})$

4.1 Lifting Game-Preserving Reductions

Let $\mathcal{R}(\mathfrak{A}, \mathfrak{B}) = (G^{ext}(\mathfrak{B}), \mathcal{T}, G^{int}(\mathfrak{A}))$ be a classical reduction. Let $\hat{G}^{ext}(\hat{\mathfrak{B}})$ and $\hat{G}^{int}(\hat{\mathfrak{A}})$ be extended games in the quantum setting that are restricted to classes of quantum machines $\hat{\mathfrak{B}}$ and $\hat{\mathfrak{A}}$. We consider the case that $\hat{G}$ and G are the same in this section. We want to know if there is a reduction $\hat{\mathcal{R}}(\hat{\mathfrak{A}}, \hat{\mathfrak{B}})$ that preserves nice properties of $\mathcal{R}$. Since we are dealing with the same games applied to different classes of machines, one may expect that simple tweaks on $\mathcal{R}$ should work. This intuition is indeed true to some extend, which we formalize next.

Definition 1 (G-equivalent machines). *Two machines M and N are called G-equivalent if $\omega_G(M) \equiv \omega_G(N)$.*

Definition 2 ($[G, \mathfrak{C}]$-realizable classical machines). *A classical machine M is called $[G, \mathfrak{C}]$-realizable, if there is a machine $N \in \mathfrak{C}$ s.t. $\omega_G(M) = \omega_G(N)$. We denote $E_G(\mathfrak{C})$ as the collection of classical machines that are $[G, \mathfrak{C}]$-realizable.*

We put forward *class-respectful* reductions as a template for quantum-friendly reductions in the game-reserving case.

Definition 3 (β-$(\hat{\mathfrak{A}}, \hat{\mathfrak{B}})$-respectful reductions). *Let $\mathcal{R}$ be a classical reduction $(G^{ext}(\mathfrak{B}), \mathcal{T}, G^{int}(\mathfrak{A}))$. We say $\mathcal{R}$ is β-$(\hat{\mathfrak{A}}, \hat{\mathfrak{B}})$-respectful for some $\beta \in \mathbb{R}^+$ if the following hold:*

1. $(\beta, \hat{\mathfrak{A}})$-*extendable*: $\mathcal{R}$ is $E_{G^{int}}(\hat{\mathfrak{A}})$-*compatible and* $(\beta, E_{G^{int}}(\hat{\mathfrak{A}}))$-*effective. That is,*
   $\forall \mathcal{A} \in E_{G^{int}}(\hat{\mathfrak{A}})$, $G^{ext}(\mathcal{T}(\mathcal{A}))$ *and* $G^{int}(\mathcal{A})$ *are well-defined*[3], *and* $\omega_{G^{ext}}(\mathcal{T}(\mathcal{A}))$
   $\geq \beta(\omega_{G^{int}}(\mathcal{A}))$.
2. $(\hat{\mathfrak{A}}, \hat{\mathfrak{B}})$-*closed*: $\mathcal{R}$ *is* $(E_{G^{int}}(\hat{\mathfrak{A}}), E_{G^{ext}}(\hat{\mathfrak{B}}))$-*consistent. Namely,* $\forall \mathcal{A} \in E_{G^{int}}(\hat{\mathfrak{A}})$,
   $\mathcal{T}(\mathcal{A}) \in E_{G^{ext}}(\hat{\mathfrak{B}})$.

The theorem below follows (almost) immediately from this definition.

Theorem 1 (Quantum lifting for game-preserving reductions). *If* $\mathcal{R}(\mathfrak{A}, \mathfrak{B})$ *is* β-$(\hat{\mathfrak{A}}, \hat{\mathfrak{B}})$-*respectful, then there exists an* $(\hat{\mathfrak{A}}, \hat{\mathfrak{B}})$-*consistent reduction* $\hat{\mathcal{R}}(\hat{\mathfrak{A}}, \hat{\mathfrak{B}}) :=$ $(G^{ext}(\hat{\mathfrak{B}}), \hat{\mathcal{T}}, G^{int}(\hat{\mathfrak{A}}))$ *that is* $(\beta, \hat{\mathfrak{A}})$-*effective.*

Proof. Consider any $\hat{\mathcal{A}} \in \hat{\mathfrak{A}}$. Let $\mathcal{A}$ be a classical machine such that $\mathcal{A}$ is G^{ext}-equivalent to $\hat{\mathcal{A}}$. Since $\mathcal{R}$ is $(\hat{\mathfrak{A}}, \hat{\mathfrak{B}})$-closed, we know that $\mathcal{T}(\mathcal{A}) \in E_{G^{ext}}(\hat{\mathfrak{B}})$ and hence there is a machine $N_{\hat{\mathcal{A}}} \in \hat{\mathfrak{B}}$ s.t. $\omega_{G^{int}}(N_{\hat{\mathcal{A}}}) = \omega_{G^{int}}(\mathcal{T}(\mathcal{A}))$. Define $\hat{\mathcal{T}}$ to be a quantum machine such that, given $\hat{\mathcal{A}} \in \hat{\mathfrak{A}}$, outputs $N_{\hat{\mathcal{A}}}$. Namely $\hat{\mathcal{T}}(\hat{\mathcal{A}}) := N_{\hat{\mathcal{A}}}$. Let $\hat{\mathcal{R}} := (G^{ext}(\hat{\mathfrak{B}}), \hat{\mathcal{T}}, G^{int}(\hat{\mathfrak{A}}))$. Clearly $\hat{\mathcal{R}}$ is $(\hat{\mathfrak{A}}, \hat{\mathfrak{B}})$-consistent due to the way we defined $\hat{\mathcal{T}}$. It is also $(\beta, \hat{\mathfrak{A}})$-effective because $\omega_{G^{ext}}(\hat{\mathcal{T}}(\hat{\mathcal{A}})) = \omega_{G^{ext}}(\mathcal{T}(\mathcal{A})) \geq \beta(\omega_{G^{int}}(\mathcal{A})) = \beta(\omega_{G^{int}}(\hat{\mathcal{A}}))$.

To apply the theorem, we need to check the two conditions of respectful reductions. The "extendability" condition is usually easy to verify. However, the "closure" property can be challenging and subtle, depending on the classes of players we care about. We will be mostly interested in poly-time machines. Namely let $\mathfrak{A} = \mathfrak{B}$ be poly-time classical machines and $\hat{\mathfrak{A}} = \hat{\mathfrak{B}}$ be the collection of poly-time quantum machines, denote it by $\mathcal{Q}$. In this case, we propose a simple criteria that is easy to check in existing classical security reductions. When combined with a few other easily verifiable conditions, we can show class-respectful reductions. This in a way justifies a common belief that most post-quantum schemes are indeed quantum-secure, due to some simple form in their classical security reductions which seem "quantum-friendly".

Let $\mathcal{R} = (G^{ext}, \mathcal{T}, G^{int})$ be a classical black-box reduction. We say that $\mathcal{R}$ is *straight-line* if the output machine of $\mathcal{T}$ on $\mathcal{A}$, which as before is denoted $T^{\mathcal{A}}$, runs $\mathcal{A}$ in straight-line till completion. Namely, other than the flexibility of choosing $\mathcal{A}$'s random tape, T behaves exactly like a honest challenger in G^{int} when it invokes $\mathcal{A}$. This type of reduction, due to its simple structure, is amenable to getting lifted.

Theorem 2 (Straight-line reduction: a useful condition for class-closure). *Let* $\mathcal{R} = (G^{ext}(\mathfrak{B}), \mathcal{T}, G^{int}(\mathfrak{A}))$ *be a classical reduction with* $\mathfrak{A}$ *and* $\mathfrak{B}$ *both being classical poly-time machines. Let* $\hat{\mathfrak{A}} = \hat{\mathfrak{B}}$ *be quantum poly-time machines. If* $\mathcal{R}$ *is black-box straight-line,* $\hat{\mathfrak{A}}$-*compatible and value-dominating, then* $\mathcal{R}$ *is* $(\hat{\mathfrak{A}}, \hat{\mathfrak{B}})$-*closed.*

Proof. For any $\mathcal{A} \in E_{G^{int}}(\hat{\mathfrak{A}})$, let $\hat{\mathcal{A}} \in \hat{\mathfrak{A}}$ be such that $\mathcal{A}$ and $\hat{\mathcal{A}}$ are G^{int}-equivalent. We argue that $T^{\mathcal{A}}$ and $T^{\hat{\mathcal{A}}}$ are G^{ext}-equivalent and hence $T^{\mathcal{A}} \in E_{G^{ext}}(\hat{\mathfrak{B}})$. Since $\mathcal{A}$ and $\hat{\mathcal{A}}$ are G^{int}-equivalent and $\mathcal{R}$ is value-dominating, $\omega_{G^{ext}}(T^{\hat{\mathcal{A}}}) = \omega_{G^{ext}}(T^{\mathcal{A}})$. $T^{\hat{\mathcal{A}}} \in$

---

[3] Most classical games we deal with are actually well-defined for all machines. But we explicitly state this requirement in case of some artificial examples.

$\mathfrak{B}$, i.e., it is quantum poly-time, since T is classical poly-time, and runs any oracle in straight-line. Finally, note that we need the compatibility condition so that all objects above are well-defined.

Combine the extendibility condition, we get the corollary below from Theorem 1.

Corollary 1. *Let* $\mathcal{R}$ *be a classical black-box reduction for classical poly-time players. Let* $\hat{\mathfrak{A}} = \hat{\mathfrak{B}}$ *be quantum poly-time machines. If* $\mathcal{R}$ *is* $(\beta, \hat{\mathfrak{A}})$-*extendible, straight-line, and value-dominating, then* $\mathcal{R}$ *is* β-$(\hat{\mathfrak{A}}, \hat{\mathfrak{B}})$-*respectful. As a consequence, there is a reduction* $\hat{\mathcal{R}}(\hat{\mathfrak{A}}, \hat{\mathfrak{B}})$ *that is* $(\beta, \hat{\mathfrak{A}})$-*effective.*

Note that in this scenario, $\hat{\mathcal{R}}$ is also straight-line and $\hat{\mathcal{T}}(\hat{A}) = T^{\hat{A}}$. Loosely speaking, the very same reduction carries over to the quantum setting.

4.2 Lifting Game-Updating Reductions

Sometimes we need to update $\hat{G}^{\mathsf{ext}}$ or $\hat{G}^{\mathsf{int}}$ or both, in order to capture the right computational assumption and the security property against quantum players. In this case, the classical transformation procedure may become totally inappropriate and give little clue about how to restore a quantum reduction (if there exists one).

We view this issue as a matter of "language-barrier". One way to establish a reduction $\hat{\mathcal{R}}(\hat{\mathfrak{A}}, \hat{\mathfrak{B}})$ is to introduce an *interpreter* $\hat{\mathcal{I}}$ that translates the "languages" between the players in the original (classical) and updated (quantum) games. Namely, $\hat{\mathcal{I}}$ translates an adversary $\hat{A}$ in $\hat{G}^{\mathsf{int}}$ to an adversary $\hat{A}'$ in the classical game G^{int}. Then we can reduce the issue to the game-preserving case and consider a class of quantum adversaries $\hat{\mathfrak{A}}' := \hat{\mathcal{I}}(\hat{\mathfrak{A}})$. Suppose we can lift the classical reduction to work with adversaries in $\hat{\mathfrak{A}}'$, then we end up with a quantum adversary in game G^{ext}. Next, by the same token, $\hat{\mathcal{I}}$ translates the adversary into a quantum one compatible in $\hat{G}^{\mathsf{ext}}$. This procedure gives a quantum transformer $\hat{\mathcal{T}} := \hat{\mathcal{I}} \circ \hat{\mathcal{T}}_0 \circ \hat{\mathcal{I}}$ that operates as follows

$$\hat{A} \in \hat{\mathfrak{A}} \xrightarrow{\hat{\mathcal{I}}} \hat{A}' \xrightarrow{\hat{\mathcal{T}}_0} \hat{\mathcal{T}}_0(\hat{A}') \xrightarrow{\hat{\mathcal{I}}} \hat{B} \in \hat{\mathfrak{B}}.$$

We formalize this idea, and propose *class-translatable* reductions as a template for quantum-friendly reductions in the game-updating case. For simplicity, we assume only G^{int} is updated to $\hat{G}^{\mathsf{int}}$ and G^{ext} stays the same. We want to investigate if a reduction of the form $(G^{\mathsf{ext}}(\hat{\mathfrak{B}}), \hat{\mathcal{T}}, \hat{G}^{\mathsf{int}}(\hat{\mathfrak{A}}))$ can be derived. It is straightforward to adapt the treatment to the scenario where G^{ext} (or both) gets updated.

Definition 4 $((\beta, \beta')$-$(\hat{\mathfrak{A}}, \hat{\mathfrak{B}})$-**translatable reductions**)**.** *Let* $\mathcal{R}$ *be a classical reduction* $(G^{\mathsf{ext}}(\hat{\mathfrak{B}}), \mathcal{T}, G^{\mathsf{int}}(\hat{\mathfrak{A}}))$ *and* β, β' *be two functions. Let* $\hat{G}^{\mathsf{int}}$ *be a quantum game, and* $(\hat{\mathfrak{A}}, \hat{\mathfrak{B}})$ *be classes of quantum machines. We say* $\mathcal{R}$ *is* (β, β')-$(\hat{\mathfrak{A}}, \hat{\mathfrak{B}})$-*translatable, if there exists a machine (i.e. Interpreter)* $\hat{\mathcal{I}}$, *such that the following hold:*

- $\mathcal{R}$ *is* β-$(\hat{\mathfrak{B}}, \hat{\mathfrak{A}}')$-*respectful, where* $\hat{\mathfrak{A}}' := \hat{\mathcal{I}}(\hat{\mathfrak{A}})$.
- $(G^{\mathsf{int}}, \hat{\mathcal{I}}, \hat{G}^{\mathsf{int}})$ *is a* $(\beta', \hat{\mathfrak{A}})$-*effective reduction. Namely* $\forall \hat{A} \in \hat{\mathfrak{A}}$, $\omega_{G^{\mathsf{int}}}(\hat{\mathcal{I}}(\hat{A})) \geq \beta'(\omega_{\hat{G}^{\mathsf{int}}}(\hat{A}))$.

Theorem 3 (Quantum lifting for game-updating reductions). *If* $\mathcal{R}(\mathfrak{A}, \mathfrak{B})$ *is* (β, β')-$(\hat{\mathfrak{A}}, \hat{\mathfrak{B}})$-*translatable, then there exists an* $(\hat{\mathfrak{A}}, \hat{\mathfrak{B}})$-*consistent reduction* $\hat{\mathcal{R}}(\hat{\mathfrak{A}}, \hat{\mathfrak{B}})$:=$(G^{\text{ext}}(\hat{\mathfrak{B}}), \hat{\mathcal{T}}, \hat{G}^{\text{int}}(\hat{\mathfrak{A}}))$ *that is* $(\beta \cdot \beta', \hat{\mathfrak{A}})$-*effective.*

Proof. By the hypothesis, we know there is an interpreter $\hat{\mathcal{I}}$. Since $\mathcal{R}$ is β-$(\hat{\mathfrak{B}}, \hat{\mathfrak{A}}')$-respectful, by Theorem 1, there is a $\hat{\mathcal{T}}_0$ s.t. $(G^{\text{ext}}(\hat{\mathfrak{B}}), \hat{\mathcal{T}}_0, G^{\text{int}}(\hat{\mathfrak{A}}'))$ is $(\beta, \hat{\mathfrak{A}}')$-effective. Define $\hat{\mathcal{T}} := \hat{\mathcal{T}}_0 \circ \hat{\mathcal{I}}$ and $\hat{\mathcal{R}} := (G^{\text{ext}}, \hat{\mathcal{T}}, \hat{G}^{\text{int}})$. Clearly, $\hat{\mathcal{R}}$ is $(\hat{\mathfrak{A}}, \hat{\mathfrak{B}})$-consistent because for any $\hat{\mathcal{A}} \in \hat{\mathfrak{A}}$, $\hat{\mathcal{T}}(\hat{\mathcal{A}}) = \hat{\mathcal{T}}_0(\hat{\mathcal{I}}(\hat{\mathcal{A}})) \in \hat{\mathfrak{B}}$. On the other hand, for any $\hat{\mathcal{A}} \in \hat{\mathfrak{A}}$ it holds that $\omega_{G^{\text{ext}}}(\hat{\mathcal{T}}(\hat{\mathcal{A}})) \geq \beta \cdot \omega_{G^{\text{int}}}(\hat{\mathcal{I}}(\hat{\mathcal{A}})) \geq \beta\beta' \cdot \omega_{\hat{G}^{\text{int}}}(\hat{\mathcal{A}})$.

In contrast to the game-preserving setting, applying lifting theorem for game-updating reductions typically needs non-trivial extra work. The main difficulty comes from showing existence of an interpreter $\hat{\mathcal{I}}$ with the desired properties. In Sect. 5.2, we give an example that demonstrates potential applications of Theorem 3.

5 Applications

We give a few examples to demonstrate our framework for "quantum-friendly" reductions. In the game-preserving setting (Section 5.1), we show two versions of quantum-secure hash-based signatures schemes assuming quantum-resistant one-way functions. One follows the generic construction that builds upon Lamport's OTS and Merkle's original hash-tree idea. The other is an efficient variant proposed in [10] that uses a more compact one-time signature scheme and a more sophisticated tree structure. In the game-updating setting (Section 5.2), we give an alternative proof for Full-Domain Hash (FDH) in the Quantum RO model as shown in [47]. We stress that this proof is meant to illustrate how our lifting theorem can be potentially applied, as apposed to providing new technical insights. Unless otherwise specified, all players are either classical or quantum poly-time machines.

5.1 Quantum Security for Hash-based Signatures

Classically, there are generic constructions (and efficient variants) for EU-CMA-secure signature schemes based on one-way functions. We show that security reductions there can be lifted easily, using our *class-respecful* characterization. It follows that there are classical signature schemes that are secure against quantum attacks, merely assuming existence of quantum-resistant one-way functions.

Generic Hash-Tree Signature Schemes. A generic approach for constructing EU-CMA-secure signature scheme from OWFS goes as follows:

- A one-time signature (OTS) is constructed based on OWFS. There are various ways to achieve it. We consider Lamport's construction (L-OTS) here [28].
- A family of universal one-way hash functions (UOWHFS) is constructed based on OWFS. This was shown by Rompel [37] and we denote the hash family R-H.

- An OTS scheme is converted to a full-fledged (stateful) signature scheme using UOWHFS. The conversion we consider here is essentially Merkle's original hash-tree construction [32].

We show next that each step can be "lifted" to the quantum setting using our lifting theorem for game-preserving reductions (Theorem 1) and the straight-line characterization (Theorem 2). Note that we do not intend to optimize the construction here. For instance, one can use a pseudorandom function to make the signature scheme stateless. Verifying whether these still hold in the quantum setting is left as future work, though we believe it is the case, following the framework and tools we have developed.

LAMPORT'S OTS. Consider the (classical) reduction $\mathcal{R} := (G^{\mathrm{INV}}, \mathcal{T}, G^{\mathrm{OT\text{-}FOR}})$, where G^{INV} is the inversion game and $G^{\mathrm{OT\text{-}FOR}}$ is the one-time forgery game. It is straight-line and value-dominating. Both games are compatible with $\mathcal{Q}$ and $\omega_{G^{\mathrm{ext}}}(T^{\mathcal{A}}) \geq \beta \cdot \omega_{G^{\mathrm{int}}}(\mathcal{A})$ for any $\mathcal{A}$ with $\beta(x) = \frac{1}{2\ell(n)}x$ and $\ell(n)$ a polynomial representing the length of the messages. Hence $\mathcal{R}$ is $(\beta, \mathcal{Q})$-effective as well. Thus we claim that:

Proposition 1. $(G^{\mathrm{INV}}, \varepsilon_{\mathcal{Q}} = \mathsf{negl}(n))_{\mathrm{OWF}}$ *implies* $(G^{\mathrm{OT\text{-}FOR}}, \varepsilon_{\mathcal{Q}} = \mathsf{negl}(n))_{\mathrm{L\text{-}OTS}}$. *Namely, assuming quantum-resistant* OWFS, *there exists* EU-CMA-*secure* OTS *against quantum attackers* $\mathcal{Q}$.

UOWHFS FROM OWFS. Rompel's construction is complicated and the proof is technical (or rather tedious). However, the key ingredients in which security reductions are crucial are actually not hard to check. Basically, there are four major components in the construction:

1. From a given OWF f^0, construct another OWF f with certain structure. Basically, f is more "balanced" in the sense that sampling a random element in the range of f and then sub-sampling its pre-images is not much different from sampling a random element in the domain directly.
2. From f, construct $\mathcal{H} = \{h_s\}$ such that for any x, it is hard to find a collision in the so called "hard-sibling" set. The hard-sibling set should comprise a noticeable fraction of all possible collisions.
3. Amplifying the hard-sibling set so that finding any collision of a pre-determined x is hard.
4. Final refinements such as making the hash functions compressing.

The second step is the crux of the entire construction. There are three reductions showing that finding a hard-sibling is as hard as inverting f which we will discuss in a bit detail below, whereas showing that the hard-sibling set is noticeably large is done by a probabilistic analysis and holds information-theoretically. Other steps either do not involve a security reduction and relies purely on some probabilistic analysis, or the reductions are clearly liftable.

The three reduction in step 2 involve four games: G^{INV}–the standard inversion game for OWFS; $G^{\mathrm{INV'}}$–a variant of G^{INV} in which y is sampled according to another distribution, as opposed to sampling a domain element x uniformly at random and setting $y := f(x)$; $G^{\mathrm{COL'}}$, a variant of the collision game for UOWHFS, in which an adversary is supposed to find a collision x' in a special set (we don't specify it here); and $G^{\mathrm{COL''}}$, which further modifies $G^{\text{COL}'}$ in the distribution that s is sampled (instead of uniformly at random). Then $\mathcal{R}_1 = (G^{\text{INV}}, \mathcal{T}_1, G^{\text{INV}'})$, $\mathcal{R}_2 := (G^{\text{INV}'}, \mathcal{T}_2, G^{\text{COL}''})$ and $\mathcal{R}_3 = (G^{\text{COL}''}, \mathcal{T}_3, G^{\text{COL}'})$ are constructed. $\mathcal{R}_1$ and $\mathcal{R}_3$ essentially follow from the "balanced" structure of f, and $\mathcal{R}_2$ comes from the construction of $\mathcal{H} = \{h_s\}$. All three reductions are black-box straight-line, value-dominating, and $(\beta_i, \mathcal{Q})$-effective with $\beta_i \geq 1/p_i(n)$ for some polynomial $p_i, i \in \{1, 2, 3\}$. For concreteness, we can set $p_1 = \ell'(n)$–the length of the input string of f^0, $p_2 = 3$ a constant, and $p_3(n) = 5\ell'(n) + \log \ell'(n) + 2$. Our exposition here and parameter choices are adapted from [25].

Proposition 2. $(G^{\text{INV}}, \varepsilon_{\mathcal{Q}} = \text{negl}(n))_{\text{OWF}}$ *implies* $(G^{\text{COL}}, \varepsilon_{\mathcal{Q}} = \text{negl}(n))_{\text{R-H}}$. *Namely, assuming quantum-resistant* OWFS, *there exist* UOWHFS *secure against quantum attackers* $\mathcal{Q}$.

HASH-TREE: CONVERTING OTS TO FULL-FLEDGED SIGNATURES. Once a family of UOWHFS and an OTS are at hand, we can get a full-fledged signature scheme based on Merkle's hash-tree construction. Basically, one constructs a depth-k binary tree and each leaf corresponds to a message. Each node in the tree is associated with a key-pair (pk_w, sk_w) of the OTS scheme. The signature of a message m consists of $\sigma_m := \text{Sign}(sk_m, m)$ and an authentication chain. For each node w along the path from the root to the message, we apply $\mathcal{H} = \{h_s\}$ to the concatenation of its children's public keys and then sign the resulting string with its secret key sk_w. The authentication chain contains all these $(pk_{w0}, pk_{w1}, \sigma_w := \text{Sign}(sk_w, pk_{w0} \| pk_{w1}))$. Let M-TREE be the resulting tree-based scheme and G^{FOR} be the forgery game. The classical security analysis builds upon two reductions $(G^{\text{COL}}, \mathcal{T}, G^{\text{FOR}})$ and $(G^{\text{OT-FOR}}, \mathcal{T}', G^{\text{FOR}})$. It is easy to check that both satisfy the conditions in Corollary 1.

Proposition 3. $(G^{\text{COL}}, \varepsilon_{\mathcal{Q}} = \text{negl}(n))_{\text{UOWHFS}}$ *and* $(G^{\text{OT-FOR}}, \varepsilon_{\mathcal{Q}} = \text{negl}(n))_{\text{OTS}}$ *imply* $(G^{\text{FOR}}, \varepsilon_{\mathcal{Q}} = \text{negl}(n))_{\text{M-TREE}}$. *Namely, assuming quantum-resistant* UOWHFS *and* OTS, *there exist an* EU-CMA-*secure signature scheme against quantum attackers* $\mathcal{Q}$.

Combining Propositions 1, 2, and 3, we get

Theorem 4. *Assuming quantum-resistant* OWFS, *there exists* EU-CMA-*secure signature schemes against quantum poly-time attackers* $\mathcal{Q}$.

XMSS: an efficient variant. The XMSS scheme [10] can be seen an efficient instantiation of the generic construction above. It uses a different one-time signature scheme called Winternitz-OTS (W-OTS for short), which can be based on a family of pseudorandom functions, which in turn exists from the "minimal" assumption that OWFS exist. The hash-tree (which is called XMSS-tree in [10]) also differs slightly. We now show that both the security of W-OTS and the conversion by XMSS-tree are still valid against quantum adversaries.

QUANTUM SECURITY OF W-OTS. Classically, existence of OWF imply the EU-CMA-security of W-OTS. This is established in three steps: 1) By standard constructions, a pseudorandom generator (PRG) can be constructed from OWFS [24], and then one can construct a pseudo-random function (PRF) from a PRG [16]. 2) A PRF is shown to be also key-one-way (KOW, defined later). 3) Show that KOW implies EU-CMA-security of W-OTS by a reduction.

The first step is known to be true in the presence of quantum adversaries [46][4]. Informally the game for KOW of a function family F goes as follows: $\mathcal{C}$ samples a random function $f_k \in_R F$ and a random element x in the domain. $(x, y := f_k(x))$ is sent to an adversary $\mathcal{A}$, who tries to find k' such that $f_{k'}(x) = y$. The PRF to KOW reduction is straight-line and value-dominating. Extendibility is trivial. Therefore it is $\mathcal{Q}$-respectful. This is also the case in the KOW to EU-CMA-security of W-OTS reduction. In addition β is 1 for both reductions, which means that the effectiveness (i.e., tightness in terms of success probability) in the classical analysis carries over unchanged to the quantum setting.

Proposition 4. $\left(G^{\text{PRF}}, \varepsilon_{\mathcal{Q}} = \mathsf{negl}(n)\right)$ *implies* $\left(G^{\text{OT-FOR}}, \varepsilon_{\mathcal{Q}} = \mathsf{negl}(n)\right)_{\text{W-OTS}}$. *Namely, assuming a quantum-resistant* PRF, W-OTS *is one-time* EU-CMA-*secure against quantum attackers* $\mathcal{Q}$.

XMSS-TREE. The XMSS-tree modifies Merkle's hash-tree construction with an XOR-technique. Loosely speaking, each level of the tree is associated with two random strings, which mask the two children nodes before we apply the hash function to produce an authentication of a node. This tweak allows one to use a second-preimage resistant (SPR) hash function, instead of collision-resistant hash functions or UOWHFS. Theoretically universal one-way implies second-preimage resistance. But in practice people typically test second-preimage resistance when a hash function is designed. Despite this change, the security proof is not much different. Reductions are given that convert a forger either to a forger for W-OTS or to an adversary that breaks SPR-hash functions. They are straight-line, value-dominating and $(1, \mathcal{Q})$-extendible. By Corollary 1, we have

Proposition 5. $\left(G^{\text{SPR}}, \varepsilon_{\mathcal{Q}} = \mathsf{negl}(n)\right)$ *and* $\left(G^{\text{OT-FOR}}, \varepsilon_{\mathcal{Q}} = \mathsf{negl}(n)\right)_{\text{W-OTS}}$ *imply* $\left(G^{\text{FOR}}, \varepsilon_{\mathcal{Q}} = \mathsf{negl}(n)\right)_{\text{XMSS}}$. *Namely, assuming quantum-resistant* PRF *and* SPR *hash functions,* XMSS *signature is* EU-CMA-*secure against quantum attackers* $\mathcal{Q}$.

As mentioned above, UOWHFS are by definition second-preimage resistant. As a result, quantum-resistant SPR hash functions can be constructed from quantum-resistant OWFS as well. Thus, we obtain that the XMSS signature scheme is EU-CMA-secure against efficient quantum attackers $\mathcal{Q}$, assuming quantum-resistant OWFS.

5.2 Full-Domain Hash in Quantum Random-Oracle Model

Full domain hash (FDH) is a generic approach of constructing signature schemes based on trapdoor permutations (TDPs) in the RO model [4]. The classical proof cleverly "programs" the random-oracle, so that a challenge of inverting a TDP gets embedded as one output value of the random-oracle. However when we consider FDH in the quantum random-oracle (QRO) model, in which one can query the random-oracle in superposition, we lose the "programable" ability in the proof. Zhandry [47] resolved this issue

---

[4] It is easy to verify that the security reduction from PRG to PRF in GMM construction is quantum friendly. The security analysis in the HILL PRF construction from OWFS is much more complicated. To the best of our knowledge, no rigorous argument has appeared in the literature. It would be a nice exercise to apply our framework and give a formal proof.

by some quantum "programing" strategy, which built upon lower bounds on quantum query complexity. This is summarized as follows.

Theorem 5 ([47, Theorem 5.3]). *Let F be a quantum-resistant trapdoor permutation. If we model H as a quantum random-oracle, then Π is quantum EU-CMA-secure.*

We note that Zhandry's proof fits our framework for lifting game-updating reductions. Namely, let G^{TDP} the inversion game for a TDP. We can construct an interpreter $\hat{\mathcal{I}}$ for any adversary in the forgery game $G^{\text{QRO-FOR}}$, and show that the classical reduction $(G^{\text{TDP}}, \mathcal{T}, G^{\text{RO-FOR}})$ is translatable. Applying Theorem 3 proves the theorem here. We describe a proof in Appendix A for completeness. This illustrates how to apply our framework and get (in our opinion) more modular security analysis.

5.3 Quantum Security of Classical Cryptographic Protocols

So far, we have been focusing on basic cryptographic primitives such as UOWHFS and signatures. However, our framework is not limited to these scenarios, and actually can be applied to analyzing more complicated cryptographic protocols as well. Specifically an abstraction called simple-hybrid arguments, which characterize a family of classical proofs for two-party secure computation protocols in the computational setting that go through against quantum adversaries [23], can be derived easily in our framework. We defer the details in Appendix B.

6 Discussions

We have proposed a general framework to study which security reductions are quantum-friendly. The lifting theorems we developed can be used to analyze security against computationally bounded quantum adversaries for post-quantum cryptography. As an application, we have shown the quantum security of a generic hash-tree based signature scheme and an efficient variant (which is a promising candidate for post-quantum signature schemes to be implemented in practice).

However, this note concerns mostly the feasibility of lifting classical security proofs to the quantum setting, and there are many important aspects missing and many interesting directions to be investigated. For example, we did not consider much about the "quality" of the resulting proofs for quantum adversaries. Say, can we preserve the tightness of the classical reduction when we lift it? Tightness of security reduction is of great practical impact. Not only it affects how to set the parameters in implementations, it may render security meaningless in some cases [11]. Interestingly, there are also examples where we get tighter reduction in the quantum setting, as demonstrated in the quantum Goldreich-Levin theorem [1]. This is also a nice example of game-updating reductions beyond the QRO model. Along the same line, another game-updating reduction that is fundamental in cryptography arises from constructing a pseudorandom permutation (PRP) from a pseudorandom function (PRF). It is not clear if the classical construction remains valid if the game defining PRP allows superposition queries to distinguish it from a truly random permutation.

There are many concrete questions left for quantum-secure signature schemes as well. We showed a quantum EU-CMA-secure signature scheme based on quantum-resistant OWFS. Can we make it strongly-unforgeable? The XMSS scheme is also known to be *forward*-secure. Is it still true against quantum adversaries? We believe both answers are positive, by similar analysis from this note. Moreover, there are generic transformations that augments a signature scheme with stronger security guarantees (e.g., from EU-CMA-secure to SU-CMA-secure). Do they hold in the quantum setting? We also note that the applications we have shown in the game-updating case are not very exciting in the sense that designing an interpreter appears no easier than coming up with a quantum reduction directly. It is helpful to further explore along this line to find more interesting applications.

Finally, we remark that quantum attacks could reduce the security level of a system, using for example Grover's quantum search algorithm. Although not covered in this note, this issue needs to be addressed with care as well.

Acknowledgments. The author is grateful to Michele Mosca for encouraging him to write up this note. F.S. would like to thank the anonymous reviewers for valuable comments and John Schank for joyful discussions on lattice-based signature schemes. F.S. acknowledges support from Ontario Research Fund, Industry Canada and CryptoWorks21.

References

1. Adcock, M., Cleve, R.: A quantum Goldreich-Levin theorem with cryptographic applications. In: Alt, H., Ferreira, A. (eds.) STACS 2002. LNCS, vol. 2285, pp. 323–334. Springer, Heidelberg (2002)
2. Barthe, G., Grégoire, B., Heraud, S., Béguelin, S.Z.: Computer-aided security proofs for the working cryptographer. In: Rogaway, P. (ed.) CRYPTO 2011. LNCS, vol. 6841, pp. 71–90. Springer, Heidelberg (2011)
3. Barthe, G., Grégoire, B., Zanella Béguelin, S.: Formal certification of code-based cryptographic proofs. ACM SIGPLAN Notices 44(1), 90–101 (2009)
4. Bellare, M., Rogaway, P.: Random oracles are practical: A paradigm for designing efficient protocols. In: Proceedings of the 1st ACM Conference on Computer and Communications Security, pp. 62–73. ACM (1993)
5. Bellare, M., Rogaway, P.: The security of triple encryption and a framework for code-based game-playing proofs. In: Vaudenay, S. (ed.) EUROCRYPT 2006. LNCS, vol. 4004, pp. 409–426. Springer, Heidelberg (2006)
6. Bernstein, D.J., Buchmann, J., Dahmen, E.: Post-quantum cryptography. Springer (2009)
7. Blanchet, B.: A computationally sound mechanized prover for security protocols. IEEE Transactions on Dependable and Secure Computing 5(4), 193–207 (2008)
8. Boneh, D., Dagdelen, Ö., Fischlin, M., Lehmann, A., Schaffner, C., Zhandry, M.: Random oracles in a quantum world. In: Lee, D.H., Wang, X. (eds.) ASIACRYPT 2011. LNCS, vol. 7073, pp. 41–69. Springer, Heidelberg (2011)
9. Boneh, D., Zhandry, M.: Secure signatures and chosen ciphertext security in a quantum computing world. In: Canetti, R., Garay, J.A. (eds.) CRYPTO 2013, Part II. LNCS, vol. 8043, pp. 361–379. Springer, Heidelberg (2013)
10. Buchmann, J., Dahmen, E., Hülsing, A.: XMSS - A practical forward secure signature scheme based on minimal security assumptions. In: Yang, B.-Y. (ed.) PQCrypto 2011. LNCS, vol. 7071, pp. 117–129. Springer, Heidelberg (2011)
11. Chatterjee, S., Menezes, A., Sarkar, P.: Another look at tightness. In: Miri, A., Vaudenay, S. (eds.) SAC 2011. LNCS, vol. 7118, pp. 293–319. Springer, Heidelberg (2012)

12. Crépeau, C., Salvail, L., Simard, J.R., Tapp, A.: Two provers in isolation. In: Lee, D.H., Wang, X. (eds.) ASIACRYPT 2011. LNCS, vol. 7073, pp. 407–430. Springer, Heidelberg (2011)

13. Damgård, I., Lunemann, C.: Quantum-secure coin-flipping and applications. In: Matsui, M. (ed.) ASIACRYPT 2009. LNCS, vol. 5912, pp. 52–69. Springer, Heidelberg (2009)

14. Fehr, S., Katz, J., Song, F., Zhou, H.-S., Zikas, V.: Feasibility and completeness of cryptographic tasks in the quantum world. In: Sahai, A. (ed.) TCC 2013. LNCS, vol. 7785, pp. 281–296. Springer, Heidelberg (2013)

15. Gentry, C., Wichs, D.: Separating succinct non-interactive arguments from all falsifiable assumptions. In: Proceedings of the Forty-Third Annual ACM Symposium on Theory of Computing, pp. 99–108. ACM (2011)

16. Goldreich, O., Goldwasser, S., Micali, S.: How to construct random functions. Journal of the ACM (JACM) 33(4), 792–807 (1986)

17. Goldwasser, S., Micali, S.: Probabilistic encryption. Journal of Computer and System Sciences 28(2), 270–299 (1984)

18. Goldwasser, S., Micali, S., Rivest, R.L.: A digital signature scheme secure against adaptive chosen-message attacks. SIAM Journal on Computing 17(2), 281–308 (1988)

19. van de Graaf, J.: Towards a formal definition of security for quantum protocols. PhD thesis, Départment d'informatique et de recherche opérationnelle, Université de Montréal (1997)

20. Haitner, I., Holenstein, T.: On the (im)possibility of key dependent encryption. In: Reingold, O. (ed.) TCC 2009. LNCS, vol. 5444, pp. 202–219. Springer, Heidelberg (2009)

21. Halevi, S.: A plausible approach to computer-aided cryptographic proofs. Cryptology ePrint Archive, Report 2005/181 (2005)

22. Hallgren, S.: Polynomial-time quantum algorithms for Pell's equation and the principal ideal problem. J. ACM 54(1), 1–19 (2007)

23. Hallgren, S., Smith, A., Song, F.: Classical cryptographic protocols in a quantum world. In: Rogaway, P. (ed.) CRYPTO 2011. LNCS, vol. 6841, pp. 411–428. Springer, Heidelberg (2011)

24. Håstad, J., Impagliazzo, R., Levin, L.A., Luby, M.: A pseudorandom generator from any one-way function. SIAM Journal on Computing 28(4), 1364–1396 (1999)

25. Katz, J., Koo, C.Y.: On constructing universal one-way hash functions from arbitrary one-way functions. IACR Cryptology ePrint Archive 2005, 328 (2005)

26. Katz, J., Lindell, Y.: Introduction to modern cryptography: principles and protocols. CRC Press (2007)

27. Kilian, J., Rogaway, P.: How to protect des against exhaustive key search (an analysis of DESX). Journal of Cryptology 14(1), 17–35 (2001)

28. Lamport, L.: Constructing digital signatures from a one-way function. Tech. Report: SRI International Computer Science Laboratory (1979)

29. Lunemann, C., Nielsen, J.B.: Fully simulatable quantum-secure coin-flipping and applications. In: Nitaj, A., Pointcheval, D. (eds.) AFRICACRYPT 2011. LNCS, vol. 6737, pp. 21–40. Springer, Heidelberg (2011)

30. Lyubashevsky, V.: Lattice-based identification schemes secure under active attacks. In: Cramer, R. (ed.) PKC 2008. LNCS, vol. 4939, pp. 162–179. Springer, Heidelberg (2008)

31. Lyubashevsky, V.: Fiat-Shamir with aborts: Applications to lattice and factoring-based signatures. In: Matsui, M. (ed.) ASIACRYPT 2009. LNCS, vol. 5912, pp. 598–616. Springer, Heidelberg (2009)

32. Merkle, R.C.: A certified digital signature. In: Brassard, G. (ed.) CRYPTO 1989. LNCS, vol. 435, pp. 218–238. Springer, Heidelberg (1990)

33. Micciancio, D., Regev, O.: Lattice-based cryptography. In: Post-quantum cryptography, pp. 147–191. Springer (2009)

34. Naor, M.: On cryptographic assumptions and challenges. In: Boneh, D. (ed.) CRYPTO 2003. LNCS, vol. 2729, pp. 96–109. Springer, Heidelberg (2003)

35. Pass, R.: Limits of provable security from standard assumptions. In: Proceedings of the Forty-Third Annual ACM Symposium on Theory of Computing, pp. 109–118. ACM (2011)
36. Peikert, C.: Some recent progress in lattice-based cryptography. In: Reingold, O. (ed.) TCC 2009. LNCS, vol. 5444, p. 72. Springer, Heidelberg (2009)
37. Rompel, J.: One-way functions are necessary and sufficient for secure signatures. In: Proceedings of the Twenty-Second Annual ACM Symposium on Theory of Computing, pp. 387–394. ACM (1990)
38. Sendrier, N.: Code-based cryptography. In: Encyclopedia of Cryptography and Security, pp. 215–216. Springer (2011)
39. Shor, P.W.: Polynomial-time algorithms for prime factorization and discrete logarithms on a quantum computer. SIAM J. Comput. 26(5), 1484–1509 (1997)
40. Shoup, V.: Sequences of games: a tool for taming complexity in security proofs. Cryptology ePrint Archive, Report 2004/332 (2005)
41. Stump, A.: Proof checking technology for satisfiability modulo theories. Electronic Notes in Theoretical Computer Science 228, 121–133 (2009)
42. Unruh, D.: Universally composable quantum multi-party computation. In: Gilbert, H. (ed.) EUROCRYPT 2010. LNCS, vol. 6110, pp. 486–505. Springer, Heidelberg (2010), preprint on arXiv:0910.2912 [quant-ph]
43. Unruh, D.: Quantum proofs of knowledge. In: Pointcheval, D., Johansson, T. (eds.) EUROCRYPT 2012. LNCS, vol. 7237, pp. 135–152. Springer, Heidelberg (2012), preprint on IACR ePrint 2010/212
44. Watrous, J.: Zero-knowledge against quantum attacks. SIAM J. Comput. 39(1), 25–58 (2009), preliminary version in STOC 2006
45. Yao, A.C.: Theory and application of trapdoor functions. In: 23rd Annual Symposium on Foundations of Computer Science, SFCS 2008, pp. 80–91. IEEE (1982)
46. Zhandry, M.: How to construct quantum random functions. In: 2012 IEEE 53rd Annual Symposium on Foundations of Computer Science (FOCS), pp. 679–687. IEEE (2012)
47. Zhandry, M.: Secure identity-based encryption in the quantum random oracle model. In: Safavi-Naini, R., Canetti, R. (eds.) CRYPTO 2012. LNCS, vol. 7417, pp. 758–775. Springer, Heidelberg (2012)

A   (Alternative) Proof of Theorem 5: FDH in QRO

We first review a technical tool in [47] called *semi-constant* distribution. Loosely speaking, it allows us to "program" a function, which still looks like a random function even to a quantum observer.

Definition 5 (Semi-Constant Distribution [47, Definition 4.1]). *Let X and Y be sets and denote $\mathcal{H}_{X,Y}$ the set of functions from X to Y. The semi-constant distribution SC_λ is defined as the distribution over $\mathcal{H}_{X,Y}$ resulting from the following process:*

- *Pick a random element y from Y.*
- *For each $x \in X$, set $H(x) = y$ wth probability λ. Otherwise set $H(x)$ to be a random element in Y.*

Theorem 6 ([47, Corollary 4.3]). *The distribution of the output of a quantum algorithm making q_H queries to an oracle drawn from SC_λ is at most a distance $\frac{8}{3}q_H^4\lambda^2$ away from the case when the oracle is drawn uniformly from $\mathcal{H}_{X,Y}$.*

We are now ready to give a proof for Theorem 5 using our framework for game-updating reductions.

Proof. Classically there is $\mathcal{R} = (G^{\text{TDP}}, \mathcal{T}, G^{\text{RO-FOR}})$ that inverts the TDP with a forger for the FDH-Sign scheme. We construct an interpreter $\hat{\mathcal{I}}$ as follows, and show that $\mathcal{R}$ is $(\hat{\mathfrak{A}}, \hat{\mathfrak{B}})$-translatable with $\hat{\mathfrak{A}} = \hat{\mathfrak{B}} = \mathcal{Q}$.

Interpreter $\hat{\mathcal{I}}$

Input: Adversary $\hat{\mathcal{A}}$ for a quantum EU-CMA-game. Let q_S and a_H be upper bounds on the number of signing queries and hash queries of $\hat{\mathcal{A}}$.

Output: An adversary $\hat{\mathcal{A}}' := \hat{\mathcal{I}}(\hat{\mathcal{A}})$ that operates as follows:

1. Receive pk from a challenger, which indexes a permeation f_{pk}.
2. Pick an arbitrary message a. Query $H(\cdot)$ and get $b := H(a)$.
3. Emulate (internally) a quantum EU-CMA-game with $\hat{\mathcal{A}}$.
   - Use b to create an oracle $\hat{H}$ from a semi-constant distribution SC_λ which handles (quantum) hash queries from $\hat{\mathcal{A}}$. Specifically, let $\mathcal{O}_2$ be a random oracle outputting 1 with probability λ and $\mathcal{O}_1$ be a random oracle mapping a message to an input of f_{pk}. Let $\hat{H}(x) = b$ if $\mathcal{O}_2(x) = 1$ and $\hat{H}(x) = f_{pk}(\mathcal{O}_1(x))$ otherwise.
   - On signing query m_i, if $\mathcal{O}_2(m_i) = 1$ abort. Otherwise respond with $\sigma_i := \mathcal{O}_1(m_i)$.
4. On output (m^*, σ^*) from $\hat{\mathcal{A}}$, if $\mathcal{O}_2(m^*) = 1$ output (a, σ^*).

Fig. 1. Construction of the Interpreter

Clearly, $\hat{\mathcal{A}}'$ is a well-defined (quantum) adversary for the original forgery game $G^{\text{RO-FOR}}$ (i.e., the hash queries are classical). If $\hat{\mathcal{A}}$ outputs a valid forgery (m^*, σ^*) such that $\hat{H}(m^*) = f_{pk}(\sigma^*)$ and $\mathcal{O}_2(m^*) = 1$, we know that $\hat{H}(m^*) = b = H(a)$ and hence (a, σ^*) forms a valid forgery in the classical forgery game. Note that the view of $\hat{\mathcal{A}}$ in $\hat{\mathcal{A}}'$ differs from a true interaction with a challenger in game $G^{\text{QRO-FOR}}$ in two places: a truly random oracle is replaced by $\hat{H}$ drawn from SC_λ and the signing query fails with probability λ. By picking λ a proper inverse polynomial in q_H and q_S, we can obtain from Theorem 6 that $\omega_{G^{\text{RO-FOR}}}(\hat{\mathcal{I}}(\hat{\mathcal{A}})) \geq \omega^2_{G^{\text{QRO-FOR}}}(\hat{\mathcal{A}})/p(n)$ for some polynomial $p(\cdot)$. Thus $(G^{\text{RO-FOR}}, \hat{\mathcal{I}}, G^{\text{QRO-FOR}})$ forms a $(\beta', \mathcal{Q})$-effective reduction for a suitable β'. Since the two random oracles $(\mathcal{O}_1, \mathcal{O}_2)$ can be simulated efficiently by k-wise indecent functions (C.f. [47, Theorem 6.1]), $\mathcal{R}$ is clearly β-$(\mathcal{Q}, \hat{\mathcal{I}}(\mathcal{Q}))$-respectful with $\beta = 1$. Therefore we obtain that $\mathcal{R}$ is $(\mathcal{Q}, \mathcal{Q})$-translatable, which by Theorem 3 can be lifted to a reduction $(G^{\text{TDP}}(\mathcal{Q}), \hat{\mathcal{T}}, G^{\text{QRO-FOR}}(\mathcal{Q}))$. This shows that the FDH-Signature scheme is quantum EU-CMA-secure, assuming quantum-resistant trapdoor permutations.

B   Details on Sect. 5.3

Security definitions in this setting usually follows the *simulation paradigm*. In particular, there is not a simple game capturing them[5]. Roughly speaking, we require the

---

[5] In some sense, the security definitions we discussed earlier that are specified by games are *falsifiable*, which does not seem to be so here.

existence of an imaginary entity (called the simulator) with certain properties for any possible adversary. The main ingredient of a security proof is often a hybrid argument, in which a sequence of imaginary experiments (a.k.a. *hybrids*) are defined in terms of an adversary and the simulator. The goal is to show each adjacent pair of hybrids is indistinguishable. Whenever this is done by a reduction of breaking a computational assumption, we can define a distinguishing game (as our internal game) and study if the reduction can be lifted using our framework.

Consider zero-knowledge proof protocols as a concrete example. Zero-knowledge property requires that for any dishonest verifier V^*, there is a simulator S, such that the output of S is indistinguishable from the view of V^* in real protocol with honest prover. At this moment, it looks quite alien to our framework. However, once we start the security proof, it naturally fits our framework. Basically, if we fix a dishonest V^*, and a specific construction of a simulator, showing that the simulator works can be thought of as a distinguishing game.

ZK Distinguishing Game $G^{ZK}_{V^*,S}$

Two parties: Challenger C and distinguisher D.

- C flips a random coin $b \in_R \{0,1\}$. If $b = 0$ simulates an execution of the ZK protocol and sends D the view of V^*. If $b = 1$, run the simulator S and sends D the output of S.
- D receives the message from C, generate one bit b' and send it to C.
- C outputs succ if $b = b'$ and fail otherwise.

The security proof will then proceed in the familiar fashion. Namely a reduction $(G^{ext}, \mathcal{T}, G^{int} := G^{ZK}_{V^*,S})$ is constructed for some computational assumption captured by G^{ext}. We can then ask if we can "lift" the reduction to the quantum setting. One subtlety, however, is that the distinguishing game is specific to V^* and S. Because of issues like rewinding, we have to update the games. The challenge then lies in constructing a simulator $\hat{S}$ for any dishonest quantum verifier $\hat{V}^*$, which gives the updated distinguishing game $\hat{G}^{ZK}_{\hat{V}^*,\hat{S}}$ in the presence of quantum verifiers.

Sometimes we end up in the simpler game-preserving case. A concrete example is an abstraction proposed in [23], called *simple-hybrid arguments* (SHA).

SIMPLE HYBRID ARGUMENTS. SHA formalizes a family of classical proofs that can go through against quantum adversaries in the computational UC model. The essence is a simple observation: if two adjacent hybrids only differs by a small change such as chaining the plaintext of an encryption, then quantum security immediately follows as long as computational assumptions are made quantum-resistant. Using our framework, each adjacent pair of hybrid induce a distinguishing game G^{int} that can be defined similarly to $G^{ZK}_{V^*,S}$, and a classical reduction $\mathcal{R} := (G^{ext}, \mathcal{T}, G^{int})$ is already at hand for some computational assumption defined by G^{ext}. The conditions in SHA, e.g., changing only the plaintext, ensure that $\mathcal{R}$ satisfy the definition of $(\hat{\mathfrak{A}}, \hat{\mathfrak{B}})$-respectful reductions with $\hat{\mathfrak{A}} = \hat{\mathfrak{B}} = \mathcal{Q}$. As a result, these reductions can be lifted by Theorem 1.

Towards Side-Channel Resistant Implementations of QC-MDPC McEliece Encryption on Constrained Devices

Ingo von Maurich and Tim Güneysu

Horst Görtz Institute for IT-Security, Ruhr University Bochum, Germany
{ingo.vonmaurich,tim.gueneysu}@rub.de

Abstract. Recent advances in code-based cryptography paved new ways for efficient asymmetric cryptosystems that combine decent performance with moderate key sizes. In this context, Misoczki et al. recently proposed the use of quasi-cyclic MDPC (QC-MDPC) codes for the McEliece cryptosystem. It was shown that these codes can provide both compact key representations and solid performance on high-end computing platforms. However, for widely used low-end microcontrollers only slow implementations for this promising construction have been presented so far.

In this work we present an implementation of QC-MDPC McEliece encryption providing 80 bits of equivalent symmetric security on low-cost ARM Cortex-M4-based microcontrollers with a reasonable performance of $42\,ms$ for encryption and $251\text{-}558\,ms$ for decryption. Besides practical issues such as random error generation, we demonstrate side-channel attacks on a straightforward implementation of this scheme and finally propose timing- and instruction-invariant coding strategies and countermeasures to strengthen it against timing attacks as well as simple power analysis.

Keywords: Code-based cryptography, public key encryption, side-channel attacks, software, microcontroller, post-quantum cryptography.

1 Introduction

Although it is well-known that factoring or the discrete logarithm problem can be solved in polynomial time by Shor's quantum computing algorithm [17], they still found the basis for virtually all public key cryptosystems used today. Needless to say that alternative cryptosystems which (a) provide the same security services at (b) a comparable level of computational efficiency and (c) similar costs for storing keys, are urgently required.

In this context, code-based cryptosystems introduced by McEliece [12] and Niederreiter [15] are among the most promising alternative public key cryptosystems. Having been regarded for a long time as impractical for memory-constrained platforms due to their large key sizes, recent advances showed that reducing the key-sizes to practical levels is possible. Using (QC-)MDPC codes in the McEliece cryptosystem was first proposed in [13] and was later published

M. Mosca (Ed.): PQCrypto 2014, LNCS 8772, pp. 266–282, 2014.

with small changes in the parameter sets in [14]. Yet it needs to be investigated if all requirements of constrained platforms can be met with QC-MDPC codes.

The first implementations of this scheme appeared in [8] for AVR microcontrollers and Xilinx FPGAs along with some optimized decoding techniques, followed by a lightweight FPGA implementation [22]. Cyclosymmetric (CS-)MDPC codes in combination with the Niederreiter cryptosystem were recently proposed in [4], including an implementation for a small PIC microcontroller.

The results from [8] indicated that it seems to be a hard challenge to provide a reasonably fast implementation of QC-MDPC codes on low-cost 8-bit AVR ATxmega256A3 microcontrollers. The authors reported that their code for this platform runs the encryption and decryption in 830 ms and 2.7 s, based on the former 80-bit secure parameter set ($n_0 = 2, n = 9600, r = 4800, w = 90, t = 84$). In particular, decryption is obviously too slow to be of any practical interest for most real-world applications.

Despite sufficient performance, other highly relevant properties need further investigation as well to enable the deployment of QC-MDPC McEliece in practical systems. First, QC-MDPC on-chip key-generation has never been implemented on constrained devices. Second, McEliece as a probabilistic scheme requires a secure random number generator capable of producing error vectors of a certain Hamming weight during the encryption operation which has not been considered yet. Third, the parameter set was recently updated by [14] as shown in Sect. 2.2 due to advances in cryptanalysis. Fourth, the timing and the instruction flow of all previously presented implementations of the encryption and decryption operations depend on secret data. Fifth, all microcontroller implementations of QC-MDPC McEliece encryption reported so far have not been investigated with regard to side-channel attacks.

Side-channel attacks on the McEliece cryptosystem have mostly targeted Goppa codes and exploited differences in the timing behavior [18,20,21]. Improved timing attacks and corresponding countermeasures were presented in [2]. First practical power analysis attacks on Goppa-code McEliece implementations for 8-bit microcontrollers were presented in [7]. A very recent work investigated differential side-channel attacks on a lightweight QC-MDPC FPGA implementation [5].

Contribution. In this work, we intend to address the aforementioned problems. We present an implementation of QC-MDPC McEliece encryption providing 80 bits of equivalent symmetric security on a low-cost ARM Cortex-M4-based microcontroller with a reasonable performance of 42 *ms* for encryption and 251-558 *ms* for decryption (1). The parameter set we considered for implementation takes latest advances in cryptanalysis into account (2). We briefly discuss how to employ true random number generation for McEliece encryption (3). We demonstrate side-channel attacks on a straightforward implementation of this scheme and finally propose coding strategies and countermeasures to harden it against timing attacks (4) and simple power analysis (5).

Outline. Our work is outlined as follows. We summarize the background on QC-MDPC McEliece encryption in Sect. 2 and describe improvements in implementing the scheme in Sect. 3. Side-channel attacks on QC-MDPC McEliece are demonstrated on two microcontroller platforms in Sect. 4. We propose countermeasures to strengthen our implementations against these attacks and provide implementation results in Sect. 5. We conclude our work in Sect. 6.

2   Background on QC-MDPC McEliece

An in-depth description of McEliece based on (QC-)MDPC codes is given in [14]. Here, we give a short summary of the cryptosystem and its underlying code.

2.1   (QC-)MDPC Codes

A binary linear $[n, k]$ error-correcting code C of length n is a subspace of $\mathbb{F}_2^n$ of dimension k and co-dimension $r = n - k$. Code C can either be defined by a generator matrix or by a parity-check matrix. The generator matrix $G \in \mathbb{F}_2^{k \times n}$ defines the code as $C = \{mG \in \mathbb{F}_2^n \mid m \in \mathbb{F}_2^k\}$ and the parity-check matrix $H \in \mathbb{F}_2^{r \times n}$ defines the code as $C = \{c \in \mathbb{F}_2^n \mid cH^T = 0^r\}$. The syndrome $s \in \mathbb{F}_2^r$ of a vector $x \in \mathbb{F}_2^n$ is defined as $s = Hx^T$. It follows that if $x \in C$ then $s = 0^r$ otherwise $s \neq 0^r$.

If there exists some integer n_0 such that every cyclic shift of a codeword $c \in C$ by n_0 positions results in another codeword $c' \in C$ then code C is called quasi-cyclic (QC). If $n = n_0 p$ for some integer p, both generator and parity-check matrix are composed of $p \times p$ circulant blocks. It suffices to store one row (usually the first) of each circulant block to completely describe the matrices.

A (n, r, w)-MDPC code is a binary linear $[n, k]$ code defined by a parity-check matrix with constant row weight w. A (n, r, w)-QC-MDPC code is a (n, r, w)-MDPC code that is quasi-cyclic with $n = n_0 r$.

2.2   The QC-MDPC McEliece Cryptosystem

In this section we describe the key-generation, encryption and decryption of the McEliece cryptosystem based on a t-error correcting (n, r, w)-QC-MDPC code. The following parameters are proposed for a 80-bit security level in [14]:

$$n_0 = 2, n = 9602, r = 4801, w = 90, t = 84.$$

With these parameters a 4801-bit plaintext block is encoded into a 9602-bit codeword to which $t = 84$ errors are added. The parity-check matrix H has constant row weight $w = 90$ and consists of $n_0 = 2$ circulant blocks, the redundant part Q of the generator matrix G consists of $n_0 - 1 = 1$ circulant block. The public key has a size of 4801-bit and the secret key has a size of 9602-bit which can be compressed to 1440 bit since it is very sparse. For a detailed discussion of the security of this scheme we refer to [14].

Key-Generation. Key-Generation is equal to generating a (n, r, w)-QC-MDPC code with $n = n_0 r$. The public key is the generator matrix G and the secret key is the parity-check matrix H.

In order to generate a (n, r, w)-QC-MDPC code with $n = n_0 r$, select the first rows $h_0, \ldots, h_{n_0-1}$ of the n_0 parity-check matrix blocks $H_0, \ldots, H_{n_0-1}$ with weight $\sum_{i=0}^{n_0-1} wt(h_i) = w$ uniformly at random. The parity-check matrix blocks $H_0, \ldots, H_{n_0-1}$ are then generated by $r - 1$ quasi-cyclic shifts of $h_0, \ldots, h_{n_0-1}$. A horizontal concatenation forms the parity-check matrix $H = H_0, \ldots, H_{n_0-1}$.

Generator matrix $G = [I_k | Q]$ is computed from H in row reduced echelon form by concatenating the identity matrix I_k and matrix

$$
Q = \begin{pmatrix} (H_{n_0-1}^{-1} \cdot H_0)^T \\ (H_{n_0-1}^{-1} \cdot H_1)^T \\ \cdots \\ (H_{n_0-1}^{-1} \cdot H_{n_0-2})^T \end{pmatrix}.
$$

Since both matrices are quasi-cyclic, it suffices to store their first rows instead of the full matrices. Note, when using a CCA2 conversion such as [10,16], G is allowed to be of systematic form without reducing the security of the scheme.

Encryption. Given a message $m \in \mathbb{F}_2^k$, generate a random error vector $e \in \mathbb{F}_2^n$ with $wt(e) \leq t$ and compute $x = mG + e$.

Decryption. Given a ciphertext $x \in \mathbb{F}_2^n$, compute $mG \leftarrow \Psi_H(x)$ using a t-error correcting (QC-)MDPC decoder Ψ_H. Since G is of systematic form, plaintext m can be extracted from the first k positions of mG.

2.3   Decoding (QC-)MDPC Codes

Compared to the simple operations involved in encryption (i.e., a vector-matrix multiplication followed by an addition), decoding is the more complex operation. Several decoders have been proposed for (QC-)MDPC codes in [3,6,8,9,14]. Here, we refer to the results obtained in [8] where an optimized bit-flipping decoder based on [6] was identified as the most suitable for the constrained computing environment of microcontrollers. This decoder works as follows:

1. Compute the syndrome of the received ciphertext $s = Hx^T$.
2. Count the unsatisfied parity-checks for every ciphertext bit.
3. If the number of unsatisfied parity-checks for a ciphertext bit exceeds a precomputed threshold, flip the ciphertext bit and update the syndrome.
4. If $s = 0^r$, the codeword was decoded successfully. If $s \neq 0^r$, go to Step 2. or abort after a defined maximum of iterations with a decoding error.

The precomputed thresholds are derived from the code parameters as proposed by [6].

3 Platform and Implementation Details

The STM32F4 Discovery board is equipped with a STM32F407 microcontroller which features a 32-bit ARM Cortex-M4F CPU with 1 Mbyte flash memory, 192 Kbytes SRAM and a maximum clock frequency of 168 MHz. It sells at roughly the same price of USD 5-10 as the AVR ATxmega256A3, depending on the ordered quantity. It is based on a 32-bit instead of a 8-bit architecture, can be clocked at higher frequencies, offers more flash and SRAM storage, comes with DSP and floating point instructions, provides communication interfaces such as CAN-, USB-/ and Ethernet controllers, and has a built-in true random number generator (TRNG).

3.1 Implementing QC-MDPC McEliece for the STM32F407

Our implementations of the QC-MDPC McEliece cryptosystem for the STM32F407 microcontroller cover key-generation, encryption, and decryption and aim for a reasonable time/memory trade-off.

Key-Generation. Secret key generation starts by selecting a first row candidate for H_{n_0-1} with w/n_0 set bits. The indexes in the range of $0 \leq i \leq r-1$ at which bits are set are generated using the microcontroller's TRNG. Since $r = 4801$ is not a power of two, we sample error indexes e_i with $\lceil \log_2(r) \rceil = 13$ bits from the TRNG and only use them if $e_i \leq r-1$ holds (i.e., rejection sampling).

The public key computation requires that $H_{n_0-1}^{-1}$ exists. Hence, we apply the extended Euclidean algorithm to the first row candidate and $x^r - 1$. If the inverse does not exist, we select a new first row candidate for H_{n_0-1} and repeat. If the inverse exists, the first row of H_{n_0-1} is converted into a sparse representation where w/n_0 counters point to the positions of set bits.

Next, we randomly select first rows for $H_0, \ldots, H_{n_0-2}$ as described for H_{n_0-1}, convert and store them in their sparse representation, and compute $(H_{n_0-1}^{-1} H_i)^T$, $0 \leq i \leq n_0 - 2$. Note, since the matrices involved are quasi-cyclic, the result is quasi-cyclic as well. The resulting generator matrix is not sparse and hence its first row is stored in full length.

Encryption. Encryption is divided into encoding a message and adding an error of weight t to the resulting codeword. To compute the redundant part of the codeword, set bits in message m select rows of the generator matrix G that have to be XORed. Starting from the first row of the generator matrix, we parse m bit-by-bit and decide whether or not to XOR the current row to the redundant part. Then the next row is generated by rotating it one bit to the right and the following message bit is processed. This implementation approach was originally introduced in [8].

After computing the redundant part of the codeword, we append it to the message and generate t random indexes at which we flip bits (i.e., the error addition) to transform the codeword into a ciphertext. We retrieve the required randomness directly from the microcontroller's internal TRNG and again use rejection sampling, this time with $\lceil \log_2(n) \rceil = 14$-bit random numbers, to get a uniform distribution of error positions.

In Sect. 4.2 we describe the shortcomings of this implementation approach with regard to side-channel attacks and present countermeasures in Sect. 5.1.

Decryption. We implement the decoder as described in Sect. 2.3 to decrypt ciphertexts. First, the syndrome is computed, which is a similar operation to encoding a message, except for the fact that the secret key is stored in a sparse representation. The ciphertext is split into n_0 parts that correspond to the n_0 blocks of the parity-check matrix. The ciphertext blocks are processed in parallel bit-by-bit. If a ciphertext bit is set, the corresponding row of the parity-check matrix is added to the syndrome otherwise the syndrome remains unchanged. The following rows of the parity-check matrix blocks are generated directly in the sparse representation by incrementing the counters.

If the computed syndrome $s \neq 0^r$ then we proceed by counting how many parity-check equations are violated by a ciphertext bit. This is given by the number of bits that are set in both the syndrome and the row of the parity-check matrix block that corresponds to the ciphertext bit. If the number of unsatisfied parity-check equations exceeds a precomputed threshold b_i, then the ciphertext bit is flipped and the row of the parity-check matrix block is added to the syndrome.

If the syndrome is zero after a decoding iteration, decoding was successful. Otherwise we continue with further iterations until we reach a defined maximum upon which a decoding error is returned. In Sect. 4.3 we describe the shortcomings of such an implementation with regard to side-channel attacks and present corresponding countermeasures in Sect. 5.2.

4   Side-Channel Attacks

In the following we present power analysis attacks on the QC-MDPC McEliece cryptosystem and describe how we modified two development boards to allow meaningful power measurements. We used the freely available source code from [8] and compiled it for the Atmel AVR XMEGA-A1 Xplained board. The board features a 8-bit Atmel ATxmega128A1 microcontroller that can be clocked at a maximum frequency of 32 MHz and which is technically equivalent to the ATxmega256A3 used in [8] except for less flash and SRAM memory.

Power analysis attacks exploit the fact that when cryptographic operations are executed on a physical device, information about the processed data and the executed instructions may be recovered from the consumed electrical energy at different points in time. Simple power analysis (SPA) attacks [11] are based on the idea that certain operations can be distinguished from each other by visual inspection or pattern recognition.

In this work we target and distinguish two side-channel attack (SCA) scenarios: first a message recovery attack demonstrates that an on-chip generated, secret message (e.g., a secret key for hybrid encryption) can be easily obtained using its significant SCA-leakage during encryption. Second, we investigate an SCA-attack on the leakage obtained during the decryption operation to identify the private key.

4.1 Preparation of the Evaluation Boards

Since our goal is to observe power traces from the respective microcontroller, we modified the boards to allow unfiltered power measurements as explained below. Note, we only modified external components on the board, leaving the microcontrollers untouched.

For our measurements we use a PicoScope 5203 with two channels that can obtain 500 MS/s for each channel sampling a bandwidth of 250 MHz. One probe measures the power consumptions at an inserted measurement resistor in the VDD path, the other probe is used to signal the beginning and end of the cryptographic operation via an I/O pin of the respective microcontroller (i.e., a trigger signal).

Atmel AVR XMEGA-A1 Xplained Board. We removed all capacitors[1] connected between the microcontroller's VCC and GND and we placed a 2.7 Ω resistor onto the power supply measurement header that connects the board's 3.3 V to the VCC pins of the microcontroller. Furthermore, we added three capacitors in parallel (100 μF, 100 nF, 10 nF) right before our measurement resistor between the board's 3.3 V and GND to account for the removed capacitors. The modified AVR board is shown in Fig. 1a.

STM32F4 Discovery Board. Again, we removed all capacitors and coils[2] that are connected between the microcontroller's VDD pins and GND and placed a 2.7 Ω resistor onto the power supply measurement header (IDD) that connects the board's 3 V to the VDD pins of the microcontroller. Similarly, we added three capacitors in parallel (100 μF, 100 nF, 10 nF) right before our measurement resistor between the board's 3 V and GND. The modified STM board is shown in Fig. 1b.

4.2 Message Recovery Attack

Imagine an implementation in which the microcontroller generates a symmetric key to encrypt bulk data. The symmetric key is encrypted under the public key of the intended receiver using asymmetric encryption. After exchanging the

---

[1] A total of ten 100nF capacitors (C102-C111) were removed, cf. [1].
[2] One coil (L1) and 16 capacitors (C21-C26,C28-C37) were removed, cf. [19].

(a) Modified Atmel AVR XMEGA-A1 Xplained board with connected probes

(b) Modified STM32F4 Discovery board with connected probes

Fig. 1. Measurement setups for our side-channel attacks

symmetric key, all communication is encrypted using symmetric encryption for performance reasons.

If an attacker is able to perform a message recovery attack on the asymmetric encryption, he is in possession of the symmetric (session-) key which allows him to decrypt and forge symmetric ciphertexts until the symmetric key is updated. Although this attack is not considered in many SCA-related works, it has indeed a high practical relevance.

General Considerations. Recall that when encrypting a message m using QC-MDPC McEliece, the message is multiplied with the generator matrix G and an error e is added to the result.

$$x = m \cdot G + e$$

Message m selects rows of G which are accumulated to compute the redundant part of the codeword. A message recovery attack is successful if it is possible to detect if a certain row of G is accumulated or not, since each accumulation can be directly mapped to a specific message bit.

The implementations under test perform QC-MDPC McEliece encryptions as follows: if a message bit is set, the corresponding row of G is added to the redundant part, otherwise this step is skipped. Afterwards, the next row of G is generated and the process is repeated for the following message bit. The addition of one row of G to the redundant part involves hundreds of `load`, `xor`, and `store` operations on both platforms.

Hence, our goal is to detect if this memory-intense operation is being executed or not by inspection of the power trace.

Experiment on the AVR. We recorded a power trace while encrypting a randomly selected message that begins with `0x8F402` under a valid public key

   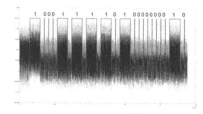

(a) Plain power trace   (b) Power trace with marked message bits

Fig. 2. Power trace of the encryption of a message starting with 0x8F402 on an ATxmega128A1 microcontroller

on an ATxmega128A1 microcontroller. The power trace as shown in Fig. 2a allows to distinguish three reoccurring patterns. Two of these patterns can be attributed to the performed or skipped row accumulation from G, the third pattern corresponds to the generation of the next row of G. Since the addition of a row of G corresponds to a set message bit, the message that is encrypted can be read more or less directly from a single power trace. We highlighted the different patterns and message bits in Fig. 2b. Note, this attack is independent of the public key under which the message is encrypted.

Experiment on the STM. We repeated the attack on the STM32F407 microcontroller with the same message and public key as before. The power trace is shown in Fig. 3a. Here, the patterns cannot be identified as clear as on the ATxmega, but there is still an observable difference in the power trace when a row of G is added to the redundant part of the codeword. We highlighted the repeating pattern in Fig. 3b and map the corresponding message bits to the power trace. Since in this case there is no visible pattern for a message bit being zero, we use the distance between two set message bits to determine how many zeros lie in-between. This is done by cross-correlating the "one"-pattern with the recorded power trace and then dividing the distance from peak to peak by the time it takes to skip one accumulation and generate the next row of G. The exact duration of skipping one accumulation was obtained in a profiling phase and only has to be done once.

4.3   Secret Key Recovery Attack

For the secret key recovery attack we assume that we are given a device that decrypts some known ciphertext (knowledge of the corresponding plaintext is not required) and that we are able to observe the power consumption of the device during decryption. The goal is to recover the secret key of the device from this information.

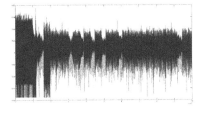 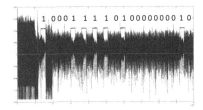

(a) Plain power trace   (b) Power trace with marked message bits

Fig. 3. Power trace of the encryption of a message starting with `0x8F402` on an STM32F407 microcontroller

General Considerations. Recall that at the beginning of a QC-MDPC McEliece decryption, the syndrome s of the received ciphertext x is computed by multiplying the secret parity-check matrix H with x^T.

$$s = H \cdot x^T$$

Since we are in a quasi-cyclic setting with $n_0 = 2$, the first rows of the two parity-check matrix blocks define the parity-check matrix. Following the implementation in [8], each row of the secret key is stored using a series of counters that point to the positions of set bits (here: 2×45 counters). To generate the next row, all counters are incremented by one. If a counter exceeds r, it overflowed and has to be reset to zero (equal to the carry bit of a rotated row).

Using SPA, at least two things should be observable from a power trace that is recorded during syndrome computation:

1. A set ciphertext bit determines if a row of the secret key is being added to the syndrome or not (similar to the message recovery attack described before). But since the ciphertext usually is assumed to be known to an attacker, recovering the ciphertext from a power trace is not a meaningful attack.
2. Incrementing the counters that resemble (parts of) the secret key must include an overflow check so that the counter is reset to zero if necessary. If it is possible to detect such an overflow, this reveals the positions of set bits in the secret key and can be used for full key recovery.

Both implementations store the position of the secret key bits in counters which are incremented to generate the next row of the quasi-cyclic parity-check matrix blocks. The counters are ordered such that the last counter stores the position of the most significant bit in the secret key. When rotating a row of the secret key, there is a conditional branch depending on whether the last counter overflowed or not. If an overflow occurred, all counter values are moved to the next counter and the first counter is reset. This reduces the overall complexity to testing only the last counter on an overflow condition.

We set the ciphertext to the all-zero vector in our experiments to remove the influence of additions of secret key rows to the syndrome on the power trace. Our

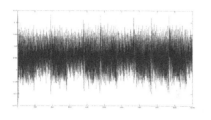

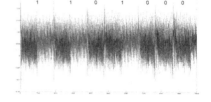

(a) Plain power trace.   (b) Power trace with marked secret key bits

Fig. 4. Power traces recorded during syndrome computation on an ATxmega128A1 microcontroller. The secret key in this example starts with $(1101000\ldots)_2$.

attack still works if any other ciphertext is used and would require to profile how long it takes to add a row of the secret key to the syndrome which to be done only once. Another option would be to just set bits at the end of the ciphertext, extract the secret key up to this point and then find the remaining secret key bits by smart brute-force (cf. [5]). Note that our attacks are independent of the implemented decoding algorithm since we attack the syndrome computation that all decoders share as a first step.

Experiment on the AVR. A power trace of the first few rounds of the syndrome computation is shown in Fig. 4a for a secret key starting with $(1101000\ldots)_2$ on the ATxmega128A1 microcontroller.

Two different repeating patterns can be distinguished in the power trace. Our experiments showed that the first pattern occurs when the device is checking whether the current ciphertext bit is set (which does not happen when we set the ciphertext to the all-zero vector) and all counters are incremented by one. The second pattern can only be detected in the power trace if the highest counter overflowed. Hence, we can distinguish if an overflow occurred or not. In case both patterns appear after each other, the highest counter overflowed. If only the first pattern appears, the highest counter did not overflow.

An overflow means that the most significant bit of the secret key was set. Since the secret key is rotated bit-by-bit, every bit of the secret key will be the most-significant bit at some point during the syndrome computation. Hence, it is possible to recover the secret key from a power trace as shown in Fig. 4b where we highlight the two patterns and mark the corresponding secret key bits.

Experiment on the STM. Fig. 5a shows the beginning of a power trace that was recorded during syndrome computation on the STM32F407 microcontroller. The first two set bits of the secret key in this example are at positions 4790 and 4741.

Again, two different patterns can be distinguished. Both patterns are negative peaks in the power trace which differ in length compared to reoccurring shorter peaks. Our experiments showed that the short peaks appear when there is no

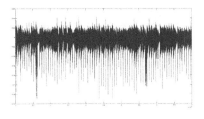

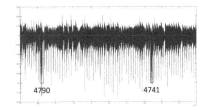

(a) Plain power trace.   (b) Power trace with marked secret key bits

Fig. 5. Power traces recorded during syndrome computation on a STM32F407 micro-controller. The secret key starts with set bits at positions 4790 and 4741.

counter overflow and the long peaks appear when there is an overflow. Thus, it is again possible to map the power trace to bits of the secret key. We highlight the two set bits at positions 4790 and 4741 in Fig. 5b. In between the two set bits there are 49 small peaks, which translate to 49 zeros in the secret key.

5   Countermeasures and Implementation Results

In this section we describe countermeasures that mitigate the attacks described in Sect. 4 and take other possible information leaks into account. The countermeasures are implemented for the STM32F4 microcontroller using the ARM Thumb-2 assembly language to have full control over the timings and the instruction flow.

5.1   Protecting the Encryption

As shown in Sect. 4.2, the encrypted message can be recovered from a single power trace if it is possible to decide whether a row of G is being accumulated or not.

Our proposed countermeasure is to always perform an addition to the redundant part, independent of whether the corresponding message bit is set. Of course we cannot simply accumulate all rows of the generator matrix, as this would map all messages to the same codeword.

Since the addition of a row of G to the redundant part is done in 32-bit steps on the ARM microcontroller, we use the current message bit m_i to compute a 32-bit mask $(0 - m_i)$. If $m_i = 0$, then the mask is zero, otherwise all 32 bits of the mask are set. Before the 32-bit blocks of the current row of G are XORed to the redundant part, we compute the logical AND of them with the mask. This either results in the current row being added if the message bit is set, or in zero being added if the message bit was not set.

This countermeasure leads to a runtime that is independent of the message and the public key. Furthermore, as the same instructions are executed for set and cleared message bits, a constant program flow is achieved. Hence, it is not

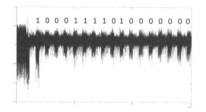
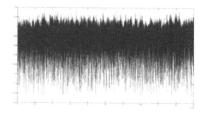

(a) Power trace of the protected encryption on the STM32F407 microcontroller. The message starts with 0x8F402, the first bits are given as reference.

(b) Power trace of the protected syndrome computation on the STM32F407 microcontroller. The secret key starts with set bits at positions 4790 and 4741

Fig. 6. Power traces recorded during encryption and decryption with enabled counter-measures

possible anymore to extract the message bits from a power trace by means of a SPA attack (cf. Fig 6a).

5.2 Protecting the Decryption

As shown in Sect. 4.3, the secret key leaks while it is being rotated in an unprotected implementation. A possible countermeasure would be to simply refrain from rotating the rows of the secret key and instead to store the full parity-check matrix in memory. However, storing H would require $2 \times (4801 \times 4801)$ bit = 5.5 Mbyte. Since this is infeasible on the platform under investigation, we are left with protecting the rotation of a row of the secret key.

To protect the secret key rotation, we still use counters that point to set bits in the secret key, but we remove the concept of having ordered counters and thus get rid of the need to copy the counter values on an overflow. After incrementing a counter, we check for an overflow by comparing the counter value to the maximum r. We load the negative flag N from the program status register, use it to compute a 32-bit mask $(0 - N)$, and store the logical AND of the counter value and the mask back to the counter. If the counter value is smaller than r, the N flag is set and the incremented counter value is stored. If the counter value is greater or equal to r, the N flag is zero and the counter is reset to zero.

The introduced countermeasure removes timing dependencies based on overflowed counters and executes the same program flow independent of whether a counter is reset or not. Fig. 6b shows the same part of the syndrome computation as was shown for the unprotected version in Fig. 5b.

With the leakage mitigation of the secret key rotation one important step towards SPA-resistant implementations was achieved. However, there are more dependencies on secret data when decoding. Even though we are currently not aware of a way to exploit these dependencies we want to avoid them in the first place.

After syndrome computation and after every decoding iteration the 4801-bit syndrome has to be compared to zero to check whether decoding was successful. This comparison should be done in constant-time, as an early abort of the comparison could leak information about the current state of the syndrome (e.g., about the first non-zero positions). We implemented the comparison by computing the OR of all 32-bit blocks of the syndrome and then check whether the result is zero or not.

Counting unsatisfied parity-check equations for a ciphertext bit is equal to counting how many bits are set at the same positions in both the current row of the secret key and the syndrome. Since we know the position of set bits in the secret key from the counters that represent the current row of the secret key, we extract the bits of the syndrome at the same positions and accumulate them. We do this by loading the 32-bit part of the syndrome which holds the bit the counter is pointing to and by shifting and masking the 32-bit part so that the bit in question is singled out and moved to the least significant bit position. We then accumulate the result which is either 0 or 1. As we use 16-bit counters for the secret key and operate on a 32-bit architecture, the upper 11-bit can be used to address a 32-bit memory cell of the syndrome. The remaining 5 bits point to the bit position within the cell. This approach computes the number of unsatisfied parity-check equations with an instruction flow (and hence a timing) that is independent of the syndrome and the current row of the secret key.

Comparing the number of unsatisfied parity-check equations to the threshold for the current iteration is implemented as a function

$$\text{ge\_u32}(x, y) = (1 \oplus ((x \oplus ((x \oplus y)|((x - y) \oplus y))) >> 31))$$

which returns 1 if x is greater or equal to y and 0 otherwise in constant time. The result of this comparison decides whether we have to flip a ciphertext bit and to update the syndrome with the current row of the secret key or not. If an attacker would be able to trace the points in time when these operations are executed, he likely would be able to recover the error that was added to the codeword and hence to reconstruct the plaintext. To circumvent this possible leakage, we always XOR the ciphertext bit at the current position with the result of the comparison which is either 1 or 0. In addition we always perform the syndrome update, in which we XOR the bit that resulted from the comparison to the positions of the syndrome which are stored in the secret key counters. Since an XOR of a value with zero results in the same value, we actually do not change the ciphertext and the syndrome in case the number of unsatisfied parity-check equations is below the decoding threshold but still execute the exact same instructions.

Last but not least, the decoding algorithm can take a variable number of iterations before it terminates. In most cases decoding is finished after either 2 or 3 decoding iterations (on average 2.4 iterations, cf. [8]) and in rare cases it requires up to a fixed maximum of five iterations. We remark that it is unclear yet if it is possible to recover secret data only from the number of decoding iterations. This needs to be investigated in future work. To be on the safe side we propose an implementation where we simply do not test the syndrome for zero after a decoding iteration. The decoding algorithm always performs the specified maximum number of iterations where it stops modifying the ciphertext once the syndrome becomes zero. In combination with the techniques introduced above this leads to a fully constant time implementation of the bit-flipping decoder.

5.3 Implementation Results

The results of our implementations are listed in Tab. 1. Encrypting a messages takes $42\,ms$ and decrypting a ciphertext takes $558\,ms$ in a fully constant-time implementation. Key-generation takes $884\,ms$ on average, but usually key-generation performance is not an issue on small embedded devices since they generate few (if even more than one) key-pairs in their lifetime. The combined code of key-generation, encryption, and decryption, requires 5.7 kByte (0.6%) flash memory and 2.7 kByte (1.4%) SRAM, including the public and the secret key. Since $w << r$ for all QC-MDPC parameter sets, storing the secret key in a sparse representation saves memory and at the same time allows fast row rotations. For the 80-bit parameter set with $n_0 = 2$ we only need $w = 90$ 16-bit counters to store the secret key (1440 bit instead of 9602 bit).

Compared to the vulnerable C implementation of the encryption, we were able to achieve a speed up of 50%, to make its execution time and instruction flow independent of secret data, and to add a true random error.

Our hardened implementations of the decoder are between 1.1-2.5 times slower than the vulnerable C implementation but mitigate the side-channel attacks from Sect. 4 and take further possible information leaks into account. Version ct_3 is completely constant-time independent of the ciphertext and secret key. Version ct_2 accelerates the first syndrome computation by skipping accumulations if ciphertext bits are not set. As discussed in Sect. 4.3, the computation only depends on set bits in the ciphertext (selecting which rows of the parity-check matrix are XORed) which is usually assumed to be known to an attacker anyways. Version ct_1 of the decoder tests the syndrome for zero after each decoding iteration and exits if decoding was successful before reaching the maximum iterations.

Compared to the QC-MDPC McEliece implementation in [8], our encryption function is 20 times faster and includes a true random error addition. Decryption performance is improved to a much more realistic 251-558 ms instead of 2.7 s. Furthermore, our implementations are protected against timing and simple power analysis attacks. Please note that the microarchitecture of the STM32F407 used in this work and the ATxmega256 in [8] are completely different – but similarly expensive in terms of cost (which is usually a most relevant factor for practical applications). The implementations are made available online to allow independent refinement and verification of our results[3].

6   Conclusion

In this work we presented implementations of QC-MDPC McEliece encryption providing 80 bits of equivalent symmetric security on low-cost ARM Cortex-M4-

---

[3] http://www.sha.rub.de/research/projects/code/

Table 1. Results of our QC-MDPC microcontroller implementations. The compiler optimization level was set to -O2. A combined implementation of key generation, encryption, and decryption occupies 5.7 kByte flash and 2.7 kByte SRAM.

Scheme	Platform	Cycles/Op	Time
This work [enc]	STM32F407	16,771,239	100 ms
This work [dec]	STM32F407	37,171,833	221 ms
This work [enc, ct]	STM32F407	7,018,493	42 ms
This work [dec, ct_1]	STM32F407	42,129,589	251 ms
This work [dec, ct_2]	STM32F407	85,571,555	509 ms
This work [dec, ct_3]	STM32F407	93,745,754	558 ms
This work [keygen]	STM32F407	148,576,008	884 ms
McEliece [enc] [8]	ATxmega256	26,767,463	836 ms
McEliece [dec] [8]	ATxmega256	86,874,388	2,71 s

based microcontrollers with a reasonable performance for encryption and decryption, respectively. We demonstrated side-channel attacks on a straightforward implementation of this scheme and finally proposed timing- and instruction-invariant coding strategies and countermeasures to strengthen it against timing attacks and simple power analysis. Future work includes differential power analysis (DPA) as well as investigations with respect to fault-injection attacks.

Acknowledgments. This work is supported by grant 01ME12025 SecMobil of the German Federal Ministry for Economic Affairs and Energy.

References

1. Atmel. Atmel AVR1924: XMEGA A1 Xplained Hardware User Guide (2010), http://www.atmel.com/Images/AVR1924.zip
2. Avanzi, R., Hoerder, S., Page, D., Tunstall, M.: Side-channel attacks on the McEliece and Niederreiter public-key cryptosystems. Journal of Cryptographic Engineering 1(4), 271–281 (2011)
3. Berlekamp, E., McEliece, R., van Tilborg, H.: On the Inherent Intractability of Certain Coding Problems (Corresp.). IEEE Transactions on Information Theory 24(3), 384–386 (1978)
4. Biasi, F., Barreto, P., Misoczki, R., Ruggiero, W.: Scaling efficient code-based cryptosystems for embedded platforms. Journal of Cryptographic Engineering, 1–12 (2014)
5. Chen, C., Eisenbarth, T., von Maurich, I., Steinwandt, R.: Differential Power Analysis of a McEliece Cryptosystem. Cryptology ePrint Archive, Report 2014/534 (2014), http://eprint.iacr.org/
6. Gallager, R.: Low-density Parity-check Codes. IRE Transactions on Information Theory 8(1), 21–28 (1962)

7. Heyse, S., Moradi, A., Paar, C.: Practical Power Analysis Attacks on Software Implementations of McEliece. In: Sendrier, N. (ed.) PQCrypto 2010. LNCS, vol. 6061, pp. 108–125. Springer, Heidelberg (2010)
8. Heyse, S., von Maurich, I., Güneysu, T.: Smaller Keys for Code-Based Cryptography: QC-MDPC McEliece Implementations on Embedded Devices. In: Bertoni, G., Coron, J.-S. (eds.) CHES 2013. LNCS, vol. 8086, pp. 273–292. Springer, Heidelberg (2013)
9. Huffman, W.C., Pless, V.: Fundamentals of Error-Correcting Codes (2010)
10. Kobara, K., Imai, H.: Semantically Secure McEliece Public-Key Cryptosystems-Conversions for McEliece. In: Kim, K.-c. (ed.) PKC 2001. LNCS, vol. 1992, pp. 19–35. Springer, Heidelberg (2001)
11. Kocher, P.C., Jaffe, J., Jun, B.: Differential Power Analysis. In: Wiener, M. (ed.) CRYPTO 1999. LNCS, vol. 1666, pp. 388–397. Springer, Heidelberg (1999)
12. McEliece, R.J.: A Public-Key Cryptosystem Based On Algebraic Coding Theory. Deep Space Network Progress Report 44, 114–116 (1978)
13. Misoczki, R., Tillich, J.-P., Sendrier, N., Barreto, P.S.L.M.: MDPC-McEliece: New McEliece Variants from Moderate Density Parity-Check Codes. Cryptology ePrint Archive, Report 2012/409 (2012), http://eprint.iacr.org/
14. Misoczki, R., Tillich, J.-P., Sendrier, N., Barreto, P.S.L.M.: MDPC-McEliece: New McEliece variants from Moderate Density Parity-Check codes. In: ISIT, pp. 2069–2073. IEEE (2013)
15. Niederreiter, H.: Knapsack-type cryptosystems and algebraic coding theory. Problems Control Inform. Theory/Problemy Upravlen. Teor. Inform. 15(2), 159–166 (1986)
16. Nojima, R., Imai, H., Kobara, K., Morozov, K.: Semantic security for the McEliece cryptosystem without random oracles. Des. Codes Cryptography 49(1-3), 289–305 (2008)
17. Shor, P.W.: Polynomial-Time Algorithms for Prime Factorization and Discrete Logarithms On a Quantum Computer. SIAM J. Comput. 26(5), 1484–1509 (1997)
18. Shoufan, A., Strenzke, F., Molter, H.G., Stöttinger, M.: A Timing Attack against Patterson Algorithm in the McEliece PKC. In: Lee, D., Hong, S. (eds.) ICISC 2009. LNCS, vol. 5984, pp. 161–175. Springer, Heidelberg (2010)
19. STMicroelectronics. UM1472 User manual - Discovery kit for STM32F407/417 lines (2014) http://www.st.com/st-web-ui/static/active/en/resource/technical/document/user_manual/DM00039084.pdf
20. Strenzke, F.: A Timing Attack against the Secret Permutation in the McEliece PKC. In: Sendrier, N. (ed.) PQCrypto 2010. LNCS, vol. 6061, pp. 95–107. Springer, Heidelberg (2010)
21. Strenzke, F., Tews, E., Molter, H.G., Overbeck, R., Shoufan, A.: Side Channels in the McEliece PKC. In: Buchmann, J., Ding, J. (eds.) PQCrypto 2008. LNCS, vol. 5299, pp. 216–229. Springer, Heidelberg (2008)
22. von Maurich, I., Güneysu, T.: Lightweight code-based cryptography: QC-MDPC McEliece encryption on reconfigurable devices. In: DATE, pp. 1–6. IEEE (2014)

Author Index